LEGENDS OF THE SUFIS

Mevlānā Jelālu-'d-Dīn Rūmī.

یا حضرت مولانا

LEGENDS OF
THE SUFIS

SELECTED ANECDOTES

From the Work Entitled

THE ACTS OF THE ADEPTS
(MENĀQIBU 'L 'ĀRIFĪN)

By
SHEMSU-'D-DĪN AHMED, EL EFLĀKĪ

Translated by
JAMES W. REDHOUSE

Preface by
IDRIES SHAH

THE THEOSOPHICAL PUBLISHING HOUSE LTD
68 Great Russell Street, London, WC1B 3BU
ADYAR, INDIA   WHEATON, ILL-USA

First published by Trubner & Co., London, 1881
Reprinted by Coombe Springs Press 1965
Third and Revised Edition 1976
By The Theosophical Publishing House Ltd
Preface Copyright © 1976 by Idries Shah

ISBN 7229 5050 0

Filmset in 'Monophoto' Times 11 on 12 pt by
Richard Clay (The Chaucer Press), Ltd, Bungay, Suffolk
and printed in Great Britain by
Fletcher & Son Ltd, Norwich

CONTENTS

PUBLISHER'S NOTE

In presenting this edition of the Holy Mesnevī it has been thought best to adhere to the spelling used by Sir James Redhouse in his translation first published in 1881. The modern equivalents will readily spring to mind. There appear to be some discrepancies in rendering A.H. dates into A.D., and these have been kept as he reckoned them.

PREFACE

THERE is no controversy about Maulana (Arabic for Our Master) Jalaluddin Rumi being one of the very greatest saints and mystics of all peoples, as well as a Master of the Way to the Sufis. This book is a selection of anecdotes about his forbears and origins, his teachings and his associates, as well as his successors in what came, after him, to be called the Mevlevi School. This text is regarded as one of the five source-books for material on this tradition: the others being the Mathnavi, The Divan of Shamsi-i-Tabriz, the Letters of Rumi and Fihi ma Fihi ("In it what is in it").

As with many other medieval works, there is no authoritative version of the original book, and many compilations, or recensions, of its contents exist. When it is read by a contemporary Western student, it is worth bearing certain points in mind. The book's original title, *Manaqib al-Arifin*, literally means "qualities" or "eulogies" of the "Mystic-Wise Ones". It is therefore almost exactly, within its own context, what Western people call a hagiography. To get the best from it one has to bear in mind the premises which underlie the operation of a Sufi school. Not the least of these is the well-established technique of proffering stories, legends and so on not necessarily for teaching purposes, but also often to test the mentality and reactions of the hearer. This kind of story, sometimes erroneously taken as really intended by its author, certainly does appear in this selection. This is not to say that even the most feeble or improbable tales are such artefacts. It is true in some cases that these have been included because they represent what was thought and reported about Rumi and others after his death, irrespective of the character and degree of spiritual attainment of the reporters.

These selections were translated by James Redhouse and published in 1881. When the Coombe Springs Press in 1965 asked me to concur in their reissuing it, I gladly did so; subject to the inclusion of a note such as the present one, to make the book more useful to serious students and to help prevent misunderstandings. The latter range from the wholesale adoption of this text as a sort of 'gospel' to the spurning of its contents as chaotic and naive. Due, no doubt, to the exigiencies of production, only a highly summarized form of this disclaimer appeared, and that on the front flap of the 1965 reprint. With the vastly increased interest in Sufi thought and action now evidenced throughout the world, one feels that the observing of suitable attitudes towards the work is no less important.

Rumi's work is generally recognized as being a timely adaptation and restatement of Sufism for the purpose of applying it to the people of his time and laying a foundation for the succeeding phases: a tradition of working which has always characterized Sufi undertakings, sometimes called the doctrine of relevance and supercession. Seen in this light, it is useful to note the continuing disparity between those students of Sufism who are slavish imitators (so detested by Rumi) and those who are able to render the materials and the experiences in present-day terms. In this respect Sufism can be seen in its overt projections as following a course similar to that of all human systems. There are the traditionalists, for whom form is sacrosanct, the innovators, who try to adapt materials without insight, the rejecters of part or whole, and the real successors to the tradition, who work through insight as well as externals.

For those who are interested in the relevance of materials such as some of those contained in the *Manaqib* to today's concerns, there is a value in emphasizing certain basics which are often ignored.

Following Rumi's dictum in Persian *Qalib az ma hast, na ma az u*—"Form is from us, not we from it"—and his many other statements to this effect, it should be observed that this Sufi persuasion insists that matter comes from mind, mind does not come from matter. Miraculous interventions involving matter or immaterial things, therefore, as we find them here, are to be seen as the working of the mind, not the operation of matter. This operation, too, is sometimes to a purpose and sometimes deceptive, mere trickery, intended or otherwise. So miracles, whatever their effect or intention, may arise from the working of mental or spiritual forces. This explanation makes it possible for the reader to understand, for instance, how Rumi's miracles or wonders can be regarded as significant while those produced by people trying to oppose him are discounted. The difference lies in the quality and purpose of the wonders.

This operation of apparently supernatural events for definite purposes and not merely to impress people in an emotional manner, not only sets Sufism very much apart from miracle-centred systems but also helps to explain how Rumi, like many other Moslem teachers, could have so many non-Moslem disciples, Christians and Jews among them. It is true that he constantly reproaches scholastic theologians and scholars as such for being unable to understand that Sufi experience neither conflicts with religions nor undermines them. But he stays within his Islamic tradition and emphasises that Sufi understanding has operated within all faiths. In the following pages there is a striking account of telepathic rapport between a Christian saint and Rumi, whom the saint regarded as his mentor through spiritual communication.

The diversity of forms under which Sufi schools have operated, and the multiplicity of their exercises and even the alleged dissonance of their teachings one to the other, has always worried externalist scholars: whom the Mevlevis call 'men of appearances'. In this book, as also elsewhere, we find a very frank statement that the so-called Dervish Dancing and other exercises are very limited activities, designed only as aids for those people who have certain local or temperamental peculiarities. It is worth noting that although this information has been publicly available for at least seven hundred years, people of all kinds prefer to believe that by imitating the physical and mental actions of some people in thirteenth-century Konya they will derive spiritual benefits. This is, to a Sufi, rather like believing that if you behave like a Pharoah you will be able to build the pyramids, without taking enough notice of what the originators of the enterprise actually said, or even were reported to have said, about it: including the purpose.

Legends of the Sufis, then, can well be described in the words of the title of Rumi's book of table-talk: "(There is) In it what is in it (for you)." May its undoubted value find its full expression in this incarnation.

Idries Shah

THE ACTS OF THE ADEPTS[1]

CHAPTER I

Bahā'u-'d-Din, Veled, Sultānu-'l-'Ulemā (The Beauty of the Religion of Islām, Son, Sultan of the Doctors of the Law)

THE king of Khurāsān,[2] 'Alā'u-'d-Dīn Muhammed, Khurrem-Shāh, uncle of Jelālu'd-Dīn Muhammed Kh'ārezm-Shāh, and the proudest, as he was the most handsome man of his time, gave his daughter, Melika'i-Jihān (Queen of the World), as to the only man worthy of her, to Jelālu-'d-Dīn Huseyn, el Khatībī, of the race of Abū-Bekr.

An ancestor of his was one of the original Muslim conquerors of Khurāsān. He was himself very virtuous and learned, surrounded with numerous disciples. He had not married until then; which gave him many an anxious and self-accusing thought.

He himself, the king, the king's daughter, and the king's vazīr were all four warned in a dream by the Prince of the Apostles of God (Muhammed) that he should wed the princess; which was done. He was then thirty years old. In due course, nine months afterwards, a son was born to him, and was named Bahā'u-'d-Dīn Muhammed. He is commonly mentioned as Bahā'u-'d-Dīn Veled.

When adolescent, this latter was so extremely learned that the family of his mother wished to raise him to the throne as king; but this he utterly rejected.

By the divine command, as conveyed in the selfsame night,

[1] There is an allusion in the word 'Arifīn (Adepts) to the name of Eflākī's patron, the Chelebi Emīr 'Arif (well-knowing).

[2] Eastern Persia.

and in an identical dream, to three hundred of the most learned men of the city of Balkh'[1] the capital of the kingdom, where he dwelt, those sage doctors unanimously conferred upon him the honorific title of Sultānu-'l-'Ulemā, and they all became his disciples.

Such are the names and titles by which he is more commonly mentioned; but he is also styled Mevlānāyi Buzurg (the Greater or Elder Master). Many miracles and prodigies were attributed to him; and some men were found who conceived a jealousy at his growing reputation and influence.

2

In A.H. 605 (A.D. 1208) he, Bahā'u-'d-Dīn Veled, began to preach against the innovations of the king and sundry of his courtiers, declaiming against the philosophers and rationalists, while he pressed all his hearers to study and practise the precepts of Islām. Those courtiers maligned him with the king, calling him an intriguer who had designs on the throne. The king sent and made him an offer of the sovereignty, promising to retire elsewhere himself. Bahā answered that he had no concern with earthly greatness, being a poor recluse; and that he would willingly leave the country, so as to remove from the king's mind all misgivings on this score.

He accordingly quitted Balkh, with a suite of about forty souls, after delivering a public address in the great mosque before the king and people. In this address he foretold the advent of the Moguls to overturn the kingdom, possess the country, destroy Balkh, and drive out the king, who would then flee to the Roman [2] land, and there at length be killed.

So he left Balkh, as the prophet (Muhammed) had fled from Mekka [3] to Medīna. His son Jelālu'd-Dīn was then five, and the elder brother, 'Alā'u-'d-Dīn, seven years old.

The people everywhere on his road, hearing of his approach or forewarned in dreams of his coming, flocked to meet him and do him honour. Thus he drew near to Bagdād.

---

[1] The ancient *Bactra*, sometimes called *Zuriaspa*, the capital of Bactria.
[2] See p. 3.
[3] Incorrectly written Mecca by Europeans.

Here he was met by the great Sheykh Shahābu-'d-Dīn, 'Umer, Suherverdī, the most eminent man of the place, deputed by the Caliph Musta'zim to do him honour. He became the guest of the sheykh.

The Caliph sent him a present of three thousand sequins, but he declined the gift as being money unlawfully acquired. He also refused to visit the Caliph; but consented to preach in the great mosque after the noon service of worship on the following Friday, the Caliph being present. In his discourse he reproached the Caliph to his face with his evil course of life, and warned him of his approaching slaughter by the Moguls with great cruelty and ignominy. The Caliph again sent him rich presents in money, horses, and valuables, but he refused to accept them.

Before Bahā'u-'d-Dīn quitted Bagdād, intelligence was received there of the siege of Balkh, of its capture, and of its entire destruction, with its twelve thousand mosques, by the Mogul army of five hundred thousand men commanded by Jengīz in person (in A.H. 608, A.D. 1211). Fourteen thousand copies of the Qur'ān were destroyed, fifteen thousand students and professors of the law were slain, and two hundred thousand adult male inhabitants led out and shot to death with arrows.

Bahā'u-'d-Dīn went from Bagdād to Mekka, performed the greater pilgrimage there, proceeding thence to Damascus, and next to Malatia (Melitene, on the Upper Euphrates), where, in A.H. 614 (A.D. 1217), he heard of the death of Jengīz. The Seljūqī sultan, 'Alā'u-'d-Dīn Keyqubād, was then sovereign of the land of Rome (Rūm, *i.e.*, Asia Minor), and was residing at Sīwās (Sebaste). In A.H. 620 (A.D. 1223) Sultan Jelālu-'d-Dīn, the dispossessed monarch of Kh'ārezm (Chorasmia) was killed in a battle fought by him in Azerbāyjān (Atropatene) against the sultans of Rome, Syria, and Egypt, when his forces were totally defeated. And thus ended that great dynasty, after ruling about a hundred and forty years.

Bahā'u-'d-Dīn went from Malatia and remained four years near Erzinjān (the ancient Aziris, on the Western Euphrates),

in Armenia, at a college built for him by a saintly lady, 'Ismet
Khātūn. She was the wife of the local sovereign, Melik
Fakhru-'d-Dīn. She and her husband both died, and then
Bahā'u-'d-Dīn passed on to Larenda (in Cataonia), in Asia
Minor, and remained there about seven years at the head of a
college, the princess Melika'i-Jihān, his mother, being still
with him.

Here it was that his younger son, Jelālu-'d-Dīn
Muhammed, the future author of the Mesnevī, attained to
man's estate, being then eighteen years old; when, in A.H. 623
(A.D. 1226), he married a young lady named Gevher Khātūn,
daughter of the Lala Sherefu-'d-Dīn, of Samarqand. She gave
birth in due course to Jelāl's eldest son, 'Alā'u-'d-Dīn.

The king had now returned to his capital, Qonya (the
ancient Iconium). Hearing of Bahā'u-'d-Dīn's great learning
and sanctity, the king sent and invited him to the capital,
where he installed him in a college, and soon professed himself a disciple. Many miracles are related as having been
worked at Qonya by Bahā'u-'d-Dīn, who at length died there
on Friday, the 18th of Rebī'u-'l-ākhir, A.H. 628 (February
A.D. 1231). The sultan erected a marble mausoleum over his
tomb, on which this date is recorded. Many miracles continued to occur at this sanctuary. The sultan died also a few
years later, in A.H. 634 (A.D. 1236).

(After the death of Bahā'u-'d-Dīn Veled, and the acquisi-
tion of still greater fame by his son Jelālu-'d-Dīn, who
received the honorific title of Khudāvendgār—*Lord*—the
father was distinguished from the son, among the disciples,
by the customary title of Mevlānā Buzurg—*the Greater or
Elder Master*. The traditions collected by Eflākī, relating to
this period, vary considerably from one another on minor
points of date and order of succession, though the main facts
come out sufficiently clear.)

3

Jelāl's son, Sultān Veled, related to Eflākī that his father
Jelāl used frequently to say, "I and all my disciples will be
under the protection of the *Great Master*, my father, on the

day of resurrection; and under his guidance we shall enter the divine presence; God will pardon all of us for his sake."

4

It is related that when the *Great Master* departed this life, his son, Jelālu-'d-Dīn, was fourteen years old. (This is apparently a copyist's error for "twenty-four." Jalāl is said to have been born in A.H. 604—A.D. 1207.) He married when seventeen (or eighteen); and often did he say in the presence of the congregation of his friends, "The *Great Master* will remain with me a few years. I shall be in need of Shemsu-'d-Dīn of Tebrīz (the capital of Azerbāyjān); for every prophet has had an Abū-Bekr, as Jesus had his apostles."

5

Shortly after the death of the Great Master Bahā'u-'d-Dīn Veled, news was received by the Sultan 'Alā'u-'d-Dīn of Qonya of the arrival of Sultan Jelālu-'d-Dīn Kh'ārezm-Shāh on the borders of Asia Minor. The sultan went and prayed at the tomb of the deceased saint, and then prepared to meet the Kh'ārezmians, who were in the neighbourhood of Erzenu-'r-Rūm (Erzen of the Romans, the ancient Arzes, now Erzerum). Scouts brought in the intelligence that the Kh'ārezmians were very numerous; and great anxiety prevailed among the sultan's troops. He resolved to see for himself.

He put on a disguise and set out with a few followers, on fleet horses, for the Kh'ārezmian camp. They gave out that they were nomad Turks of the neighbourhood, their ancestors having come from the Oxus; that latterly the sultan had withdrawn his favour from them; and that, in consequence, they had for some time past been looking for the Kh'ārezmian advent. This was reported to the king, Jelālu-'d-Dīn, who sent for them and received them kindly, giving them tents and assigning them rations.

During the night King Jelālu-'d-Dīn began to reflect that every one had hitherto spoken well of Sultan 'Alāu-'d-Dīn, and a doubt arose in his mind in consequence respecting the

story of these newcomers, especially as he learned that the
sultan was on his march to meet him. Consulting with the
Prince of Erzenu-'r-Rūm, further perquisition was postponed
until the morrow.

But at midnight the deceased saint of Qonya, Bahā-Veled,
appeared in a dream to Sultan 'Alā'u-'d-Dīn, and warned
him to fly at once. The sultan awoke, found it was a dream,
and went to sleep again. The saint now appeared a second
time. The sultan saw himself seated on his throne, and the
saint coming to him, smiting him on the breast with his staff,
and angrily saying, "Why sleepest thou? Arise!"

Now the sultan did arise, quietly called his people, saddled
horses, and stole away out of the camp. Towards morning
King Jelāl caused guards to be placed round the tents of the
strangers to watch them. But afterwards, when orders were
given to bring them to the king's presence to be questioned,
their tents were found to be empty. Pursuit was attempted,
but in vain.

After an interval the two armies came into collision. The
Sultan of Qonya was victorious. From that time forward,
whenever difficulties threatened, he always betook himself to
the shrine of the saint, Bahā Veled, who always answered his
prayers.

(As Sultan Jelālu-'d-Dīn Kh'ārezm-Shāh has already been
stated to have died in battle in Azerbāyjān in A.D. 1223,
whereas the saint of Qonya did not die until A.D. 1231, eight
years afterwards, the discrepancy of that date with the
present anecdote is irreconcilable.)

6

The Great Master, Bahā Veled, used to say that while he
himself lived, no other teacher would be his equal, but that
when his son, Jelālu-'d-Dīn, should succeed him at his death,
that son of his would equal and even surpass him.

7

Seyyid Burhānu-'d-Dīn Termīzī [1] is related to have said

---

[1] Of Termīz (Tirmez), on the north bank of the Oxus, near to Balkh.

that one night the door of the mausoleum of Bahā Veled opened of itself, and that a great glory shone forth from it, which gradually filled his house, so that no shadow fell from anything. The glory then gradually filled the city in like manner, spreading thence over the whole face of nature. On beholding this prodigy the Seyyid swooned away.

This vision is a sure indication that the whole human race will one day own themselves the disciples of the descendants of the great saint.

8

Before he quitted Balkh, Bahā Veled one day saw a man performing his devotions in the great mosque in his shirt sleeves, with his coat upon his back. Bahā reproved him, telling him to put on his coat properly and decently, then to continue his devotions. "And what if I will not?" asked the man in a disdainful tone. "Thy dead-like soul will obey my command, quit thy body, and thou wilt die!" answered Bahā. Instantly the man fell dead; and crowds flocked to become disciples to the saint who spoke with such power and authority.

9

When Sultan 'Alā'u-'d Dīn had fortified Qonya, he invited Bahā Veled to mount to the terraced roof of the palace, thence to survey the walls and towers. After his inspection, Bahā remarked to the sultan, "Against torrents, and against the horsemen of the enemy, thou hast raised a goodly defence. But what protection hast thou built against those unseen arrows, the sighs and moans of the oppressed, which overleap a thousand walls and sweep whole worlds to destruction? Go to, now! strive to acquire the blessings of thy subjects. These are a stronghold, compared to which the walls and turrets of the strongest castles are as nothing."

10

On one occasion Sultan 'Alā'u-'d-Dīn paid a visit to Bahā Veled. In lieu of his hand the latter offered the tip of his staff to be kissed by the sultan, who thought within himself: "The proud scholar!" Bahā read the sultan's thoughts as a seer, and remarked in reply thereto: "Mendicant students are bound to be humble and lowly. Not so a sultan of the Faith who has attained to the utmost circumference of the orbit thereof, and revolves therein."

11

A certain Sheykh Hajjāj, a disciple of Bahā Veled and one of God's elect not known to the herd of mankind, quitted the college after the decease of his teacher, and betook himself to his former trade of a weaver, therewith to gain an honest livelihood. He used to buy the coarsest brown bread of unsifted flour, mash this up with water, and break his fast with this sop alone. All the rest of his earnings he saved up until they would reach to two or three hundred piastres. This sum he would then carry to the college, and place it in the shoes of his teacher's son, Jelālu-'d-Dīn, the new rector. This practice he continued so long as he lived.

At his death a professional washer was appointed to perform the last ablution for Sheykh Hajjāj. In the execution of his office the washer was about to touch the privities of the deceased, when the defunct seized his hand with so strong a grip as to make him scream with pain and fright. The friends came to rescue him, but they were unable to release the imprisoned hand. They therefore sent word to Jelālu-'d-Dīn of what had occurred. He came and saw, knew the reason, and whispered into the ear of the deceased man: "The poor simpleton has been unaware of the high station of thy sanctity. Pardon his unintentional transgression for my sake." Immediately the poor washer's hand was released; but three days afterwards he was himself washed and borne lifeless to his grave.

12

The sultan had a governor of his childhood still living, the Emīr Bedru-'d-Dīn Guhertāsh, commonly known as the dizdār (castellan), whom he held in great esteem. One day, as

Bahā Veled was lecturing in the mosque, in presence of the sultan and his court, he suddenly called upon the dizdār to recite any ten verses of the Qur'ān, saying he would then expound them to the congregation. The dizdār had been admiring the eloquence of the preacher's expositions. Upon this sudden call, without the slightest hesitation and without ever having committed them to memory, he recited the first ten verses of chapter xxiii., "The believers have attained to prosperity," &c., which Bahā forthwith explained in such a manner as to draw down the plaudits of the assembly. The dizdār, with the sultan's permission, went to the foot of the pulpit and declared himself a disciple to Bahā. "Then," said the preacher, "as a thank-offering for his happy event, do thou build and endow a college where my descendants shall teach their disciples after me." The dizdār did so, and richly endowed it. This is the college where Jelālu-'d-Dīn afterwards lived. When the dizdār died he left all his possessions to enrich the foundation. (See chap. iii. No. 69.)

13

The sultan had a dream (something like one of Nebuchadnezzar's). He saw himself with a head of gold, a breast of silver, a belly of brass, thighs of lead, and shanks of tin. Bahā Veled explained the dream as follows:—"All will go well in the kingdom during thy lifetime. It will be as silver in the days of thy son; as brass in the next generation, when the rabble will get the upper hand. Troubles will thicken during the next reign; and after that the kingdom of Rome will go to ruin, the house of Seljūq will come to an end, and unknown upstarts will seize the reins of government."

CHAPTER II

Seyyid Burhānu-'d-Dīn, Sirr-Dān, el Muhaqqiq, el Huseynī, of the posterity of Yā-Sīn (Muhammed) [1]

(HE is called Seyyid, the "*Syud*" of our East India authorities, for the reason that he was a descendant of the prophet, of whom Yā-Sīn is one of the titles, as it is also the name of the thirty-sixth chapter of the Qur'ān, at the head of which the two letters stand which form the name. Burhānu-'d-Dīn means *The Proof of the Religion*; Sirr-Dān signifies *The Confidant*, one who possesses a knowledge of a secret or secrets, a mystery or mysteries. Muhaqqiq is one who verifies, who probes the truth; and Huseynī indicates that the seyyid was of the branch of Huseyn, the younger of the two sons of Fātima, Muhammed's only child that left posterity.)

1

Seyyid Burhānu-'d-Dīn was popularly known by the name of Sirr-Dān at Balkh, Bukhārā (Alexandria Oxiana?), and Termīz. His discourse was continually running upon the subjects of spiritual and metal phenomena, of the mysteries of earth and of heaven.

When Bahā Veled quitted Balkh, the seyyid went to Termīz, and there secluded himself as a hermit. After a while again he began to lecture in public on the significations of knowledge. Suddenly, one morning, that of Friday the 18th of Rebī'u-'l-ākhir, A.H. 628 (February, 1231 A.D.), he cried out most bitterly, in a flood of tears, "Alas! my master has passed away from his tabernacle of dust to the abode of sincerity!" His words and the date were noted down, and, on

---

[1] The two letters Yā and Sīn heading the thirty-sixth chapter of the Qur'ān are said to stand for the words, Yā insān, *O man!* as Muhammed is there addressed.

inquiry, after his arrival in Qonya, were found to correspond exactly with the moment of Bahā Veled's decease.

2

For forty days the disciples at Termīz mourned for the death of the great teacher. At the end of that period the seyyid said: "The son of my master, his successor, Jelālu-'d-Dīn Muhammed, is left alone and is wishing to see me. I must go to the land of Rome and place myself at his service, delivering over to him the trust which my teacher confided to my safe-keeping."

3

When the seyyid reached Qonya, Bahā Veled had been dead about a year, and Jelāl had gone to Larenda. The seyyid applied himself for several months to devotional seclusion in one of the mosques of Qonya; after which he sent off a letter to Jelāl by the hands of two mendicants, saying: "Come and meet this stranger to thee at the resting-place of thy father, for Larenda is not a place of permanency for thee. From that hill (on which Bahā's mausoleum was built) a fire will shower down on the city of Qonya."

After reading this epistle Jelāl returned to Qonya with all possible despatch. There he went at once to visit the seyyid, who came forth from the mosque to receive him. They embraced. They now entered into conversation on various subjects. So delighted was the seyyid with the expositions set forth by Jelāl that he kissed the soles of his feet, and exclaimed: "A hundredfold hast thou surpassed thy father in all knowledge of the humanities; but thy father was versed also in the mysteries of mute reality and ecstasy. From this day forward my desire is that thou shouldest also acquire that knowledge—the knowledge possessed by the prophets and the saints, which is entitled *The Science of Divine Intuition*—the science spoken of by God (in Qur'ān xviii. 64): 'We have taught him a science from within us.' This knowledge did I acquire from my teacher; do thou receive it from me, so that thou mayest be the heir to thy father in spiritual matters as well as in things temporal. Thou wilt then be his second self."

Jelāl complied with all the syyid pressed upon him. He took the seyyid to his college, and for nine years received instruction from him. Some accounts make it appear that Jelāl first became the seyyid's disciple at this time; but others go to show that Bahā Veled gave Jelāl as a pupil to the seyyid at Balkh, and that the seyyid used now and then to carry Jelāl about on his shoulders, like as is practised by the nursing-tutors—*lala*—of children. (Compare chap. iii., Nos. 6 and 8.)

<h1 style="text-align:center">4</h1>

Husāmu-'d-Dīn told us that Jelāl had informed him of the following occurrence:—

The syyid once arrived at a certain city in Khurāsān named Sāmānek. The chief people went forth to meet him and show him honour, all excepting the Sheykhu-'l-Islām of the place (the local vice-chancellor). Nevertheless the seyyid went to pay his respects to the legal functionary. The latter went barefoot to the door of the house to meet the seyyid, whose hand he kissed, and to whom he offered excuses for his seeming lack of courtesy.

In reply, the seyyid said to him: "I am come to inform you that, on the 10th day of next month, Ramazān, you will have occasion to go forth to a hot bath. On your way thither you will be assassinated by the emissaries of the *Old Man of the Mountain*. This I communicate to thee, that thou mayest set thy affairs in order, and repent thee of thy sins."

The Sheykhu-'l-Islām fell at the seyyid's feet, wailing; but the latter remarked: "This is of no avail. Events are in God's hands, and he has so ordered it. Still, as thou showest so much contrition, I may add, for thy consolation, that thou wilt die in the faith, and shalt not be cut off from the divine mercy and grace."

And so it happened as thus predicted. The assassins took his life on the very day foretold by the seyyid.

(The stronghold, Alamūt, of the *Old Man of the Mountain*, was stormed by forces sent against it by Helagū, grandson of

Jengīz, in about the year A.H. 654 (A.D. 1256). The last prince
of the dynasty was sent to China, and there put to death by
the emperor; and thus these detestable scourges of humanity
were at length suppressed.)

5

After a certain time the seyyid asked permission of Jelāl to
go for a while to Qaysariyya (Cæsarea), but Jelāl could not
spare him. So he remained at Qonya still.

Somewhat later a party of friends took the seyyid out for a
ride among the vineyards. The thought occurred to him that,
without saying anything to anybody, he might now easily
abscond and get away to Qaysariyya. Scarcely had he conceived this vagabond idea than his beast reared with him,
threw him, and broke his leg. His friends raised him, set him
again on his horse, and conducted him to a neighbouring
country-house to which Jehāl had also come.

On seeing Jelāl the seyyid exclaimed to him, "Is this the
proper way to reward your teacher—to break his leg?" Jelāl
at once ordered the seyyid's boot to be removed, and saw
that his foot and toes were crushed. He now passed his hands
along the injured limb and blew on it. The limb was at once
restored whole. Jelāl now granted permission, and the seyyid
forthwith proceeded to Qaysariyya.

6

When the time was come that the seyyid should die, he told
his servant to prepare for him an ewer of warm water, and to
go. The water was made ready, placed in the seyyid's room,
and the servant went forth. The seyyid called after him: "Go
and proclaim that the stranger seyyid has departed to the
other world." He then bolted the door, that none should
enter to him.

The servant, however, had his curiosity excited by those
words, and went back to the door, to listen and to see what
might happen. Through a chink he saw his master perform
an ablution, arrange his dress, lie down on his couch, and cry
out: "All ye angels, saints, and heavens, who have at any time

intrusted to me a secret, come to me now and receive back your charges. Ye are here all present."

He then recited the following hymn:—

"God, my beloved, darling God, adored, to me incline;
 My soul receive; intoxicate, release poor me distraught.
 In thee alone my heart finds peace; it fire with love divine;
 Take it unto thyself; to it both worlds are naught."

These were the seyyid's last words, ere he yielded up his spirit. The servant carried the news to the seyyid's friends, who gathered together, carried him forth, and buried him.

A mausoleum was raised over his grave by a rich and powerful disciple. The departed saint would not allow a cupola to stand. Twice the dome was shaken down by earthquakes, and in a dream the seyyid himself forbade its third edification.

After the usual forty days of mourning, a letter was sent to Jelāl, who at once journeyed from Qonya to Qaysariyya, and prayed at the tomb of his deceased teacher, returning home again afterwards.

CHAPTER III

Mevlānā Jelālu-'d-Dīn Muhammed, the Revered Mystery of God upon Earth[1]

1

JELĀLU-'D-DĪN is related to have been born at Balkh on the 6th of Rebī'u-'l-evvel, A.H. 604 (29th September 1207).

When five years old, he used at times to become extremely uneasy and restless, so much so that his attendants used to take him into the midst of themselves.

The cause of these perturbations was that spiritual forms and shapes of the absent (invisible world) would arise before his sight, that is, angelic messengers, righteous genii, and saintly men—the concealed ones of the bowers of the True One (spiritual spouses of God), used to appear to him in bodily shape, exactly as the cherubim and seraphim used to show themselves to the holy apostle of God, Muhammed, in the earlier days, before his call to the prophetic office; as Gabriel appeared to Mary, and as the four angels were seen by Abraham and Lot; as well as others to other prophets.

His father, Bahā'u-'d-Dīn Veled, the Sultānu-'l-'Ulemā, used on these occasions to coax and soothe him by saying: "These are the Occult Existences. They come to present themselves before you, to offer unto you gifts and presents from the invisible world."

These ecstasies and transports of his began to be publicly known and talked about; and the affectionately honorific title of Khudāvendgār, by which he is so often mentioned, was conferred upon him at this time by his father, who used to address him and speak of him by this title, as "My Lord."

---

[1] The truly eminent author of the Mesnevī.

2

His son, Sultan Veled, related that there was a paper in the
handwriting of his father, Bahā Veled, which set forth that at
Balkh, when Jelāl was six years old, he was taking the air one
Friday, on the terraced roof of the house, and reciting the
Qur'ān, when some other children of good families came in
and joined him there.

After a time, one of these children proposed that they
should try and jump from thence on to a neighbouring terrace, and should lay wagers on the result.

Jelāl smiled at this childish proposal, and remarked: "My
brethren, to jump from terrace to terrace is an act well
adapted for cats, dogs, and the like, to perform; but is it not
degrading to man, whose station is so superior? Come now, if
you feel disposed, let us spring up to the firmament, and visit
the regions of God's realm." As he yet spake, he vanished
from their sight.

Frightened at Jelāl's sudden disappearance, the other children raised a shout of dismay, that some one should come to
their assistance; when lo, in an instant, there he was again
in their midst; but with an altered expression of countenance
and blanched cheeks. They all uncovered before him, fell to
the earth in humility, and all declared themselves his
disciples.

He now told them that, as he was yet speaking to them, a
company of visible forms, clad in green raiment, had led him
away from them, and had conducted him about the various
concentric orbs of the spheres, and through the signs of the
Zodiac, showing him the wonders of the world of spirits, and
bringing him back to them so soon as their cries had reached
his ears.

At that age, he was used not to break his fast more often
than once in three or four, and sometimes even seven, days.

3

A different witness, a disciple of Jelāl's father, related that
Bahā Veled frequently affirmed publicly that his Lord, Jelāl,
was of exalted descent, being of the lineage of a king, and

also of an hereditary saint.

His maternal grandmother was a daughter of the great Imām Es-Sarakhsī[1] (died at Damascus A.H. 571, A.D. 1175), who was of the lineage of the Prophet. The mother of Es-Sarakhsī was descended from the Caliph 'Alī; and Jelāl's paternal grandmother was a daughter of the King of Kh'ārezm, who resided at Balkh.

Jelāl's paternal great-great-grandmother, also, the mother of Ahmed, El-Khatībī, grandfather of Jelāl's father, was a daughter of a king of Balkh. These particulars establish that Jelāl was well descended on both sides, in a mundane and in a spiritual sense. The well-known proverb—

"Hereditary disposition ever insinuates itself,"

proved fully true in his most illustrious case.

4

When Jelāl was seven years old, he used every morning to recite the very short chapter, cviii., of the Qur'ān—

"Verily we have given unto thee the abounding good. Therefore, do thou perform thy devotions unto thy Lord, and slaughter victims. Verily, he who evil entreateth thee is one who shall leave no issue after him."

He used to weep as he recited these inspired words.

Suddenly, God one day vouchsafed to appear to him visibly. On this he fainted away. Regaining consciousness, he heard a voice from heaven, that said—

"O Jelālu-'d-Dīn! By the majesty (jelāl) of our glory, do thou henceforward cease to combat with thyself; for we have exalted thee to the station of ocular vision."

Jelāl vowed, therefore, out of gratitude for this mark of grace, to serve the Lord to the end of his days, to the utmost of his power; in the firm hope that they who followed him would also attain to that high grade of favour and excellence.

5

Two years after the death of his father, Jelāl went from

[1] From the city of Sarakhs in Khurāsān.

Qonya to Haleb (Aleppo) to study. (This account is altogether subversive, as to time and date, of that already given in chap. ii. No. 3.)

As he was known to be a son of Bahā'u-'d-Dīn Veled, and was also an apt scholar, his professor showed him every attention.

Others were offended, and evinced their jealousy at the preference thus accorded to him. They complained to the governor of the city that Jelāl was immoral, as he was in the habit, each night, of quitting his cell at midnight for some unknown purpose. The governor resolved to see and judge for himself. He therefore hid himself in the porter's room.

At midnight, Jelāl came forth from his room, and went straight to the locked gate of the college, watched by the governor. The gate flew open; and Jelāl, followed at a distance by the governor, went through the streets to the locked city gate. This, too, opened of itself; and again both passed forth.

They went on and came to the tomb of Abraham (at Hebron, about 350 miles distant), the "Friend of the All-Merciful." There a domed edifice was seen, filled with a large company of forms in green raiment, who came forth to meet Jelāl, and conducted him into the building.

The governor hereupon lost his senses through fright, and did not recover until after the sun had risen.

Now, he could see nothing of a domed edifice, nor one single human being. He wandered about on a trackless plain for three days and three nights, hungry, thirsty, and footsore. At length he sank under his sufferings.

Meanwhile, the porter of the college had given intelligence of the governor's pursuit after Jelāl. When his officers found that he did not return, they sent a numerous party of guards to seek him. These, on the second day, met Jelāl. He told them where they would find their master. The next day, late, they came up with him, found him to be nearly dead, and brought him home.

The governor became a sincere convert, and a disciple to Jelāl for ever after.

(A parallel tale is told of Jelāl's fetching water from the Tigris for his father by night when he was a little child at Bagdad. There, too, all the gates opened to him of themselves.)

6

It is related that the Seyyid Burhānu-'d-Dīn was often heard to narrate that, when Jelāl was a child, the seyyid was his governor and tutor. He had often taken Jelāl up on his shoulder, and so carried him to the empyrean. "But now," he would add, "Jelāl has attained to such eminence of station that he carries me up." These sayings of the seyyid were repeated to Jelāl, who confirmed them with the remark: "It is quite true; and a hundredfold more also; the services rendered to me by that man are infinite."

7

When Jelāl went to Damascus to study, he passed by Sīs in Upper Cilicia. There, in a cave, dwelt forty Christian monks, who had a great reputation for sanctity, but in reality were mere jugglers.

On the approach of Jelāl's caravan to the cave, the monks caused a little boy to ascend into the air, and there remain standing between heaven and earth.

Jelāl noticed this exhibition, and fell into a reverie. Hereupon, the child began to weep and wail, saying that the man in the reverie was frightening him. The monks told him not to be afraid, but to come down."Oh!" cried the child, "I am as though nailed here, unable to move hand or foot."

The monks became alarmed. They flocked around Jelāl, and begged him to release the child. After a time, he seemed to hear and understand them. His answer was: "Only through the acceptance of Islām by yourselves, all of you, as well as by the child, can he be saved."

In the end they all embraced Islām, and wished to follow Jelāl as his disciples. He recommended them, however, to remain in their cave, as before, to cease from practising jugglery, and to serve God in the spirit and in truth. So he proceeded on his journey.

8

Jelāl remained seven years, or four years, at Damascus; and there he first saw his great friend Shemsu-'d-Dīn of Tebrīz, clothed in his noted black felt and peculiar cap. Shems addressed him; but he turned away, and mixed in the crowd. Soon afterwards, he returned to Qonya by way of Qaysariyya. At this latter place, under the guiding supervision of his spiritual teacher, the Seyyid Burhānu-'d-Dīn, Jelāl fasted three consecutive periods of forty days each, with only a pot of water and two or three loaves of barley bread. He showed no signs of suffering. Burhān now pronounced him perfect in all science, patent and occult, human and spiritual. (Compare chap. ii. No. 3.)

9

In the year A.H. 642 (A.D. 1244), Shemsu-'d-Dīn of Tebrīz came to Qonya.

This great man, after acquiring a reputation of superior sanctity at Tebrīz, as the disciple of a certain holy man, a basket-maker by trade, had travelled about much in various lands, in search of the best spiritual teachers, thus gaining the nickname of Perenda (the *Flier*, *Bird*, &c.).

He prayed to God that it might be revealed to him who was the most occult of the favourites of the divine will, so that he might go to him and learn still more of the mysteries of divine love.

The son of Bahā'u-'d-Dīn Veled, of Balkh, was designated to him as the man most in favour with God. Shems went, accordingly, to Qonya; arriving there on Saturday, the 26th of Jemādà-'l-ākhir, A.H. 642 (December A.D. 1244). He engaged a lodging at an inn, and pretended to be a great merchant. In his room, however, there was nothing but a broken water-pot, an old mat, and a bolster of unbaked clay. He broke his fast once in every ten or twelve days, with a damper soaked in broth of sheep's trotters.

One day, as he was seated at the gate of the inn, Jelāl came by, riding on a mule, in the midst of a crowd of students and disciples on foot.

Shemsu-'d-Dīn arose, advanced and took hold of the mule's bridle, addressing Jelāl in these words: "Exchanger of the current coins of recondite significations, who knowest the names of the Lord! Tell me: Was Muhammed the greater servant of God, or Bāyezīd of Bestām?"

Jelāl answered him: "Muhammed was incomparably the greater—the greatest of all prophets and all saints."

"Then," rejoined Shemsu-'d-Dīn, "how is it that Muhammed said: 'We have not known Thee, O God, as Thou rightly shouldest be known,' whereas Bāyezīd said: 'Glory unto me! How very great is my glory'?"

On hearing this question, Jelāl fainted away. On recovering his consciousness, he took his new acquaintance home with him. They were closeted together for weeks or months in holy communications.

Jelāl's disciples at length became impatient, raising a fearful and threatening tumult; so that, on Thursday, the 21st of Shewwāl, A.H. 643 (March A.D. 1246), Shemsu-'d-Dīn mysteriously disappeared; and Jelāl adopted, as a sign of mourning for his loss, the drab hat and wide cloak since worn by the dervishes of his order.

It was about this time, also, that he first instituted the musical services observed by that order, as they perform their peculiar waltzing. All men took to music and dancing in consequence. Fanatics objected, out of envy. They said Jelāl was gone mad, even as the chiefs of Mekka had said of old of the Prophet. His supposed malady was attributed to the malefic influence of Shemsu-'d-Dīn of Tebrīz.

10

The widow of Jelāl, Kirā (*or* Girā) Khātūn, a model of virtue, the Mary of her age, is related to have seen, through a chink in the door of the room where he and Shems were closeted in spiritual communion, that the wall suddenly opened, and six men of majestic mien entered by the cleft.

These strangers, who were of the occult saints, saluted, bowed, and laid a nosegay at the feet of Jelāl, although it was then in the depth of the midwinter season. They remained until near the hour of dawn worship, when they motioned to Shemsu-'d-Dīn to act as leader on the occasion of the service. He excused himself, and Jelāl performed the office. The service of worship over, the six strangers took leave, and passed out by the same cleft in the wall.

Jelāl now came forth from the chamber, bringing the nosegay in his hand. Seeing his wife in the passage, he gave her the nosegay, saying that the strangers had brought it as an offering to her.

The next day, she sent her servant, with a few leaves from her nosegay, to the perfumers' mart of the city, to inquire what might be the flowers composing it, as she had never seen their like before. The merchants were all equally astonished; no one had ever seen such leaves. At length, however, a spice merchant from India, who was then sojourning in Qonya, saw those leaves, and knew them to be the petals of a flower that grows in the south of India, in the neighbourhood of Ceylon.

The wonder now was: How did these Indian flowers get to Qonya; and in the depth of winter, too?

The servant carried the leaves back, and reported to his lady what he had learnt. This increased her astonishment a hundredfold. Just then Jelāl made his appearance, and enjoined on her to take the greatest care of the nosegay, as it had been sent to her by the florists of the lost earthly paradise, through those Indian saints, as a special offering.

It is related that she preserved them as long as she lived, merely giving a few leaves, with Jelāl's express permission, to the Georgian wife of the king. If any one suffered with any disease of the eyes, one leaf from that nosegay, applied to the ailing part, was an instant cure. The flowers never lost their fragrance or freshness. What is musk compared with such?

11

To prove that man lives through God's will alone, and not by blood, Jelāl one day, in the presence of a crowd of physicians and philosophers, had the veins of both his arms opened, and allowed them to bleed until they ceased to flow.

He then ordered incisions to be made in various parts of his body; but not one drop of moisture was anywhere obtainable. He now went to a hot bath, washed, performed an ablution, and then commenced the exercise of the sacred dance.

12

One of Jelāl's disciples died, and there was a consultation among his friends as to whether he should be buried in a coffin or without one.

Another disciple, after Jehāl had been consulted, and had told them to do as they pleased, made the observation that it would be better to bury their relative without a coffin. On being asked why, he answered: "A mother can better nurse her child, than can her child's brother. The earth is the mother of the human race, and the wood of a coffin is also the earth's child; therefore, the coffin is the man's brother. Man's corpse should be committed, then, not to a coffin, but to mother earth, his loving affectionate parent."

Jelāl expressed his admiration for this apposite and sublime doctrine, which, he said, was not to be found written in any then extant book.

The name of the disciple who made this beautiful remark was Kerīmu-'d-Dīn, son of Begh-Tīmūr.

13

Many of the chief disciples of Jelāl have related that he himself explained to them, as his reasons for instituting the musical service of his order, with their dancing, the following reflections:—

"God has a great regard for the Roman people. In answer to a prayer of the first Caliph, Abū-Bekr, God made the Romans a chief receptacle of his mercy; and the land of the Romans (Asia Minor) is the most beautiful on the face of the earth. But the people of the land were utterly void of all idea of the riches of a love towards God, and of the remotest shade of a taste for the delights of the inner, spiritual life. The great Causer of all causes caused a source of affection to arise, and out of the wilderness of causelessness raised a means by which I was attracted away from the land of Khurāsān to the country of the Romans. That country he made a home for my children and posterity, in order that, with the elixir of his grace, the copper of their existences might be transmuted into gold and into philosopher-stone, they themselves being received into the communion of saints. When I perceived that they had no inclination for the practice of religious austerities, and no knowledge of the divine mysteries, I imagined to arrange metrical exhortations and musical services, as being captivating for men's minds, and more especially so for the Romans, who are naturally of a lively disposition, and fond of incisive expositions. Even as a sick child is coaxed into taking a salutary, though nauseous medicine, so, in like manner, were the Romans led by art to acquire a taste for spiritual truth."

14

As an instance of the great value attached to the poetry of Jelāl, the following anecdote is related:—

Shemsu-'d-Dīn Hindī, Prince of Shīrāz in the province of Fars, Southern Persia), wrote a flattering letter to the re-nowned poet, Sheykh Sa'dī, of Shīrāz (who lived A.H. 571–691, A.D. 1175–1291, and was consequently a contemporary of Jelāl's), begging him to select the best ode, with the most sublime thoughts, that he knew of as existing in Persian, and to send it to him, for presentation to the great Khān of the Moguls (who then ruled over nearly all Asia).

It so happened that the ode by Jelāl had just become known at Shīrāz, which commences:—

"Divine love's voice each instant left and right is heard to sound,
We're bound for heaven. To witness our departure who'll be found?"

This ode had captivated the minds of all the men of culture in the city; and this ode Sa'dī selected, wrote it out, and sent it to the prince, with the remark: "A monarch, of auspicious advent, has sprung up in the land of Rome, from whose privacy these are some of the breathings. Never have more beautiful words been uttered, and never will be. Would that I could go to Rome, and rub my face in the dust under his feet!"

The prince thanked Sa'dī exceedingly, and sent him valuable presents in return. Eventually, Sa'dī did go to "Rome," arrived in Qonya, and had the gratification to kiss the hand of Jelāl. He was well received in that city by the dervish circle.

The prince was himself a disciple of Sheykh . . . . 'd-Dīn, of Bakharz (in Khurāsān, about midway between Tūrshīz and Herāt), to whom he sent a copy of the ode, to learn what the sheykh would think of it. All the learned men of Bakharz assembled round the sheykh. He read the ode attentively, and then burst out into exclamations of the wildest delight and most fervid admiration, rending his garments, and acting as though mad. At length he calmed down and said: "O wonderful man! O thou champion of the Faith! Thou pole of the heavens and of the earth! Verily, thou art a wonderful sultan, who hast appeared on earth! In good sooth, all the sheykhs of bygone ages who were seers, have been frustrated in not having seen this man! They would have supplicated the Lord of Truth to allow them to meet him! But it was not to be; and this mercy will last until the end of time, as has been sung:—

"A fortune, by the men of ancient times in dreams long sought,
Has been vouchsafed to modern men; without their efforts caught."

"One ought to put on ironed shoes, and take in hand an ironed staff, to set out at once and visit this great light. I make it a legacy to all my friends to do so without the least delay, if they have the means and the strength, so as to achieve the happiness and secure the honour of making the acquaintance of this prince, so obtaining the grace and favour of hearing him. His father, Bahā Veled, and his ancestors, were great sheykhs and most illustrious; their great progenitor having been the first Caliph, Abū-Bekr, the glorious confirmer of the truth spoken by the apostle of God. I am myself old and infirm, unequal to the fatigues of travel. Otherwise, I would have walked, not on the soles of my feet, but on the tips of my great toes, to visit that eminent man."

The sheykh's eldest son, Muzahhiru-'d-Dīn, was there present. To him the sheykh addressed himself, saying: "My son, I do hope that thy eyes will behold this sacred visage; and, if God so will, convey to him my salutation and my respects."

After the death of the old man, his son went to Rome, had the felicity to see Jelāl, and presented his father's message. He returned to Bakharz; but it is said that a son of his lies buried at Qonya.

15

Kirā Khātūn, the widow of Jelāl, is reported to have related to a friend that there was in their household a candlestick of the height of a man, before which Jelāl used to stand on foot the night through, until daydawn, studying the writings of his father.

One night, a company of the genii, dwellers in the college where Jelāl and his wife lived, appeared to her in a body, to complain of the great inconvenience and suffering to which they were subjected by this practice of Jelāl's, and saying: "We can put up with it no longer. Take care, lest we do a mischief to some one in the college."

The lady reported this complaint of the genii to her husband. He merely smiled, and took no further notice of the matter for several days.

At the end of that time, however, he spoke of it, and told his wife to trouble herself no more about the threat of the genii, as he had converted them all. They had become disciples of his, and would certainly do no harm to any friend or dependent of their teacher.

16

It was related by one of the chief of Jelāl's disciples, a butcher by trade, a trainer of dogs for the chase, and a purveyor of horses of the best kind, which he used to sell to princes and grandees at high prices, that, at a certain time, Jelāl was much exercised by visions from the spiritual world, so that for forty days he was as though beside himself, pas-

sing through the streets with his head bare, and his turban
twisted round his neck.

After that, he came suddenly one day, bathed in perspira-
tion, to the butcher, and said he wanted a certain unbroken
horse to be saddled for him immediately. The butcher, with
the help of three stable-men, managed with the utmost difficulty to saddle the horse and bring him out. Jelāl mounted
him without opposition, and set off in a southerly direction.
The butcher asked whether he should accompany him, and
Jelāl replied: "Give me your prayers and holy good wishes."

In the evening Jelāl returned covered with dust. The poor
horse, though of gigantic frame, was reduced to mere skin
and bone, being nearly broken-backed with fatigue.

The next day he came again, and asked for another horse,
better than the one of yesterday, mounted it, and rode off.
He returned at the hour of sunset devotions, and this horse
also was reduced to a pitiable condition. The butcher dared
not offer a word of remonstrance.

On the third day he came again, mounted a third horse,
and returned as before, at sunset. He sat down now in the
most composed manner possible, and called out cheerily:
"Good news! Glad tidings, O ye of the Faith! That dog of
hell has gone back to his pit of fire!"

The butcher was too much astonished at his manner to feel
any inclination to inquire what these words might mean; but
a certain number of days afterwards, a large caravan came
into Qonya from Syria, and brought news that the Mogul
army had besieged Damascus, and had reduced it to straits.

Helaw Khan (Holagu, Helagu) had taken Bagdad in A.H.
655 (A.D. 1257–58). Two years later, A.H. 657 (A.D. 1259–60),
he advanced against Aleppo and Syria, sending his general,
Ketbuga, against Damascus with a numerous army. He laid
siege to the city. But the inhabitants witnessed, with their
very own eyes, that Jelāl came and joined himself there to the
forces of Islām. He inflicted defeat on the Mogul forces, who
were compelled to retreat, totally frustrated.

The butcher was overjoyed at this welcome intelligence,
and went forthwith to communicate the news to Jelāl. The

latter smilingly replied: "Yes, yes! Jelālu-'d-Dīn was the horse-man who obtained a victory over the enemy, and showed himself a sultan in the eyes of the people of Islām." On hearing this, his disciples rent the air with their shouts of joy and triumph, and the townspeople of Qonya decked out and illuminated the city, holding public rejoicings.

This miracle of power became noised abroad, and every-where Jelāl's friends and adherents were transported with ecstasy at its occurrence.

17

On one occasion a rich merchant of Tebrīz came to Qonya. He inquired of his agents there who was the most eminent man of learning and piety in the city, as he wished to go and pay his respects to him. He remarked to them: "It is not merely for the sake of making money that I travel about in every country on earth; I desire also to make the acquain-tance of every man of eminence I can find in each city."

His correspondents told him that the Sheykhu-'l-Islām of the capital had a great reputation for learning and piety, and that they would be proud to present him to that celebrated luminary. Accordingly, he selected a number of rarities from among his store, to the value of thirty sequins; and the party set out to visit the great lawyer.

The merchant found the dignitary lodged in a great palace, with guards at the gate, crowds of servants and attendants in the courtyard, and eunuchs, pages, grooms, ushers, chamber-lains, and the like, in the halls.

Turning to his conductors, he expressed some doubt as to whether they had not, by mistake, brought him to the king's palace. They quieted his fears, and led him into the presence of the great fountain of legal erudition. He felt a very great dislike for all he saw; and he remarked to his friends: "A great lawyer is never anything the worse for possessing a clear conscience. A physician may himself indulge in sweet-meats; but he does not prescribe them to a patient suffering with fever."

He now offered his presents; and then inquired of the great

lawyer whether he could solve a doubt under which he was then labouring. This he stated as follows:—"Of late, I have been sustaining a series of losses. Can you indicate a way by which I may escape from that unfortunate position? I give, every year, the fortieth part of my liable possessions to the poor; and I distribute alms besides, to the extent of my power. I cannot conceive, therefore, why I am unfortunate."

Other remarks he made also to the same effect. They appeared to be lost on the great luminary, who affected to be otherwise preoccupied. At length the merchant took leave without obtaining a solution to his difficulty.

The day following he inquired of his friends whether there did not chance to be, in the great city, some poor mendicant of exemplary piety, to whom he might offer his respects, and from whom he might, haply, learn what he longed to know, together with advice that would be of service to him. They answered: "Just such a man as thou describest is our Lord, Jelālu-'d-Dīn. He has forsaken all pleasures, save only his love towards God. Not only has he given up all concern for worldly matters, he has also renounced all care as to a future state. He passes his nights, as well as his days, in the worship of God; and he is a very ocean of knowledge in all temporal and spiritual subjects."

The Tebrīz merchant was enchanted with this information. He begged to see that holy man, the bare mention of whose virtues had filled him with delight. They accordingly conducted him to the college of Jelāl, the merchant having privately furnished himself with a rouleau of fifty sequins in gold as his offering to the saint.

When they reached the college, Jelāl was sitting alone in the lecture-hall, immersed in the study of some books. The party made their obeisances, and the merchant felt himself completely overpowered at the aspect of the venerable teacher; so that he burst into tears, and could not utter a word. Jelāl addressed him, therefore, as follows:—

"The fifty sequins thou hast provided as thy offering are accepted. But better for thee than these are the two hundred sequins thou hast lost. God, whose glory be exalted, had determined to visit thee with a sore judgment and a heavy trial; but, through this thy visit here, he hath pardoned thee, and the trial is averted from thee. Be not dismayed. From this day forth thou shalt not suffer loss; and that which thou hast already suffered shall be made up to thee."

The merchant was equally astonished and delighted at these words; more so, however, when Jelāl proceeded with his discourse: "The cause and reason of thy bygone losses and misfortunes was, that, on a certain day thou wast in the west of Firengistān (Europe), where thou wentest into a certain ward of a certain city, and there sawest a poor Firengī (European) man, one of the greatest of God's cherished saints, who was lying stretched out at the corner of a market-place. As thou didst pass by him, thou spattest on him, evincing aversion from him. His heart was grieved by thy act and demeanour. Hence the visitations that have afflicted thee. Go thou, then, and make thy peace with him, asking his forgiveness, and offering him our salutations."

The merchant was petrified at this announcement. Jelāl then asked him: "Wilt thou that we this instant show him to thee?" So saying, he placed his hand on the wall of the apartment, and told the merchant to behold. Instantly, a doorway opened in the wall, and the merchant thence perceived that man in Firengistān, lying down in a market-place. At this sight he bowed down his head and rent his garments, coming away from the saintly presence in a state of stupor. He remembered all these incidents as facts.

Immediately commencing his preparations, he set out without delay, and reached the city in question. He inquired for the ward he wished to visit, and for the man whom he had offended. Him he discovered lying down, stretched out as Jelāl had shown him. The merchant dismounted from his beast, and made his obeisance to the prostrate Firengī dervish, who at once addressed him thus: "What wilt thou that I do? Our Lord Jelāl suffereth me not; or otherwise, I had a desire to make thee see the power of God, and what I am. But now, draw near."

The Firengī dervish then clasped the merchant to his

bosom, kissed him repeatedly on both cheeks, and then
added: "Look now, that thou mayest see my Lord and
Teacher, my spiritual Master, and that thou mayest witness a
marvel." The merchant looked. He saw the Lord Jelāl immersed in a holy dance, chanting this hymn, and entranced
with sacred music:—

"His kingdom's vast and pure; each sort its fitting place finds there;
 Cornelian, ruby, clod, or pebble be thou on his hill.
 Believe, he seeks thee; disbelieve, he'll haply cleanse thee fair;
 Be here a faithful Abū-Bekr; Firengī there; at will."

When the merchant happily reached Qonya on his return,
he gave the salutations of the Firengī saint, and his respects,
to Jelāl; and distributed much substance among the disciples.
He settled at Qonya, and became a member of the fraternity
of the Pure Lovers of God.

18

Jelāl was one day passing by a street, where two men were
quarrelling. He stood on one side. One of the men called out
to the other: "Say what thou will; thou shalt hear from me a
thousandfold for every word thou mayest utter."

Hereupon Jelāl stepped forward and addressed this
speaker, saying: "No, no! Whatsoever thou have to say, say it
to me; and for every thousand thou mayest say to me, thou
shalt hear from me one word."

On hearing this rebuke, the adversaries were abashed, and
made their peace with one another.

19

One day, a very learned professor brought all his pupils to
pay their respects to Jelāl.

On their way to him, the young men agreed together to put
some questions to Jelāl on certain points of Arabic grammar,
with the design of comparing his knowledge in that science
with that of their professor, whom they looked upon as
unequalled.

When they were seated, Jelāl addressed them on various

fitting subjects for a while, and thereby paved the way for the
following anecdote:—

"An ingenuous jurist was once travelling with an Arabic
grammarian, and they chanced to come to a ruinous well.

"The jurist hereupon began to recite the text (of Qur'ān
xxii. 44): 'And of a ruined well.'

"The Arabic word for 'well' he pronounced 'bīr,' with the
vowel long. To this the grammarian instantly objected, telling
the jurist to pronounce that word with a short vowel and
hiatus—bi'r, so as to be in accord with the requirements of
classical purity.

"A dispute now arose between the two on the point. It
lasted all the rest of the day, and well on into a pitchy dark
night; every author being ransacked by them, page by page,
each sustaining his own theory of the word. No conclusion
was arrived at, and each disputant remained of his own opinion still.

"It so happened in the dark, that the grammarian slipped
into the well, and fell to the bottom. There he set up a wail of
entreaty: 'O my most courteous fellow-traveller, lend thy help
to extricate me from this most darksome pit.'

"The jurist at once expressed his most pleasurable wil-
lingness to lend him that help, with only one trifling condition—that he should confess himself in error, and consent
to suppress the hiatus in the word 'bi'r.' The grammarian's
answer was 'Never.' So in the well he remained."

"Now," said Jelāl, "to apply this to yourselves. Unless you
will consent to cast out from your hearts the '*hiatus*' of
indecision and of self-love, you can never hope to escape
from the noisome pit of self-worship—the well of man's
nature and of fleshly lusts. The dungeon of 'Joseph's well' in
the human breast is this very 'self-worship;' and from it you
will not escape, nor will you ever attain to those heavenly
regions—'the spacious land of God' " (Qur'ān iv. 99, xxix.
56, xxxix. 13).

On hearing these pregnant words, the whole assembly of
undergraduates uncovered their heads, and with fervent zeal
professed themselves his spiritual disciples.

20

There was a great and good governor (apparently) of
Qonya, of the name of Mu'īnu-'d-Dīn, whose title was the
Perwāna (moth or fly-wheel, viz., of the far-distant Mogul
Emperor, resident at the court of the king). He was a great
friend to the dervishes, to the learned, and to Jelāl, whose
loving disciple he was.

One day, a company of the dervishes and learned men
united in extolling the perwāna to the skies, in Jelāl's
presence. He assented to all they advanced in that respect,
and added: "The perwāna merits a hundredfold all your
eulogiums. But there is another side to the question, which
may be exemplified by the following anecdote:—

"A company of pilgrims were once proceeding towards
Mekka, when the camel of one of the party fell down in the
desert, totally exhausted. The camel could not be got to rise
again. Its load was, therefore, transferred to another beast,
the fallen brute was abandoned to its fate, and the caravan
resumed its journey.

"Ere long the fallen camel was surrounded by a circle of
ravenous wild beasts—wolves, jackals, &c. But none of these
ventured to attack him. The members of the caravan became
aware of this singularity, and one of them went back to in-
vestigate the matter. He found that an amulet had been left
suspended on the animal's neck; and this he removed. When
he had retreated to a short distance, the hungry brutes fell
upon the poor camel, and soon tore him piecemeal."

"Now," said Jelāl, "this world is in an exactly similar
category with that poor camel. The learned of the world are
the company of pilgrims, and our (Jelāl's) existence among
them is the amulet suspended round the neck of the camel—
the world. So long as we remain so suspended, the world will
go on, the caravan will proceed. But so soon as the divine
mandate shall be spoken: 'O thou submissive spirit, come
thou back to thy Lord, content and approved' (Qur'ān lxx-
xix. 27–8), and we be removed from the neck of the world-
camel, people will see how it shall fare with the world—how
its inhabitants shall be driven—what shall become of its

sultans, its doctors, its scribes."

It is said that these words were spoken a short time before Jelāl's death. When he departed this life, not much time elapsed ere the sultan, with many of his great men of learning and nobles, followed him to the grave, while troubles of all kinds overwhelmed the land for a season, until God again vouchsafed it peace.

21

During one of his expositions, Jelāl said: "Thou seest naught, save that thou seest God therein."

A dervish came forward and raised the objection that the term "therein" indicated a receptacle, whereas it could not be predicated of God that he is comprehensible by any receptacle, as this would imply a contradiction in terms. Jelāl answered him as follows:—

"Had not that unimpeachable proposition been true, we had not proffered it. There is therein, forsooth, a contradiction in terms; but it is a contradiction in time, so that the receptacle and the recepted may differ—may be two distinct things; even as the universe of God's qualities is the receptacle of the universe of God's essence. But, these two universes are really one. The first of them is not he; the second of them is not other than he. Those, apparently, two things are in truth one and the same. How, then, is a contradiction in terms implied? God comprises the exterior and the interior. If we cannot say he is the interior, he will not include the interior. But he comprises all, and in him all things have their being. He is, then, the receptacle also, comprising all existences, as the Qur'ān (xli. 54) says: 'He comprises all things.' "

The dervish was convinced, bowed, and declared himself a disciple.

22

Jelāl was one day seated in the shop of his great disciple the Goldbeater, Salāhu-'d-Dīn; and was surrounded by a circle of other disciples, listening to his discourse; when an old man came rushing in, beating his breast, and uttering loud lamentations. He entreated Jelāl to help him in his endeavours to recover his little son, a child seven years old, lost for several days past, in spite of every effort made to find him.

Jelāl expressed his disapprobation at the extreme importance the old man appeared to attach to his loss; and said: "Mankind in general have lost their God. Still, one does not hear that they go about in quest of him, beating their breasts and making a great noise. What, then, has happened to thee so very particular, that thou makest all this fuss, and degradest thyself, an elder, by these symptoms of grief for the loss of a little child? Why seekest thou not for a time the Lord of the whole world, begging assistance of him, that peradventure thy lost Joseph may be found, and thou be comforted, as was Jacob on the recovery of his child?"

The old man at once followed Jelāl's advice, and begged forgiveness of God. Just then, news was brought him there that his son had been found. Many who were witnesses of these circumstances became devoted followers of Jelāl.

23

Jelāl was one day lecturing, when a young man of distinction came in, pushed his way, and took a seat higher up than an old man, one of the audience.

Jelāl at once remarked: "In days of yore it was the command of God, that, if any young man should take precedence of an elder, the earth should at once swallow him up; such being the divine punishment for that offence. Now, however, I see that young men, barely out of leading-strings, show no respect for age, but trample over those in years. They have no dread of the earth's swallowing them up, nor any fear of being transformed into apes.[1] It happened, however, that one morning the Victorious Lion of God, 'Alī, son of Abū-Tālib, was hasting from his house to perform his devotions at dawn in the mosque of the Prophet. On his way, he overtook an old man, a Jew, who was going in the same direction. The future

[1] As related of certain Sabbath-breaking Jews, in Qur'ān ii. 61.

Caliph, out of innate nobility and politeness of nature, had respect for the Jew's age, and would not pass him, though the Jew's pace was slow. When 'Alī reached the mosque, the Prophet was already bowed down in his devotions, and was about to chant the '*Gloria;*' but, by God's command, Gabriel came down, laid his hand on the Prophet's shoulder, and stopped him, lest 'Alī should lose the merit attaching to his being present at the opening of the dawn service; for it is more meritorious to perform that early service once, than to fulfil the devotions of a hundred years at other hours of the day. The Prophet has said: 'The first act of reverence at dawn worship is of more value than the world and all that is therein.'

"When the Apostle of God had concluded his *worship*, offered up his *customary prayers*, and recited his usual *lessons* from the Qur'ān, he turned, and asked of Gabriel the occult cause of his interruption at that time. Gabriel replied that God had not seen fit that 'Alī should be deprived of the merit attaching to the performance of the first portion of the dawn worship, through the respect he had shown to the old Jew he had overtaken, but whom he would not pass.

"Now," remarked Jelāl, "when a saint like 'Alī showed so much respect for a poor old misbelieving Jew, and when God viewed his respectful consideration in so highly favourable a manner, you may all infer how he will view any honour and veneration shown to an elderly saint of approved piety, whose beard has grown grey in the service of God, and whose companions are the elect of their Maker, whose chosen servant he is; and what reward he will mete out in consequence. For, in truth, glory and power belong to God, to the Apostle, and to the believers, as God hath himself declared (Qur'ān lxiii. 8): 'Unto God belongeth the power, and to the apostle, and to the believers.'

"If then," added he, "ye wish to be prosperous in your affairs, take fast hold on the skirts of your spiritual elders. For, without the blessing of his pious elders, a young man will never live to be old, and will never attain the station of a spiritual elder."

24

One day Jelāl took as his text the following words (Qur'ān xxxi. 18):—"Verily, the most discordant of all sounds is the voice of the asses." He then put the question: "Do my friends know what this signifies?"

The congregation all bowed, and entreated him to expound it to them. Jelāl therefore proceeded:—

"All other brutes have a *cry*, a *lesson*, and a *doxology*, with which they commemorate their Maker and Provider. Such are, the *yearning cry* of the camel, the *roar* of the lion, the *bleat* of the gazelle, the *buzz* of the fly, the *hum* of the bee, &c.

"The angels in heaven, and the genii, have their doxologies also, even as man has his doxology—his *Magnificat*, and various forms of worship for his heart (or mind) and for his body.

"The poor ass, however, has nothing but his *bray*. He sounds this bray on two occasions only: when he desires his female, and when he feels hunger. He is the slave of his lust and of his gullet.

"In like manner, if man have not in his heart a doxology for God, a cry, and a love, together with a secret and a care in his mind, he is less than an ass in God's esteem; for he has said (Qur'ān vii. 178): 'They are like the camels; nay, they are yet more erring.'" He then related the following anecdote:—

"In bygone days there was a monarch, who, by way of trial, requested another sovereign to send him three things, the worst of their several kinds that he could procure; namely, the worst article of food, the worst dispositioned thing, and the worst animal.

"The sovereign so applied to sent him some *cheese*, as the worst food; an Armenian slave, as the worst-dispositioned thing; and an ass, as the worst of animals. In the superscription to the epistle sent with these offerings, the sovereign quoted the verse of Scripture pointed out above."

25

On a certain day, the Lord Jelālu-'d-Dīn went forth to the country residence of the saint Husāmu-'d-Dīn, riding on an ass. He remarked: "This is the saddle-beast of the righteous. Several of the prophets have ridden on asses: as Seth, Ezra, Jesus, and Muhammed."

It so chanced that one of his disciples was also mounted on an ass. The creature suddenly began to bray; and the rider, annoyed at the occurrence, struck the ass on the head several times.

Jelál remonstrated: "Why strike the poor brute? Strikest thou him because he bears thy burden? Returnest thou not thanks for that thou art the rider, and he the vehicle? Suppose now, which God forbid, that the reverse were the case. What wouldst thou have done? His cry arises from one or the other of two causes, his gullet or his lust. In this respect, he shares the common lot of all creatures. They are all continually thus actuated. All, then, would have to be scolded and beaten over the head."

The disciple was abashed. He dismounted, kissed the hoof of his ass, and caressed him

26

On a certain occasion, one of his disciples complained to Jelál of the scantiness of his means and the extent of his needs. Jelál answered: "Out upon thee! Get thee gone! Henceforward, count me not a friend of thine; and so, peradventure, wealth may come to thee." He then related the following anecdote:—

"It happened, once, that a certain disciple of the Prophet said to him: 'I love thee!' The Prophet answered: 'Why tarriest thou, then? Haste to put on a breastplate of steel, and set thy face to encounter misfortunes. Prepare thyself, also, to endure straitness, the special gift of the friends and lovers (of God and his Apostle)!'"

Another anecdote, also, he thus narrated: "A Gnostic adept once asked of a rich man which he loved best, riches or sin. The latter answered that he loved riches best. The other replied: 'Thou sayest not the truth. Thou better lovest sin and calamity. Seest thou not that thou leavest thy riches behind, whilst thou carriest thy sin and thy calamity about with thee,

making thyself reprehensible in the sight of God! Be a man!
Exert thyself to carry thy riches with thee, and sin not; since
thou lovest thy riches. What thou has to do is this: Send thy
riches to God ere thou goest before him thyself; peradventure, they may work thee some advantage; even as God hath
said (Qur'ān lxxiii. 20): 'And that which ye send before, for
your souls of good works, shall ye find with God. He is the
best and the greatest in rewarding.' "

27

It is related that one day the perwāna, Mu'īnu-'d-Dīn, held
a great assembly in his palace. To this meeting were collected
together all the doctors of the law, the sheykhs, the men of
piety, the recluses, and the strangers who had congregated
from various lands.

The chiefs of the law had taken their places in the highest
seats. The perwāna had had a great desire that Jelāl should
honour the assembly with his presence. He had a son-in-law,
Mejdu-'d-Dīn, governor to the young princes, the sons of the
king. This son-in-law of his was a disciple of Jelāl's, and a
man of very eminent qualities, with great faith in his teacher.
He offered to go and invite Jelāl to the meeting.

Hereupon, the arch-sower of doubts and animosities in the
human breast spread among the chiefs of the law, there
present, the suspicion that, if Jelāl should come, the question
of precedence would arise: "Where should he be seated?"
They all agreed that they were themselves in their proper
places, and that Jelāl must find a seat where he could.

Mejdu-'d-Dīn delivered the perwāna's courteous message
to his teacher. Jelāl, inviting Husāmu-'d-Dīn and others of
his disciples to accompany him, set out for the perwāna's
palace. The disciples went on a little ahead, and Jelāl brought
up the procession.

When Husām entered the apartment of the perwāna, all
present rose to receive him, making room for him in the upper
seats. Lastly, Jelāl made his appearance.

The perwāna and other courtiers crowded forward to
receive Jelāl with honour, and kissed his lordship's blessed

hands with reverence, expressing regret that he had been put to inconvenience by his condescension. He returned compliment for compliment, and was shown upstairs.

On reaching the assembly room, he saw that the grandees had occupied the whole of the sofa, from end to end. He saluted them, and prayed for God's grace to be showered upon them; seating himself then in the middle of the floor. Husāmu-'d-Dīn immediately rose from his seat, descended from the sofa, and took a place by the side of Jelāl.

The grandees of the assembly now arose also, excepting those who, in spite and pride, had formed the confederacy mentioned above. These kept their seats. Some of them were of the greatest eminence in learning; and one, especially, was not only very learned, but also eloquent, witty, and bold.

He, seeing what had taken place, and that all the men of rank had quitted the sofa, to seat themselves on the floor, asked in a jocose manner: "Where, according to the rules of the Order, is the chief seat in an assembly?"

Some one answered him: "In an assembly of the learned, the chief seat is in the middle of the sofa, where the professor always sits." Another added: "With recluses, the cell of solitude is the chief seat." A third said: "In the convents of dervish brethren, the chief seat is the lower end of the sofa, where, in reality, people put off their shoes."

After these remarks, some one present, as an experiment, asked Jelāl, saying: "In your rule and opinion, where is the chief seat?' His answer was: "The chief seat is that where one's beloved is found." The interrogator now asked: "And where is your beloved?" Jelāl replied: "Thou must be blind, not to see."

Jelāl then arose, and began to sing. Many joined; and the singing became so enthusiastic, that the nobles rent their garments.

It so happened that, after Jelāl's death, this interlocutor of his went to Damascus, and there became blind. Friends flocked to visit him, and to condole with him. He wept bitterly, and cried aloud: "Alas, alas! what have I not suffered? That very moment, when Jelāl gave me that fatal answer, a black veil seemed to fall down over my eyes, so that I could not distinguish objects clearly, or their colours. But I have hope and faith in him, that, out of his sublime generosity, he will yet take pity on me, and pardon my presumption. The goodness of the saints is infinite; and Jelál himself hath said: 'Despair not because of one sin; for the ocean of divine mercy accepteth penitence.' "

The foregoing incident is also related with the following variation:—

Shemsu-'d-Dín of Tebríz had just then returned to Qonya, and was among those who accompanied Jelál to the per-wāna's palace, sitting down near him on the floor. When the question was put: "Where is your beloved?" Jelál arose, and cast himself on the breast of Shems. That occurrence it was that made Shems, from that time forward, a man of mark in all Qonya.

28

There was in Qonya a great physician, of eminence and ability, who used occasionally to visit Jelál.

On one of those days, Jelál requested him to prepare seventeen purgative draughts by a certain time, propitious for taking medicine, as that number of his friends required them.

When the specified time came, Jelál went to the physician's house, and received the seventeen draughts. He immediately began, and, in the physician's presence, drank off the whole seventeen in succession, thence returning home.

The physician followed him there, to render the assistance he felt sure would be wanted. He found Jelál seated as usual, in perfect health, and lecturing to his disciples. On inquiring how he felt, Jelál answered, in the words so often repeated in the Qur'ān (ii. 23, &c.): "Beneath which rivers flow." The physician recommended Jelál to abstain from water. Jelál instantly ordered ice to be brought and broken up small. Of this ñe swallowed an inordinate quantity, while the physician looked on.

Jelál then went to a hot bath. After bathing, he began to sing and dance; continuing in those exercises three whole days and nights, without intermission.

The physician declared this to be the greatest miracle ever wrought by prophet or by saint. With his whole family, and with many of the greatest in the medical profession, he joined himself to the multitude of Jelāl's disciples of the most sincere.

29

The perwāna is related to have said publicly, in his own palace, that Jelāl was a matchless monarch, no sovereign having ever appeared in any age like unto him; but that his disciples were a very disreputable set.

These words were reported to them, and the company of disciples were greatly scandalized at the imputation. Jelāl sent a note to the perwāna, of which the following is the substance:—

"Had my disciples been good men, I had been their disciple. Inasmuch as they were bad, I accepted them as my disciples, that they might reform and become good—of the company of the righteous. By the soul of my father, they were not accepted as disciples until God had made himself responsible that they would attain to mercy and grace, admitted among those accepted of him. Until that assurance was given, they were not received by me, nor had they any place in the hearts of the servants of God. 'The sons of grace are saved; the children of wrath are sick; for the sake of thy mercy, we, a people of wrath, have come to thee.'"

When the perwāna had read and considered these words, he became still more attached to Jelāl; arose, came to him, asked pardon, and prayed for forgiveness of God, distributing largely of his bounty among the disciples.

30

Another great and good man once observed: "Jelāl is a great saint and a sovereign; but he must be dragged forth from among his disciples." This was reported to Jelāl, who smiled, and said: "If he can!"

Soon afterwards he added: "Why, then, is it that my followers are looked upon with spite by the men of the world? It is because they are beloved of God, and favourably regarded by him. I have sifted all mankind; and all have fallen through my sieve, excepting these friends of mine. They have remained. My existence is the life of my friends, and the existence of my friends is the life of the men of the world whether they know this, or whether they ignore it."

31

There was a young merchant, whose house was near Jelāl's college, and who had professed himself a sincere and ardent disciple.

He conceived a desire and intention to make a voyage to Egypt; but his friends tried to dissuade him. His intention was reported to Jelāl, who strictly and rigorously prohibited his undertaking the voyage.

The young man could not divest himself of his desire, and had no peace of mind; so one night he clandestinely stole away, and went off to Syria. Arrived at Antioch, he embarked in a ship, and set sail. As God had willed, his ship was taken by Firengī pirates. He was made prisoner, and was confined in a deep dungeon, where he had a daily portion of food doled out to him, barely sufficient to keep his body and soul together.

He was thus kept imprisoned forty days, during which he wept bitterly, and reproached himself for having been disobedient to the injunction of Jelāl; saying: "This is the reward of my crime. I have disobeyed the command of my sovereign, following after my own evil propensity."

Precisely on the night of the fortieth day, he saw Jelāl in a dream, who addressed him, and said: "To-morrow, to whatever questions these misbelievers may ask thee, do thou return the answer: 'I know.' By that means shalt thou be released." He awoke bewildered, returned thanks to Heaven, and sat down in holy meditation, awaiting the solution of the dream.

Shortly, he saw a company of Firengī people come to him, with whom was an interpreter. They asked him: "Knowest thou aught of philosophy, and canst thou practise therapeutics? Our prince is sick." His answer was: "I know."

They immediately took him out of the pit, led him to a bath, and dressed him in a handsome vestment of honour. They then conducted him to the residence of the sick man.

The young merchant, inspired of God, ordered them to bring him seven fruits. These be prepared with a little scammony, and made the whole into a draught, which he administered to the patient.

By the grace of God, and the intercession of the saints, his treatment was crowned with success, after two or three visits. The Firengī prince recovered; and by reason that the favour of Jelāl was upon that young merchant, though he was utterly illiterate, he became a philosopher. Jelāl assisted him.

When the Firengī prince had entirely recovered his health, and had arisen from his sick-bed, he told the young merchant to ask of him whatsoever he might wish. He asked for his freedom, and for leave to return home, that he might rejoin his teacher. He then related all that had befallen him—his disobedience, his vision, and the assistance of Jelāl. The whole audience of Firengīs, without sight of Jelāl, became believers in him, and wooers of him.

They set the young merchant free, and allowed him to depart, bestowing on him rich presents and a bountiful outfit.

On his arrival at the metropolis, before going to his own house, he hastened to pay his respects to Jelāl. On beholding the sacred features from afar, he threw himself on the earth, embraced Jelāl's two feet, kissed them, rubbed his face upon them, and wept. Jelāl raised him, kissed both his cheeks, and said: "It was a narrow escape through thy curing the Firengī prince. Thou didst abscond; but henceforward, do thou remain at home, and occupy thyself in earning what is lawful. Take contentment as thy exemplar. The sufferings of the sea, the commotion of the ship, the calamity of captivity, and the darkness of the dungeon, are so many evils. Contentment is a very blessing from God."

32

Jelāl one day was going from his college into the town, when by chance he met a Christian monk, who made him an obeisance. Jelāl asked him which was the elder, himself or his beard. The monk replied: "I am twenty years older than my beard. It came forth that number of years later." Jelāl answered him: "Then I pity thee. Thy young beard has attained to maturity, whereas thou has remained immature, as thou wast. Thou art as black, and as weak, and as untutored as ever. Alas for thee, if thou change not, and ripen not!"

The poor monk at once renounced his rope girdle, threw it away, professed the faith of Islām, and became a believer.

33

A company of black-habited ones (Christian priests or monks) chanced to meet Jelāl one day, as they came from a distant place. When his disciples espied them afar off, they expressed their aversion from them by exclaiming: "O the dark-looking, disagreeable things!"

Jelāl remarked: "In the whole world, none are more generous than they are. They have given over to us, in this life, the faith of Islām, purity, cleanliness, and the various modes of worshipping God; while, in the world to come, they have left to us the everlasting abodes of paradise, the large-eyed damsels, and the pavilions, as well as the sight of God, of which they will enjoy no share; for God hath said (Qur'ān vii. 48): 'Verily God hath made both of them forbidden things to the misbelievers!' They walk in darkness and misbelief, willingly incurring the torments of hell. But, let only the sun of righteousness rise upon them suddenly, and they will become believers."

Being now come near enough, they all made their obeisances to Jelāl, entered into conversation with him, and professed themselves true Muslims. Jelāl now turned to his disciples, and added: "God swallows up the darkness in the light, and the light in the darkness. He also makes in the darkness a place for the light." The disciples bowed, and rejoiced.

34

A certain well-known disciple related that, on one occasion, Jelāl and his friends went forth to the country seat of

Husām, and there held a grand festival of holy music and dancing until near daybreak. Jelāl then left off, to give his followers a little rest.

They dispersed about the grounds; and the narrator took a seat in a spot from whence he could see and observe Jelāl. The others all fell asleep; but he occupied himself with reflections on the miracles performed by various of the prophets and of the saints. He thought to himself: "I wonder whether this holy man works miracles. Of course he does: only, he keeps the fact quiet, to avoid the inconveniences of notoriety."

Hardly had the thought crossed his mind, when Jelāl called him by name. On his approaching Jelāl, the latter stooped, picked up a pebble from the earth, placed it on the back of his own hand, and said to him: "Here, take this; it is thy portion; and be thou one of the thankful" (Qur'ān vii. 141).

The disciple examined the pebble by the light of the moon, and saw that it was a large ruby, exceedingly clear and brilliant, not to be found in the treasuries of kings.

Utterly astounded, he shrieked out, and swooned away; awaking the whole company with his shout; for he was a very loud-voiced man. On recovery, he told the others what had occurred. He also expressed to Jelāl his contrition for the temerity of his reflections.

Jelāl told him to carry the stone to the queen, and to mention how he had become possessed of it. The queen accepted it, had it valued, and gave to him a hundred and eighty thousand pieces of silver in return, besides rich gifts. She also distributed presents to all the members of the fraternity.

35

A certain sheykh, son of a sheykh, and a man of great reputation for learning, came to Qonya, and was respectfully visited by all the people of eminence residing there.

It so happened that Jelāl and his friends were gone that day to a mosque in the country; and the new-comer, offended at Jelāl's not hasting to visit him, made the remark in public:

"Has Jelāl never heard the adage: 'The newly-arrived one is visited'?"

One of Jelāl's disciples chanced to be present, and heard this remark. On the other hand, Jelāl was expounding sublime truths in the mosque to his disciples, when suddenly he exclaimed, "My dear brother! I am the newly-arrived one, not thou. Thou and those like thee are bound to visit me, and so gain honour to yourselves."

All his audience were surprised at this apostrophe; wondering to whom it was addressed. Jelāl then spake a parable: "One man came from Bagdād, and another went forth out of his house and ward; which of the two ought to pay the first visit to the other?"

All agreed in opinion that the man from Bagdād ought to be visited by the other. Then Jelāl explained, thus: "In reality, I am returned from the Bagdād of *nulliquity*, whereas this dearly beloved son of a sheykh, who has come here, has gone forth from a ward of this world. I am better entitled, therefore, to be visited than is he. I have been hymning in the Bagdād of the world of spirits the heavenly canticle: 'I am the Truth,' since a time anterior to the commencement of the present war, ere the truth obtained its victory." The disciples expressed their concurrence, and rejoiced exceedingly.

By and by, the sheykh's son was informed of this wonder. He at once arose, went on foot to visit Jelāl, uncovered his head, and owned that Jelāl was right. He further declared himself Jelāl's disciple, and said: "My father enjoined me to put on ironed sandals, taking an iron-shod staff in my hand, and go forth in quest of Jelālu-'d-Dīn, since it is a duty of all to visit and reverence him who has spoken the truth and reposes on the truth. But the majesty of Jelāl is a hundredfold greater than what my father explained to me."

36

Jelāl once commanded one of his attendants to go and arrange a certain matter. The attendant answered: "God willing."

Upon this, Jelāl was wroth, and shouted to him: "Stupid,

garrulous fool!" The attendant fainted and foamed at the mouth.

The disciples interceded. Jelāl expressed his forgiveness; and the attendant recovered.

37

On the occasion of a grand religious commemoration at the house of the perwāna, in the presence of the Sultan Ruknu-'d-Dīn, this monarch was taken unwell, and the exercises were suspended, only, one of the disciples continued to sing and shout.

The sultan remarked: "How ill-behaved is that man! Does he pretend to be more ecstatic than his teacher Jelālu-'d-Dīn?"

Jelāl heard this, and answered the king: "Thou art unable to withstand an attack of fever. How then canst thou expect a man devoured with an enthusiasm that threatens to swallow up even heaven itself, to calm down on a sudden?"

When the disciples heard this, they set up a shout; and the sultan, after himself witnessing one or two of the mighty signs wrought by Jelāl, made his obeisance to him, and became a disciple.

38

It has been related by some that the final overthrow of the rule of the Seljūqī dynasty in Asia Minor (in A.H. 700, A.D. 1300), was in this manner:—

The Sultan Ruknu-'d-Dīn had adopted Jelāl as his (spiritual) father. After a while, he held a great dervish festival in the palace. But, about that period, a certain Sheykh Bāba had created for himself a great name in Qonya, and certain intriguers had led the king to visit him.

It was shortly after that visit that the king held the revival in honour of Bāba in the Hall of the Bowls.

The sheykh was met and introduced in state by the court officials, and was then installed on the throne, with the sultan seated on a chair by his side. Jelāl now made his appearance, saluted, and took his seat in a corner of the hall. Portions of the Qur'ān were recited, and exhortations were delivered, with hymns.

The sultan then turned to Jelāl, and spoke: "Be it known to the Lord Jelāl, to the doctors of the law, and to the grandees, that I have adopted the Sheykh Bāba as my (spiritual) father, who has accepted me as his dutiful and affectionate son."

All present shouted their approval, and prayed for a blessing on the arrangement. But Jelāl, burning with divine jealousy, instantly exclaimed (in words traditionally related of the prophet, Muhammed): "Verily, Sa'd is a jealous man; but I am more jealous than Sa'd; and God is still more jealous than I am." To this he further added: "Since the sultan has made the sheykh his father, we will make some other our son." So saying, he gave his usual religious shout of ecstasy, and stalked out from the assembly.

Husāmu-'d-Dīn related that he saw the sultan, when Jelāl thus quitted the presence, turn pale, as though shot with an arrow.

The grandees ran to stop Jelāl; but he would not return.

A few days afterwards, the officers of state adopted the resolution to invite the sultan to go to another city, that they might take measures to get rid of Sheykh Bāba. The sultan now went to consult Jelāl, and ask for his blessing before setting out. Jelāl advised him not to go. The matter had, however, been officially promulgated, and there was no possibility to alter arrangements.

On arriving at the other town, the sultan was conducted to a private apartment, and forthwith strangled with a bowstring. Ere his breath failed, he invoked the name of Jelāl.

At that moment Jelāl was at his college, lost to consciousness in the enthusiasm of a musical service. Suddenly, he put his two forefingers into his two ears, and ordered the trumpets and chorus to join in. He then shouted vociferously, and recited aloud two of his own odes, of which one commences thus:

"My words were: 'Go not; I'm thy friend; the world is rife
  With threats of dire destruction; I'm the Fount of Life.'"

When the service was over, the disciples requested Jelāl's son, Sultan Veled, to inquire of his father what all this might signify. In reply, he merely put off his cloak, and said aloud: "Let us perform the service for the burial of the dead."

He acted as precentor in the service, and all present joined in. Then, without waiting for his son to put any question, he addressed the assembly, saying: "Yea, Bahā'u-'d-Dīn and my friends! They have strangled the poor Sultan Ruknu-'d-Dīn. In his agony, he called on me, and shrieked. God had so ordained. I did not wish his voice to ring in my ears, and interrupt my devotions. He will fare better in the other world."

(There is a serious anachronism in the foregoing account. Sultan Ruknu-'d-Dīn, whose name was Suleyman son of Key-Khusrew, was put to death by order of the Mogul emperor Abaqa Khān, in A.H. 664 (A.D. 1265), thirty-six years before the final extinction of the dynasty by order of Qāzān Khān, between Abaqa and whom no less than four emperors reigned. Besides this, Jelāl himself died in A.H. 672 (A.D. 1273), twenty-seven years before the last of the Seljūqī sovereigns, Key-Qubād son of Ferāmurz son of Key-Kāwus, was slaughtered, together with all living members of the race. Historians differ much respecting the names and order of succession of the last sovereigns of the dynasty; and the present anecdote shows how confused had become on the spot the legend of these puppets. Ruknu-'d-Dīn caused his own brother to be poisoned, as he had become jealous of the favour shown to that brother by the Mogul emperor. His own death was the reward of that act.)

39

One day, in lecturing on self-abasement and humility, Jelāl spake a parable from the trees of the field, and said: "Every tree that yields no fruit, as the pine, the cypress, the box, &c., grows tall and straight, lifting up its head on high, and sending all its branches upwards; whereas all the fruit-bearing trees droop their heads, and trail their branches. In like manner, the apostle of God was the most humble of men. Though he carried within himself all the virtues and excellencies of the ancients and of the moderns, he, like a fruitful tree, was more humble, and more of a dervish, than any other prophet. He is related to have said: 'I am commanded to show consideration to all men, to be kind to them; and yet, no prophet was ever so ill-treated by men as I have been.' We know that he had his head broken, and his teeth knocked out. Still he prayed: 'O our Lord God, guide thou my people aright; for they know not what they do.' Other prophets have launched denunciations against the people to whom they were sent; and certainly, none have had greater cause to do so, than Muhammed.''

"Old Adam's form was moulded first of clay from nature's face;
Who's not, as mire, low-minded's not true son of Adam's race.''

In like manner, Jelāl also had the commendable habit to show himself humble and considerate to all, even the lowest; especially so to children, and to old women. He used to bless them; and always bowed to those who bowed to him, even though these were not Muslims.

One day he met an Armenian butcher, who bowed to him seven times. Jelāl bowed to him in return. At another time he chanced upon a number of children who were playing, and who left their game, ran to him, and bowed. Jelāl bowed to them also; so much so, that one little fellow called out from afar: "Wait for me until I come." Jelāl moved not away, until the child had come, bowed, and been bowed to.

At that time, people were speaking and writing against him. Legal opinions were obtained and circulated, to the effect that music, singing, and dancing, are unlawful. Out of his kindly disposition, and love of peace, Jelāl made no reply; and after a while all his detractors were silenced, and their writings clean forgotten, as though they had never been written; whereas, his family and followers will endure to the end of time, and will go on increasing continually.

40

Jelāl once wrote a note to the perwāna, interceding for a

disciple who had been involved in an act of homicide, and
had taken refuge in the house of another.

The perwāna demurred; saying it was a very grave matter,
a question of blood. Jelāl thereupon facetiously replied: "A
homicide is popularly termed 'a son of 'Azrā'īl (the angel of
death).' Being such, what on earth is he to do, unless he kill
some one?"

This repartee so pleased the perwāna, that he pardoned the
culprit, and paid himself to the heirs of the slain man the
price of his blood.

41

Jelāl one day went forth and preached in the market.
Crowds collected round him. But he continued until night
fell around him; so he was at length left alone.

The dogs of the market-place now collected in a circle
about him, wagging their tails and whining.

Seeing this, Jelāl exclaimed: "By the Lord, the Highest, the
Strongest, the All-Compelling One, besides whom none is
high, or strong, or powerful! These dogs comprehend my
discourse, and the truths I expound. Men call them dogs; but
henceforward let them not be so termed. They are of the
family of the '*Seven Sleepers*.' " [1]

42

The perwāna much wished Jelāl to give him private
instruction at his palace; and requested Jelāl's son, Sultan
Veled, to intercede for him in the matter; which he did.

Jelāl replied to his son: "Bahā'u-'d-Dīn! He cannot bear
that burden." This was thrice repeated. Jelāl then remarked
to his son: "Bahā'u-'d-Dīn! A bucket, the water of which is
enough for forty, cannot be drained by one."

Bahā made the reflection: "Had I not pressed the matter, I
had never heard this wonderful saying."

43

At another time, the perwāna, through Bahā'u-'d-Dīn,

[1] Qur'ān xviii. 8, &c.

requested Jelāl to give a public lecture to all the men of
science of the city, who were desirous to hear him.

His answer was: "A tree laden with fruit, had its branches
bowed down to the earth therewith. At the time, doubts and
gainsayings prevented the gardeners from gathering and
enjoying the fruit. The tree has now raised its head to the
skies, and beyond. Can they hope, then, to pluck and eat of
its fruit?"

44

Again, the perwāna requested Jelāl himself to instruct him
and give him counsel.

After a little reflection, Jelāl said: "I have heard that thou
hast commited the Qur'ān to memory. Is it so?" "I have." "I
have heard that thou hast studied, under a great teacher, the
Jāmi'u-'l-Usül, that mighty work on the 'Elements of
Jurisprudence.' Is it so?" "It is."

"Then," answered Jelāl, "thou knowest the Word of God,
and thou knowest all the words and acts reported of his
apostle. But thou settest them at naught, and actest not up to
their precepts. How, then, canst thou expect that words of
mine will profit thee?"

The perwāna was abashed, and burst into tears. He went
his way; but from that day he began to execute justice, so as
to become a rival of the great Chosroes. He made himself the
phœnix of the age, and Jelāl accepted him as a disciple.

45

A company of pilgrims arrived one year at Qonya from
Mekka, on their way home elsewhere. They were taken in
succession to visit all the chief men of rank and learning in
the capital, and were received with every demonstration of
respect.

At last they were conducted to Jelāl also, in his college. On
seeing him seated there, they all screamed out and fainted
away.

When they were recovered, Jelāl began to offer excuses,

saying to them: "I fear you have been deceived, either by an impostor, or by some person resembling me in feature. There are men who strongly resemble one another."

The pilgrims one and all objected: "Why talks he thus? Why strive to make us doubt our eyes? By the God of heaven and earth, he was with us in person, habited in the very dress he now wears, when we all assumed the pilgrim garb at Mekka. He performed with us all the ceremonies of the pilgrimage, there and at 'Arafāt.[1] He visited with us the tomb of the Prophet at Medīna; though he never once ate or drank with us. Now he pretends that he does not know us or we know him."

On hearing this declaration, Jelāl's disciples were transported with joy, a musical festival ensued, and all those pilgrims became disciples.

46

A certain rich merchant of Qonya, a disciple, as was his wife, of Jelāl's, went to Mekka one year for the pilgrimage.

On the day when the victims are slaughtered, the lady had a dish of sweetmeat prepared, and sent some of it in a china bowl to Jelāl, to be eaten at dinner. She made the request that, when he partook of the food, he would favour her absent husband with his remembrance, his prayers, and his blessing.

Jelāl invited his disciples to the feast; and all ate of the lady's sweetmeat to repletion. But the bowl still remained full.

Jelāl then said: "Oh, he too must partake of it." He took the bowl, ascended to the terraced roof of the college with it, returning immediately empty-handed. His friends asked him what he had done with the bowl and the food. "I have handed them," said Jelāl, "to her husband, whose property they are." The company remained bewildered.

In due course of time, the pilgrims from Qonya returned home from Mekka; and out of the baggage of the merchant, the china bowl was produced, and sent in to the lady, who

---

[1] The mount where the victims are slaughtered by the pilgrims.

was much astonished at sight of it. She inquired of her husband how he had become possessed of that identical dish. He replied: "Ah! I also am at a loss to know how it happened. But, on the eve of the slaughter of the victims, I was seated in my tent, at 'Arafāt, with a company of other pilgrims, when an arm projected into the tent, and placed this dish before me, filled with sweetmeat. I sent out servants to see who had brought it to me; but no one was found." The lady at once inferred the truth, and guessed what had happened. Her husband was more and more astonished at such miraculous power.

Next day, husband and wife went to Jelāl, stood bareheaded before him, wept for joy, and related what had occurred. He answered:

"The whole thing is the effect of your trust and belief. God has merely made use of my hand as the instrument wherewith to make manifest his power."

47

Jelāl was accustomed to go every year for about six weeks to a place near Qonya, called "*The Hot Waters*," where there is a lake or marsh inhabited by a large colony of frogs.

A religious musical festival was arranged one day near the lake, and Jelāl delivered a discourse. The frogs were vociferous, and made his words inaudible. He therefore addressed himself to them, with a loud shout, saying: "What is all this noise about? Either do you pronounce a discourse, or allow me to speak." Complete silence immediately ensued; nor was a frog ever once heard to croak again, so long as Jelāl remained there.

Before leaving, he went to the marsh, and gave them his permission to croak again now as much as they pleased. The chorus instantly began. Numbers of people, who were witnesses of this miraculous power over the frogs, became believers in Jelāl, and professed themselves his disciples.

48

A party of butchers had purchased a heifer, and were leading her away to be slaughtered, when she broke loose from them, and ran away, a crowd following and shouting after her, so that she became furious, and none could pass near her.

By chance Jelāl met her, his followers being at some distance behind. On beholding him, the heifer became calm and quiet, came gently towards him, and then stood still, as though communing with him mutely, heart to heart, as is the wont with saints; and as though pleading for her life. Jelāl patted and caressed her.

The butchers now came up. Jelāl begged of them the animal's life, as having placed herself under his protection. They gave their consent, and let her go free.

Jelāl's disciples now joined the party, and he improved the occasion by the following remarks:—"If a brute beast, on being led away to slaughter, break loose and take refuge with me, so that God grants it immunity for my sake, how much more so would the case be, when a human being turns unto God with all his heart and soul, devoutly seeking him. God will certainly save such a man from the tormenting demons of hell-fire, and lead him to heaven, there to dwell eternally."

Those words caused such joy and gladness among the disciples that a musical festival, with dancing, at once commenced, and was carried on into the night. Alms and clothing were distributed to the poor singers of the chorus.

It is related that the heifer was never seen again in the meadows of Qonya.

49

A meeting was held at the perwāna's palace, each guest bringing his own waxlight of about four or five pounds' weight. Jelāl came to the assembly with a small waxtaper.

The grandees smiled at the taper. Jelāl, however, told them that their imposing candles depended on his taper for their light. Their looks expressed their incredulity at this. Jelāl, therefore, blew out his taper, and all the candles were at once extinguished; the company being left in darkness.

After a short interval, Jelāl fetched a sigh. His taper took fire therefrom, and the candles all burnt brightly as before. Numerous were the conversions resulting from this miraculous display.

50

One day, the poet-laureate, Qāni'ī, came to visit Jelāl at his college. He was the very Khāqānī [1] of the age, and was accompanied by a crowd of noble admirers.

After much conversation, Qāni'ī remarked that he did not like the writings of the poet Sanā'ī, [2] and Jelāl inquired the reason. The poet-laureate replied: "Sanā'ī was not a Muslim." Again Jelāl asked why he had formed that opinion; and Qāni'ī replied: "He has quoted passages from the Qur'ān in his poetry, and has even used them as his rhymes."

Jelāl hereupon rebuked him most severely, as follows:—

"Do hold thy peace. What sort of a Muslim art thou? Could a Muslim perceive the grandeur of that poet, his hair would stand on end, and his turban would fall from his head. That Muslim, and thousands such as he—such as thee—out of this lower world, and out of the land of spirits, would become real Muslims. His poetry, which is an exposition of the mysteries of the Qur'ān, is so beautifully embellished, that one may apply to it the adage: 'We have drawn from the ocean, and we have poured out again into the ocean.' Thus hast not understood his philosophy; thou hast not studied it; for thou art a Qāni'ī (Follower of one who is satisfied). The vicars of God have a technology, of which the rhetoricians have no knowledge. Hence these truths appear to be imperfect, because men of crude minds are prevented from comprehending them. Though thou hast no part in the lot of the recondite mysteries of the saints, it does not thence follow that thou shouldest deny their position, and so place thyself

[1] The great Persian poet Khāqānī, born at Shirwān, died and was buried at Tebrīz A.H. 582 (A.D. 1186).

[2] Sanā'ī, of Gazna in Afgānistān, surnamed "the Wise" or "the Phillosopher," died and was buried at the place of his birth, A.H. 576 (A.D. 1180).

in a position where destruction may be brought down upon
thee. On the contrary, shouldest thou fix thy faith upon them,
and act with true sincerity, thou shalt find in the day of
judgment no heavy burden on thy shoulders. In lieu thereof,
a burden-bearer will be present at thy side—a refuge, who
will prove thy most earnest intercessor."

Struck with these words, the poet-laureate arose, uncovered,
begged forgiveness, confessed contrition for his disrespect,
and became one of Jelāl's disciples.

51

A discipe of Husāmu-'d-Dīn wished to make a vow never
to do an act not expressly authorized by the Canon Law of
Islām. For the purpose of administering the oath to him,
instead of the Qur'ān, a copy of the Ilāhī-nāma (Divine
Hymns) of the philosopher Sanā'ī was placed on a lectern,
covered over with a cloth, and tendered as "the Book" on
which he came to swear.

Just then, Jelāl came into the room, and asked what was
going on. Husām replied:: "One of my disciples is going to
make a vow against backsliding. We shrank from swearing
him on the Qur'ān, and have therefore prepared a copy of the
Ilāhī-nāma for the occasion."

Jelāl observed: "Indeed! Why, the Ilāhī-nāma would draw
down on a forswearer a more severe chastisement than the
Qur'ān itself. The Word of God is but milk, of which the
Ilāhī-nāma is the cream and the butter!"

52

When Adam was created, God commanded Gabriel to
take the three most precious pearls of the divine treasury, and
offer them in a golden salver to Adam, to choose for himself
one of the three.

The three pearls were: *wisdom, faith*, and *modesty*.

Adam chose the pearl of *wisdom*.

Gabriel then proceeded to remove the salver with the
remaining two pearls, in order to replace them in the divine

treasury. With all his mighty power, he found he could not lift the salver.

The two pearls said to him: "We will not separate from our beloved wisdom. We could not be happy and quiet away from it. From all eternity, we three have been the three compeers of God's glory, the pearls of his power. We cannot be separated."

A voice was now heard to proceed from the divine presence, saying: "Gabriel! leave them, and come away."

From that time, wisdom has taken its seat on the summit of the brain of Adam; faith took up its abode in his heart; modesty established itself in his countenance. Those three pearls have remained as the heirlooms of the chosen children of Adam. For, whoever, of all his descendants, is not embellished and enriched with those three jewels, is lacking of the sentiment and lustre of his divine origin.

So runs the narrative reported by Husām, Jelāl's successor, as having been imparted to him by the latter.

53

A certain flute-player named Hamza, much beloved by Jelāl, happened to die. Jelāl sent some of his disciples to array the defunct in his grave-clothes. He himself followed them to the house of the deceased.

On entering the room, Jelāl addresses the dead body: "My dear friend Hamza, arise!" Instantly, the deceased arose, saying: "Lo, here I am!" He then took his flute, and for three whole days and nights a religious festival was kept up in his house.

Above a hundred Roman misbelievers were thereby converted to the faith of Islām. When Jelāl left the house, life departed from the corpse also.

54

Among the disciples there was a hunchback, a devout man, and a player on the tambourine, whom Jelāl loved.

On the occasion of a festival, this poor man beat his tam-

bourine and shouted in ecstasy to an unusual degree. Jelāl
was also greatly moved in the spirit with the holy dance.

Approaching the hunchback, he said to him: "Why erec-
test thou not thyself like the rest?" The infirmity of the hunch
was pleaded. Jelāl then patted him on the back, and stroked
him down. The poor man immediately arose, erec: and
graceful as a cypress.

When he went home, his wife refused him admittance,
denying that he was her husband. His companions came, and
bare witness to her of what had happened. Then she was
convinced, let him in, and the couple lived together for many
years afterwards.

55

It was once remarked to Jelāl, with respect to the burial
service for the dead, that, from the earliest times, it had been
usual for certain prayers and Qur'ānic recitations to be said
at the grave and round the corpse; but, that people could not
understand why he had introduced into the ceremony the
practice of singing hymns during the procession towards the
place of burial, which canonists had pronounced to be a
mischievous innovation.

Jelāl replied: "The ordinary reciters, by their services, bear
witness that the deceased lived a Muslim. My singers, however, testify that he was a Muslim, a believer and a lover of
God."

He added also: "Besides that; when the human spirit, after
years of imprisonment in the cage and dungeon of the body,
is at length set free, and wings its flight to the source whence
it came, is not this an occasion for rejoicings, thanks, and
dancings? The soul, in ecstasy, soars to the presence of the
Eternal; and stirs up others to make proof of courage and
self-sacrifice. If a prisoner be released from a dungeon and be
clothed with honour, who would doubt that rejoicings are
proper? So, too, the death of a saint is an exactly parallel
case.

56

One of Jelāl's chief disciples related that, when he first began to study under that teacher, a company of pilgrims from Mekka came to Qonya, and among them was a very handsome young man of this latter city, son to one of the chief professors there.

This young man brought rich presents to Jelāl, and gifts for the disciples, relating to the latter the following adventure:—

"We were travelling in the desert of Arabia, and I chanced to fall asleep. The caravan went on without me. When I awoke, I found myself alone in the trackless sands. I knew not which way to turn. I wept and lamented for a considerable time, took a direction at hazard, and walked until I was thoroughly exhausted.

"To my surprise and joy I espied a large tent at a distance, with a great smoke rising by it. I made for the tent, and there encountered a most formidable-looking personage, to whom I related my misadventure. He bid me welcome, asked me in, and invited me to rest myself. Within the tent I observed a large kettle, full of fresh-cooked sweetmeat of the finest kind, and a plentiful supply of cool clear water.

"My wonder was great. I asked my host what these preparations might mean, and he answered: "I am a disciple of the great Jelālu-'d-Dīn of Qonya, son of Bahā'u-'d-Dīn of Balkh. He is used to pass by here every day. I have therefore pitched this tent for him, and I prepare this food. Perchance, he may honour and bless me with his presence, partaking of hospitality here.'

"As he yet spake, in walked Jelāl. We saluted; and he was begged to partake of the food. He took a little morsel, no larger than a filbert, giving me some also. I fell at his feet, and told him I was from Qonya on pilgrimage, and had missed the caravan by falling asleep. 'Well,' answered he, 'as we are fellow-townsmen, be of good cheer.' He then bade me close my eyes. I did so; and on opening them again I found myself in the midst of my companions of the caravan. I am now come here, on my return home in safety, to offer my thanks for

that miraculous kindness, and to profess myself a disciple of
the holy man."

57

A man of great learning came once to visit Jelāl. By way of
a test, he asked Jelāl two questions: "Is it correct to speak of
God as '*a living soul?*' since God hath said (Qur'ān iii. 182):
'Every living soul shall taste death!' " and: "If one ought
not to call God 'a living soul,' what did Jesus mean when he
said (Qur'ān v. 116): 'Thou knowest what is in my soul, but I
know not what is in thy soul'?" The second question was:
"Can God properly be called 'a thing'? If he can be so called,
what is the signification of his word (Qur'ān xxviii. 88):
'Every thing shall perish, save his cause'?"

Jelāl immediately replied: " 'But I know not what is in thy
soul' means *in thy knowledge, in thy absentness,* or, as we
seers say, *in thy secrecy.* Thus the passage would be paraph-
rased: *Thou knowest what is in my secrecy; but I know not
what is in the secret of thy secrecy;* or, as '*the people of heart*'
would put it: *Thou knowest what issues from me in the world;
but I know not the secret of what issues from thee in the world
to come.* It is quite proper to speak of God as 'a thing;' for he
hath said (Qur'ān vi. 19): 'What thing is greatest in
testimony? Say thou: "God;" ' *i.e.,* God is the greatest thing
in testimony; 'God will be a witness between me and you in
the day of the resurrection.' The signification of the passage
'Every thing shall perish' is: *every created thing shall perish;*
not the Creator, *i.e.,* 'save he.' The thing excepted from the
general category is 'he'. But God knows best."

The man of learning instantly professed himself a disciple,
and composed a panegyric on Jelāl.

58

The legend goes that Jelāl made a practice of seeing the
new moon of the Arabian new year, and always uttered the
following prayer on seeing it:—"O our Lord God! Thou art
the Past-eternal One, the Future-eternal One, the Ancient
One! This is a new year. I beg of thee therein steadfastness to

withstand the lapidated Satan,[1] and assistance against the rebellious spirit (within me); also, occupation in what will approximate me to thee, and an avoidance of what might elongate me from thee. O God! O the All-merciful One, the All-compassionate One! Through thy mercy, O Most-compassionate of the merciful ones! O thou Lord of majesty and of honour!"

59

It is related that Jelāl cured one of his disciples of an intermittent fever by writing down the following invocation on paper, washing off the ink in water, and giving this to the patient to drink; who was, under God's favour, immediately relieved from the malady:—"O Mother of the sleek one (a nickname of the tertian ague)! If thou hast believed in God, the Most Great, make not the head to ache; vitiate not the swallow; eat not the flesh; drink not the blood; and depart thou out of so-and-so, betaking thyself to some one who attributes to God partners of other false gods. And I bear witness that there is not any god save God, and I testify that Muhammed is his servant and apostle."

60

One day Jelāl paid a visit to a great sheykh. He was received with the utmost respect, and seated with the sheykh on the same carpet, both together falling into ecstatic heart-communion with the world of spirits.

A certain dervish was there present also, who had repeatedly performed the pilgrimage at Mekka. The dervish addressed Jelāl, and inquired: "What is poverty?" Jelāl returned no answer; and the question was thrice repeated.

When Jelāl took his leave, the great sheykh accompanied him to the street door. On his return to his room, he reprimanded the dervish severely for his insolent intrusion on the guest; "especially," said the sheykh, "as he fully answered

[1] "*Satan, the Lapidated One*," is the chief title of the accursed one. Muslims believe that the "shooting stars" are missiles cast by angels at demons who attempt to approach heaven for eavesdropping purposes.

thy question the first time thou puttest it." The dervish, surprised, asked what the answer had been. "The poor man,"
said the sheykh, "when he hath known God, hath his tongue
tied. That is being a real dervish; who, when in the presence
of saints, speaks not; neither with the tongue, nor with the
heart. This is what is signified by (Qur'ān xlvi. 28): 'Hold ye
your peace.' But now, prepare thyself for thy end. Thou art
struck by a shaft from heaven.'

Three days later, the dervish was met by a gang of repro-
bates, who attacked and killed him, carrying off every thing
he had about him. *Salve fac nos, Domine!*

61

In the days of Jelāl there was in Qonya a lady-saint, named
Fakhru-'n-Nisā (the Glory of Women). She was known to all
the holy men of the time, who were all aware of her sanctity.
Miracles were wrought by her in countless numbers. She constantly attended the meetings at Jelāl's home, and he occasionally paid her a visit at her house.

Her friends suggested to her that she ought to go and
perform the pilgrimage at Mekka; but she would not undertake this duty unless she should first consult with Jelāl about
it. Accordingly she went to see him. As she entered his
presence, before she spoke, he called out to her: "Oh, most
happy idea! May thy journey be prosperous! God willing, we
shall be together." She bowed, but said nothing. The disciples
present were puzzled.

That night she remained a guest at Jelāl's house, convers-
ing with him till past midnight. At that hour he went up to
the terraced roof of the college to perform the divine service
of the vigil. When he had completed that service of worship,
he fell into an ecstasy, shouting and exclaiming. Then he
lifted the skylight of the room below, where the lady was, and
invited her to come up on to the roof also.

When she was come, he told her to look upwards, saying
that her wish was come to pass. On looking up, she beheld
the Cubical House of Mekka in the air, circumambulating
round Jelāl's head above him, and spinning round like a

dervish in his waltz, plainly and distinctly, so as to leave no
room for doubt or uncertainty. She screamed out with astonishment and fright, swooning away. On coming to herself,
she felt the conviction that the journey to Mekka was not one
for her to perform; so she totally relinquished the idea.

62

Jelāl was once standing at the edge of the moat round the
city of Qonya, when a company of students, undergraduates
of one of the colleges in the neighbourhood, seeing him,
agreed to try him by asking the question: "Of what colour
was the dog of the Seven Sleepers?"

Jelāl's immediate, unpremeditated answer was: "Yellow. A
lover is always yellow (sallow); as am I; and that dog was a
lover." The students bowed to him, and all became disciples.

63

The Superior of the monks of the monastery of Plato was
an old man, and was held in the very highest esteem for his
learning in all Constantinople and Firengistān, in Sīs, Jānik,
and other lands. (Sīs was capital of the kingdom of Lower
Armenia, and Jānik was the secondary "Roman Empire" of
Trebizond.) From all those lands did disciples flock to learn
wisdom from him.

This Superior related the following anecdote:—

"One day, Jelāl came to the monastery of Plato, situated at
the foot of a hill, with a cavern therein, from whence issued a
stream of cold water. Jelāl entered the cavern, and proceeded
to its farther extremity. The Superior remained at the
cavern's mouth, watching for what might happen. For seven
whole days and nights Jelāl remained there, seated in the
midst of the cold water. At the end of that period he came
forth from the cavern, and walked away, singing a hymn.
Not the slightest change was apparent in his features, nor in
his eyes."

The Superior made oath that all he had read about the
person and qualities of the Messiah, as also in the books of
Abraham and Moses, were found in the person of Jelāl, as

well as the grandeur and mien of the prophets, as set forth in books of ancient history, and far more besides.

64

Shemsu-'d-Dīn of Tebrīz once asserted, in Jelāl's college, that whosoever wished to see again the prophets, had only to look on Jelāl, who possessed all their qualifications; more especially of those to whom revelations were made, whether by angelic communications, or whether in visions; the chief of such qualities being serenity of mind with perfect inward confidence and consciousness of being one of God's elect. "Now," said he, "to possess Jelāl's approbation is heaven; while hell is to incur his displeasure. Jelāl is the key of heaven. Go then, and look upon Jelāl, if thou wish to comprehend the signification of that saying '*the learned are the heirs of the prophets*,' together with something beyond that, which I will not here specify. He has more learning in every science than any one else upon earth. He explains better, with greater tact and taste, as also more exhaustively, than all others. Were I, with my mere intellect, to study for a hundred years, I could not acquire a tenth part of what he knows. He has intuitively thought out that knowledge, without being aware of it, in my presence, by his own subtlety."

65

One of the greatest teachers of Qonya was one day giving a lecture on a terraced roof, when suddenly he heard the sound of a lute. He exclaimed: "These lutes are an innovation on the prophetic usages. They must be interdicted."

Forthwith, the form of Jelāl appeared before him, and answered: "That must not be." On this the teacher fainted away.

When he regained his consciousness, he sought to make his peace with Jelāl, by sending an apology and a recantation to him, through the medium of Jelāl's son, Sultan Veled; but Jelāl would not accept them. He answered: "It would be easier to convert seventy Roman bishops to Islām, than to clear away from the mind of that teacher the stains of hate, and so set him on the right road. His soul is as foul as the paper on which children practise their writing exercises."

At length, however, he allowed himself to be appeased by his son; so that he permitted the teacher, with his pupils, to constitute themselves his disciples.

66

Jelāl one day addressed his son, saying: "Bahā'u-'d-Dīn, dost thou wish to love thy enemy, and to be loved of him? Speak well of him, and extol his virtues. He will then be thy friend; and for this reason: In like manner as there is a road open between the heart and the tongue, so also is there a way from the tongue to the heart. The love of God may be found by bearing his *comely names*. God hath said: 'O my servants, take ye heed that ye often commemorate me, so that sincerity may abound.' The more that sincerity prevails, the more do the rays of the light of truth shine into the heart. The hotter a baker's oven is, the more bread will it bake; if cool, it will not bake at all."

67

Sultan Veled, Bahā'u-'d-Dīn, is said to have recounted of his father, Jelāl, this saying: "A true disciple is he who holds his teacher to be superior to all others. So much so, that, for instance, a disciple of Bāyezīd of Bestām was once asked whether Bāyezīd or Abū-Hanīfa was the greater, and he replied that his teacher, Bāyezīd, was the greater. 'Then,' said the questioner, 'is Bāyezīd the greater, or is Abū-Bekr?' 'My teacher is the greater.' 'Bāyezīd or Muhammed?' 'Bāyezīd.' 'Bāyezīd or God?' 'I only know my teacher; I know no other than him; and I know that he is greater than all others.'

"Another was asked the last question, and his reply was: 'There is no difference between the two.' A third was asked it also, and he replied: 'It would require a greater one than either of the two to determine which of them is the greater.'

"As God does not walk in this world of sensible objects, the prophets are the substitutes of God. No, no! I am wrong! For if thou suppose that those substitutes and their principal are two different things, thou has judged erroneously, not rightly."

68

Sultan Veled is reported to have said: 'My grandfather, the Great Master, used to recommend to his disciples to honour his son Jelāl exceedingly, as one of noble extraction and exalted pedigree, of an eternal descent in the past; since the mother of his mother was the daughter of the Imām Sarakhsī, a descendant from Huseyn, son of 'Alī, and grandson of the Prophet."

69

Sultan Veled is also reported to have said: "My father told his disciples that I was seven, and my brother 'Alā'u-'d-Dīn eight years old, when the Dizdār Bedru-'d-Dīn Guhertāsh had us circumcised at Qara-Hisār." (See chap. i., No. 12.)

He is also reported to have declared: "When the sultan invited my grandfather to Qonya, a year passed, and then the Emīr Mūsa invited my grandfather to Larenda, and took my father to be his own son-in-law; so that I was born in that town." (See chap. i., No. 2. The account now given here is at variance with that mentioned in the preface, which makes 'Alā'u-'d-Dīn and Bahā'u-'d-Dīn to have been born at Larenda before Jelāl and his father went to Qonya. Moreover, their mother, Gevher Khātūn, is there said to have been the daughter of Lala Sherefu-'d-Dīn of Samarqand. Is that an alias of the Emīr Mūsa of the present anecdote; or did Jelāl marry two ladies of Larenda at different times? There are several difficulties here. Sultan Veled puts only one year as the difference of age between himself and his elder brother. If the daughter of the Emīr Mūsa was the mother of both these brothers, Jelāl's stay at Larenda must have been of about two years at least. If they were by different mothers, and born, the one before, the other after Bahā Veled's settling at Qonya, there must have been a greater difference in their ages. Jelāl's age at his marriage is also variously stated. These discrepancies show that the anecdotes were collected from traditions of various sources, long after the events recorded.)

70

Sultan Veled is said to have related that one day, two Turks, law-students, brought to Jelāl an offering of a few lentils, excusing the paucity of the gift, as the result of their poverty. Jelāl thereupon narrated the following anecdote:—

"God revealed to Mustafa (Muhammed) that the believers should contribute of their possessions, for the service of God, as much as they could spare. Some brought the half, some the third part; Abū-Bekr brought the whole of what he possessed. Thus a large treasure was collected, of money, beasts, and arms, for God's service.

"A poor woman, too, brought three dates and a cake of bread—all she had on earth.

"The disciples smiled. Mustafa perceived their action, and said that God had showed him a vision, which he desired to tell to them. They all begged he would favour them with the recital. He therefore thus proceeded:

" 'God hath removed the veils from before me. And lo, I saw that the angels had placed in one scale of a balance the whole of your very liberal offerings together, and in the other scale the three dates and one cake of this poor woman. The latter scale was preponderant; its contents outweighed all the rest.'

"The disciples bowed, thanked the prophet, and inquired the hidden explanation of this mystery. He answered: 'This poor woman has parted with her all, whereas my disciples have kept back a part of their possessions. Proverbs say: The generous one is generous out of what he possesses," and, "A little, in the eyes of the Most Great, is much." You put into the earth a single date-stone, intrusting it to God. He makes that stone become a tree, which yields fruits without number; because the stone was confided to him. Therefore, let your alms be given to the poor, and to God's servants, as a trust committed unto God. For it is said: "Alms fall first into God's hand, before reaching the hands of the poor;" and again: "Alms for the poor and the destitute." '

"The poor of Mekka and Medina, refugees and auxiliaries, shouted their admiration as they heard these words."

When the two Turkish students heard this anecdote related, they professed themselves disciples of Jelāl.

71

When Jelāl was quite young, he was one day preaching on the subject of Moses and Elias (Qur'ān xviii. 59–81). One of his disciples noticed a stranger seated in a corner, paying great attention, and every now and then saying: "Good! Quite true! Quite correct! He might have been the third one with us two!" The disciple surmized that the stranger might be Elias. (Elias is believed by Muslims to be always visible somewhere, but that people know him not. Did they recognize him, they could obtain from him a knowledge of the secret of eternal life, which he possesses.) He therefore seized hold of the stranger's skirt, and asked for his spiritual aid. "Oh," said the stranger, "rather seek assistance from Jelāl, as we all do. Every occult saint of God is the loving and admiring friend of him." So saying, he managed to disengage his skirt from the disciple's hold, and instantly disappeared. The disciple went to pay his respects to Jelāl, who at once addressed him, saying: "Elias, and Moses, and the prophets, are all friends of mine." The disciple understood the allusion, and became more and more devoted at heart to Jelāl than he even was before.

72

It is related that when the burial service was about to be performed over the corpse of Jelāl, the precentor gave a shriek, and swooned away. After a while, he recovered, and then performed his office, weeping bitterly.

On being asked the cause of his emotion, he answered: "As I stood forward to perform my office, I perceived a row of the most noble of spiritual saints of the spiritual world, as being present, and as being engaged in reciting the prayers for the dead over the departed one. Those angels of heaven wore robes of blue (the mourning of some sects of Muslims), and wept."

For forty days, that precentor and others daily visited Jelāl's grave.

73

At Damascus, when a young student, Jelāl was frequently seen by others to walk several arrow-flights' distance in the air, tranquilly returning to the terraced roof on which they were standing.

Those fellow-pupils were among his earliest believers and disciples.

74

A friend of Jelāl's once took leave of him at Qonya, and went to Damascus. On his arrival there, he found Jelāl seated in a corner of his room. Asking for an explanation of this surprising phenomenon, Jelāl replied: "The men of God are like fishes in the ocean; they pop up into view on the surface here and there and everywhere, as they please."

75

Jelāl once met a Turk in Qonya, who was selling foxskins in the market, and crying them: "dilku! dilku!" (fox! fox! in Turkish.)

Jelāl immediately began to parody his cry, calling out in Persian: "dil kū! dil kū!" (heart, where art thou?) At the same time he broke out into one of his holy waltzes of ecstasy.

76

In the time of Sultan Veled (A.D. 1284–1312), a young man, of the descendants of the Prophet, and son of the guardian of the holy tomb of Muhammed at Medīna, came to Qonya with a company of his fellow-descendants, belonging to that city. He was presented to Sultan Veled, and became his disciple.

He wore a most singular head-dress. One end of his turban hung down in front to below his navel; while the other end was formed into the *sheker-āvīz* [1] of the Mevlevī dervishes.

---

[1] I have not met with an explanation of this word in any Persian dictionary. Literally it signifies *sugar-hanging*. In the Bahāri-'Ajem alone is it mentioned, with a distich from Hāfiz; but it is left unexplained.

When they had become somewhat intimate, Sultan Veled asked him how it happened that he wore the *sheker-āvīz* of the Mevlevis, when nobody else but those dervishes wear it, in imitation of their founder, Jelāl.

The young man explained that his family were descended from the Prophet. That the Prophet, on the night of his ascension to heaven, after seeing God and many mysteries, had returned a certain distance, and, as is well known, then went back to intercede with God for his people. He now perceived, on the pinnacle of God's throne, the ideal portrait of a form, so beautiful, that he had not hitherto witnessed anything so charming among the angels and inhabitants of heaven.

After contemplating the lovely vision, in amazement, for some time, Muhammed was able to notice that the ideal form wore on its head a *sheker-āvīz*. He asked Gabriel what that ideal portrait might portend, which was so attractive in its beauty as to surpass all the wonders he had witnessed in all the nine heavens. "Is it the portrait of an angel, a prophet, or a saint?" Gabriel replied: "It is the portrait of a personage of the descendants of Abū-Bekr, who will appear in the latter days among the people of thy Church, and will fill the whole world with the effulgence of the knowledge of thy mysteries. To him will God vouchsafe a precedency, and a pen, and a breath, such that kings and princes will profess themselves his disciples; and he will be a most pure upholder of thy religion, being, in every respect, the counterpart of thyself in aspect and in morals. His name will be Muhammed, as is thine; and his surname will be Jelālu-'d-Dīn. His words will explain thy sayings, and will expound thy Qur'ān."

On his return home, the Prophet adopted the form of turban he had seen worn in that ideal portrait, making one end hang down a span in front, and binding the other end behind into a *sheker-āvīz*.

"From that day to this," said the young man, "the fathers of our family have followed that fashion, so adopted by the Prophet; and we continue to do so too."

It is said that when Abū-Bekr heard this narrative from the

Prophet, respecting his great descendant that was thus fore-told, he gave the whole of his possessions to the Prophet, to be expended in God's cause.

When Muhammed died, Abū-Bekr wept long and bitterly. But the Prophet appeared to him, and consoled him by say-ing: "One day I will reappear among my people from out of the collar of one of thy race."

The young man continued: "From that time onwards, our family were on the outlook for the manifestation of the holy personage whose ideal portrait the Prophet so saw. Thank God that I have witnessed the realization of their hope."

The Qonya pilgrims published this communication to all the disciples there present.

77

In the days of Sultan Veled, a great merchant came to Qonya to visit the tomb of Jelāl. He offered many rich gifts to Sultan Veled, making presents also to the disciples. He related to them many anecdotes of adventures encountered by him in his travels, such as the following:—

He once went to Kīsh and Bahreyn in quest of pearls and rubies. "An inhabitant told me," said he, "that I should find some in the hands of a certain fisherman. I went to him, and the fisher showed me a chest, containing pearls of inestimable value, such as impressed me with astonishment. I asked him how he had collected them; and he told me, calling God to witness, that he, his three brothers, and his father, were for-merly poor fishermen. One day they hooked something that gave them immense trouble before they could bring it to land.

"They now found they had captured a 'lord of the waters,' also named a 'marvel of the sea,' as is commonly known.[1]

"We wondered," said he, "what we could do with the beast. We wept for the ill fortune that had brought us such a disap-pointment. The creature looked at us as we spoke. Suddenly my father cried out: 'I have it! I will put him on a cart, and exhibit him all over the country at a penny a head!'

[1] Apparently a "*merman*" is intended.

"Through the miraculous power of him who has endowed man with speech and his creatures with life, the beast broke forth and exclaimed: 'Make me not a staring-block in the world, and I will do anything you may wish of me, so as to suffice for you and your children for many years to come!'

"Our father answered: 'How should I set thee free, when thou art so strange and unparalleled a creature?' The beast replied: 'I will make an oath.' Our father said: 'Speak! Let us hear thy oath.'

"The beast now said: 'We are of the faith of Muhammed, and disciples of the holy Mevlānā. By the soul of the Mevlānā, the holy Jelālu-'d-Dīn of Rome, I will go, and I will return.'

"Our father fainted away with astonishment. I, therefore, now asked: 'How hast thou any knowledge of him?' The beast replied: 'We are a nation of twelve thousand individuals. We have believed in him, and he frequently showed himself to us at the bottom of the sea, lecturing and sermonizing to us on the divine mysteries of the truth. He brought us to a knowledge of the true faith; so that we continually practise what he taught us.'

"Our father instantly told him he was free. He went back, therefore, into the water, and was lost to sight. But two days later he returned, and brought with him innumerable pearls and precious stones. He asked whether he had been true and faithful to his promise; and on our expressing our satisfaction on that score, he took an affectionate farewell from us.

'We were thus raised from the depths of poverty to the pinnacle of wealth. We became merchant princes, and our slaves are the great merchants of the earth. Every dealer who wishes for pearls and rubies comes to us. We are known as the *Sons of the Fisherman*. Our father went to Qonya, and paid his respects to the Mevlānā.

"Through his narrative, I formed the design, now carried into effect, to visit the son of that great saint."

This wonderful narrative has been handed down ever since in the mouths of the merchants of Qonya.

78

(The following appears to be an account of one of the first visits of the Perwāna to Jelāl, to whom he subsequently became so devotedly attached.)

One of the most eminent among the men of learning in Qonya was visited by the perwāna. The learned man held forth eloquently on several exalted themes, and then informed the perwāna that he had, the night before, been taken up into the highest heaven, and had there learnt many mysteries. He said that he there saw Jelāl hold a higher station of proximity to God than any other saint, as he stood on a level with God's throne.

A day or two later, the perwāna, filled with reverence for Jelāl's unequalled sanctity, went and paid him a visit with the utmost deference. Before the perwāna could broach any subject of conversation, Jelāl said to him: "Mu'īnu-'d-Dīn! the vision related to you by your learned friend is quite true in the main facts, though I never saw him there at any time." He then extemporized the following ode:—

"Fellow-visitant wert thou? Then say what thou sawest there last night.
'Twixt my heart and inspiring loved darling what passed in thy sight?
And if thou, in thy dream, with thy eyes sawest my beautiful love,
Tell us then, in the earrings he wore there what jewels were wove.
If with me thou be fellow in coat, as in thoughts and in creeds,
Let us hear the details of that ragged old mendicant's weeds.
If thou poverty's son be, and unspoken mysteries hear,
Thou'lt recount all the words that were thought by my silent compeer,
If thou'st learnt whence the source of mankind and of souls did proceed.
Since the source was but one, what then means all this search, all this greed?
And if thou hast not seen any place of his form and face free,
Say then what, in the thoughts of his lovers, that face and form be.
And if I head the lists of those lovers, as thou seemest to say,
Tell us, What are those lists? What his messages, words, answers? Pray!"

A musical service was then got up, this ode being chanted during its performance. The perwāna was so utterly bewildered by this incident, that he could say nothing. He therefore rose, bowed, and took his leave.

79

One day, it is said, the Prophet (Muhammed) recited to 'Alī in private the secrets and mysteries of the "Brethren of Sincerity" (who appear to be the "Freemasons" of the Muslim dervish world), enjoining on him not to divulge them to any of the uninitiated, so that they should not be betrayed; also, to yield obedience to the rule of implicit submission.

For forty days, 'Alī kept the secret in his own sole breast, and bore therewith until he was sick at heart. Like a pregnant woman, his abdomen became swollen with the burden, so that he could no longer breathe freely.

He therefore fled to the open wilderness, and there chanced upon a well. He stooped, reached his head as far down into the well as he was able; and then, one by one, he confided those mysteries to the bowels of the earth. From the excess of his excitement, his mouth filled with froth and foam. These he spat out into the water of the well, until he had freed himself of the whole, and he felt relieved.

After a certain number of days, a single reed was observed to be growing in that well. It waxed and shot up, until at length a youth, whose heart was miraculously enlightened on the point, became aware of this growing plant, cut it down, drilled holes in it, and began to play upon it airs, similar to those performed by the dervish lovers of God, as he pastured his sheep in the neighbourhood.

By degrees, the various tribes of Arabs of the desert heard of this flute-playing of the shepherd, and its fame spread abroad. The camels and the sheep of the whole region would gather around him as he piped, ceasing to pasture that they might listen. From all directions, north and south, the nomads flocked to hear his strains, going into ecstasies with delight, weeping for joy and pleasure, breaking forth in transports of gratification.

The rumour at length reached the ears of the Prophet, who
gave orders for the piper to be brought before him. When he
began to play in the sacred presence, all the holy disciples of
God's messenger were moved to tears and transports, burst-
ing forth with shouts and exclamations of pure bliss, and
losing all consciousness. The Prophet declared that the notes
of the shepherd's flute were the interpretation of the holy
mysteries he had confided in private to 'Alī's charge.[1]

Thus it is that, until a man acquire the sincere devotion of
the linnet-voiced flute-reed, he cannot hear the mysteries of
the Brethren of Sincerity in its dulcet notes, or realize the
delights thereof; for "faith is altogether a yearning of the
heart, and a gratification of the spiritual sense."

"To whom, alas, the pangs my love for thee excites, to breathe?
My sighs, like 'Alī, I'll to some deep well's recess bequeathe.
Perchance some reeds may spring therefrom, its brink to over-
    grow;
Those reeds may moaning flutes become, and so betray my woe.
Who hear will say: 'Be silent, flutes! We're not love's confidants;
To that sweet tyrant make excuse for us and for those plants!' "

80

One of Jelāl's disciples possessed a slave girl of Roman
origin, whom Jelāl had named Siddīqa (after Muhammed's
virgin wife 'Ā'isha). Occasionally she had miraculous visions.
She used to see aureolas of heavenly light, green, red, and
black. Various of the angels used to visit her, and souls of the
departed.

Her master was vexed at her being so favoured above himself. Once he was visited by Jelāl, and expressed his chagrin
to him on the subject. Jelāl replied: "True! There is a
heavenly light resides in the pupils of some eyes. These occasionally mislead a few with visions of beauteous form, with
which they fall in love. Others they preserve in chastity, and
lead them to their adored Maker. Others, again, they may

---

[1] This is a much more poetical account of the origin of the reed-flute
than the pagan Greek myths of Orpheus and his lyre, Pan and his pipe, for
which no reasons are assigned.

lead to take delight in exterior objects, so as to cast their eyes on every pretty face they see, while the wife at home is curtained away from her husband. Thus, whenever God opens a way to any one, appearing to him, and showing him glimpses of the hidden world, he is apt to become entranced therewith, and to lose all power of further progress, saying to himself: 'How greatly in favour am I!' Others, in short, use every endeavour; but nothing is vouchsafed to them in visions, until they be favoured with a special sight of God himself, and they be admitted to a near approach unto him."

The girl's master was comforted, and bowed to his teacher, whose disciples then broke out into a holy service of psalmody and dancing.

81

There was once a wise monk in the monastery of Plato, who was on very friendly terms with Jelāl's grandson 'Ārif. He was very aged, and used to be visited by the dervishes of his neighbourhood, to whom he was very polite, and towards whom he exhibited great confidence; so much so that, one day, some of them inquired of him how he had found Jelāl, and what he had thought of him.

The monk replied to them: "What do you know of him, as to who or what he was? I have seen signs and miracles without number worked by him. I became his devoted servant. I had read in the gospel and in the prophets the lives and the works of the saints of old, and I saw that he compassed them all. I therefore had faith in the truth of his reality.

"One day he came here, conferring on me the honour of a visit. For forty days he shut himself up in ecstatic seclusion. When at length he came forth from his privacy, I laid hold of his skirt, and said to him: 'God, in his holy scripture hath said (Qur'ān xix. 72): "And there is none of you but shall come to it (hellfire)." Now, since it is incontestable that all shall come to the fire of hell, what preference is there in Islām over our faith?'

"For a little time he made no answer. At length, however, he made a sign towards the city, and went away in that direction. I followed after him leisurely. Near the city, we came to a bakehouse, the oven of which was being heated. He now took my black cassock, wrapped it in his own cloak, and threw the bundle into the oven. He then withdrew for a time into a corner, sunk in meditation.

"I saw a great smoke come out of the oven, such that no one had the power of utterance. After that, he said to me: 'Behold!' The baker withdrew the bundle from the oven, and assisted the saint to put on his cloak, which had become exquisitely clean; whereas my cassock was, as it were, branded and scorched, so as to fall in pieces. Then he said: 'Thus shall we enter therein, and thus shall you enter!'

"That self-same moment I made my bow to him and became his disciple."

82

The reason why the Mesnevī was written is related to have been the following:—

Husāmu-'d-Dīn learnt that several of the followers of Jelāl were fond of studying the Ilāhī-nāma of Senā'ī, the Hakīm, and the Mantiqu-'t-Tayr of 'Attār, as also the Nasībnāma of the latter.

He therefore sought and found an opportunity to propose that Jelāl should indite something in the style of the Ilāhī-nāma, but in the metre of the Mantiqu-'t-Tayr; saying that the circle of friends would then willingly give up all other poetry, and study that alone.

Jelāl immediately produced a portion of the Mesnevī, saying that God had forewarned him of the wishes of the brethren, in consequence of which he had already begun to compose the work. That fragment consisted of the first eighteen couplets of the introductory verses:—

> "From reed-flute hear what tale it tells,
> What plaint it makes of absence' ills," &c.

It is of the metre *remel*, hexameter contracted:

$$- \smile - - \mid - \smile - - \mid - \smile - \| - \smile - - \mid - \smile - - \mid - \smile - \|$$

Jelāl frequently mentions Husām as the cause of the work's having been begun and continued. In the fourth book he addresses him in the opening couplet:—

"Of Truth, the light; of Faith, the sword: Husāmu-'d-Dīn aye be;
Above the lunar orb has clomb my Mesnevī, through thee."

And again the sixth book has for its opening verse the following apostrophe:—

"O thou, Husāmu-'d-Dīn, my heart's true life! Zeal, for thy sake,
I feel springs up in me sixth book hereby to undertake."

Often they spent whole nights at the task, Jelāl inditing, and Husām writing down his inspirations, chanting it aloud, as he wrote it, with his beautiful voice. Just as the first book was completed, Husām's wife died, and an interval ensued.

Two years thus passed without progress. Husām married again; and in that year, A.H. 662 (A.D. 1263), the second book was commenced. No other interval occurred until the work was brought to a conclusion. The third couplet of the second book mentions Husām in these terms—

"When thou, of Truth the light, Husāmu-'d-Dīn, thy courser's rein
Didst turn, descending earthward from the zenith's starry plain."

The third, fifth, and seventh books have similar addresses to Husām in their opening verses. His name is also mentioned cursorily in the third tale of the first book.

83

On the death of Jelāl, a party of zealots went in a body to the perwāna, explaining to him that the new practices of music and dancing, introduced by Jelāl, were innovations altogether contrary to the canonical institutes, and begging him to use his utmost endeavours to suppress them.

The perwāna called on the learned Mufti of Qonya, Sheykh Sadru-'d-Dīn, and consulted him on the subject. The mufti's answer was: "Do nothing of the kind. Listen not to such biased suggestions. There is an apostolical saying to this effect: 'A laudable innovation, introduced by a perfect follower of the prophets, is of the same nature with the cus-

tomary practices of the prophets themselves.' " The perwāna
resolved, therefore, to do nothing towards suppressing Jelāl's
institutions.

84

A certain great man, who esteemed Jelāl, was nevertheless
shocked that he should, with all his learning and piety, sanc-
tion the use of music and dancing.

He had occasion to visit Jelāl, who at once addressed him
as follows:—"It is an axiom in the sacred canons that a
Muslim, if hard pressed, and in danger of death, may eat of
carrion and other forbidden food, so that the life of a man be
not sacrificed. This rule is admitted and approved by all the
authorities of the law. Now, we *men of God* are exactly in that
position of extreme danger to our lives; and from that danger
there is no escape, save by song, by music, and by the dance.
Otherwise, through the awful majesty of the divine manifestations, the bodies of the saint would melt away as wax,
and disappear like snow under the beams of a July sun."

The personage thus addressed was so struck with the ear-
nestness of Jelāl's manner, and the cogency of his reasoning,
that he became convinced, and thenceforward was a defender
and upholder of Jelāl's institutions, so that these formed, as it
were, the very nourishment of his heart. Many of the learned
followed his example, and joined themselves to Jelāl's followers and disciples.

85

Kālūmān and 'Aynu-'d-Devla were two Roman painters.
They were unrivalled in their art of painting portraits and
pictures. Both were disciples of Jelāl.

Kālūmān one day narrated that in Constantinople, on a
certain tablet, the portraits of the Lady Meryem and of Jesus
were painted, in such style as to be matchless. From all parts
of the world artists came and tried their best; but none could
produce the equal of those two portraits.

'Aynu-'d-Devla undertook, therefore, to journey to
Constantinople, and see this picture. He made himself an

inmate of the great church of Constantinople for a whole year, and served the priests thereof in various ways.

One night, then, he spied his opportunity, took the tablet under his arm, and absconded with it.

On reaching Qonya, he paid his respects to Jelāl, who inquired of him where he had been. He narrated to Jelāl all that had occurred with the tablet, which he exhibited.

Jelāl found the picture exceedingly beautiful, and gazed on it long with the utmost pleasure. He then spake as follows:—

"These two beautiful portraits complain of you, saying that you are not a faithful admirer of theirs, but are an untrue lover." The artist asked: "How?" Jelāl replied: "They say they are not supplied with food and rest. On the contrary, they are kept sleepless every night, and fasting every day. They complain: 'Aynu-'d-Devla leaves us, sleeps himself all night, and takes his meals by day, never remaining with us to do as we do!'"

The artist remarked: "Food and sleep are to them impossibilities. Neither have they speech, with which to say anything. They are mere lifeless effigies."

Jelāl now replied: "Thou art a living effigy. Thou hast acquired a knowledge of various arts. Thou art the handiwork of a limner whose hand has framed the universe, the human race, and all things on earth and in heaven. Is it right that thou forsake him, and enamour thyself of an insignificant lifeless effigy? What profit is there in these portraits? What advantage can accrue to thee from them?"

Touched by these reproaches, the artist vowed repentance of his sin, and professed himself a Muslim.

86

When the time of Jelāl's death drew near, he cautioned his disciples to have no fear or anxiety on that account; "for," said he, "as the spirit of Mansūr [1] appeared, a hundred and

[1] Mansūr, son of 'Ammār, thus mentioned by D'Herbelot: "Scheikh des plus considérés parmi les Musulmans. On le cite au sujet d'un passage du chapitre Enfathar de l'Alcoran (lxxxii.), où Dieu est introduit faisant ce reproche aux hommes: *Qu'est-ce qui vous rend si orgueilleux contre votre*

fifty years after his death, to the Sheykh Ferīdu-'d-Dīn 'Attār, and became the sheykh's spiritual guide and teacher, so, too, do you always be with me, whatever may happen, and remember me, so that I may show myself to you, in whatever form that may be—that I may always belong to you, and ever be shedding in your breasts the light of heavenly inspiration. I will simply remind you now that our dear Lord, Muhammed, the Apostle of God, said to his disciples: 'My life is a blessing unto you, and my death will be a blessing unto you. In my life I have guided you, and after my death I will send blessings on you.' "

Jelāl's friends shed tears all, and broke out into sighs and lamentations; but bowed their heads in reverence.

It is said that he gave directions to get ready his grave-clothes, and that his wife, Kirā Khātūn, began to wail, tearing her clothes, and exclaiming: "O thou light of the world, life of the human race; unto whom wilt thou commit us? Whither wilt thou go?"

He answered her: "Whither will I go? Verily, I shall not quit your circle." She then asked: "Will there be another like unto thee, our Lord? Will another become manifest?" He replied: "If there be, he will be I." After a while he added: "While in the body, I have two attachments; one, to you; the other, to the flesh. When, by the grace of the unique Spirit, I become disembodied—when the world of unbodied spirits, unity, and singleness, shall appear—my attachment to the flesh will become attachment to you, and I shall then have but one sole attachment."

87

With his last breath Jelāl recommended to Husāmu-'d-Dīn to lay him in the upper part of his tomb, so that he might be the first to rise at the last day.

maître qui vous fait tant de biens? (v. 6). Ce Scheikh disait: Quand Dieu me fera ce reproche, je lui repondrai: *Ĺe sont ces biens et ces graces mêmes que vous me faites, qui me rendent si superbe.*" As Sheykh 'Attār lived about A.H. 600, Mansūr must have died about A.H. 400 (A.D. 1020). He is mentioned in No. 51, p. 68, of the *Nafahātu-'l-Uns.*

As he lay in his extreme sickness, there were earthquakes for seven days and nights, very severe, so that walls and houses were overthrown. On the seventh occasion, all his disciples were alarmed. He, however, calmly remarked: "Poor earth! it is eager for a fat morsel! It shall have one!"

He then gave his last instructions to his disciples, as follows:—"I recommend unto you the fear of God, in public and in private; abstemiousness in eating and in sleeping, as also in speaking; the avoidance of rebelliousness and of sin; constancy in fasting, continuous worship, and perpetual abstinence from fleshly lusts; long-suffering under the ill-treatment of all mankind; to shun the companionship of the light-minded and of the common herd; to associate with the righteous and with men of worth. For verily *the best of mankind is he who benefiteth men,*[1] and *the best of speech is that which is short and to the purpose.*"[2]

88

The following is a prayer taught by Jelāl, on his death-bed, to one of his friends, to be used whenever affliction or care might weigh upon him:—

"O our Lord God, I breathe but for thee, and I stretch forth my spirit towards thee, that I may recite thy doxologies abundantly, commemorating thee frequently. O our Lord God, lay not on me an ailment that may make me forgetful to commemorate thee, or lessen my yearning towards thee, or cut off the delight I experience in reciting the litanies of thy praise. Grant me not a health that may engender or increase in me presumptuous or thankless insolence. For thy mercy's sake, O thou Most-Merciful of the compassionate. Amen."

89

A friend was seated by Jelāl's pillow, and Jelāl leaned on that friend's bosom. Suddenly a most handsome youth appeared at the door of the room, to the utmost astonishment of the friend.

[1] Khayru 'n nāsi, men yenfa 'u 'n nāsa.—*Arabic Proverb.*
[2] Khayru 'l kelāmi, qasīruhu 'l mufīdu.—*Arabic Proverb.*

Jelāl arose and advanced to receive the stranger. But the friend was quicker, and quietly asked his business. The stranger answered: "I am 'Azrā'īl, the angel of departure and separation. I am come, by the divine command, to inquire what commission the Master may have to intrust to me."

Blessed are the eyes that can perceive such sights!

The friend was near fainting at this answer. But he heard Jelāl call out: "Come in, come in, thou messenger of my King. Do that which thou art bidden; and, God willing, thou shalt find me one of the patient."

He now told his attendants to bring a vessel of water, placed his two feet therein, and occasionally sprinkled a little on his breast and forehead, saying: "My beloved (God) has proffered me a cup of poison (bitterness). From his hand I drink that poison with delight."

The singers and musicians now came in, and executed a hymn, while the whole company of friends wept, and sobbed loudly.

Jelāl observed: "It is as my friends say. But, were they even to pull down the house, what use? See my panting heart; look at my delight. The sun sheds a grateful light on the moth. My friends invite me one way; my teacher Shemsu-'d-Dīn beckons me the other way. Comply ye with the summoner of the Lord, and have faith in him. Departure is inevitable. All being came out of nothing, and again it will be shut up in the prison of nullity. Such is God's decree from all eternity; and, to decree belongeth unto God, the Most High, the All-Great!"

His son Sultan Veled had been unremitting in his attentions. He wept and sobbed. He was reduced to a shadow. Jelāl therefore said to him: "Bahā'u-'d-Dīn, my son, I am better. Go and lie down a little. Rest thyself, and sleep awhile!"

When he was gone, Jelāl indited his last ode; thus:—

"Go! head on pillow lay; alone, in peace, me leave,
Loved tyrant, plague by night, while all around thee grieve.
That peerless beauty (God) has no need kind care to show;
But, sallow lovers, ye must patient faith still know.

Perplexity is ours to bear; 'tis his to own hard heart;
Shed he our blood; what sin? He'll not pay murder's smart.
To die's hard, after all; but remedy there's none;
How, then, to crave a remedy? The evil's done.
Last night, in dream, a warder, from my love's abode,
Made sign to me, and said: 'This way! Hold thou my lode.' "

90

It is related that, after his death, when laid on his bier, and
while he was being washed by the hands of a loving and
beloved disciple, while others poured the water for the ablution of Jelāl's body, not one drop was allowed to fall to the
earth. All was caught by the fond ones around, as had been
the case with the Prophet at his death. Every drop was drunk
by them as the holiest and purest of waters.

As the washer folded Jelāl's arms over his breast, a tremor
appeared to pass over the corpse, and the washer fell with his
face on the lifeless breast, weeping. He felt his ear pulled by
the dead saint's hand, as an admonition. On this, he fainted
away, and in his swoon he heard a cry from heaven, which
said to him: "Ho there! Verily the saints of the Lord have
nothing to fear, neither shall they sorrow. Believers die not;
they merely depart from one habitation to another abode!"

91

When the corpse was brought forth, all the men, women,
and children, who flocked to the funeral procession, smote
their breasts, rent their garments, and uttered loud lamentations. These mourners were of all creeds, and of various
nations; Jews and Christians, Turks, Romans, and Arabians
were among them. Each recited sacred passages, according to
their several usages, from the Law, the Psalms, or the Gospel.

The Muslims strove to drive away these strangers, with
blows of fist, or staff, or sword. They would not be repelled.
A great tumult was the result. The sultan, the heir-apparent,
and the perwāna all flew to appease the strife, together with
the chief rabbis, the bishops, abbots, &c.

It was asked of these latter why they mixed themselves up with the funeral of an eminent Muslim sage and saint. They replied that they had learnt from him more of the mysteries shrouded in their scriptures, than they had ever known before; and had found in him all the signs and qualities of a prophet and saint, as set forth in those writings. They further declared: "If you Muslims hold him to have been the Muhammed of his age, we esteem him as the Moses, the David, the Jesus of our time; and we are his disciples, his adherents."

The Muslim leaders could make no answer. And so, in all honour, with every possible demonstration of love and respect, was he borne along, and at length laid in his grave.

He had died as the sun went down, on Sunday, the fifth of the month Jumāda-'l-ākhir, A.H. 672 (16th December A.D. 1273); being thus sixty-eight (lunar) years (sixty-six solar years) of age.

92

Sultan Veled is reported to have related that, shortly after the death of his father, Jelāl, he was sitting with his step-mother, Jelāl's widow, Kirā Khātūn, and Husāmu-'d-Dīn, when his step-mother saw the spirit of the departed saint, winged as a seraph, poised over his, Sultan Veled's, head, to watch over him.

93

Jelāl had a female disciple, a saint, named Nizāma Khātūn, an intimate friend of his wife's.

Nizāma formed the design to give a spiritual party to Jelāl, with an entertainment for his disciples. She possessed nothing but a Thevr (*or* Sevr)[1] veil, which she had destined to be her own winding-sheet.

She now ordered her servants to sell this veil, and so procure the necessaries for the projected feast. But, that same

[1] *Thevr* is the name of a tribe of Arabians, and of two hills, one at Mekka, the other at Medīna; but the explanation of the term "a *Thevr* or *Sevr veil*" I have not met with.

morning, Jelāl came to her house with his disciples, and, addressing her, said: "Nizāma Khātūn, sell not thy veil; to thee it is a piece of necessary furniture. Lo! we are come to thy entertainment."

He and his disciples remained with her, engaged in spiritual exercises, three whole days and nights.

94

After Jelāl's death, Kīgātū Khān, a Mogul general, came up against Qonya, intending to sack the city and massacre the inhabitants. (He was emperor from A.H. 690 to 696, A.D. 1290–1294.)

That night, in a dream, he saw Jelāl, who seized him by the throat, and nearly choked him, saying to him: "Qonya is mine. What seekest thou from its people?"

On awaking from his dream, he fell on his knees and prayed for mercy, seeking also for information as to what that portent might signify. He sent in an ambassador to beg permission for him to enter the city as a friendly guest.

When he arrived at the palace, the nobles of Qonya flocked to his court with rich offerings. All being seated in solemn conclave, Kīgātū was suddenly seized with a violent tremor, and asked one of the princes of the city, who was seated on a sofa by himself: "Who may the personage be that is sitting at your side on your sofa?" The prince looked about, right and left; but saw no one. He replied accordingly. Kīgātū answered: "What? How sayest thou? I see by thy side, seated, a tall man with a grisly beard and a sallow complexion, a grey turban, and an Indian plaid over his chest, who looks at me most pryingly."

The prince sagaciously suspected forthwith that Jelāl's shade was there present by his side, and made answer: "The sacred eyes of majesty alone are privileged to witness that vision. It is the son of Bahā'u-'d-Dīn of Balkh, our Lord Jelālu-'d-Dīn, who is entombed in this land."

The Khān replied: "Last night I saw him in my dream. He went nigh choking me, and told me Qonya is his possession. Now, prince, thee I call my adoptive father; and I entirely forego my intention to devastate this city. Tell me; has that holy man any son or descendant alive here?"

The prince told him of Bahā Veled, now sheykh of the city, and the peerless saint of God. Kīgātū expressed the wish to go and visit the sheykh. The prince conducted him and his suite of nobles to Sultan Veled. They all declared themselves his disciples, and assumed the dervish turban. Bahā recounted to the khān the history of his grandfather's expulsion from Balkh, and of all that followed. The khān offered him royal presents, and accompanied him on a visit of reverence to the shrine of the deceased saint.

CHAPTER IV

Shemsu-'d-Dīn Tebrīzī, Muhammed son of 'Alī son of Melik-dād

1

SHEMSU-'D-DĪN of Tebrīz was surnamed the Sultan of Mendicants, the Mystery of God upon earth, the Perfect in word and deed. Some had styled him the Flier, because he travelled about so much; and others spoke of him as the Perfect One of Tebrīz.

He went about seeking for instruction, human and spiritual. He had visited many of the chief spiritual teachers of the world; but he had found none equal to himself. The teachers of all lands became, therefore, pupils and disciples to him.

He was always in quest of the beloved object of the soul (God). His corporeal frame he habited in coarsest felt, shrouding his eminent greatness from all eyes in what are really the jewelled robes of spirituality.

At Damascus it was, where he was then studying, that he first saw Jelālu-'d-Dīn by chance in a crowded market-place; but Jelāl, who was at that time a student also, avoided him.

Ultimately, he was led to Qonya in Jelāl's traces, and first arrived there at dawn, on Saturday, the twenty-sixth of Jumāda-'l-ākhir, A.H. 642 (28th November, A.D. 1244), Jelāl being then professor at four colleges there. They met as is related in a former chapter (chap. iii. Nos. 8, 9).

At the end of three months' seclusion together, passed in religious, scientific, and spiritual disquisitions and investigations, Shemsu-'d-Dīn became satisfied that he had never met Jelāl's equal.

2

When Shemsu-'d-Dīn was quite worn out by a series of divine manifestations and the consequent ecstasies, he used to break away, hide himself, and work as a day-labourer at the water-wheels of the Damascus gardens, until his equanimity would be restored. Then he would return to his studies and meditations.

In his supplications to God, he was constantly inquiring whether there was not in either world, corporeal and spiritual, one other saint who could bear him company. In answer thereto, there came at length from the unseen world the answer, that the one holy man of the whole universe who could bear him company was the Lord Jelālu-'d-Dīn of Rome.

On receiving this answer, he set out at once from Damascus, and went in quest of his object to the land of Rome (Asia Minor).

3

Chelebī Emīr 'Ārif related that his father, Sultan Veled, told him that one day, as a trial and test, Shemsu-'d-Dīn requested Jelāl to make him a present of a slave. Jelāl instantly went and fetched his own wife, Kirā Khātūn, who was as extremely beautiful as virtuous and saintlike, offering her to him.

To this act of renunciation Shemsu-'d-Dīn replied: "She is my most esteemed sister. What I want is a youth to wait on me." Jelāl thereupon produced his own son, Sultan Veled, who, he said, would be proud to carry the shoes of Shems, placing them before him for use when required for a walk abroad. Again Shems objected: "He is as my son. But, perhaps, you will supply me with some wine. I am accustomed to drink it, and am not comfortable without it."

Jelāl now took a pitcher, went himself to the Jews' ward of the city, and returned with it full of wine, which he set before Shems.

"I now saw," continued Sultan Veled in his recital, "that Shemsu-'d-Dīn, uttering an intense cry, rent his garment, bowed down to Jelāl's feet, lost in wondering admiration at this implicit compliance with the behests of a teacher, and then said: 'By the truth of the First, who had no beginning, the Last, who will have no end, there never has been, from the commencement of creation, and there never, until the end of time, will be, in the universe of substance, a lord and master, heart-captivating and Muhammed-like, as thou art.' "

He now bowed down again, declared himself a disciple to Jelāl, and added: "I have tested and tried to the utmost the patient long-suffering of our Lord; and I have found his greatness of heart to be totally unlimited by any bounds."

4

Jelāl is reported to have said: "When Shemsu-'d-Dīn first came, and I felt a mighty spark of love for him lighted up in my heart, he took upon himself to command me in the most despotic and peremptory manner.

" 'Study,' said he, 'the writings of thy father.' For a while I studied nothing else. 'Keep silent, and speak to no one.' I ceased from all intercourse with my fellows.

"My words were, however, the food of my disciples; my thoughts were the nectar of my pupils. They hungered and thirsted. Thence, ill feelings were engendered amongst them, and a blight fell upon my teacher.

"He came to me another day as I was, by his command, studying the writings of my father. Thrice he called out to me: 'Study them not.' From his sacred features the effulgence of spiritual wisdom streamed. I laid down the book, and never since have I opened it."

5

Jelāl is said to have related that Shemsu-'d-Dīn forbade him to study any more the writings of his father, Bahā Veled, and that he punctually obeyed the injunction.

But one night he dreamt that he was in company with a number of friends, who were all studying and discussing with him those very writings of Bahā Veled.

As he woke from his dream, Shems was entering the room with a severe look. Addressing Jelāl, he asked: "How hast thou dared to study that book again?" Jelāl protested that, since his prohibition, he had never once opened his father's works.

"Yes," retorted Shems, "there is a study by reading, and there is also a study by contemplating. Dreams are but the shadows of our waking thoughts. Hadst thou not occupied thy thoughts with those writings, thou wouldst not have dreamt about them."

"From that time forward," remarked Jelāl, "I never again busied myself with my father's writings, so long as Shemsu-'d-Dīn remained alive."

6

Jelāl is related to have informed his disciples that Shemsu-'d-Dīn was a scholar in every science known to man, and also a great alchemist; but that he had renounced them all, to devote himself to the study and contemplation of the mysteries of divine love.

7

Shemsu-'d-Dīn was one day sitting with his disciples, when the public executioner passed by. Shems remarked to those around him: "There goes one of God's saints."

The disciples knew the man, and told Shems that he was the common headsman. Shems replied: "True! In the exercise of his calling, he put to death a man of God, whose soul he thus released from the bondage of the body. As a recompense for this kind act of his, the saint bequeathed to him his own saintship."

On the following day the executioner relinquished his office, vowed repentance, came to Shemsu-'d-Dīn, made his bow, and professed himself a disciple.

8

Sheykh Husāmu-'d-Dīn was originally a young man who showed great respect and humility towards Shemsu-'d-Dīn, to whom he rendered services of every kind.

One day Shems said to him: "Husām, this is not the way. Religion is a question of money. Give me some coin, and offer your services to the Lord; so, peradventure, thou mayest rise in our order."

Husām at once went forth to his own house, collected all his own valuables and money, with his wife's jewels, and all the provisions of the house, brought them to Shems, and laid them at his feet. He furthermore sold a vineyard and country seat he possessed, bringing their price also to his teacher, and thanking him for having taught him a duty, as also for having deigned to accept so insignificant a trifle from his hand.

"Yes, Husām," said Shems, "it is to be hoped that, with God's grace, and the prayers of the saints, thou wilt henceforth attain to such a station, as to be the envy of the most perfect men of God, and be bowed down to by the *Brethren of Sincerity*. It is true that God's saints are not in want of anything, being independent of both worlds. But, at the outset, there is no other way to test the sincerity of one we love, and the affection of a friend, than to call upon him to sacrifice his worldly possessions. The next step is, to summon him to give up all that is not his God. No disciple who wishes to rise, has ever made progress by following his own devices. Advancement is earned by rendering service, and by spending in God's cause. Every pupil who sacrifices possessions at the call of his teacher, would also lay down his life, if needs were. No lover of God can retain both mammon and religion."

Shems then restored to Husām the whole of his goods, keeping back only one piece of silver. Nine times as much more did he bestow upon Husām from first to last; and, as the results of all things are in God's hands, so did Husām at length become the ruler of God's saints, and Jelāl made him the keeper of God's treasury. He it was who wrote down the twenty-four thousand six hundred and sixty couplets contained in the six books of the Mesnevī.

9

Shemsu-'d-Dīn left Qonya, at the end of his first visit, on

Thursday, the twenty-first day of the month of Shawwal, A.H.
643 (14th March, A.D. 1246), after a stay of about sixteen
months.

He returned to Damascus; and his departure left Jelāl in a
state of great uneasiness and excitement. (Compare a conflicting date given in No.13, further on.)

10

Shemsu-'d-Dīn was one day at Bagdād, and entered one of
the palaces there. A eunuch who saw him enter, without
being himself visible, made a sign to a slave to go and drive
away the mendicant.

The slave drew his sword, and raised it to strike; but his
arm withered, and fell palsied.

The eunuch then motioned to another slave to execute the
commission; and he, too, became similarly incapacitated.

Shems them went away of himself, and none dared to
pursue him. Two days later, the eunuch died also.

11

Jelāl's father, Bahā Veled, had a disciple, who, for some
reason, gave offence to Shemsu-'d-Dīn; the latter, in punishment, inflicted a deafness on both the disciple's ears.

After a time, Shems pardoned the offender, and restored
his hearing. But the man bore him a grudge in his heart,
nevertheless. One day, Shems said to him: "Friend, I have
pardoned thee; wherefore art thou still cast down? Be comforted." Notwithstanding this, his rancour remained.

One day, however, he met Shems in the midst of a market.
Suddenly, he felt a new faith glow within him, and he shouted
out: "There is no god save God; Shemsu-'d-Dīn is the apostle
of God."

The market-people, on this, raised a great hubbub, and
wished to kill him. One of them came forward to cut him
down; but Shems uttered so terrific a shout, that the man at
once fell down dead. The rest of the market-people bowed,
and submitted.

Shems now took the disciple by the hand, and led him

away, remarking to him: "My good friend; my name is
Muhammed. Thou shouldest have shouted: 'Muhammed is
the apostle of God.' The rabble will not take gold that is not
coined."

12

One beautiful moonlight night, Jelāl and Shems were together on the terraced roof of the college, and all the inhabitants of Qonya were sleeping on their housetops.

Shems remarked: "See all these poor creatures! They are
dead to every sense of their Creator on this beautiful night of
God's decree. Wilt thou not, Jelāl, of thy infinite compassion,
wake them up, and let them gain a share in the shower of
blessings of this night?"

Thus appealed to, Jelāl faced toward Mekka, and offered
up this prayer to God: "O thou Lord of heaven, and of earth,
for the love of thy servant Shemsu-'d-Dīn, vouchsafe
wakefulness to this people."

Immediately a black cloud gathered from the unseen
world. Thunders and lightnings burst forth; and so heavy a
rain fell, that all the sleepers, catching up what clothing they
could find, quickly took refuge in their houses below. Shems
smiled at the saintly joke, and was greatly amused.

When daylight dawned, the disciples gathered round,
numerous as the raindrops of that shower; and Shems related
to them the story, with the following remarks:—

"Hitherto, all the prophets and saints have ever sought to
hide from vulgar eyes the miraculous powers they have possessed, so that none should be aware of the fact. But now,
our Lord and Master, Jelāl, has been so successful in secretly
following up the path of mystic love, that his miraculous
powers have hitherto escaped the searching eyes of even the
chiefest of God's elect, even as it hath been said: 'Verily, God
hath saints of whom no man knoweth.'"

13

Kimiyā Khātūn, the wife of Shemsu-'d-Dīn, was a very
beautiful, and also a very virtuous, woman. One day, how-

ever, it so happened that, without his permission or knowledge, the grandmother of Sultan Veled, and her attendant
ladies, took Kimiyā with them for an outing to the vineyards
of the city.

As chance would have it, Shems came home while she was
still away. He asked for her, and was informed where she had
gone, and with whom. He was exceedingly annoyed at her
absence.

Kimiyā had scarcely returned home, ere she began to feel
unwell. Her limbs stiffened like dry firewood, and became
motionless. She continued screaming and moaning for three
days, and then gave up the ghost, in the month of Sha'bān,
A.H. 644 (December, A.D. 1246. But compare a conflicting
date given in No. 9, further back.)

14

It is related that, a second time, Shems and Jelāl shut
themselves up for a whole six months in Jelāl's room at the
college, without partaking of meat or drink, and without the
entrance of a single individual to interrupt them, or either of
them coming forth, Sultan Veled and one other disciple alone
excepted.

15

Shemsu-'d-Dīn was extremely bitter in his preachings and
lectures to the learned auditory who used to gather around
him in Qonya. He likened them to oxen and asses. He
reproached them with being further than ever astray from the
path of living love, and taxed them with the presumption of
supposing themselves the equals of Bāyezīd of Bestām.

He once went to Erzen-of-Rome (Erzrūm), the prince of
which city had a son so extremely stupid, though very handsome, that he could be taught nothing, or next thereto.

Shems let no one know who or what he was; but opened a
school for children. Inquiries were made by the prince, and
Shems undertook to instruct the child, and enable him, in one
month, to recite the whole Qur'ān by heart.

He kept his promise. The young prince acquired, further,

during the same period, a beautiful handwriting, and sundry other accomplishments.

It began to be suspected, now, that he was a saint in disguise. He therefore quietly slipped away from that city.

16

There is a tradition that Jelāl one day called his son Sultan Veled, gave him a large sum of money, and bade him go, with a suite of the disciples, to Damascus, and request Shems to return to Qonya.

Jelāl told his son that he would find Shems in a certain inn, playing at backgammon with a young Firengī (European, Frank), also one of God's saints. Sultan Veled went, found Shems exactly so occupied, and brought him back to Qonya, the Firengī youth returning to his own country, there to preach Jelāl's doctrines, as his vicar.

Sultan Veled walked the whole way from Damascus to Qonya, at the stirrup-side of Shems, as a groom walks by the side of a prince's charger. The whole city went forth to receive them. Jelāl and Shems embraced each other. Jelāl became more than ever devoted to his friend; and his disciples resented his neglect of them, as they had done before. Not long afterwards, the dolorous event occurred that terminated the life of Shemsu-'d-Dīn.

17

The Vazīr of Qonya had built a college. On its completion, he gave a great entertainment, in the college, of religious music and dancing, all the learned men of the city being present.

The Qur'ān was first recited in its entirety; after which, the holy waltzing began. The vazīr and Shemsu-'d-Dīn both joined in the dance. Several times they came into collision; or, the vazīr's skirt swept against Shems's person, as he observed no caution in his gyrations.

Jelāl expressed great indignation at this want of courtesy and reverence for his guest and friend. He took Shems by the hand, to lead him away. The grandees present essayed to appease him, but their entreaties were of no avail. The police of the sultan were therefore sent for; and when they arrived, they instantly seized Shems, led him forth a prisoner with every mark of indignity, and put him to death without further inquiry or formality.

18

Chelebī Emīr 'Ārif related, as informed by his mother, Fātima Khātūn, that when Shemsu-'d-Dīn was thus made a martyr, his executioners threw his corpse down a well.

Sultan Veled saw Shems in a dream, and was informed by him where the body would be found. Sultan Veled went therefore at midnight with some friends, recovered the corpse, washed it, and privately buried it in the college grounds, by the side of the founder.

19

Forty days after the disappearance of Shemsu-'d-Dīn, Jelāl, wishing to appease his own sorrow, and quell the mutinous spirit that had broken out among the disciples, appointed Husāmu-'d-Dīn his local deputy, and set out to seek Shems at Damascus for the third time. All the learned men of Syria became his disciples, and he was absent about a year, more or less.

The Sultan and the nobles grew impatient at this long absence, and wrote him an urgent petition, begging him to return to Qonya. With this request he complied.

Naturally, he had failed to find Shemsu-'d-Dīn in the flesh at Damascus; but he had found within himself what was still greater. He went to the lodging of Shems, and wrote on the door, with red ink: "This is the station of the beloved one of Elias, on whom be peace!"

It is said that the body of Shemsu-'d-Dīn disappeared, and that he was buried by the side of Jelāl's father, Sultan Bahā Veled the Elder.

CHAPTER V

Sheykh Salāhu-'d-Dīn [1] *Ferīdūn, surnamed Zer-Kūb*
(Goldbeater)

1

SHEYKH SALĀHU-'D-DĪN was originally a fellow-disciple with
Jelāl, as pupils to Seyyid Burhānu-'d-Dīn. He afterwards
became a goldbeater, as his parents were poor.

After a while, when Jelāl's reputation became great, Salāh
went and paid him his respects. Jelāl knew how highly
Burhān had esteemed Salāh, when his pupil. He therefore
received him in a very friendly manner, and their intercourse
became warmly renewed.

One day, after the murder of Shemsu-'d-Dīn, and the return
of Jelāl from Damascus, he sent for Salāh, and appointed
him his own assistant in the government and instruction of
the disciples, presenting him also to the king in that capacity.

2

Jelāl's first royal protector, 'Alā'u-'d-Dīn Keyqubād, was
now dead, and his son, Gayāsu-'d-Dīn Key-Khusrev, reigned
in his stead.

The monarch one day made a feast in the vineyards, and
went forth into the fields for a walk, alone. He picked up a
young snake, carried it indoors, placed it in a gold box, sealed
this up, and then rejoined his courtiers.

To those attendants the king exhibited the sealed packet,

---

[1] Saladin of European writings. The words mean: *the Fitness of the*
Religion (of Islām).

as having just then been privately received from the Qaysar [1] of Constantinople with a message to this effect: "If your religion of Islām be the true faith, some one of your wise men will be able to see into this packet without breaking its seals, and to tell what it contains."

The king then called upon his ministers to prove their loyalty to him, and their faithfulness to their religion, by solving this riddle. None of them was able.

The packet was now sent round in succession to all the eminent teachers and theologians of the city; but none could unravel the enigma.

At last it was brought to Jelāl, as Sheykh Ferīdūn and he were sitting together. Jelāl invited Ferīdūn to tell them the contents of the packet; and he immediately replied: "It is not a dignified act in the king to imprison a young snake in a gold box, sealing this up as a packet, and then tempting his courtiers, ministers, and learned men with a false pretence. A saint, however, knows not only the solution of so paltry a trick as this, but is also aware of every thought in the king's heart, and every secret of earth and heaven."

When this answer was reported to the king, he came to the college, and professed himself a disciple, remarking: "If the disciples of Shemsu-'d-Dīn possess such power, and work such miracles, how great must have been the sanctity of the murdered martyr."

Ferīdūn acted for ten years as assistant to Jelāl.

3

Fātima, the daughter of Sheykh Salāhu-'d-Dīn Ferīdūn, was married to Sultan Veled, Jelāl's son. Jelāl used to teach her to read the Qur'ān and other books.

Jelāl used to call Fātima his *right eye*; her sister Hediyya, his *left eye*; and their mother, Latīfa Khātūn, *the personification of God's grace*.

When Fātima's marriage was solemnized, all the angels of

[1] The Muslim world knows but one *Qayser* (Cæsar), the Emperor of Rome (Old or New).

heaven were present, and wished the young couple all happiness.

She was a saint, and continually worked miracles. She fasted by day and watched by night, tasting food only once in three days. She was very charitable to the poor, the orphans, and the widows, distributing to them food and raiment.

Sheykh Ferīdūn died on New Year's Day, A.H. 657 (28th December, A.D. 1258).

CHAPTER VI

Chelebī Husāmu-'l-Haqqi-wa-'d-Dīn, Hasan, son of Mu-hammed, son of Hasan, son of Akhī-Turk,[1] *related to Esh-Sheykhu-'l-Mukerrem*[2]

1

ON the death of Sheykh Ferīdūn, Chelebī Husāmu-'d-Dīn was appointed by Jelāl his assistant in place of the deceased saint. For another ten years these two spiritual friends worked together in perfect unity as superior and assistant. Husām was surnamed "the Juneyd and the Bāyezīd[3] of the age," "the Key of the Treasuries of God's throne," "the Trustee of the Treasures on earth," and "God's next Friend in the World."

2

Husām once made his obeisance to Jelāl, and related to him that, when the disciples recited the poetry of the Mesnevī, and became entranced, he had himself seen a company of invisible ones, armed with clubs and scimitars, keeping guard over them. If any one did not listen to those sacred words with reverence and believing, the clubs and swords were brought into play, and he was hurled into the pit of hell-fire. Jelāl confirmed, as being a fact, all Husām had related.

[1] I have not met with any notice of Akhī-Turk.

[2] *The Honoured Elder*; by which Abū-Bekr is probably intended; but see a note to the Preface of the Mesnevī.

[3] Juneyd and Bāyezīd of Bestām were two great doctors of mysticism; the latter died in A.H. 234 or 261 (A.D. 848 or 874), and the former in A.H. 297–8 (A.D. 909–10).

3

Husāmu-'d-Dīn was very eloquent, pious, and God-fearing. He would never use the water, even, of the college, for drink or for ablutions; but always brought his water from his own home for those purposes. He distributed, to the very last farthing, the whole of the revenues of the college among the disciples.

4

Sultan Veled and his friends went one day to Husām's garden. Some of the disciples felt a desire to eat of some honey, but had said nothing on the subject. Husām read their thoughts. He therefore ordered his gardener to bring some new honeycomb from a certain hive. More, and more, and still more comb was brought, until all were satisfied; still, the hive was yet full. When they left his garden, Husām sent the hive with them; and for a long time it supplied all their wants.

5

A severe drought afflicted Qonya and its environs. Prayers for rain were publicly offered without avail.

Recourse was now had to Husāmu-'d-Dīn, who was begged to intercede for the people, and to pray for rain.

He first went to Jelāl's tomb, there performed his devotions to God, and then put up the prayer for rain, his disciples weeping as they chanted "Amen."

Clouds now began to collect and lower; shortly after which an abundance of rain was vouchsafed.

6

Not only were all the revenues of the college, arising from its endowments, committed by Jelāl to the sole administration of Husām, but, whatever gifts and contributions were offered by princes and friends, in money or in kind, they were all consigned to his care, to augment the resources of the general fund. Jelāl's family, and also his son, though often pinched, fared as the disciples.

7

The disciples were both surprised and scandalised, at one time, by Husām's publicly speaking very much in praise of certain individuals who bore an extremely bad character, while he disparaged certain others who were noted for their pious lives.

They complained to Jelāl; but he confirmed what Husām had said, and remarked to them: "God looks only to man's heart. Those seemingly lewd fellows are really God-loving saints, while those outwardly pious livers are merely inward hypocrites."

8

One day Husām was lecturing. Suddenly he beckoned to one of the disciples, and told him to go with all speed to the royal palace, ask to see the queen, give her his greeting, and say to her: "Instantly quit this apartment thou art in, if thou wouldest avoid impending destruction, the result of God's decree."

The queen believed his word, and at once removed to another part of the palace. The apartment was speedily stripped of its furniture; and scarcely had the last loads been removed, when, with a loud crash, the building fell in. Her faith in his miraculous power was thenceforward increased a hundredfold.

9

A certain sheykh died at Qonya, who was rector of two different colleges. The prince who was the trustee of both, elected to nominate Husāmu-'d-Dīn as rector of one of them; and a great entertainment was prepared by the prince for the occasion.

Jelāl was informed of the arrangement, and he expressed the intention to bear himself Husām's carpet to his new college, and himself spreading it for Husām in his new seat.

A certain brawler, a kinsman of Husām's, Akhī Ahmed by name, was of the company; and he had felt nettled at Husām's appointment. He came forward, snatched away

Husām's carpet, gave it to one of his companions to cast out of the building, and exclaimed: "We will not suffer this fellow to be installed here as sheykh."

Great confusion ensued. Several nobles of the Akhī clan, who were present, drew their swords and knives, a scene of blood appearing to be about to commence.

Jelāl now addressed the crowd, reproaching them for such behaviour. He told them that their family and college would not prosper, but that the Mevlevī order, founded by himself, and his lineal posterity would go on ever steadily increasing. He then related the following anecdote:—

"A certain sheykh from Samarqand, Abū-'l-Lays by name, went on his travels for about twenty years, with a view to study, partly at Mekka. At length he set out on his return home, whither his reputation, as well as numerous disciples, had preceded him.

"Arrived at the outskirts of his native place, he went to the riverside to perform an ablution. There he found a number of women, occupied with laundry work. From among these, one old woman advanced, looked at him attentively, and then exclaimed: 'Why, if here isn't our little Abū-'l-Lays come back again! Go quickly, girls, and carry the news to our family.'

"The sheykh returned forthwith to his party of fellow-travellers, and gave orders for their beasts to be at once reloaded for an immediate return to Damascus. On being questioned as to his reason for this sudden change of intention he answered: 'My people still think of me as "*little Abū-'l-Lays*," and will treat me with familiar indignity accordingly, esteeming me of small account, and thereby committing a grievous sin; for it is an incumbent duty on all to honour the learned and the wise. To respect them is to show reverence to the apostle of God, and to revere him is to serve the Creator.'

"Now, the truth was that, when a child, his father had always called him 'little Abū-'l-Lays.' But strangers would not so understand that term of endearment; they would think it one of too free and easy familiarity, and as likely to draw down on the city and its inhabitants the divine displeasure. It was not consistent with true affection to allow the possibility of such a visitation to occur."

Having delivered himself of this constructive reprimand, Jelāl left the college barefoot, and in high dudgeon. The chief people came after him to intercede, but he would not be pacified. Their intervention was declined, and he refused to be reconciled with the broiler, Akhī Ahmed. He would not consent to go near that offender, who died soon afterwards; though most of his sons, relatives, and even his fellow-revellers, became disciples of Jelāl's.

The sultan would have caused him to be put to death at once; but Jelāl would not permit that.

Akhī Ahmed was never again allowed to show himself at any public reception, and was shunned by all, like the wandering Jew.

Eventually, Husāmu-'d-Dīn was appointed rector of both the colleges in question; and Ahmed's son, Akhī 'Alī, was a disciple of Sultan Veled.

10

Jelālu-'d-Dīn was of the school of Abū-Hanīfa; but Husām belonged to that of Shāfi'ī.[1] He thought of joining the Hanefī school, out of deference to his teacher. Jelāl, however, recommended him to remain what he had always been, and to strive to inculcate to all the doctrine of divine love, as set forth by Jelāl.

11

After Jelāl's death, his widow, Kirā Khātūn, suggested to her stepson, Sultan Veled Bahā'u-'d-Dīn, that he ought to have succeeded his father as rector of the fraternity, and not Husām.

Sultan Veled answered that it had been his father's bequest

---

[1] These are two of the four orthodox schools of Islām; they differ in certain details. There are reputed to be seventy-two schismatic or heretical sects.

that Husām should succeed, that he himself had sworn the oath of fealty to Husām, and that Husām was now become a kind of spiritual beehive, through the incessant and multitudinous visitations of angelic ministers sent to him with messages from on high.

12

Husāmu-'d-Dīn had a gardener, whose name was Sheykh Muhammed. About four years after Jelāl's death, Husām had reason to reprimand the gardener, who took offence at this, and went away to another garden, resolved never to return to Husām's service.

As he sat reflecting, he fell asleep. In his dreams he saw Jelāl coming towards him, with an executioner by his side, who held up an axe. Jelāl ordered the executioner to cut off Muhammed's head, as the punishment for his having offended Husām.

This was done; and Muhammed saw his own head fall off, and his own blood flow. He knew that he was dead.

After a while he saw Jelāl return, pick up Muhammed's decapitated head, place it in proper junction with the neck of the corpse, and utter the exclamation: "In the name of God, with God, from God, and to God." Muhammed saw himself instantly alive again, felt very penitent, threw himself at Jelāl's feet, and cried out piteously.

He now awoke and arose. No one was in sight. All traces of blood had vanished, and no sign of a wound was discernible on his neck. In all speed he returned to Husām's garden, and resumed his work with alacrity.

But now he saw Husām approaching, who said to him: "Well, Sheykh Muhammed! Until Jelālu-'d-Dīn chastised thee, thou wert no Muslim, and wert given over to stiffneckedness. Had not I interceded for thee, thou hadst been dead to all eternity, shut out from every hope of heaven."

Muhammed protested his sincere repentance, became a dervish, and professed himself a disciple.

13

When Husāmu-'d-Dīn had faithfully executed for ten years, as a just and wise steward, all his duties as successor to Jelālu-'d-Dīn, he one day went, with his companions and disciples, to visit the shrine of his predecessor.

As he drew near to the mausoleum, information was brought to him that the gilt crescent surmounting the cupola had fallen down.

On the moment, Husām felt himself to be stricken. He asked for an examination of dates to be made, and found that ten years previously Jelāl had departed this life. He therefore said to those around him: "Lead me back home. The time for my dissolution is at hand."

He was conducted to his chamber, where, a few days later, on Thursday, the twenty-second of Sha'bān, in the year A.H. 683 (4th November, A.D. 1284), he breathed his last exactly at the time when the gilt crescent was replaced over Jelāl's tomb, and the works brought to a close.

14

Shortly after the death of Husāmu-'d-Dīn, the widow of Jelāl, Kirā Khātūn, too, departed this life, and was buried by the side of her husband.

As her corpse was being borne towards its last resting-place, the procession passed through one of the gates of the town. Here, the bearers found themselves arrested by some unseen power, so that they could not move, hand or foot. This singular effect lasted for about half an hour.

Her stepson, Sultan Veled, with the other mourners, struck up a hymn, and commenced a holy dance. Soon after this, the bearers recovered the use of their limbs, and found themselves able to proceed. All now went well, and the interment was completed.

That same night, a holy man of the fraternity saw Kirā Khātūn in heaven near to her husband.[1] He inquired of her

---

[1] This anecdote directly contradicts the foolish idea, so common in Europe, that, in the religious system of Islām, women are held to have no souls, and no hope of paradise.

concerning the arrestation of the funeral. She informed him thus: "The day previous, a man and a woman had been stoned to death at that gate for the sin of adultery. I took compassion on them, interceded for their forgiveness, and obtained for them admittance to paradise. My preoccupation in their cause was the reason of the delay met with by the funeral procession."

15

One day, while Jelál was yet living, Satan appeared in person to Husámu-'d-Dín, and complained bitterly of the torments inflicted on him by the continuous pious exercises of Jelál. He said that such was his deep reverence for Jelál and his followers, that he dared not attempt to seduce one of them; and that, had he known that, of the seed of Adam, so holy a race of men were to spring, he never would have tempted the father of mankind. He further added: "I entertain a hope that the kindness of heart of his sons will lead them to intercede with Jelál for me, and so obtain my eventual release and salvation."

Husám related this occurrence to Jelál, who smiled, and said: "There is reason to hope that he need not despair. God forbid that he should despair!"

16

Whenever the grandees of Qonya entertained a desire to have an audience of the Sheykh Shemsu-'d-Dín of Tebríz, during his lifetime, they used to request Husám to beg Jelál to intercede for them with Shems, and so obtain for them the desired interview.

Jelál and Husám used to tax those nobles for this favour, according to their means and circumstances.

On one occasion the Grand Vazír solicited an audience, and was taxed at forty thousand pieces of silver; which, after much chaffering, was reduced to thirty thousand.

At this audience with Shems, the vazír was so charmed with the mysteries revealed to him, that, on his return there from, he voluntarily sent the ten thousand pieces of silver to Husām, which had been abated from the sum originally fixed.

These monies were always expended by Husām, as he saw fit, in relieving the necessities of the holy community, and the families of Jelāl, the goldbeater, and their various dependants.

CHAPTER VII

The Sultan of them who attain to the Truth, in whom are manifested the mysteries of Positive Knowledge, Bahā'u-'l-Haqqiwa-'d-Dīn,[1] El Veled

1

WHILE Sultan Veled was yet a child, his father, Jelālu-'d-Dīn, was once discoursing on the miracle of the rod of Moses, which swallowed up the rods and other engines of Pharaoh's magicians, related to have been in such quantities as to form seventy camel-loads, and yet that staff became no thicker or longer than before.

Turning to Sultan Veled, his father asked how this could be, and to what it could be likened for the sake of illustration.

The child at once replied: "In a very dark night, if a lighted taper be brought into a large room or hall, it instantly devours all the darkness, and yet remains a little taper."

Jelāl jumped up from his seat, ran to his son, took the child to his bosom, kissed him with effusion, and then said: "May God bless thee, my child! Verily, thou has strung a pearl of the very first water on the string of illustration."

2

Sultan Veled's elder brother, 'Alā'u-'d-Dīn, was killed in the tumult for which the police authorities of Qonya put to death the Sheykh Shemsu-'d-Dīn of Tebrīz. Sultan Veled ruled the dervish community, in room of his father (after the death of Husāmu-'d-Dīn), for many years (from A.H. 683 to

---

[1] The Beauty of the Truth and of the Religion (Of Islām).

712, being twenty-nine lunar years). He composed three volumes of poetry in couplets, like the Mesnevī (hence styled *Mesneviyāt*, Mesnevian Poems), and a volume (*Dīwān*) of odes in the Arabian style, arranged in the alphabetical order of their rhymes.

3

It is related that when Husāmu-'d-Dīn was in his last illness, Sultan Veled came to visit him. Finding the sickness was unto death, he began to wail and lament, asking what would become of himself after the removal of so dear a friend and so able a director.

Husām collected himself, and, leaning on Sultan Veled, sat up. He then addressed the latter thus: "Be of good cheer, and let not thy heart be dismayed through my departure in the body. In another form, I will ever be near thee still. Thou shalt never be in need of counsel from another. In all difficulties and troubles that may beset thee, I will always be present, and in the visions of the night will I solve every doubt, and direct thee in each matter, whether it relate to the spirit and religion, or whether it pertain to the flesh and mundane affairs. Whenever thou shalt receive counsel in this manner, know of a surety that it is I who suggest it to thee—it will be none other than I myself. I will show myself to thee in thy visions; and I will be thy counsel and thy guide."

Sultan Veled was the first who narrated his dreams in his poems. Seek them there; there shalt thou find them consigned.

4

One day a great man asked Sultan Veled whether God ever speaks to his servant—man.

This inquirer had frequently had the idea to send an offering to Sultan Veled; but had hesitated between a gift of money and one of Indian muslins.

Sultan Veled answered his inquiry thus: "God does certainly speak to his servants. And as to the method by which he addresses them, I will relate to thee an anecdote."

"There was in Balkh a preacher, who was also one of God's most precious saints. He had many disciples, who loved him dearly. I heard him once say, during one of his discourses: 'Long hath God spoken to you in words; but you will not hearken to him. This conduct is strangely improper on the part of obsequious servants. In God's name, therefore, I warn you that you ought to hearken to God's words, and yield obedience to his commands.'

"Just then, a dervish in the congregation stood up, and begged that some one would bestow on him a handkerchief.

"A merchant, who was seated in a corner of the mosque, thrice conceived the resolve to give the dervish a handkerchief; but thrice he failed to carry that design into effect.

"That merchant now rose, and, addressing the preacher, said: 'Sir, how does God speak to his servants? Pray explain this, that the method may be known unto us.'

"The preacher answered: 'For one handkerchief, God does not speak more than three times!'

"The merchant was petrified. He cried aloud, and cast himself at the feet of the preacher. What he had thrice resolved to do, and had not performed, he now carried out, giving a handkerchief to the dervish; and professing himself a disciple to the preacher."

"Now,' added Sultan Veled, "I say unto thee, O grandee, do thou also hearken unto the words of God. Give the Indian handkerchiefs, and distribute also the money. When thou shalt have hearkened to the words of God, he will listen also to that which thou mayest say unto him. All thou mayest ask of him, God will give thee; and whatsoever thou seekest of him, thou shalt find."

Forthwith that grandee became a sincere convert and disciple. Similar miraculous works of Sultan Veled are beyond all count.

5

Sultan Veled died on Saturday, the tenth day of Rejeb, A.H. 712 (11th November, A.D. 1312). He had as many as a dozen children by his wife Fātima, daughter of the Sheykh Salāhu-

'd-Dīn Ferīdūn, the goldbeater; but they all died in infancy, immediately after birth, or ere they were six months old. At length, on a Monday, the eighth day of the month of Zū-'l-Qa'da, A.H. 670 (6th May, A.D. 1272), his son and successor Chelebī Emīr 'Ārif, was born.

Soon after his birth, or when only a few months old, the Emīr 'Ārif, at the invitation of his grandfather, Jelālu-'d-Dīn, and in the hearing of a numerous circle of assembled friends, thrice pronounced, audibly and distinctly, God's great name. His grandfather prophesied thence that he would be a very great saint, and would sit in the seat of his own successorship, after his father Sultān Veled. The Emīr 'Ārif lived about fifty years, surviving his father, however, but the short term of eight or nine summers.

CHAPTER VIII

Chelebī Emīr 'Ārīf, Jelālu-'d-Dīn

(NINETY pages of the volume by Eflākī give more than two hundred anecdotes of the acts and miracles, of various kinds, of this illustrious grandson of Jelālu-'d-Dīn, the teacher and friend of the author, who vouches as an eye-witness for the truth and correctness of some of the narratives.

The Emīr 'Ārif passed the far greater portion of his life in travelling about to various cities in central and eastern Asia Minor, and north-western Persia, countries then subject to the great khāns, descendants of Jengīz. He appears to have been of a more energetic or bellicose character than his father, and to have ruled with vigour during his short rectorship.)

1

On the last day but one of the period of the greater pilgrimage at Mekka, the eve of the Festival of Sacrifices, the ninth of the month of Zū-'l-Hijja, A.H. 717 (11th February, A.D. 1318), the Emīr 'Ārif, and the historian Eflākī, his disciple, were together at Sultāniyya, in the north of Persia, the new capital of the great western Mogul empire.

They were visiting at the convent of a certain Mevlevī dervish, named Sheykh Suhrāb,[1] with sundry of the friends and saints, all of whom were engaged in the study of different books, at about the hour of midday, excepting 'Ārif, who was enjoying a siesta.

Suddenly, 'Ārif raised his head, and gave one of his loud, awe-inspiring shouts, which caused all present to tremble.

---

[1] Europeanized Armenians have made this into *Zohrab*, as their own family name.

Without a word, however, he again composed himself to sleep.

When he at length fully roused himself, and finally woke up from his sleep, Sheykh Eflākī ventured to inquire what it was that had disturbed him.

He answered: "I had gone in the spirit to pay a visit to the tomb of my great-grandfather, when there I saw the two Mevlevī dervishes, Nāsiru-'d-Dīn and Shujā'u-'d-Dīn Chanāqī, who had seized each other by the collar, and were engaged in a violent dispute and struggle. I called out to them to desist; and two men, with one pious woman, being there present, saw me."

Eflākī at once made a note of this narrative, putting down the date and hour of the occurrence.

Some time afterwards, 'Ārif returned to the land of Rome, and went to the town of Lādik (*Laodicæa Combusta*, not far from Qonya); and there they met the above-named Nāsiru-'d-Dīn. In the presence of all the friends, 'Ārif asked Nāsir to relate to them the circumstances of his quarrel with Shujā'.

Nāsir replied: "On the eve of the Festival of Sacrifices, I was standing at the upper end of the mausoleum, when Shujā' came there, and committed an unseemly act, for which I reprehended him. He immediately collared me, and I him; when suddenly, from the direction of the feet of the holy Bahā Veled, the voice of 'Ārif was heard shouting to us, and made us tremble. In awe thereat, we immediately embraced each other, and bowed in reverence. That is all I know of the matter."

'Ārif then addressed Eflākī, and said: "Pray relate to our friends what thou knowest thereof, that they may be edified."

Eflākī now produced his memorandum-book, and showed the entry he had made, with the date. The friends marvelled at this, and rejoiced exceedingly, their spirits being refreshed with an influence from the invisible world.

'Ārif then said: "By the soul of my ancestor, I dislike exceedingly to make a display of any miraculous power. But, now and then, for the edification of my disciples, such scenes will slip out. Then Eflākī takes note thereof."

Such miracles are known by the names of "manifestations," and "ektasis of the spirit."

When Qonya was reached, three friends, one a lady, bore
testimony to having seen 'Ārif at the tomb on that day, and
to their having heard him shout.

2

'Ārif's last journey was from Lārenda to Aq-Serāy (on the
road to Qonya). In the latter place he remained about ten
days; when, one night, he laid his head on his pillow, and
wept bitterly, continuously moaning and sobbing in his sleep.

In the morning his friends inquired the cause. He said he
had seen a strange dream. He was seated in a vaulted chamber, with windows looking on to a garden as beautiful as
paradise, with all kinds of flowering shrubs and fruit-bearing
trees, beneath the shade of which the youths and maidens of
heaven were walking and disporting themselves. Melodious
voices were also heard. In one direction he noticed a flower-
garden, and there he saw his grandfather, Jelālu-'d-Dīn. He
wondered at his appearance; when lo, Jelāl looked towards
him, and beckoned him to approach. On his drawing near,
Jelāl asked him what had brought him there; and then added:
"The time is come; the end of thy term. Thou must come to
me."

It was from joy and delight at this kind invitation of his
grandfather, that 'Ārif had wept and sobbed.

He then said: "It is time for me to make my journey to
heaven,—to drink of the cup of God's might."

Two days later, they continued their journey towards
Qonya, and 'Ārif showed some slight symptoms of indisposi-
tion. These daily grew more severe. He reached Qonya. One
morning he came out of his house, and stood in the gateway
of his great-grandfather's mausoleum, silent, in the midst of
his disciples. It was Friday, the last day of the month of Zū-
'l-qaʻda, A.H. 719 (13th January, A.D. 1320).

The orb of the sun rose like a disk of gold, careering over
the azure vault from an impulse given to it by the bat of
God's decree. It attained the altitude of a lance-length. 'Ārif

contemplated it, and smiled. Shortly afterwards, he spoke as follows:—

"I am tired of this lower world, and have no wish to remain beneath the sun, surrounded with dust and misery. The time is come for me to trample on the stars that encircle the pole, mounting beyond the sun, to occupy myself with the mysteries of the heavenly choir, and to be entirely delivered from the instabilities of this world of change."

His disciples burst into tears, and he continued—

"There is no remedy hereto, but to die. During life, my pleasure has been to journey and wander about, in outward space, and in inward self-exploration. For idle spirits come into the world of material forms to contemplate the marvels of the horizons, and the wonders of men's minds,—to acquire knowledge, and attain to certainty. Through the gravity of the body I have been impeded in the investigation, and I shall not be able to travel again. Let me, then, wend my way to the future state, for here below I have no real companion. My only anxiety is, to be with my father and grandfather. How long shall I be severed from them in this world of suffering? I long to behold my grandfather, and I will certainly depart."

He then cried aloud. After which he slowly returned to his chamber, and there continued to moan.

He managed to crawl, as well as he could, to the congregational service of worship of that Friday at noon. Thence he proceeded to the mausoleum, kissed the shrine, sang a hymn, performed a holy dance, and uttered ecstatic cries. He then laid himself down at full length on the floor, under which he is now buried, and said: "Where the man falls, there let him be interred. Bury you the deposit of my corpse in this spot."

That day was as though the last judgment were at hand. A tempest arose; all creation, mortal and immortal, seemed to be groaning.

The day following, Saturday, the traces of his malady were but too visible in 'Ārif's features. He strove to battle with it, and to converse, as if he were in perfect health.

His sickness lasted about five and twenty days. On the

twenty-second of Zū-'l-Hijja there was a violent shock of earthquake.

There was then in Qonya a certain saint, commonly known as "*the Student*," a successor of the legist Ahmed. In his youth he had made himself a great reputation for learning, in all its branches. But, for forty years, he had been paralysed, and had never risen from his seat, summer or winter. He was well versed in all mysteries, and now began to say: "They are taking away the lamp of Qonya! Alas, the world will go to utter confusion! I, too, will follow after that holy man!"

Shocks followed after shocks of the earthquake; and 'Ārif exclaimed: "The hour of departure is at hand! See, the earth yawns for the mouthful it will make of my body. It shows signs of impatience for its food!"

He then asked: "Look! what birds are these that are come here?" His eyes remained fixed for a time on the angelic visions which he now saw. From time to time he would start, as though about to fly. The assembled disciples, men and women, wept bitterly. But he again spoke, and said—

"Sheykhs, be not troubled! Even as my descent into this world was for the regulation of the affairs of your community, so is my existence of equal advantage to you, and I will at all times be with you, never absent from you. Even in the other world will I be with you. Here below, separation is a thing unavoidable. In the other world there is union without disrupture, and junction without a parting. Let me go without a pang. To outward appearance, I shall be absent; but in truth, I shall not be away from you. So long as a sword is in its sheath, it cuts not; but, when it shall be drawn, you shall see its effects. From this day forward, I dash my fist through the curtain that veils the invisible world; and my disciples shall hear the clash of the blows."

As he spake these words, his eldest son, Shāh-Zāda, and his own half-brother, Chelebī 'Ābid, entered the room. Sheykh Eflākī asked him what commands he had to give for them. 'Ārif replied: "They belong to the Lord, and have no longer a relation to me; he will take care of them."

Eflākī now asked: "And what are your wishes with respect

to me, your most humble servant?" The answer was: "Do thou remain in the service of the mausoleum. Forsake it not. Go not elsewhere. That which I have commanded thee to do, as to collecting in writing all the memoirs of my ancestors and family, that do thou in all diligence until its completion. So mayest thou be approved of the Lord, and blessed by his saints."

All wept.

'Ārif now recited some verses; pronounced thrice the holy name of God, with a sigh; recited some more verses; and then, between the noon and afternoon hours of worship, having recited two short chapters of the Qur'ān, he departed, in peace and rejoicing, to the centre of his existence, on Tuesday, the twenty-fourth day of Zū-'l'Hijja, A.H. 719 (5th February, A.D. 1320). Unto God be all glory, now and for ever!

He was buried on the 25th, where he had himself indicated, by the side of his grandfather. His half-brother 'Ābid succeeded him.

CHAPTER IX

Genealogy of Jelālu-'d-Dīn, Rūmī

On his father's side, the remote ancestor of Jelālu-'d-Dīn, during Islāmic times, was Abū-Bekr, the dearest and most faithful friend of Muhammed the Arabian lawgiver, and his successor in the government of the community of Islām, as the first of the long line of Caliphs.

Like Muhammed himself, Abū-Bekr was of the tribe of Quraysh, which claims descent, through Ishmael, from Abraham, the chosen friend of God, and father of the faithful. The stem of Abū-Bekr's branch of the tribe unites with that of Muhammed in Murra, ancestor to Muhammed in the seventh degree, and to Abū-Bekr in the sixth.

Abū-Bekr was, furthermore, one of Muhammed's fathers-in-law, as his daughter 'Ā'isha was the Prophet's only virgin bride.

A son or grandson of Abū-Bekr is said to have been among the Arabian conquerors of Khurāsān during the caliphate of 'Uthmān (Osmān), about A.H. 25 (A.D. 647), and to have settled at Balkh (the capital of the ancient Bactria), where his family flourished until after the birth of Jelālu-'d-Dīn.[1]

---

[1] A genealogy is given in the Turkish preface to my copy of the Mesnevī, which traces the descent of Jelālu-'d-Dīn Muhammed from Abū-Bekr in ten degrees, as follows:—"Jelālu-'d-Dīn, son of Bahā'u-'d-Dīn, son of Huseyn, son of Ahmed, son of Mevdūd, son of Sābit (Thābit), son of Museyyeb, son of Mutahhar, son of Hammād, son of 'Abdu-'r-Rahmān, son of 'Abū-Bekr." Now, Abdu-'r-Rahmān, the eldest of all the sons of Abū-Bekr, died and was buried at Mekka in A.H. 53 (A.D. 672), and Jelālu-'d-Dīn was born at Balkh in A.H. 604 (A.D. 1207). Between these two there

At an uncertain period subsequent to A.H. 491 (A.D. 1097), a daughter of one of the Kh'ārezmian kings of Central Asia was given in marriage to Jelālu-'d-Dīn's great-great-grandfather, whose name is either not mentioned by Eflākī, or I have missed it. She gave birth to Jelāl's great-grandfather, Ahmed, surnamed El-Khatībī (as being, apparently, a son or descendant, or a client, of a public preacher, Khatīb).

Nothing more is mentioned of Ahmed by Eflākī, than that he had a son Huseyn, surnamed Jelālu-'d-Dīn, who married a daughter of a certain Khurrem-Shāh, King of Khurāsān, and became grandfather, by her, to the author of the Mesnevī. His son, Muhammed, surnamed Bahā'u-'d-Dīn, styled Sultānu-'l-'Ulemā, and commonly known as Bahā'u-'d-Dīn Veled, or shorter as Bahā Veled, appears also to have married a lady, by whom he had three children, a daughter and two sons.

Bahā Veled's eldest child, his daughter, was married off, and remained at Balkh, when Bahā Veled, his mother, and two sons left it, a year or so before it was taken and devastated by Jengīz Khān in A.H. 608 (A.D. 1211). His elder son is not again mentioned by Eflākī after their departure from Balkh. Neither is the mother of his children once mentioned. But his own mother, the princess, was alive, and was still with him in about A.D. 1230; after which, she too is not again mentioned.

Bahā Veled's youngest child, his most celebrated son Muhammed, surnamed Jelālu-'d-Dīn, Mevlānā, Khudā-vendgār, and Rūmī, the principal personage of these memoirs, the founder of the order of the Mevlevī dervishes, and author of the Mesnevī, had four children, three boys and a girl, by two wives. His eldest son was killed in the broil that caused the murder of his father's friend Shemsu-'d-Dīn of

---

are nine degrees of descent given, for a period of 535 years, or 66 years for each life after the birth of the next link. This alone suffices to show that the genealogy is not to be depended on. Supposing the names given to be true, many other links must be missing; as many, probably, as those given.

Tebrīz. His youngest son is not taken further notice of; but his daughter was married off to a local prince, and left Qonya.

His second son, and eventually his successor as principal or abbot of his order, was named Muhammed, and surnamed Bahā'u-'Dīn. He is commonly known as Sultan Veled.

Sultan Veled had six children, a boy and two girls by his wife Fātima, daughter of Sheykh Ferīdūn the goldbeater, and three boys, of whom two were twins, by two slave women. The daughters married well, and all his sons, or three of them, succeeded him as abbot, one after the other. The eldest was Mīr 'Ārif (Chelebī Emīr 'Ārif), the second was named 'Ābid, the third Zāhid, and the fourth Wāhid.

Chelebī Emīr 'Arif, the eldest, and Eflākī's patron, had two sons and a daughter. His eldest son, Emīr 'Ālim, surnamed Shāh-zāda, succeeded eventually to the primacy after his uncles. With him, Eflākī's memoir is brought to a close.

Such was the natural line of this dynasty of eminent men. But Eflākī has also given the links of a spiritual series, through whom the mysteries of the dervish doctrines were handed down to and in the line of Jelālu-'d-Dīn.

In the anecdote No. 79, of chapter. iii., the account is given of the manner in which the prophet Muhammed confided those mysteries to his cousin, son-in-law, and afterwards his fourth successor, as Caliph, 'Ālī son of Abū-Tālib, the "Victorious Lion of God."

'Ālī communicated the mysteries to the Imām Hasan of Basra, who died in A.H. 110 (A.D. 728); Hasan taught them to Habīb the Persian,[1] who confided them to Dāwūd of the tribe of Tayyi'—Et-Tā'ī (mentioned by D'Herbelot, without a date, as Davud Al Thai; he died A.H. 165, A.D. 781).

Dāwūd transmitted them to Ma'rūf of Kerkh (who died A.H. 200, A.D. 815); he to Sirrī the merchant of damaged goods (Es-Saqatī?; died A.H. 253, A.D. 867); and he to the great Juneyd (who died in about A.H. 297—A.D. 909). Jun-

---

[1] Habīb the Persian, a wealthy man, converted to Islām by one word from Hasan of Basra, whose devoted disciple he became. He died A.H. 106 (A.D. 724).

eyd's spiritual pupil was Shiblī (died A.H. 334, A.D. 945); who taught Abū-'Amr Muhammed, son of Ibrāhīm Zajjāj (the glazier), of Nīshāpūr (who died in A.H. 348—A.D. 959); and his pupil was Abū-Bekr, son of 'Abdu-'llāh, of Tūs, the weaver, who taught Abū-Ahmed (Muhammed son of Muhammed, El-Gazālī (who died A.H. 504—A.D. 1110), and he committed those mysteries to Ahmed el-Khatībī, Jelāl's great-grandfather, who consigned them to the Imām Sarakhsī (who died in A.H. 571—A.D. 1175).

Sarakhsī was the spiritual teacher of Jelāl's father Bahā Veled, who taught the Seyyid Burhānu-'d-Dīn Termīzi, the instructor of Jelāl. He again passed on the tradition to Shemsu-'d-Dīn of Tebrīz, the teacher of Jelāl's son, Sultan Veled, who himself taught the Emīr 'Ārif.

At the same time that the mysteries were thus being gradually transmitted to Jelālu-'d-Dīn and his successors by these links, they were also being diffused in thousands of other channels, and are at this day widely diffused over the world of Islām, which daily boasts of its living saints and their miracles. These latter are perhaps not less veracious that those continually blazoned forth by the Church of Rome, and by its Eastern sisters. We, too, have our spiritualists. Credulity will never forsake mankind and prodigies will never be lacking for the credulous to place faith in. There is much that is human in man, all the world over.

For a moment, all looks peaceful. But then I catch movement to the east. The sharp glint of the sun glancing off metal. A flash of red.

Make that many flashes of red.

My heart pounds, and my fingers dig into the bark as a massive flock of crows explodes out of the trees twenty yards east of us and spirals into the sky, screaming their distress.

"Logan?"

A large group is traveling through the Wasteland, heading straight for Baalboden. I stare at the eastern trees for a moment, trying to count. Are we dealing with highwaymen? A battalion? Something worse?

The flashes of sun-kissed metal and red uniforms stretch as far east as I can see.

We aren't dealing with highwaymen or a battalion.

We're facing an entire army.

DECEPTION

A DEFIANCE NOVEL

C. J. REDWINE

BALZER + BRAY

An Imprint of HarperCollins*Publishers*

Balzer + Bray is an imprint of HarperCollins Publishers.

Deception

Library of Congress catalog card number: 2013012323
ISBN 978-0-06-211721-2

Typography by Alison Klapthor
14 15 16 17 18   LP/RRDH   10 9 8 7 6 5 4 3 2 1
❖
First paperback edition, 2014

*For Mandy, because without you
this book would never have seen the light of day*

CHAPTER ONE

LOGAN

"What are you going to tell them?" Rachel asks. She sits beside me, her scuffed boots touching mine while long strands of her hair rise in the early morning breeze like fine lengths of copper wire. The dark bulk of the Commander's compound crouches on the hill behind us, and the charred remains of Baalboden stretch out nearly as far as the eye can see.

"The truth." My voice sounds stronger than I feel. The truth of the situation facing the tiny group of Baalboden survivors is a complex creature full of shadows and secrets. I don't want to be the one to explain it, but I've done a lot of things I didn't want to do. Including accepting the job of leading these people in the absence of the Commander, who ran into the Wasteland the day of the fires and hasn't been heard from since.

I suppose it's too much to hope that he fell off a cliff or got eaten by wolves.

"All of it?" She sounds strong too, but her fingers clench into fists as if she's bracing herself. She looks past our camp—four rows of shelters made from cobbling together jagged slices of canvas, dead tree limbs, and bits of salvaged material that huddle beside the Commander's compound like an outcast beggar too bedraggled to have any pride—and gazes south at the ruins of Baalboden itself.

"Almost all of it." I take her hand and rub my thumb across her skin as I look away from the city. We're responsible for calling the Cursed One to Baalboden, hoping to use the device Rachel's father inadvertently took from Rowansmark to control the beast and destroy our brutal leader. It doesn't matter that we never intended for the monster to enter the city itself. It only matters that it did. And everywhere we look we see death and destruction. We're responsible, but I can't say that to the survivors who sit scattered around the clearing at the center of our camp eating their breakfasts and thinking their own thoughts as they stare at what's left of the lives they once knew. "I'm going to tell them what we're up against, and what we have to do to stay safe."

Her fingers tighten over mine. "They're going to argue."

"I'm going to win."

She smiles, a slow lifting of the corners of her mouth that makes me wish I could turn back time to happier days when her smile was as impulsive and honest as she was.

She's right. They're going to argue. And complain. And question my judgment. I'd like to think that after three weeks of being their leader I'd be used to it. That it wouldn't matter. But every argument, every sliver of doubt, simply amplifies my own.

I'm too young for this. Too inexperienced. What do I know about leading people? Until the fires destroyed our city, killing thousands of people in the process, I'd been an outcast. I have no formal education, no job experience beyond apprenticing with Rachel's father, and am far more comfortable balancing a chemistry equation than dealing with most people. I keep waiting for Baalboden's survivors to figure out my deficiencies and change their minds about electing me to lead them.

Three days ago, thirty-one of Baalboden's survivors did just that. They declared me unfit to lead and headed east in hopes of finding shelter at one of the three eastern city-states, all of which are allied with the Commander.

I watched them go with what felt like needles in my chest, expecting the rest of the group to find me lacking and go east as well. Half dreading it. Half hoping for it. But one hundred fifty-seven stayed. And now I get to put their faith in me to the test.

My stomach feels like I swallowed an unstable chemical solution on a dare. I let go of Rachel's hand and push myself to my feet.

The food wagon, one of only a handful of wagons we managed to salvage from the city's wreckage, perches on the eastern edge of the clearing. I climb onto the driver's seat, where I can be seen and heard by all.

The first time I addressed the group was the afternoon the survivors elected me as their new leader. Drake, the man who met with a small group of revolutionaries in the dark corners of Thom's Tankard and who sent his daughter, Nola, to bring me medicine and food while I was locked in the Commander's dungeon, gave a rousing speech that somehow resulted in a group of otherwise sane people voting a nineteen-year-old into a position of authority.

Maybe it was because he reminded them that I'd stood up to the Commander on the Claiming stage, escaped the dungeons—the only person in Baalboden's history to ever do so—and then blew up the gate to save us from the Cursed One. Or maybe it was because out of a city-state of thousands, only a handful remained, and most of us didn't know each other before the fires. Thanks to my public confrontation with the Commander, mine was the only face every survivor recognized. When Drake made me sound like a hero, like someone who knew exactly what to do, somehow nobody remembered that until that moment, I had been nothing but an outcast to most of them.

I doubt I'll sound like a hero now.

"Attention!" I do my best to sound as crisp and authoritative as Rachel's father, Jared, used to when he was teaching me how to use a sword. The hum of conversations slowly subsides. My stomach squeezes painfully as one hundred fifty-seven faces turn toward mine and wait.

"It's been three weeks since the Cursed One destroyed our city and the Commander disappeared into the Wasteland with his entire army of guards."

Everyone watches me in silence.

"We've buried our dead and mourned them. We've searched the buildings that weren't destroyed and stockpiled what we could salvage. We have enough medical supplies to hold us over for several months. We have canned and dried food to supplement the game we bring in each day. We have weapons, and thanks to Quinn, Willow, and Rachel, twenty-three additional people are now learning how to defend us."

Here and there people crane their necks to see Quinn and Willow, the Tree People Jared trusted to give the device to Rachel and me, but still, no one responds. I'm betting that's about to change.

A brisk breeze kicks through the camp, tugging on loose flaps of canvas. I shrug my cloak closer to my shoulders, take a deep breath, and continue. "And we *need* people to defend us if we're going to stay alive long enough to get to safety."

The crowd shifts restlessly, and people begin whispering to each other.

"You mean we aren't staying here and rebuilding? You're taking us into the Wasteland? That's a death sentence," someone calls from the left. I turn and see Adam, a boy about my age. I recognize him from the group who meets daily to spar. He stands a little apart from everyone else with his arms crossed over his chest, a clear challenge in his dark, almond-shaped eyes. The uncomfortable squirming in my stomach settles.

A challenge is much easier to face than the expectations I see written across almost every other face.

Frankie Jay, a bear of a man who worked closely with Drake before Baalboden burned, folds his huge freckled arms across his chest and stares Adam down until he looks away.

I raise my voice above the murmurs spreading across the field and say, "Rebuild with what? We don't have those kind of supplies. Besides, we'd never get the gate repaired in time to save us from our enemies."

"What enemies?" another man calls from my right. "We've never hurt anyone."

Others voice their agreement and soon conversations erupt across the field.

"Quiet!" Frankie's voice cracks through the air like a whip, and silence descends. He slaps one large, freckled fist into his other palm in a clear message that he'd be happy to gain their cooperation with or without their consent.

I nod my thanks to him and face the crowd. "There's a reason every city-state is surrounded by a wall. A reason every gate is guarded."

"Yes, and all of those reasons are in the Wasteland!" a woman yells.

"For now. But what happens when word gets around that our gate is in ruins? That our city is easily plundered? That we have girls in our camp, but we don't have enough trained guards to be able to defend them against a mob of highwaymen or worse?" I ask.

"What could be worse than highwaymen?" a girl near the front asks.

I clench my fists and prepare to lay the truth on the table, one miserable piece at a time.

"An army."

There's a beat of silence, and then a tall woman with brown skin and graying brown hair says, "What city-state would send an army to attack us? We've done nothing wrong."

"Rowansmark attacked representatives of Baalboden in an unprovoked act of war just before our city burned, and they control the south."

The words have barely left my mouth when Ian, another boy my age who trains with the sparring group, steps away from the wagon he'd been leaning on. The morning sun carves deep shadows beneath his cheekbones. "Why would Rowansmark do that?"

"Because James Rowan thinks the Commander stole a very important piece of tech. He won't stop until he gets it back," I say, and catch myself reaching toward the device strapped to my chest beneath my tunic.

"Why not just make another one? What a waste of manpower," Adam says.

"And let a theft go unpunished?" Ian shakes his head. "You don't know much about Rowansmark, do you?"

No, he doesn't. Most of us don't. Other than Rachel, I don't know anyone in our group who's been to Rowansmark.

"And you do?" I ask Ian.

He shrugs. "I know what I learned in school, just like everyone else."

Since the Commander wouldn't allow me to attend school, I have no answer for that.

"It's a stain on their honor," Rachel says from beside the food wagon. "Another city-state successfully stole one of their inventions and refuses to return it. Their honor can't be redeemed until the tech is returned and the thief pays the price for his crime."

"Plus, they may not want anyone else to be able to copy their design," Elias, a young man who often helps guard the camp, says.

I make sure my next words are very clear. "Which is another reason why we can't stay here. The Commander wants to copy their design, and he's convinced I have the stolen tech. We already know the Commander allows nothing to stand in the way of what he wants. I don't know where he went or if he's called in a favor from one of his southeastern allies, but I do know that he won't let this go."

I sweep the crowd with my gaze. "The only reason we didn't leave earlier is because those who were injured in the fire weren't well enough to travel. And because we needed enough time to find a way for us to escape these ruins without leaving a trail."

"Where will we go?"

"How on earth can we travel without leaving a trail?"

"Won't we be killed in the Wasteland?"

The questions fly at me from every corner of the clearing, and I raise my voice. "We're going north. As for traveling without leaving a trail . . ." I look at Drake, Frankie, and Thom—the burly owner of Thom's Tankard, who never has much to say but who silently guards my back with a steadfast loyalty I feel sure I haven't earned—then gaze out at the survivors again. "With the help of a handful of men, I've been working on that. We're digging a tunnel from the compound's basement as far into the northern Wasteland as we can get before surfacing. By traveling underground for at least a thousand yards, we'll be impossible to track. It will be like we just vanished off the face of the earth."

"We can't travel underground," a man near Adam shouts. "We'll be killed by the Cursed One."

"I can keep us safe."

More murmuring, more questions, more complaints from the crowd. I grit my teeth and feel an unwelcome stab of understanding for the Commander's absolute refusal to entertain any discussion on his decisions. Trying to get one hundred fifty-seven opinionated people to agree on a course of action is harder than trying to herd a bunch of fighting tomcats out of an alley.

"Listen to me. Rowansmark is coming for us from the south. The Commander will be coming from the east. A river cuts us off to the west. North is the only logical choice. We'll travel to Lankenshire. They have no alliances with the Commander or Rowansmark. We'll try to secure an alliance of our own with them."

"And if we can't?" Ian asks, and several heads nod in agreement.

"I think once they see what we bring to the table, they're going to want us on their side."

Ian laughs. "A tiny remnant of survivors with barely enough skill to find food and water? Why should they extend us any kind of protection?"

I take a deep breath. "Because we have the tech that was stolen from Rowansmark, and it will be worth a small fortune to another city-state."

I let the words fill the clearing. Let my voice ring out so no one doubts that we have to leave before our enemies arrive and that I can keep us safe while we travel. Ian stares at me in silence, and I turn to find the rest of the group staring at me as well.

"Shouldn't we give it back?" someone asks.

Others murmur their agreement, and suddenly I've had *enough*.

I straighten my spine and speak as forcefully as possible. "That piece of tech is going to keep us safe as we cross the Wasteland. And it's our only leverage for creating a new alliance. Besides, who would we give it to? To the Commander, who has already killed innocent people in his efforts to get his hands on it? He'd abuse the power in this tech just like he abuses everything else he touches. To Rowansmark? That would be giving them unlimited power over every other city-state. No one could stop them."

"What do you mean?" Adam asks.

"The tech the Commander tried to steal from Rowansmark is a device that can call and control the Cursed One," Rachel says, her voice cold, her blue eyes sharp. "Who knows how many of those they've created? If we give it back, then we voluntarily give Rowansmark the power to obliterate any city whose leader falls out of favor with James Rowan. Or to obliterate *us*."

I nod. "But if we keep it, we can protect ourselves from the Cursed One while traveling through the Wasteland, and we can prove to other city-states that Rowansmark is a true threat. And given enough time, I can duplicate it so that our new allies aren't defenseless."

"That's your plan?" Ian asks. "Duplicate stolen technology and turn it against Rowansmark?" There's a curious intensity to his voice.

"Yes." I don't try to justify myself. I don't have that luxury. I have one hundred fifty-seven people to keep safe, and two power-hungry leaders to thwart. I'll do what I must.

"Why didn't you use it?" Adam asks, and the pain in his voice echoes the pain inside of me. "If you have the tech, why didn't you save Baalboden when the Cursed One tunneled under the Wall?"

"I tried. The device malfunctioned." Before the murmurs can start up again, I throw a hand into the air, palm out, and say, "I've fixed the problem. I can't turn back time and save our city, but I can keep us safe until we make a new alliance. Our only other choice is to sit here and wait for either the Commander or Rowansmark to destroy us. I'm not willing to do that."

The people whisper and shift closer together, but no one offers another argument.

"We leave in two days. Sooner if we can manage. Drake, Nola, and Thom are in charge of packing up our supplies, loading the wagons, and completing the tunnel. If they ask for your help, you will give it to them." I wait a beat, but no one questions me. "We'll need a map of the northern territories, especially the road to Lankenshire. Has anyone been there?"

A voice speaks up from the middle of the crowd. "Many times. It's about an eighteen-day journey. Maybe twenty with a group our size."

I glance at the speaker, a short, weathered man with wispy gray hair and a brilliant purple cloth tied in a bow at his neck. He crushes a battered hat between fingers as brown and bent as twigs as he meets my gaze.

"Jeremiah Krunkel, sir. Head groom to the Commander for nigh unto thirty years. Done my fair share of travel."

I stare him down. "Thirty years of loyal service to the Commander. Why not leave with the others three days ago and seek asylum at one of the southeastern city-states? Why follow me?"

Jeremiah's pale eyes lock onto mine. "Figured thirty years of brutality was more than any man should have to bear."

"Fair enough. Can you draw me a map?"

Jeremiah stands and shoves his hat onto his head. His fingers curl and twist like hairs held too close to a fire. "Have a bit of trouble holding a quill these days, but I'll manage."

"There are drawing supplies inside the compound. Meet me there in twenty minutes, and I'll show you." I look at the rest of the crowd. "We're going out through the tunnel. I'll collapse the basement ceiling in the compound to cover our tracks. It will be like we simply vanished. Until then, though, we have two days and a lot of work to do. Let's get started."

As the crowd slowly disperses, I gaze out past the city's Wall at the vast expanse of the Wasteland that stands between us and safety.

Best Case Scenario: Everything runs smoothly, and we're able to leave within the next two days without anyone realizing where we've gone.

Worst Case Scenario: Rowansmark or the Commander arrives before we leave, and I'm forced to flee across the Wasteland with a group of untrained, inexperienced men, women, and children while an army closes in behind us.

Because I've never once known anything to go according to plan, I dismiss the group and then head to my tent, where my pack of salvaged tech supplies beckons to me. I might put most of my faith in the tunnel, Rowansmark's tech, and the steadily improving fighting abilities of those who are training each morning, but it never hurts to have a backup plan.

Just in case.

CHAPTER TWO

RACHEL

After Logan's speech, I approach the training ground, located fifteen yards away from the first line of tents that mark our camp. Willow is already waiting for me, her olive skin glowing in the sun. The rest of the survivors are hurrying toward their various job assignments, casting furtive glances at the distant Wall that surrounds Baalboden as if wondering when Rowansmark might arrive to claim their stolen tech.

Quinn, Willow's older brother, weaves around the scattering of people walking through this row of shelters, his movements graceful and controlled. I stop at the edge of the training ground and wait for him. His dark hair has grown past his shoulders, but unlike Willow, he doesn't seem to care about restraining it before our practice sessions. He still wears the leather breeches and rough-spun tunic of the Tree Village that declared him an outcast before he met up with me in the Wasteland to fulfill my father's last wish.

"I heard you screaming in your sleep last night," he says as he walks up to me. His voice is as calm and emotionless as always. "I was walking past your tent after my guard shift."

I glare at him. "What, no 'hello'? No small talk? Just straight into things that are none of your business?"

"Rachel." His tone is gentle but unyielding. "We're friends. How is it none of my business?"

I sigh. "They're just nightmares. They'll pass."

"Not until you face what causes them."

There's a glimmer of pain buried in his words, but I have to search to find it. I used to hate the way Quinn always holds himself under such tight control. Especially after he told me that, like me, he'd killed a man he wasn't sure deserved it. Back then, fury and guilt burned inside me with equal strength, and I couldn't help but scorch everything I touched.

But fires only burn until you starve them for fuel. And the ashes of my fury are as cold and silent as the streets of Lower Market.

"I'll face what causes my nightmares as soon as we drop all these people off at Lankenshire and I can search for the Commander without risking their lives." My lips feel stiff with cold, though the morning is warm. It's like the icy silence that swallowed the grief of losing Oliver, my father, and my city is leeching the warmth from my skin. I walk toward the group waiting on the practice field without a backward glance while the silence inside of me shivers.

A breeze lifts silvery bits of ash from the wreckage behind us and slaps us in the face with grit as the twenty-three survivors who've faithfully attended every practice session spread out on the field. A pile of salvaged knives and swords lies to my right, and a stack of practice sticks fashioned from tree limbs is on my left. A few have reached the point where they can train with real weapons, but most are still using the practice sticks.

I clear my throat, and twenty-three pairs of eyes lock on me. My best friend, Sylph, is here, her curly dark hair tied back with rope, along with her new husband, Smithson. Jodi, a small blonde girl I recognize from my few years at Life Skills, the domestic arts class all Baalboden girls attended in place of a real education, stands next to Thom, who must've found someone to take his place in the tunnel in order to attend this session. A small knot of boys, most of them younger than me, stand close to Willow, eyeing her hopefully. Ian stands near her as well, the sun painting his brown hair gold as he flashes a charming smile in her direction whenever she makes eye contact. Most of the girls in camp melt when Ian aims one of his smiles at them. Willow is a notable exception.

Another boy elbows his way to the front of the pack, and I roll my eyes. If we could get the rest of the survivors as interested in Willow's *instruction*, we'd have a battalion full of trained soldiers in no time.

"Are we going to get started, or what?" someone asks.

I look past Thom and see Adam. Bruises mar his golden skin, and his dark eyes glare into mine. He'd be almost pretty if someone hadn't recently used him as a punching bag.

"Get in another fight?" I ask him.

"He deserved it." His expression is mutinous.

"You always think everyone deserves it. What if you're wrong?"

Melkin's face, pale and cold, burns into my memory, and I

shove it away before I can remember the terrible wet sound of my knife sliding into his chest. Before his blood pours over my hands, a stain I'll wear beneath my skin for the rest of my life.

Adam glares at me. "I'm not wrong. This?" He gestures at the ruins behind us. "This is what's wrong."

"I know," I say, and turn away from the pain I see in his eyes. He needs comfort, and I'm all out.

"That and the fact that our *true* leader disappeared into the Wasteland, and we've got a nineteen-year-old boy trying to take his place." Adam's voice is sharp with derision, but beneath it I hear the kind of fathomless grief that drags you under until you no longer care if you ever find the surface again.

Blinking away the stark memory of my father's grave, I walk toward Adam. I recognize the fury that drives him. I once used something like it as fuel to give me a reason to face one more day. To take one more step forward, even though it meant leaving behind the life I once thought I'd have. Stopping in front of him, I ask, "Who did you lose in the fire?"

He glares at me. "Everyone." Waving a hand at the unending sea of destruction at my back, he flings his words at me like a challenge he doesn't think I'll answer. "I lost *everyone*. You?"

"I lost everyone I loved long before. Everyone but Logan."

"Lucky for you," he says, and looks away. "Must be nice not to have watched your family burn."

"Oh, yes, I'm very lucky." My voice is as unyielding as his. "I'm so incredibly fortunate that I had to watch my grandfather die in front of me because our *true* leader decided killing a harmless baker to get my cooperation was acceptable. So fortunate that my father was a man of honor who tried to stop our leader's treachery and paid for it with his life."

He meets my eyes, and I step closer. "By the time our city burned, I had no family left to lose. So don't you stand there and call me lucky. Don't you shame Logan by referring to the Commander as our true leader when all he ever delivered to us was heartbreak, fear, and death."

For one terrible instant, Adam's face blurs and bends until the Commander stands before me, his sword dripping Oliver's blood in a river of crimson that refuses to stop no matter how hard I beg.

I don't remember releasing the blade on the Switch, but it gleams silver-sharp in the sunlight as I lift my arm. Quinn is at my side a second later, his hand pressed firmly against my shoulder.

Silence holds us captive for a long moment as Adam looks from me to Quinn. Slowly, I lower my arm and step back.

"Break into three groups now, please," Quinn says, and the twenty-three survivors, now armed with practice sticks, slowly gravitate toward Willow, Quinn, and me.

Mostly toward Willow, who seems oblivious to the way the boys watch her every move with hungry, admiring eyes, or the way the girls pretend indifference but are careful to copy her stance and the tilt of her chin.

Adam stares me down for another second, then moves to Willow's side. I wish her luck.

Jodi, Thom, Sylph, and Smithson surround me in our corner of the practice field. A man old enough to be my father joins us as well, along with three boys who can't possibly be more than fourteen. The youngest, a boy named Donny Miller, keeps stealing glances at Willow like he wishes he'd joined her group instead.

We begin running practice drills, and the sharp slap of wooden sticks slamming against each other fills the air. The practice sticks are heavy enough to approximate the weight of a short sword and long enough to give our recruits a sense of the way a weapon lengthens your reach and changes your balance. I pace around my group, calling out instructions.

"Keep your grip loose." I tap Donny's white knuckles. "Hands wide apart to give you stability and power."

Hefting my Switch, I demonstrate. "You need to be able to block effectively. Watch." I nod toward Smithson. "Hit me."

"I—what?"

"Hit. Me." When he hesitates again, I snap, "Did you think this would be all safe little practice drills? Swing that stick at me, Smithson. I'm going to show everyone how to deflect a blow."

"I don't want to hurt you," he says as he lifts his stick.

"You won't." I roll to the balls of my feet and widen my stance. He swings at my side. I pivot and slam my Switch into his weapon. It goes flying out of his hand.

I swear viciously. "You'd be dead right now. Dead!" Springing forward, I get in his face. "When you swing your weapon, you give it everything you've got. Every time. Now pick up your stick and come at me again."

Smithson's face flushes red. "You're a lady—"

Swearing again, I snatch his stick off the ground and thrust it at him.

"Not with that mouth, she isn't," Jodi says with a tiny smirk on her face.

I glare at her, and then include everyone else for good measure. "The Baalboden protocol that promised protection in exchange for absolute submission is dead. Forget everything you think you know about being a girl." I look at Smithson. "Or how to treat a girl. This is battle, and despite the Commander's protests to the contrary, girls are capable of attacking, defending, and killing. *Anyone* who comes at you with intent to harm you must be put down."

Melkin's dark eyes stare at me, full of accusation. I ignore the memory and lift my Switch. "Now attack me like you mean it."

His stick whistles through the air. I whip my Switch up and block the blow. The power of it reverberates up my arms. "Good. See how I block with the middle of my weapon? My balance is still centered, and I can safely pivot to either side and deliver a blow of my own."

I swing to the left and slam the lightest end of the Switch against Smithson's thigh.

"Block me!" I pivot again and swing.

He blocks me. Barely, but it's a victory, and I reward him with a smile. Then I divide up my group and set them to sparring with each other while I study all twenty-three trainees and size them up.

Jodi has potential. So do two of the boys and, to my utter surprise, Sylph. Smithson, now that he's recovering from his gentlemanly instincts, isn't half-bad either, and neither is Thom, though I knew that already. I turn to study the other groups and find several who've developed decent instincts, strength, and agility. A man in Quinn's group can block almost any blow aimed at him. Another kicks with enough power to knock Quinn off balance. Even a few of the boys in Willow's group aren't half-bad. Elias, who is a year older than Smithson, and Derreck, a man with creases in his forehead and strength in his arms, move like they've been training for months instead of weeks.

But the real star is Ian. The flirtatious charm he uses to turn most of the girls in camp into starry-eyed idiots is gone. He fights with focused intensity, and his blows are swift and precise.

A frown digs in between my brows as I study his moves. He dances around his sparring partner, a girl of about eighteen with long brown hair and wide eyes who grips her practice stick like she isn't quite sure how it came to be in her hand. Ian jumps forward to deliver a light tap the second she drops her guard. Which is often. When she finally decides to take a swing at him, he pivots to the left and lunges forward as if his weapon is an extension of himself.

Where did he learn to fight like that? And why is he in the sparring session for beginners instead of in the postlunch session for those who are more advanced?

I'm halfway across the field, intent on pulling Ian aside and getting some answers, when the girl swings wildly at his head. He ducks, executes a half turn, and taps her smartly across the back with his own stick. She flinches and releases her stick so she can press her hand against the skin he bruised. He grabs her arm, spins her around, and drives her to her knees.

"What do you think you're doing?" he demands.

I walk faster.

"Hold the stick *steady*. Use the core of your body when you swing. And whatever you do, don't take time to deal with your injuries until your opponent is dead. Why am I having to repeat this to you? A girl your age should be able to hold her own."

My fingers curl around my Switch. "Ian!"

"She knows better than to drop her weapon," Ian says, straightening slowly. "You'd think she'd never given one thought to self-defense until we started these sessions."

"Maybe she hadn't," I say. "Certainly she never thought about it until the city burned. Have you already forgotten Baalboden had a protocol that required girls to be dependent on male Protectors?"

He looks away. "I was just trying to help." Reaching his hand out toward the girl, he says, "I'm sorry. You can take a free swing at me if it will make you feel better."

"I'm fine," the girl says as she picks up her stick and lets Ian help her to her feet. "He's right. I know better than to drop my weapon."

"Sometimes I forget that all Baalboden girls aren't as experienced as Rachel and Willow. Plus, you're beautiful, and that's an unfair distraction," he says, and she returns his smile.

Ridiculous. Between the girls throwing themselves at Ian's feet and the boys panting after Willow, you'd think we were at a Claiming ceremony instead of learning how to fight.

"I'm not a Baalboden girl," Willow says softly, and her voice carries an edge I don't often hear from her.

Ian winks at her. "You are now."

I watch to see if Willow's golden skin will turn pink as well, but she seems impervious to Ian's charms. Instead, she hefts a sword, hands it to Adam, who stands beside her, and says, "I didn't say we were finished for the day. Back to sparring."

Slowly, the twenty-three recruits regroup, some with practice sticks and some with swords. I keep my eye on Ian as he faces off with Quinn, but the skill he displayed earlier is nothing compared to the lethal force of Quinn's movements. Maybe Ian only looked good because he was sparring with a girl who can barely manage to hold on to her weapon.

Or maybe he has more experience than he wants to let on.

Either way, I decide Logan needs to know that Ian might be hiding something from us, and that Adam isn't going to stop causing trouble in camp until he accepts Logan's leadership.

I hope Logan has a plan for how to ferret out secrets and stop rebellion with typical Logan-ish practicality, because if he doesn't, I might suggest giving me and my Switch five minutes alone with each of them. We have to worry about the Commander lurking somewhere in the Wasteland, Rowansmark's bounty on our head, and gangs of highwaymen who will surely see us as easy prey. We shouldn't have to add idiots from our own camp to that list.

CHAPTER THREE

LOGAN

Striding into my tent, I toss my cloak onto my bedroll and crouch beside my tech bag. The machine I built to dig the tunnel is down.

Again.

This time, it's a stripped gear and some broken teeth. Last time, the battery cables were pulled loose. The time before that, I found my stash of spare parts strewn across the basement floor. Either some of the younger kids are getting a thrill from messing with me, or someone is disgruntled with my leadership but lacks the courage to say so to my face.

It's childish nonsense, but still, it takes time. Time we don't have. I want to tunnel at least one thousand yards into the Wasteland before we surface so that the trackers who come to Baalboden won't have any signs to follow. I can't do that if my machine keeps breaking down.

Snatching my tech bag, I flip the latch open and look inside.

I need another battery, and I only have a few left from the stash I kept at the armory with my barrels of glycerin and acid and my extra wires. I can make more, but I'm not sure I have all the supplies I'd need, and another salvage expedition through the ruins would slow me down further. The extra batteries are near the bottom of the bag. I shove my hand inside and my fingers scrape the edges of something smooth and soft.

Parchment.

Frowning, I pull out a square of parchment the size of my hand. Bold black letters across the center read, *"How will you make things right?"*

Swearing, I crumple up the note and toss it to the side of the shelter just as Rachel ducks beneath the flap.

"What's that?" she asks as she unties her cloak and tosses it on top of mine.

"Just another stupid prank." I reach into the bag and this time grab the battery. "Machine's down again."

"This is getting old. I thought you put someone in charge of the younger kids."

"I did. Jan Nelson. Used to be a cook at Jocey's Mug and Ale, remember? Tall, skinny—"

"Eyes in the back of her head." Rachel pretends to shudder. "Yes, I remember her. She never let Sylph and me get away with *anything* when she caught us in the alley between Jocey's and Oliver's."

I laugh. "I imagine you gave her plenty of trouble." I step close to her and run my fingers lightly across her arm. "I'll let her know the prankster can read and write. That should exclude the youngest in the bunch."

"And the girls," Rachel says. "Unless they had parents like mine, none of the girls were taught to read and write."

"Something we'll have to remedy once we make it to Lankenshire," I say, and lean in for a quick kiss. "I'm going to grab my lunch ration and go fix the machine."

I'm nearly out of the tent when she says, "Before I forget, you might want to keep an eye on both Adam and Ian. After today's sparring practice, I learned a few things. For one, Adam isn't willing to accept you as his leader. I don't know why he didn't just go east with the others, but he's our problem now. And Ian fights like he's been trained. I don't know why he'd hide that and pretend that he's a beginner. If you want, Willow and I could question him and have your answer in two seconds flat."

There's no softness in her eyes as she offers to torture Ian for answers, and I wonder if the loss of Oliver, Jared, and our city is slowly turning us into the kind of people we always swore we'd fight against.

I close my fist around the wire-wrapped surface of the battery as I see Ian walking toward the food wagon, surrounded as usual by several girls. "I'll handle it. In fact, I think I'll have a talk with him right now."

I walk quickly through my row of shelters and catch up to Ian just as he's accepting a portion of roasted pheasant from Thom. Frankie stands beside Thom, his eyes on the sky, clutching a lunch ration even though Quinn is clearly standing in front of him waiting for the food.

"May I have the food, please?" Quinn asks. I can tell by his tone that this isn't the first time he's asked.

"I don't serve leaf lovers." Frankie's wide mouth curls into a sneer.

"When you're on lunch duty, you serve every member of our group," I say.

Frankie looks at me, his expression mutinous, and then slowly hands the food to Quinn. He jerks his fingers back before Quinn can touch him, and I roll my eyes.

"We have bigger problems on our plate than worrying about whether someone used to be a Tree Person, Frankie." Before he can reply, I clap my hand on Ian's shoulder and say, "I'm off to fix the machine. I'd like your help."

Ian's brows rise. "Are you sure I'm the best person for the job? I don't know much about tinkering with things."

My hand tightens on his shoulder. "You'll do."

He shrugs and follows me in silence.

The iron gate at the compound's entrance stands open, and we hurry up the cobblestone drive and into the main hall. The brilliant noonday sun pours in the front windows, glowing on the white marble floor and then fading against the dark stone walls. If Ian is afraid to enter the Commander's personal residence, as so many of the group are, he doesn't show it. Instead, he strides down the hall like he owns the place and doesn't bat an eyelash when I wrench open the door that leads to the tunnel.

A steep set of damp-slick stairs leads down into the cavernous basement. Our footsteps echo loudly, and I don't try to speak until we've crossed the fifty yards of gritty stone that separate us from the gaping mouth of the tunnel I've spent the last two weeks digging.

A bag of copper parts and spare batteries lies just across the seam that separates the basement floor from the dark earth of the tunnel. I pick it up and grab two torches from the pile of extras lying against the wall. Ian strikes the flint and soon both of our torches blaze brightly against the thick darkness that waits for us.

Our footsteps don't echo in the tunnel. Every sound is absorbed, swallowed up by the dense earth surrounding us. Every three yards, a steel rib salvaged from Baalboden's wreckage is jammed against the tunnel's side to act as a support beam. Thick branches or wooden beams cut to size are wedged across the tunnel's ceiling as well, each end buried in the opposite wall. Frankie and his handpicked team of helpers have been hard at work for the last two weeks, and I'm pleased with the progress. With so much reinforcement, I'm certain the tunnel won't collapse when I bring the survivors through it.

As we pass each pair of steel ribs, I count the yards in my head. By the time we reach the solid wall of dirt at the end of the tunnel, I estimate we've traveled three hundred sixty-eight yards. That's about one hundred seventy-three yards past Baalboden's perimeter and into the northern Wasteland.

"You really *do* need to fix the machine," Ian says. He sounds surprised. When I look at him, he tugs on the silver chain he wears around his neck and says, "You've never asked for my help before. I figured you had ulterior motives."

I study him for a moment and say, "I could use the help, but yes, I had ulterior motives. I wanted to talk to you. Alone."

He grins. "Never thought the first person in camp to try to get me alone in a dark, private place would be you, but—"

"Where did you learn how to fight?"

Ian stiffens and slowly raises his gaze to mine. Torchlight flickers against the blue of his eyes. "What makes you think I know how to fight?"

I step closer. "Answering a question with a question is simply a way to gain enough time to think of a plausible lie."

His lips thin, but his voice is calm. "I wasn't trying to think of a lie. I was asking to see what gave me away."

"You have one minute to explain to me where you learned how to fight and why you've been hiding it from the rest of us before I decide *you're* the one with ulterior motives here."

"It was Rachel, wasn't it?" He slaps his hand against the wall behind him. "I knew she was watching me too closely this morning. She should be happy that someone on that practice field knows what he's doing."

"You should be happy I'm the one questioning you instead of her. You'd already be missing a few vital organs. Who are you really, and what are you hiding?"

His shoulders sag, and he seems to shrink a little before my eyes. "I want your promise that what I tell you will stay between us."

"Absolutely not."

Something flickers in his eyes, but he blinks it away before I can identify it. "If you don't—if you tell the others about this, they'll kill me in my sleep."

"If you deserve death, you won't be leaving this tunnel, never mind getting another opportunity to go to sleep."

He holds his body still, his eyes locked on mine. "I don't deserve death, Logan. But others might not see it that way."

"I'll be the judge of that."

The torchlight dances in his blue eyes like inner flames, and he nods slowly. "Judge and be judged."

"What?"

He shakes his head. "Just something my father used to say."

"Answer, Ian. Now."

Without taking his eyes from mine, he says, "My father worked for the Commander. He was . . . loyal."

He lingers over the word as if it holds some secret meaning for him as he pulls the silver chain out from under his tunic. A small copper dragon-scale charm hangs off the middle of the chain.

"What was your father's job?"

Ian looks away. "Brute Squad."

Brute Squad. The Commander's elite group of guards tasked with torturing prisoners, scaring the population into compliance, and publicly flogging those who broke the law. My palms are suddenly damp, and I clench my fists. "And you?"

"Apprenticed to take his place."

It takes every ounce of willpower I have to force my expression to remain neutral. Ian's right. Every person in our group would want him dead if they knew who he was.

When I don't reply, Ian looks me in the eye again. "In the interest of full disclosure, because I wouldn't want to be accused of having ulterior motives"—he brackets the words with air quotes—"I know more about Rowansmark than the average survivor in our camp."

"How?" The stolen Rowansmark tech I wear strapped beneath my tunic suddenly feels heavy and obvious.

"My father died in Rowansmark. Punished at the hands of a tracker for being loyal to the Commander. I was there." He dangles the dragon-scale charm between us, his gaze locked on the trinket like it hurts him to look at it. "This was the last gift my father gave to me. It's all I have left of him."

His voice is crisp. Almost emotionless. I'm not fooled. I can see the horror in his eyes. The scars that rot him from the inside out. I know what it's like to watch a parent die. To stand helpless while someone bigger and stronger destroys someone you love and leaves you with nothing. I know how the loneliness sours into bitterness until every memory is tainted with the dregs of a sorrow you can never quite shake.

I take a slow breath. "Why didn't you follow the Commander? Or leave with the group who went to find him?"

"Follow the man who put my father in that position in the first place? No."

I understand the anger. The desperation to keep his background a secret from the others. He wants a fresh start.

I do, too.

"I'm sorry about your father," I say, and step back from him. "I won't tell you it will get easier or that you'll move on or any of the other useless things people say to make you feel better."

"I'll feel better when the man responsible is punished." Ian stuffs his necklace beneath his tunic again and pushes away from the wall.

Another thing we have in common. We both want the Commander to pay for his crimes.

"Are you going to tell the others?"

"I'll tell Drake. I don't want our new society to be a place of secrets. But we won't spread news of your former occupation to others. You can have a fresh start, but you have to stop pretending to be less skilled than you are. We need you."

"Will you tell Rachel?"

I imagine Rachel's reaction to the news that we have an apprenticed member of the Brute Squad in our midst, and shake my head slowly. The Brute Squad held her captive in a wagon while the Commander tortured and killed Oliver. And then they surrounded me on the Claiming stage and nearly took my life. If I told her Ian was apprenticed to the Brute Squad, I don't know what she'd do. Maybe nothing. Maybe decide he's an acceptable proxy for the Commander and beat him with her Switch.

"Thanks." His usual flippant charm chases the seriousness from his face as he crouches beside the silent machine. "Now, are we going to fix this or stand around sharing life stories all day? I have four or five girls I've promised to eat lunch with, and I hate to disappoint the ladies."

I kneel beside him and drive my torch into the ground for light. The machine looks like a multitiered plow with a catch-tray beneath each row of teeth and a pair of pipes attached to each tray, ready to sluice dirt away from the teeth and shoot it backward at the completed tunnel in its wake. Dumping the contents of the tech bag onto the ground, I grab a new gear and exchange it for the stripped one while Ian removes the broken teeth and uses large metal scraps in their place.

The afternoon tunnel crew approaches as Ian hammers the last tooth into place. I flip the power switch, and the machine instantly hums to life. Chugging forward, it digs into the wall of soil in front of it and spews dirt out of the pipes, nearly hitting me in the face.

I step back as the tunnel crew leaps into action. We need to tunnel another seven hundred yards into the Wasteland to feel truly safe. I just hope we don't run out of time.

CHAPTER FOUR

LOGAN

"I can do it this time." I slide the arrow into place the way Rachel showed me and slowly pull the wire taut, my elbow perfectly parallel to the ground.

At first, it was nice having Rachel teach me how to use a bow and arrow to hunt. We headed south out of Baalboden immediately after lunch, carefully climbing over the slabs of steel and stone that litter the ground in front of the remains of the gate. I'd taken an extra moment to double-check that the explosives we'd removed from the compound and laced along the gate as a defensive measure were still in place, but I hadn't lingered. With Drake in charge of the camp, and an entire crew of men working in the tunnel, I figured I'd take down my first rabbit, and then we'd have plenty of afternoon to spare for . . . other things.

Five misses later, I'd adjusted my description from "nice" to "somewhat unpleasant."

Eleven misses after that, I'd decided the best word to sum up the experience was "humiliating."

"Turn your left shoulder toward the target," Rachel whispers.

"I did."

"Not enough." She nudges me to make her point. The rabbit in my sights freezes. "Now," she breathes against my ear. "Shoot now."

My fingers curve around the wire, and I quickly run through the steps in my head. One vane turned away from the bow. Body perpendicular to the target. Feet shoulder width apart. Relaxed tension—whatever that means—in my stance.

"Logan, *now*."

The rabbit will run when I shoot. The faint noise of the arrow launching from the bow will send it scrambling for safety. Which way will it go? I'll need to compensate. Aim slightly to the left, to the spot where it first nosed its way out of the undergrowth? Or to the right in case it sprints forward?

Probably to the left. He'll try to return to what he knows is safe.

The rabbit jerks its head up, ears swiveling. I try to find the anchor point along my cheekbone in time to shoot with any sort of accuracy. I release the wire, and the arrow wobbles slightly as it sails toward its target.

The rabbit dodges safely to the left.

That's what I get for ignoring logic.

I hook the bow over my shoulder and move forward to collect my arrow. Sunlight filters in through the oak branches above me and hangs in the air like golden mist before disintegrating into the deep shadows that stretch across the forest floor.

"I should've torqued my shot to the left," I say as I bend to dig the arrow out of a bush where it has gallantly speared a handful of thick green leaves. "I *knew* it was going to run."

"Well, of course it ran. You gave it a good ten minutes' notice that you were going to shoot it." Rachel steps to my side as I brush the last of the leaves off of the arrow's chiseled copper tip.

I stare her down. "I was double-checking the steps you gave me."

"You'd already done the steps." She crosses her arms and taps her fingers against her elbow. "You were wasting time."

I speak with as much dignity as a man who's missed seventeen shots in a row can possibly speak. "I was making calculations."

"You were doubting yourself." Her eyes meet mine. "Hunting with a bow and arrow isn't science, Logan. It's poetry. Let me show you."

"It's a specific algorithm of speed, mass, and velocity." There's nothing poetic about that, unless you appreciate the beauty of a well-defined mathematical equation. Which I do, but that isn't the point. The point is that hunting with a bow and arrow isn't some romanticized communion with one's inner poetic instincts. It's cold, hard science, and there's absolutely no reason why I should continually fail at it when I understand science better than I understand anything else.

Maybe even better than I understand Rachel.

She leads me to the edge of a little clearing, the towering oaks of the Wasteland circling us like silent sentries. Twigs crunch softly beneath our boots. A handful of sparrows scold us vigorously as we stop beneath their tree.

I'm still arguing my point.

"You calculate the angle between yourself and your target, factor in wind speed and direction, account for the prey's instinctual flight, and—"

She steps behind me and slides her hands over my hips to position my body, her fingers pressing against me with tiny pricks of heat.

"And what?" she asks as she reaches around my back to pull my arms into position.

I swallow against the sudden dryness in my throat and try not to dwell on the fact that her chest—her entire body—is leaning against me.

"Logan?" The wind lifts a long strand of her fiery red hair and slides it against my face. "You were giving me your list of Things That Must Be Taken into Account Before One Dares to Shoot an Arrow. What's next?"

"I don't—" I clear my throat. "I don't remember."

"Oh, really?" Her voice is low. "Maybe you wanted to warn me to always multiply the force of the arrow with the probability that the prey will jerk to the left?"

"That doesn't . . ."

She hooks her fingers around my hand and together we nock the arrow, one vane pointed away from the bow. Her skin is smooth against mine, and I try hard not to imagine anything more than her hands.

"That doesn't what?" she asks, her voice nothing but a whisper against my ear.

"That doesn't make sense. You can't multiply force with . . . whatever it was you said."

"With a probability?" Her body is molded to mine, our hands

are inseparable, and my heart feels like a hammer pounding against my chest.

"I—yes. That. Exactly."

We stand in silence for several excruciating minutes, waiting for more prey to appear. The scolding birds subside into cheerful chirping. The leafy canopy above us rustles like paper made of silk. She leans against me, and I force myself to review the proper method for creating a battery just to give my mind something other than Rachel to think about.

Assemble copper coins, silver coins, and paper discs cut to coin size.

Heat radiates from her body onto mine.

Stack them up—copper, paper, silver—eight times. Secure with copper wire.

I want to take her into my arms until both of us forget why we're even here.

Dip the stack in salt water.

She shifts her weight, and I close my eyes.

Connect the wire to the terminals, copper on one end, silver on the other.

"There." She breathes the word against my neck, and my eyes fly open. We turn six degrees to the right and see another rabbit hopping slowly along the edge of the clearing. Our fingers relax away from the wire, and the arrow streaks across the space to bury its tip into the rabbit's side.

"Got it," she says, and her lips brush the side of my neck.

All thoughts of assembling batteries fly out of my head.

I spin away from the rabbit, toss the bow onto the ground, and pull Rachel against me before she can open her mouth to tell me she was right—for once, poetry was the answer instead of math.

Kissing Rachel is like discovering a new element—one that turns my blood into lava and sends sparks shooting straight through every logical thought still lingering in my head. Forget math and poetry. Especially poetry. This is much more fun.

Her hands dig into my shoulders, anchoring me to her. Her lips are softer than her hands, but she kisses me like she's trying to win an argument.

I decide to let her.

She clings to me, and my knees are suddenly unsteady. I push her against the closest tree so that I don't do something supremely stupid like pull her down to the forest floor.

Not that there's anyone in the Wasteland with us to see what we're doing. For the first time in three weeks, we're absolutely alone, and I don't plan to waste the opportunity.

I lift my mouth from hers long enough to say, "You were right." My voice sounds like I've just run the length of Lower Market at a hard sprint.

"I know," she says, and the smug little smile at the corner of her mouth makes me want to do things I shouldn't do, even though I know the probability of being interrupted is so insignificant, it defies mathematical calculation.

She lifts her lips toward me, and I kiss her like I never want to come up for air. A strange hum fills my head.

This is what I want. Just Rachel and the wide-open space of the Wasteland. Nobody asking my opinion. Questioning my decisions. Looking at me like somehow a nineteen-year-old boy can save them from their worst fears.

This is what I want, but it isn't the life I've been given. It isn't the path my choices—and the choices of others—have put me on, and until I see it through, until the one hundred fifty-seven survivors in my care are safe and the Commander has paid for his crimes with his life, I can't turn back.

I can, however, wish with everything in me that things were different.

The rough bark behind Rachel scrapes against my knuckles as I fist my hands in the back of her cloak and tell myself I can't do more than kiss her. Not now. Not here. Not while the ruins of our lives are a mere seventy yards away.

Not when she still screams herself hoarse every night in her sleep and refuses to discuss it with me when she wakes.

Her hands slide down my shoulders and over my chest until they come to rest on the Rowansmark device I wear strapped beneath my tunic every day. She scrapes her nail over the rope binding the button that sends the sonic frequency used to repel the Cursed One and pulls back to look at me.

"You tied down the button that sends the monster back to its lair." She raises a brow. "That was smart."

"I have my moments."

"Yes, you do." Slowly she pulls her hand away from the tech. "Are you sure the device is working again? I know what you said at the camp meeting, but maybe we should test it before we actually need it."

"You want to call the Cursed One? A hundred yards from a group of survivors who might drop dead of heart failure if they have to deal with one more shock?"

"I'm just saying if I have to put my faith in something, I want to be sure it works."

"I checked the device but didn't see any reason for it to malfunction. I'm building a booster pack that will significantly increase the power of the tech's sonic pulse. Once I've finished that, we should be able to use it without any trouble." I lean closer, my eyes drifting toward her lips. "Give me a little more time, and it will be ready. You can put your faith in me, Rachel."

Before she responds, I kiss her again, and this time I'm the one trying to win an argument. The bark scrapes my hands, the hum fills my head again, and I lose myself in her. She's in every breath I take, and somehow I feel stronger than I have since I watched the last flame gutter into ash inside my city. When I pull away, she's smiling.

"We'd better go back." I shade my eyes as I peer up at the sun, just visible beyond the canopy of branches above us. Three hours until nightfall. Just enough time to return to camp, let Rachel run another sparring practice, and check on the tunnel's progress.

She walks across the clearing to collect our catch. I grab her Switch from the forest floor as she pulls the arrow out of the rabbit. We work in companionable silence as I clean the arrow and she stuffs the rabbit into a burlap sack with the other small game she caught today.

I'm sliding the arrow back into its quiver when I realize the silence between us has extended into the surrounding Wasteland as well. The hush is weighted with tension as all of the little noises that usually fill the forest fade into nothing. There's only one reason forest wildlife suddenly go silent: They're hiding. And since they'd long since adjusted to our presence, they aren't hiding from us.

Rachel meets my eyes as the realization hits us: We aren't alone.

Handing over her Switch, I grab a low-hanging branch and swing into the tallest tree I can find. The bark scrapes against my skin as I dig my boots into the trunk and shinny my way toward the top. I climb nearly fifteen yards before I'm up high enough to see over the trees around me and into the Wasteland beyond.

For a moment, all looks peaceful. But then I catch movement to the east. The sharp glint of the sun glancing off metal. A flash of red.

Make that many flashes of red.

My heart pounds, and my fingers dig into the bark as a massive flock of crows explodes out of the trees twenty yards east of us and spirals into the sky, screaming their distress.

"Logan?"

A large group is traveling through the Wasteland, heading straight for Baalboden. I stare at the eastern trees for a moment, trying to count. Are we dealing with highwaymen? A battalion? Something worse?

The flashes of sun-kissed metal and red uniforms stretch as far east as I can see.

We aren't dealing with highwaymen or a battalion.

We're facing an entire army.

CHAPTER FIVE

RACHEL

We run hard, weapons slapping our thighs, underbrush clawing at us, while more birds spill out of the trees to the northeast. Whoever is moving toward the city is traveling fast.

A thorny bush catches my cloak, and I rip the leather free without pausing. Our people are as good as dead if we can't reach them first.

Unless Logan already has a plan in place for something like this.

I leap a fallen branch and skid around a bend in the trail I'm hoping will get us to Baalboden's gate before we get cut off. "If we don't make it in time—"

"Drake knows what to do." Logan grabs my hand when I slip on a moss-covered rock. "If anyone attacks, he'll blow the gate."

When we were trapped inside Baalboden's Wall, surrounded on three sides by fire, we blew up the gate to escape death. How ironic to think we might have to blow it up again and seal ourselves back inside the Wall for the very same reason. Logan,

Drake, and Thom spent days lacing explosives taken from the Commander's personal supply and threading fuses into the gate's rubble. Some are buried in the slabs of steel and stone that are piled across the opening. Some line the jagged walls on either side.

If Drake lights the fuse, no one will be able to get inside Baalboden.

No one will be able to get out, either.

"They'll be trapped," I say as we near the rough seam of land that joins the overgrown Wasteland with the flat stretch of ground between the forest and Baalboden's western Wall.

"They'll leave through the tunnel."

"But if you aren't there to protect them from the Cursed One—"

"You and I will go to the northern Wasteland, just beyond the city's perimeter. The tech's signal is strong enough to protect them even if I'm not underground." Logan's voice is breathless. Mine is too. And we still have fifty yards between us and the gate.

I fall silent as we reach the edge of the Wasteland, directly opposite the western corner of the Wall. I strain to hear something. Birds. Footsteps. The metallic kiss of a sword leaving its sheath.

Nothing.

It's as if the army traveling through the Wasteland has disappeared.

Or as if they're lying in wait. Assessing their target. Watching for the perfect moment to attack.

I figure that perfect moment is going to be the instant Logan and I step out of the tree line.

A twig snaps somewhere behind us, a loud crack that has Logan reaching for his sword even as I spin around, searching for movement.

Everything is still.

"They must be getting into position," Logan breathes against my ear. "We have to go."

I turn back around and stare at the heap of ruined stone that marks the entrance to the city. Gulping in deep breaths of air, I wipe the sweat from my face and nod.

The gate is fifty yards ahead of us, facing west into the Wasteland. We can move out of the trees, race across the flat land separating us from the corner of the Wall, and then run along it until we reach the entrance. A movement catches my eye, and I see Thom's wide shoulders beside Drake's smaller frame as they pace along the top of the Wall beside the opening, guarding the entrance from predators they didn't really think would come.

"Let's go," I say, and run out of the trees, Logan on my heels.

We've covered half the distance between the tree line and the Wall when the entire western edge of the Wasteland explodes into motion. Wave after wave of soldiers dressed in red and gold pour out of the trees, swords drawn, and charge the city.

"Blow the gate!" Logan yells.

For a moment, I think Drake will do it. He and Thom disappear off the top of the Wall, and we wait for an explosion that never comes. Instead, Willow vaults over the pile of rubble, arrows already flying from her bow. Thom, Drake, Quinn, Ian, Frankie, and five others rush after her, swords gleaming in the dying rays of the sun, and create a small perimeter around the entrance.

"No!" I scream as I run for the gate. They're going to die. All of them. At least twenty soldiers are already closing in, with hundreds more behind them. Trying to fight them off is suicide.

"Blow the gate." Logan runs beside me, his sword out. *"Blow the gate!"*

The first wave of soldiers crashes into the tiny band of survivors and the scream of metal against metal shivers through the air. Two of our men go down immediately. Quinn, weaponless, spins with terrifying speed, swiping the legs out from underneath soldiers and kicking their weapons away. Willow's arrows slam into the attackers, though her aim seems to be off, as most of those who get hit keep rushing forward. Thom grips a sword in one beefy hand and a thick, jagged board in the other. He swings both like he's felling a tree. Ian and Frankie stand back-to-back, their swords flashing in the sunlight.

They're fighting with skill and courage. The small opening into the city works to our advantage as the fighting between our people and theirs creates a barrier the other soldiers can't penetrate or flank. But already our people are showing signs of exhaustion. And it doesn't matter how many soldiers go down, more just keep coming.

We're twenty yards from the gate when we reach the army's fringe. I swing the weighted end of my Switch into a soldier's knee and leap over him as he falls. Logan slams into another man, and their swords clash. We lunge, swing, hack, and parry with the Wall at our backs, and slowly gain ground toward the gate.

We're still ten yards away and tiring fast when a group of soldiers breaks through the perimeter as another one of our men falls to the ground. Ignoring those fighting around them, the soldiers crawl over the gate's wreckage and swarm inside Baalboden.

"Drake!" Logan's voice, furious and desperate, rises above the sound of battle. "Do it before it's too late!"

"Not without you two," Drake yells, his dark eyes lit with a fervor that turns his mild, ordinary face into something dangerous as he swings his sword into every red-and-gold uniform he can see.

I take a sharp blow to my shoulder and spin into the side of the Wall. The stone scrapes my skin as my breath leaves my body. Pain rips a path from my shoulder to my jaw. I turn my face to look at my attacker as he whips his sword toward my neck.

Instantly, I drop to the ground, feeling the sword slice the air above me as I fall. My Switch is useless now. Too long and too heavy to do any damage unless I can gain some leverage. With my back to the Wall and my attacker directly in front of me coming in for another blow, leverage isn't one of my options.

I dive forward, slam into his knees, and reach for my knife when he staggers back a step. He raises his sword. I press one hand into the ground for balance and gather myself. His sword flashes through the air, and I roll to the left, my knife hand slashing as I go.

The sword whistles past my head. I leap to my feet, and he lunges toward me on legs suddenly too weak to hold him. I follow his gaze as he stares down at the deep cut on his thigh, at the blood gushing out of his artery with every beat of his heart. Before he falls to his knees, I'm already gone. Scooping up my Switch, I battle to cross the last few yards between me and the gate.

Willow stands on top of the rubble, firing arrows at the soldiers who've climbed into the city. Quinn holds the ground below his sister, disarming those who try to reach her. He fights with lethal precision. Like a machine whose sole function is to reduce grown men to nothing.

Thom, Drake, Ian, and the two remaining Baalboden men aren't faring as well. They're backed against the Wall, cut off on all sides by soldiers, and the space between them and the teeth of the soldier's swords is steadily shrinking. Even as I watch, a soldier plunges his sword into the chest of the man beside Thom, and the man drops to the ground.

I slam my Switch into a soldier standing between me and Drake, then slice my knife across his neck as he turns. Blood spurts, and I stagger back as it arcs toward me. Logan leaps over the fallen man, his sword dripping, and together we shove our way to Drake's side.

Soldiers press around us from all sides, herding us toward the city's entrance.

I hope Logan planned for this, too.

"Get inside," he says, and our men scramble across the rubble while Willow fires two more arrows into the soldiers surrounding us.

"Time to go," she says, and leaps into the city.

Logan climbs after her, already yelling orders to whoever is on the other side of the gate to kill the soldiers who broke through or get out of the way and let him do it himself. In seconds, he's over the other side.

I grab for a handhold in the pile of steel and stone, but someone behind me wraps a fist around my hair and yanks me back. The soldier holding my hair pulls me against him, trapping my Switch with his sword arm in a movement so fluid and fast, I don't even register it until I'm already at a disadvantage. The soldiers around me step back, and a sudden silence falls across the field.

"Rachel Adams!"

My name, cut into bite-size syllables, echoes through the air, coated in fury. I know that voice. Terror and rage battle for control over my body. My limbs are too heavy. My head is too light. A distant roaring fills my ears as the soldier holding me pivots toward the Wasteland, and I see Commander Jason Chase, our former leader and the man who singlehandedly destroyed my family and my world, riding toward me on a large brown horse.

CHAPTER SIX

RACHEL

The Commander glares at me with palpable hatred.

My pulse thunders against my ears as I glare right back.

A slew of Baalboden guards dressed in crisp blue military jackets with shining silver buttons step out of the Wasteland and form ranks behind their leader.

We aren't facing one army, we're facing two.

Whose army is the Commander borrowing? I rack my brain, running through what I know of the southeastern city-states. All allied with the Commander. All places my father refused to bring me for fear one of the Commander's many spies would mention the presence of Jared Adams's daughter when I was supposed to be meekly learning domestic arts at home in Baalboden.

Red-and-gold uniforms. Horses. Carrington? Schoensville? I can't remember which of them uses red uniforms—a tremendously stupid color to wear while traveling through the Wasteland since it offers zero camouflage—and it doesn't matter. What matters is that the Commander is coming closer, and I'm still pinned.

I need to be free of this soldier before the Commander reaches me, or I'm dead. I'm not about to die without taking the Commander with me.

"You took something of mine," he says, his dark eyes burning while the thick scar that bisects his face pulls at his mouth.

The dull ache of missing Oliver and Dad throbs beneath my breastbone, and then slowly sinks into the icy silence that bloomed inside of me while I was lying on my father's grave.

The Commander can't hurt me if I refuse to feel it.

I let the memory of Dad and Oliver dissolve my terror and straighten my spine. Raising my chin, I tighten my grip on my knife while I say, "You took something of mine, too."

His laugh is a bitter poison spilling from his lips. "I suppose you think we're even now, you foolish girl."

Soldiers step aside as the horse comes closer. I have forty yards before he reaches me. Maybe less. My knife is a reassuring weight in my left hand. I lower my arm, and the soldier holding me tightens his grip. I flip my knife blade around and aim for what I hope is the artery in his thigh.

I'm only going to get one chance at this.

Meeting the Commander's eyes, I raise my voice and speak as clearly as possible. "We won't be even until you lie dead at my feet."

A faint *thwing* disturbs the air, and an arrow flies past me to bury itself in the Commander's chest. I don't know whether to celebrate that someone—most likely Willow—had such excellent aim or to be sorry that I didn't get to destroy him myself.

I don't get the chance to decide because the Commander sneers, reaches for the arrow, and yanks it free. I stare at his chest, waiting for the blood to come. *Willing* it to come, but it doesn't.

He's wearing armor. Only one city-state equips its soldiers with armor, which means the soldiers in red must be Carrington, and any blows we aim at their chests will be useless. No wonder Willow's arrows had such little effect on the attackers.

"Aim at his head!" I scream.

The Commander throws the arrow onto the ground and spurs his horse forward. Willow doesn't fire again. Either she's out, or she has her hands full defending the survivors inside the Wall from the soldiers who overran the gate. Either way, I've got seconds before the Commander reaches me. Seconds to get free of the soldier who pins me, release the blade at the end of my Switch, and prepare to kill the Commander or die trying.

I jab the knife into the soft meat of the soldier's leg, and he stiffens, his grip on my Switch arm loosening slightly. Before he can recover, I snap my head back, smashing my skull into his nose. Bright lights dance at the edge of my vision as I crush his instep with my boot and whirl around, my Switch already swinging for his head.

He lunges forward, blocking the Switch with his sword while blood pours from his nose, and then balls up his fist to punch me in the face. I whip my knife arm up to block him, but someone hurtles through the air and knocks the soldier to the ground.

Quinn sits astride him, his dark hair flying in the wind as he wrenches the man's sword arm into an impossible angle. The soldier screams in agony as the sickening crack of a bone ripping apart from its tendons fills the air. I jump over them, grip my Switch, and face the Commander. I'll have to unseat him from his horse. A slice across the back of his knee followed by a blow to his chest should do it. Once he's on the ground, I'll attack quickly and without mercy. Just the way he taught me.

"Rachel, get inside the city!" Quinn snaps at me, but I can barely hear him past the pounding of my pulse.

Fifteen yards. Fifteen yards and the Commander is mine. His dark eyes mock me as he reaches for his sword. He thinks he can crush me beneath the hooves of his horse like I'm nothing.

Like the ones he took from me were nothing.

Hatred is steel running through my blood, and it feels like courage. I lift my Switch and keep my knife pressed close to my body, ready to slash the back of his knee at the last moment.

Ten yards. I call up the memory of my father's face and hold it steady.

Eight yards.

Strong hands wrap around my waist from behind and lift me off of the ground.

"No!" I wrench myself to the left, trying to break free, but the hands just clamp down harder. "Let me go!"

Seven yards.

"You aren't sacrificing yourself today," Quinn says, and hauls me toward the pile of rubble that covers the entrance to Baalboden.

"That's not your choice." I elbow him, but he won't relent, and I don't want to fight hard enough to hurt him. "Quinn, that's not your choice."

Six yards.

Quinn's hands loosen. "Then I'll fight with you."

For a moment, I remain resolute, facing the Commander. I

can end it now. One way or the other. I can find peace.

But what good is peace if it comes at the expense of someone who doesn't deserve to die? Quinn is an exceptionally good fighter, but he can't hold off an army by himself. If I take down the Commander, the army will finish us both.

I have enough blood on my hands. I won't add Quinn's.

Swearing viciously, I grab Quinn's hand and pull him toward the gate. He moves quickly, and together we scramble over the slabs of wreckage, trying desperately to reach the top before anyone can stop us.

Hoofbeats thunder toward us as the Commander screams at his soldiers to capture me and kill Quinn. Soldiers swarm onto the rubble behind us as we climb the ruins, skid down the other side, and then run away from the gate.

Thom yells, "All clear!" and strikes a pitch-coated match. Soldiers reach the top of the gate's wreckage and begin sliding down the other side as Thom lights the fuse and then runs with us toward the relative safety of Lower Market. We've put twenty yards between us and the gate when the giant shards of stone and steel explode with enough force to drive all of us to our knees.

Thom hits the ground beside me like a load of bricks and lies still. I reach for him as a second explosion splits the stone skin of the Wall beside the gate and sends several tons of debris crashing into the gap, burying the soldiers who were climbing into the city. The Wall is sealed off once again, though it won't take long for Carrington to come up with a new plan of attack.

Thom stirs beneath my hands and coughs sharply. Frankie sinks to the ground beside him and gently brushes his fingers against the lump rising out of Thom's skull. I cough, too, and swipe tears from my watering eyes as I scan my surroundings.

Dust, ash, and the sharp tang of hot metal lie heavy on the air. Some men outside the Wall scream in pain. Others yell for medical aid and grappling hooks. Men cry out in front of us, too, as Willow yanks arrows out of dead soldiers and sends them flying into the neck, forehead, or eye sockets of the Carrington soldiers still alive inside the Wall. The last two soldiers flee toward the ruins of Lower Market. Holding a handful of arrows, Willow takes several running leaps forward, drops to her knees, and takes them both down in less than ten seconds.

I look away before I can see the blood that pours out of their wounds and spreads across the soot-stained cobblestones beneath them.

The sudden stillness feels just as loud as the explosion. I look over the group again, searching for injuries. Quinn kneels beside Willow, checking to see that his sister is okay. Ian wipes at a cut on his forehead but otherwise seems unharmed. Drake rubs his left thigh and winces as he stands. Frankie wraps an arm around Thom's shoulders and helps him to his feet. Thom sees me watching and smiles a little.

It takes everything in me to force myself to smile back.

Logan reaches my side and crouches down. "Are you okay?" His hands are stained with the blood of the soldiers he killed, and I push myself to my knees before he decides to touch me.

"Rachel, are you okay?" he asks again, and a hard little shudder works its way down my spine.

The man who brutally murdered Oliver and set in motion the chain of events that killed my father is just outside the Wall with an army of soldiers who are apparently willing to die for him. We've blown up the gate and are trapped inside our ruined city like sheep led to slaughter until the tunnel is at least one thousand yards long. And I gave up my chance to destroy the Commander because I couldn't bear to let Quinn be caught in the crossfire.

But Logan doesn't need to hear that. He has a terrified group of survivors to protect from a danger that is suddenly all too real. He has decisions to make, arguments to win, and problems to solve. The least I can do is give him one less thing to worry about.

Ignoring the voice inside my head that whispers I'm only protecting Logan so that I can protect myself from talking about things I don't want to face, I smile reassuringly and say, "I'm fine."

The lie leaves a bitter taste in my mouth as we get to our feet and check to see that the rest of our group survived the blast. I cast one more glance over my shoulder at the pile of metal and stone that seals off the entrance to Baalboden. Just outside the Wall, the object of my hatred is still breathing. Still living. Still waiting for the vengeance I promised my father when I lay on his grave.

The icy silence within me presses close as I imagine the Commander slowly bleeding to death at my feet. Holding that thought, I turn my back on the Wall and walk away, ignoring the way Quinn's eyes follow me as I go.

CHAPTER SEVEN

LOGAN

We lost four men at the gate. They were my responsibility, and now they're gone. All my planning, all my careful instruction, all for nothing because Drake refused to do his part.

That his refusal saved Rachel and me makes the guilt I feel that much worse.

I don't look at him as I give the order to strip the soldiers' bodies of anything we can use. Weapons. Scabbards. Boots. We're in no position to leave a single item of value behind.

"They're from Carrington. The Commander is with them, along with the guards who fled into the Wasteland with him like the cowardly dogs they are," Rachel says. Her voice trembles a little when she says the Commander's name, but she lifts her chin and stares me down—stares everyone down—as if daring us to call her weak. "They'll have Dragonskin on beneath their tunics."

"What's Dragonskin?" Quinn asks as he flips a body over and pulls his sister's arrow free.

"Impenetrable armor worn beneath a soldier's clothing. Kind of like a metal tunic with tiny interlocking scales," I say.

"It's thin and lightweight, almost the density of a cotton tunic, so it doesn't hamper movement or slow them down," Rachel says. "That's why Willow's arrows weren't stopping the soldiers until she aimed for their heads."

Drake bends down to tug at the bloodstained jacket of a soldier who died with Willow's arrow in his throat. Rachel balls her hands into fists and looks away.

"It's Carrington's design, and they don't trade it out to anyone. Ever," Drake says, his eyes on me. "It's their best-kept secret. They also don't leave their city-state and attack others. They don't have to. Because all of their soldiers wear Dragonskin, everyone knows attacking Carrington is futile unless—"

"Unless you have a weapon capable of destroying metal," I say without meeting his eyes.

"The Cursed One can destroy metal." Willow scrubs a handful of arrow tips against the bright green blades of grass that have pushed their way through the blackened soil at the edge of the path. "Looks like your Commander—"

"He's not our Commander. Not anymore." Rachel's voice is cold.

"Fine. The man formerly known as your Commander must have explained the facts of life to Carrington, and they're scared that if someone else gets ahold of the device to control the Cursed One, all the Dragonskin in the world won't save them from being incinerated."

"He must have promised them safety or shared control of the device in exchange for working with him," Drake says as he removes a pair of almost-new boots from the feet of a dead soldier. "What do you think, Logan?"

I think he should've blown the gate and taken the survivors out of the city the way we planned. I'm spared the necessity of answering him when Willow laughs and says, "I just met the Commander, and I can tell you I wouldn't trust him to keep his word unless I had a sword already cutting into his neck. The leader of Carrington is either stupid or is planning a double cross of his own."

"Well, that isn't going to be our problem," Drake says, and stands, the soldier's boots in his hands, while Frankie rips the bloody tunic off of the body and reveals the silvery sheath of armor underneath. "We'll be out of the Commander's reach soon. Right, Logan?" Drake reaches out to clap a hand on my shoulder, and I step back.

He nods. "Figured something was eating at you. Out with it, then."

Willow slides her arrows back into her quiver and bends to help Ian remove another soldier's Dragonskin. Thom slowly crouches down to unstrap a scabbard. Quinn unlaces a pair of boots, his eyes on Rachel, who frowns at Drake and me.

"You should've blown the gate," I say, and my words are too small, too weak to contain the sharp sting of impotent fury raging within me. I look at him, at his steady brown eyes holding my own, and my fingers curl into fists. "We had an agreement, Drake. A *plan*. And four men died today because you didn't keep your end of the bargain."

"No, four men died today because they, like the rest of us, wanted to keep you safe."

I slam my left fist into my right palm. "Do you think that reasoning makes it better? We exchanged four lives for two today. That's a poor bargain any way you look at it."

"So if the situation was reversed, and it was me and Frankie outside the Wall, you'd have blown the gate and left us to the mercy of that army?" Drake asks, his voice calm.

I glare at him.

Willow stands, tosses the Dragonskin onto the pile of goods we've assembled, and looks at me. "He's got you there."

"It's a hard thing to have someone give their life for yours," Quinn says quietly. "The debt feels impossible to repay."

"They didn't have to give their lives," I say. "We've lost so many people already. We didn't have to lose anyone else."

"It was their choice," Drake says. "Every person who went outside the gate knew their lives were in danger. One of the boys we assigned to the watchtower saw movement in the Wasteland. We had enough warning to gather a small team of people ready to keep the gate open for you." He reaches for my shoulder again, and this time I let him. "I only took volunteers, Logan. They believed you were worth it. Don't shame their sacrifice or their courage by calling their motives into question."

I can't find an answer to this, but Rachel steps forward and wraps an arm around Drake's waist. "Thank you," she says.

"You'd have done the same for me," Drake says.

"Yes, but you've earned it," she says quietly. She's right. Without Drake and Nola's aid, I might have died in the Commander's dungeon. As far as I'm concerned, Drake can ask me anything he wants for the rest of my life, and I'll do it.

"Oh, I think you've earned it, too." He smiles and wraps one arm around each of us. For a moment, I'm back in my cottage with Oliver's arm wrapped securely around my shoulders, his love for me a constant presence I'd learned to depend on. The ache of missing him grows larger when Drake lets go and steps back.

"So are we going to stand around hugging all day, or should we figure out how to tell the camp their psychotic ex-leader has returned with friends?" Willow asks.

"Maybe we should also figure out how to explain to them that we're now trapped inside the city until the tunnel is finished," Ian says as he brushes bits of grass and dirt from a scabbard and then slides the soldier's weapon back into its resting place. "Of course, I guess if you really do have a device that can control the Cursed One, we could just call the monster and set it loose on the army. Problem solved."

He flashes me a grin. My stomach clenches as I remember the desperate screams of Baalboden's people while the beast turned the city into their funeral pyre.

"We aren't using the Cursed One as a weapon," I say.

Ian shrugs. "Seems the easiest answer to our problem."

The last time I believed that line of reasoning, the device failed, and Baalboden was destroyed. I'm not risking it again. Not when I have the tunnel at my disposal.

"We'll leave through the tunnel." A glance at the sky shows that the shadows of twilight are already gathering. "I want us out of here tomorrow morning, even if we haven't reached the one-thousand-yard mark I set for us."

"Suit yourself." Ian bends to lift a handful of Dragonskin tunics. He's taller than me, all angles and sharp edges, but he's strong enough to toss five tunics over his shoulder and scoop up three swords as well.

Thom, ignoring Frankie's strident insistence that he take it easy because of the lump on his head, gathers up the knives we found strapped to the soldiers' ankles. The weapons look small in Thom's massive hands.

"We'll sleep in the compound tonight and leave at first light," I say.

"No one's going to be happy about sleeping in the Commander's home," Frankie says, his lips turning down like he's just bitten into something sour.

"It's that or stay out in the open and hope Carrington can't get into the city." I hold Frankie's gaze. "I'm sure you can find a way to convince them."

I turn to Quinn. "We need to double the guards tonight in case we didn't get every soldier that came through the gate. Use people from your sparring class if you have to."

As the rest of the group divides the supplies into bundles they can carry, I take the remaining Dragonskin tunics and jerk my chin toward the northbound road. "Let's go."

They match my pace as we leave the grass-lined path behind and enter what used to be Lower Market. The streets, a swath of broken cobblestones and haphazard piles of debris, cut a path through the burned-out husks of stores, tents, and food stalls. I turn the corner at what's left of Jocey's Mug & Ale, and my boots grind bits of glass that lie across the soot-covered cobblestones like diamonds.

Rachel's mouth is a thin, pressed line, and her eyes are shadowed by the same demons that seem to haunt her when she wakes screaming from her nightmares. I let the others move ahead of me and fall into step beside her.

"I should've waited for you," I say quietly.

She says nothing.

"When I went over the gate, I was sure you were right behind me, and I was focused on catching the soldiers who already went through. I didn't know that I'd be leaving you to face the Commander alone." I swallow hard as the unwelcome image of Rachel lying dead at the Commander's feet taunts me.

"You did the right thing," she says, but her voice sounds detached. Like she's saying the words she thinks I want to hear, but keeping the truth locked somewhere inside.

"The right thing is to protect you."

Her shoulders straighten, and she shifts the load of boots and knives she carries. "The right thing is to take care of those who can't take care of themselves. You don't have to worry about me. I could've taken him if Quinn hadn't interfered."

It takes a second for her words to register, but when they do, I have to grit my teeth to keep from raising my voice. "Are you saying you *deliberately* stayed outside the Wall so you could face him? Alone?"

"Not at first. A soldier caught me." She still sounds like the words she says mean nothing to her, and the fear that slides through me flickers into anger.

"And you got away from him. Didn't you?"

"Of course." She sounds insulted.

A gust of wind snatches her hair and flings it in my face. I swat it away, trying to figure out how to get through to her. How to make her care that she nearly sacrificed herself for vengeance and left me with yet another loved one to miss.

A sharp turn takes us north, and I clench my jaw as we walk past the ashes of Oliver's bakery. I try to remember the way his dark eyes would rest on me, filled with gentle acceptance and later with love, but already his memory blurs around the edges. I know from experience that I can't hold on to it. Not exactly. The smell of his baking, the warmth of his hand, and the way he would quietly encourage me will keep fading with every day that passes without him. But I can hold on to what he built into me—the strength to do the right thing even when it feels impos-· sible and the belief that if I put my mind to it, I can accomplish anything—I can hold on to that, and a part of him will never leave me.

I can do that for Oliver, but I don't want to have to do it for Rachel. I don't want to struggle to remember the exact shade of her eyes or the way she smiles when she thinks she's bested me. I don't want to be left with nothing but regrets and the heart-breaking certainty that if I'd only done something differently, I could've saved her.

Keeping my voice low, I say, "So you got away from the sol-dier and had a chance to follow us into the city, but you chose to stay and face the Commander?"

Something in my tone gets through to her, and she frowns at me. "He was right there. The man responsible for all of this." She gestures at the remains of Oliver's stall and then at the ruined city itself. "He took everything from us, and he was *right there*. Tell me you wouldn't have done the same thing."

I stop and face her. "I wouldn't have done the same thing."

She shakes her head, and this time, I don't bother trying to speak quietly. "No, Rachel. I wouldn't have stayed out there to face him alone. Not when an entire army was surrounding me."

"They weren't attacking anymore. They were waiting—"

"For him to kill you!"

Sudden fury blazes across her face, and her voice shakes. "I would've killed him first, Logan. In case you've forgotten, I know how to do it."

"And then what?" My voice shakes as much as hers. "If you managed to kill him first, what was your exit strategy with the entire army of Carrington surrounding you? Death?"

"If that's what it takes!" Unshed tears gather on her lashes, but her expression is fierce.

I can't breathe. Can't think beyond the terrifying realization that the pain Rachel has endured at the hands of the Commander has led her to this precipice. How can I save her if she doesn't even want to be saved?

"Rachel—"

"He deserves to die. There won't be any peace for us until he's dead."

I drop the load of supplies I'm carrying and reach for her. She doesn't pull away as I grip her shoulders and gently tug her toward my chest, but her spine is ramrod straight. I wrap my arms around her and lean my face against her hair as I search for the words I need.

"You're right," I say, and she trembles. "He deserves to die. But *you* don't. Don't you see that? You don't deserve to die, and I can't stand the thought of losing you. Please, Rachel, you're all I have left."

Her spine slowly curves toward me until she presses her

forehead to my shoulder. I hold her, all lean muscle and soft curves, and for the first time in all the years I've known her, she feels fragile in my arms.

When she pulls away, I have a hard time letting go. But she starts moving north again, so I pick up the slippery Dragonskin tunics and walk beside her. It takes a while to weave past the splintered wood, scorched brick, and shattered glass on the streets of Lower Market and into the less damaged area of Center Square. The Dragonskin grows heavy in my hands. I look away from the remains of the Claiming stage and the memories of Rachel in her beautiful blue dress trying desperately to stand up to the Commander, who was so sure he had her firmly under his control.

He was wrong, and his mistake destroyed countless lives.

I'm not going to let him destroy anyone else. Including Rachel.

"Quinn was going to fight with me," she says as we turn a street corner and see the blackened, spindly structures that were once the opulent homes of North Hub.

Forty yards past the Hub, the Commander's compound, largely undamaged, squats behind its iron fence—all fierce turrets and unblinking panes of glass. Most of the medical and food supplies we've managed to recover have come from the compound. Still, every time I see it, part of me wishes it had burned, too. It's impossible to look at it without seeing the Commander's merciless eyes as my mother lay dying on the cobblestones for the crime of leaving her home to find food for her starving child. Without feeling the damp of his dungeon and the sole of his boot against the brand he burned into the side of my neck.

Without seeing the back of his hand slam into Rachel's face.

My eyes find Quinn as he carefully navigates around a pile of debris before turning north, heading for the compound. The others are already out of sight.

"He helped me escape from the soldier who had me."

"I thought he didn't approve of violence," I say, though what I really mean is that I'm thankful he chose to stand by us.

By her.

"I don't think he does. He was trying to get me to go into the city, and when I refused, he decided to stay with me rather than leave me to face the Commander alone." Her voice catches. "I didn't ask him to put himself in danger for me."

Neither did I, but I'm grateful he did. And after witnessing just how far Rachel is willing to go for revenge, I'm hoping Quinn will be willing to watch out for her anytime my back is turned. Not that I'm going to tell Rachel that. I like my internal organs right where they are.

"We'll punish the Commander," I say. "But we'll do it with a plan. With an exit strategy that doesn't involve either one of us dying."

"Do you have a plan?" she asks as we trudge up the hill that leads to our camp.

I swallow hard and refuse to look at her, because I don't. I don't know how to punish the Commander and still get the survivors to safety like I promised. I don't know how to defeat two armies just to get to one man.

But I'm going to figure it out. I'm not going to let the Commander take another person from me. Once I deliver the survivors to Lankenshire, I'll devote every minute of every day to tracking him down. . . .

Tracking.

Wristmarks.

Sonar.

"Yes." My voice grows stronger as an idea—a bold, risky, nearly impossible idea—hits me. "I have a plan. It's going to take several weeks to build the tech I need, but I have a plan."

Her eyes meet mine as we crest the top of the hill. The camp is already in motion, with people hurrying to tear down shelters and pack up supplies. A few survivors head toward me. No doubt with questions, arguments, or worries they need me to solve.

"Can you build the tech while we travel through the Wasteland?" Rachel asks.

"Yes. As long as I have the right supplies, I can build anything."

"Too bad you can't come up with a way to let Lankenshire know we're coming. And to warn the other city-states about Rowansmark." Enthusiasm lights up her voice. "Or invent something that would let us know where Rowansmark's battalions are and how fast they're traveling. Maybe you could—"

"Hold on a second." I laugh a little. "The Cursed One destroyed the infrastructure that existed between cities in the old civilization, and we can't build more without risking another attack. If there are no wires laid between city-states, we can't build technology that would allow us to communicate with them. Or spy on them. We can, however, build tech that is individually targeted at specific people or local tasks by using sonar. The Commander used the science of sound to keep tabs on his people, and now I'm going to use it to destroy him."

"So let's get these people to Lankenshire, convince them to offer us shelter, and then hunt down the Commander and obliterate him. We'll use your plan if it's working. We'll do it my way if our other options run out. Deal?"

"Deal."

Best Case Scenario: I can build the invention that is slowly taking shape inside my mind, and we destroy the Commander before he ever sees us coming.

Worst Case Scenario: The invention fails, the Commander somehow anticipates us, or Rachel gets impatient with my plan and decides sacrificing herself is an acceptable price for delivering justice.

Before I can think of any solutions to those scenarios, a huge *boom* echoes across the ruins. We spin on our heels and scan the blackened city laid out before us. Nothing moves, but a cloud of ash and dust rises from the direction of the gate.

Seconds later, another *boom* shatters the stillness. The cloud of dust grows thicker.

"They have a battering ram," I say as yet another crash ratchets my pulse into overdrive.

"How long before they get through the gate?" Rachel asks, and the same dread that fills me is written all over her face.

"It's an unstable structure. It could take them days to make a dent, or the whole thing could slide into Lower Market in a matter of hours. We have to get everyone inside the compound *now*."

As the battering ram slams repeatedly against the pile of debris blocking the gate, I hurry into camp praying that we still have enough time to tunnel to the surface and leave this place of death and destruction behind us.

CHAPTER EIGHT

RACHEL

"Get to the compound," I shout as Logan grabs Drake's arm and begins giving him a list of instructions about the tunnel, the wagons, and erasing all traces of camp on the hillside. "Grab your travel pack and anything else that still needs to be loaded on a wagon and *move*."

"We can't sleep inside the Commander's compound!" a woman says even as she snatches up a pile of blankets that were drying on the soft spring grass and looks around to see what else she can carry. Several others voice their agreement.

"Why not?" Logan asks as Drake hurries off toward the compound.

"Because"—the woman's hand flutters toward her throat—"it's forbidden."

In the distance, the steady *boom, boom* of the battering ram echoes through the air.

Logan's voice is gentler than his words. "The Commander

isn't going to punish you for entering the compound. He's not looking over your shoulder anymore." He points west, toward the distant ruins of the gate. "He's out there with guards and the Carrington army trying to find a way inside the Wall. When he does break through, and he will, being caught out in the open is a death sentence."

"Being caught anywhere is a death sentence," Ian mutters as he hoists his pack on his shoulder and grabs his armful of Dragonskin.

I glare at him, but Logan nods. "Exactly. Which is why we'll take shelter in the compound tonight, and I'll have the tunnel ready for us to leave first thing in the morning." He scans the crowd and pays close attention to Adam, who is standing near Willow as usual.

"Why not just surface in the Wasteland now?" a young man named Keegan asks as he walks past us carrying a load of canvas. "The tunnel is far enough along to get us into the forest, right?"

"Not far enough that we could safely travel by torchlight, and we can't travel with wagons in the dark."

Boom. Boom.

Adam walks by, carrying Willow's travel bag for her and laughing at something she says. He stops laughing when he catches Logan watching him, but Logan just turns away and starts giving Jodi directions for helping Quinn pack up the weapons.

A few people stand and stare in the direction of the gate, terror rooting them to the ground. I grab their arms and give them a little shake.

"Get your stuff and get into the compound. We can outwit the Commander and his stupid army, but only if we keep our heads. Now go."

They hurry toward their shelters, and I turn to see who else might need motivating. Logan is already heading up the compound's steps. Probably to see about bringing the tunnel to the surface. No one else seems to need me to prod them into action. I cast one more glance over my shoulder toward the gate and feel torn. On the one hand, I know we need to be far away from here before the Commander gets into the city. On the other, it would be nice to dip one of my arrows in some sort of slow-acting poison and nail the Commander in the face when he rode up the hill on his horse.

It takes nearly four hours to pack up the camp and get our belongings inside the compound. We move fast, heads down, lips tight, as the constant noise of the battering ram hangs over our heads like a blade. There's no way to know how much longer the gate can withstand its incessant strikes. The faster we lock ourselves inside, the safer we'll be.

People stream out of the campsite, following the supply wagons, and head up the steep hill that leads to the compound.

Sylph walks beside Smithson in the middle of the group. Her unruly dark curls bounce against her shoulders with every step, and she smiles at those around her with genuine affection.

I don't know how she does it. She lost her parents, her grandparents, and her older brother. I know she's devastated. But instead of closing herself off to mourn her loss, she reaches out to others with an unflinching generosity that both baffles me and makes me envious.

Sylph sees me and leaves Smithson's side to hook her arm through mine so we can walk up the steep hill together. The air is heavy with the spicy-sweet perfume of apple blossoms and the drowsy buzzing of bees that move slowly through the trees. People walk the packed dirt path in clumps of twos and threes. Most walk in silence.

"I've learned a lot in sparring practice," she says.

"You're doing well."

"You hold back with us. I was in the watchtower when the army attacked. I saw you. Saw you fight your way to the gate and then get away from the soldier who grabbed you. You could've been killed."

"But I wasn't. I'm fine." I hold my hands up as if to offer proof but drop them to my sides when they start to shake.

I'm many things, but fine isn't one of them. Not when the man responsible for so much pain still breathes freely on the other side of the Wall.

"I never knew you could do that," Sylph says, her voice subdued. "Ever since seeing you fight the guards on the Claiming stage, I've been trying to figure out how I could be your best friend and still not know something so important."

I can't think of anything to say, and the silence between us begins to feel awkward.

"You were always different from the rest of the girls. You thought for yourself. I didn't mind. In fact, I admired you for it. But I think there's a lot I don't know about you."

What can I say to that? We may come from the same world, but her parents obeyed the Commander without question. Mine defied him at any cost. I won't make apologies for the way I was raised or for the intimacy I sacrificed in our friendship by hiding the truth. I had to protect my father from the consequences of breaking the law. She might understand that, but while I can let her see the girl I really was, I can't bear to let her see the hollow, silent girl I've become.

"Yes," I say, "I'm different from the other Baalboden girls."

"I want to learn." There's a quiet determination in her voice that takes me by surprise.

"What?" I look at her and find her wide green eyes fixed on me.

"I want to learn how to fight like that. I want you to stop holding back with me. This isn't the same world we grew up in." She waves her hands at the blackened streets behind us. "There aren't Protectors lined up ready to save us. We need to learn how to save ourselves."

I squeeze her arm closer to me. "It's nice to have my differences be an asset instead of something that makes me the most unfeminine girl in the room."

Sylph smiles. "You aren't unfeminine. You just stink at setting a nice table or sewing a decent dress."

"I can sew a decent dress."

"You are the worst seamstress Baalboden's ever seen. And possibly the worst cook as well."

"I can cook when I have to," I say, and return her smile.

"Well, you don't have to. We need someone who knows how to use weapons and win a fight, and you're the best girl for the job. I'll never forget the way you launched yourself into that mess on the Claiming stage. I thought you were going to die."

"So did I." I should be trembling at the memory of being

surrounded by the Brute Squad and held at the Commander's mercy, but the ashes of my fury lie cold and silent within me.

She shakes her head. "No, you knew exactly what to do. How to stand up for yourself and win. It was terrifying and amazing."

"Terrifying."

"And amazing. Who knew a girl could kill a grown man?"

In the back of my mind, Melkin's dark eyes beg me to save him as his blood flows hot and sticky over my hands. I shake my head and walk faster. Sylph matches my pace.

After a moment, she says, "I felt foolish, Rachel. All those years of friendship, and I had no idea what you were capable of. You could've told me."

"You would've told your mother." I squeeze her closer to me to take away the sting of remembering her mother's death. "Not on purpose, but you would've told her."

Her voice catches on a rasp of grief. "Maybe. She could always get the truth out of me."

I think of the way we used to walk behind her father in the market, whispering our secrets. Whispering *her* secrets. Most of mine were too dangerous to share. "I'm sorry."

"For what?"

For still having secrets. For being unable to open up and let her in anymore. For pretending to feel the things I know I should be feeling because inside of me there's nothing but darkness and the faint voices of those whose blood is on my hands.

"I'm sorry about your family," I say.

She leans her cheek against my shoulder as we step around a woman whose small child has stopped to chase a shower of flower petals teased from the branches by the late afternoon breeze. "And I'm sorry about your family, too. But I have Smithson, and you have Logan. We have more than most."

The bouncing, irrepressible Sylph of my childhood is gone. In her place, forged out of fire and loss, is a woman-girl with steady eyes and clear vision. Talking to her is like coming home and finding the furniture in every room rearranged. The same pieces are there, the same sense of comfort, but nothing is exactly where you'd expect.

Ahead of us, a woman struggles up the hill alone, her gait unsteady and her steps slow. Sylph and I lean against each other the way we used to as children when we'd walk through Lower Market, plotting how to get extra sticky buns from Oliver or how to get Corbin Smythe, the cutest boy our age, to notice us.

More apple blossoms whirl through the air as we approach the woman who can barely manage the hill. I'm about to remind Sylph of the time we bribed Corbin to eat lunch with us by promising to give him an entire loaf of raisin bread, but the words shrivel in my mouth as we flank the woman, and I look in her face.

It's Melkin's wife, Eloise, waddling slowly up the hill, her hands cupped beneath her swollen belly as if to keep the baby safe inside of her for just a little longer. Her thin brown hair falls down her shoulders in limp strands, and her eyes are puffy with exhaustion or tears. Probably both.

"Let us help you," Sylph says, and gently wraps her arm around Eloise's waist.

"Thank you." Eloise's voice is a timid, caged thing hovering uncertainly in the air before drifting away. Everything about her seems washed-out and weary. Everything but her eyes.

Her eyes are full of misery and *knowing*. I look away, my cheeks burning as if she'd slapped me.

"Rachel, put your arm around her and help me," Sylph says.

I can't touch her with the hands that ripped her husband away from her. I *can't*.

She looks at me with her tired eyes as if waiting for me to tell her something she already knows, but I can't speak.

"It's okay," Eloise says in her pale, whispery voice. "I know you tried to save him."

Who told her that lie? I shake my head and try to find the words to contradict her, but my lips stay closed, protecting my secrets even as they rise up to choke me with bloody fingers.

"Rachel?" Sylph sounds baffled. Maybe worried. I can't look at her to see which is true. I can't look at either of them.

Melkin's dark eyes burning with fury, his knife pointed at the ground. The rage that blistered through me when I knew he wanted to take the device and leave me with nothing—no way to destroy the Commander and make my father's sacrifice count. The flash of silver as I attacked him. A confusion of blows. And Melkin dropping toward me, his face a murderous mask, his sword arm hidden.

My knife. His chest. Blood covering me as I sat horrified. As I let him believe I was Eloise. As I pretended he'd saved her, when neither of us had saved anyone.

"Rachel!" Sylph's voice cuts through the memory, and something tugs on my arm.

I look down to see Eloise's small white hand pressing against my arm. My stomach surges, and I snatch my arm away before the bile reaches my throat.

"Are you okay?" Sylph asks, but I'm already moving—striding past citizens, crushing apple blossom petals beneath my boots, and pretending I can leave the ghost of Melkin behind as easily as I can leave his wife.

CHAPTER NINE

LOGAN

I spend the evening monitoring the machine's progress, helping maneuver the wagons down the slick basement steps, which are barely wide enough to accommodate them, and pressuring Jeremiah to hurry up and finish drawing a map of the northern territory.

I also spend it straining to hear any change in the constant rhythm of the battering ram. Any indication that our narrow window of opportunity is gone.

Through it all, I answer innumerable questions—*How will we get the animals through the tunnel?* Blindfold them and lead them. *Are you really going to let girls carry weapons and help guard the camp?* Absolutely. *Shouldn't we leave now?* Too dangerous. *What if the tunnel collapses? What if the Commander finds us? What if the Cursed One attacks?*

What if?

I can't assure them enough. I can't explain my plans, argue my points, or reason with panic-stricken people. Not if I also want to make sure the camp is locked down, the wagons are ready, the map is completed, and the tunnel reaches the surface in the right place. My patience feels like a stripped wire ready to snap.

When I find myself tempted to pull a page out of the Commander's rule book and tell a woman that if she doesn't like my methods she can stay behind in the dungeon, I ask Drake to keep everyone but the tunnel crew away from me, and I hide in the tunnel's depths, calculating distances, replacing batteries, and reconfiguring trajectories while the rest of the camp goes to sleep.

The battering ram is still pounding at the gate in regular intervals when I make my way up the basement stairs again. The majority of our people have settled down on bedrolls in the main banquet hall. Most of my inner circle are already sleeping, taking the opportunity to get some rest now in case they're called upon to handle a crisis later. Even Rachel is sleeping, her bedroll snugged up beside Sylph's. Their hands are clasped tightly, and I hope it's enough to keep Rachel's nightmares away.

Quinn has a pair of guards stationed by the compound's front door and another pair in the watchtower that rises above the kitchen like a castle's turret. All of them have one duty: to listen for the battering ram to fall silent.

I pace through the compound checking locks, supplies, wagons, and animals. Making sure the last of the Commander's explosives are mounted in the right places throughout the basement. Thinking through every possible scenario and doing my best to come up with a solution for each.

The pile of weapons resting against the basement wall catches my eye. Every piece is lined up and ready for one of the survivors to grab it on the way into the tunnel tomorrow. Long swords for the men. Short swords, daggers, and knives for everyone else. Even a few walking sticks for those who need the help. Rachel is proof that a walking stick in the right hands can be a formidable weapon.

At the end of the row, a walking stick in black ebony nearly blends into the dark wall behind it.

Melkin's staff.

The one he was given when he was on a mission to another city-state.

The one that can call the Cursed One.

I'm willing to bet Melkin was in Rowansmark when he received his gift. Did he know what he had? Or was James Rowan just hoping to get lucky and have Melkin accidentally call the beast to destroy Baalboden?

The metal is smooth and cold beneath my fingers. I should leave the staff. Shove it into a shadowy corner of the basement where it will be overlooked and then bury it when I bring down the ceiling.

But what if in burying it, I activate the sonic pulse that calls the Cursed One? My people would be in the tunnel. Even with the completed power booster attached to the tech I carry, I can't risk it. Besides, if the staff is capable of calling the monster, maybe it's capable of other things as well. You never know when something like that could come in handy.

Laying the staff in the back of the supply wagon, behind my extra jars of glycerin and acid and my bags of tech supplies and scrap parts, I return to the tunnel and consider the one scenario I don't have a solution for.

Every guard in Baalboden carried a tracking device and an Identidisc capable of scanning the unique ridges of our wristmarks and listing which citizens were in a seventy-yard radius. I'd be a fool not to consider that the Commander may have already used an Identidisc to scan our wristmarks to see who survived the fires and stayed behind with me. Once he has a list of our wristmark signals, he can use a tracking device to find us unless we're out of range.

We'd have to be at least five hundred yards away to be out of range. We don't have time to tunnel that far. I just have to hope the Commander doesn't realize we've left until it's too late to track us down.

I nod a silent greeting to the nighttime tunnel crew again and set about toggling the levers that control the machine's trajectory. A few minutes later, the machine is chewing through the dirt at a three percent incline, and I'm back to pacing the tunnel while I worry over every other worst case scenario that presents itself to me.

What if the machine breaks before it reaches the surface?

What if the device doesn't keep the Cursed One at bay when one hundred fifty-four pairs of boots are stomping through its domain?

What if the Commander is already tracking us?

What if?

"Thought I might find you here," a voice says behind me, and I nearly drop the torch I'm holding as I spin around to find Thom standing in the tunnel holding a torch of his own. The firelight flickers along the craggy planes of his face, and he smiles a little as I shake my head.

"Don't sneak up on me like that. You nearly gave me heart failure."

"Didn't sneak up on purpose. You weren't paying attention." He shifts his torch to his other hand. "You need sleep, Logan."

"I can't."

"If you want to lead everyone out of this place tomorrow, you don't have a choice." He nods toward the far end of the tunnel, where the faint hum of the machine drones steadily. "I'll keep watch here for you."

"You need sleep, too." And besides, I'm not awake because I think the tunnel crew needs supervision. I'm awake because there might be a scenario that I've missed. I can't afford to stop thinking through the potential problems and coming up with viable solutions.

"The group can function well enough without me for a few hours tomorrow if I have to nap in a wagon, Logan. It's you they need."

The air in the tunnel feels close and warm. I gulp it down as my throat tightens and look away. For most of my life, I wondered what it would feel like to be respected. Looked up to. Needed.

I thought it would be fulfilling, but instead it's exhausting. The expectations and hope placed on me weigh more than I think I can bear, and every single bit of the trust that's been thrust my way feels fragile in my clumsy hands.

What if I fail them?

Thom's hand wraps around my shoulder and squeezes gently. "How old are you?"

"Nineteen."

He sighs and settles himself next to me with his back against the dirt wall. His mop of brown hair falls into his eyes, but he doesn't seem to care. "That's young. Maybe too young for everything we've asked of you."

"Drake could do it better." I lean next to him and watch the way the torchlight dances in the gloom. "He's older, more experienced—he'd already started leading your group against the Commander. I just don't understand why . . ."

"Why we picked you?"

I nod.

"Drake gathered a group of like-minded people together to talk grand ideas. What if things were different? What if we could change our society?" His hand tightens against my shoulder and then slips away. "But really, what we were doing was waiting for the Commander to die. Planning for change that we could implement when our enemy was already gone."

I remain silent, and Thom takes a moment, as if he wants to choose his words with care. "But you, Logan, you didn't wait. You didn't sit in dark corners making big plans that you knew you couldn't put into motion because it would mean committing treason. You stood up to him. You saw an injustice, and you stood up to him. None of us had ever found the courage to do that."

"I just did what anyone . . . I couldn't—he was hurting *Rachel*."

Thom's voice is filled with quiet grief. "And before that, it was Drake's wife. Derreck's son. My sister. The list is endless. But we just talked. Grieved and talked. Got angry and talked some more. We were full of someday plans, because we aren't leaders."

"I think you're selling yourself short."

"I'd say that honor goes to you alone."

We fall silent, listening to the rumble of the machine and the quiet murmurs of the tunnel crew as they brace the walls and the ceiling.

"You aren't afraid when it counts," he says.

My laugh is tinged with bitterness. "I'm always afraid."

"Of what? Dying? Being tortured? The Cursed One?"

"Failing."

There's a smile in his voice. "And *that's* what makes you the right leader for us. You're driven to do the right thing, no matter what it costs you. And you're smart enough to make it happen. Never in my life seen anyone with more ideas and plans than you."

I let his words settle in my head while our torches hiss and pop. The burden of responsibility is still enormous, but somehow it feels like Thom is now shouldering a small piece of it for me. I push away from the wall and look at him. His brown eyes hold mine steadily, and he waits quietly for my next words.

"I think this is the longest conversation you and I have ever had," I say.

He looks pained. "I'd appreciate it if next time you didn't make me do most of the talking. Never really cared for it."

I grin. "I respect a man who lets his actions speak louder than his words."

"And I respect you. Never forget it. Now go get some sleep. I'll watch over the tunnel until daybreak."

I respect you. His words ring in my ears as I follow his advice and head toward the main banquet hall and my bedroll.

I was wrong. Being needed, trusted, and respected by others isn't nearly as exhausting as the fear that those who now look to me for leadership do so because they've built me up to be more than I can possibly be. Thom accepts my fears and my shortcomings and still wants me as his leader for reasons that make sense to me. I underestimated him, and as I lie down with nothing but a thin blanket between me and the cold marble floor of the banquet hall, I have to wonder if it's possible that I've underestimated the rest of my people as well.

I hope to keep them safe long enough to find out.

CHAPTER TEN

RACHEL

I wake in the predawn gray with the rest of the camp, pack up my bedroll, and take my breakfast ration—a chunk of yesterday's bread—to the wide steps leading to the compound's entrance while Logan supervises the final preparations for our journey. The air is heavy with the promise of rain, and faint beams of sunlight waver uncertainly between thick ribbons of gray cloud.

Boom. Boom.

The pair of second-shift guards who are standing at the door listening to the battering ram's steady assault against the gate gaze longingly at my bread, and I take pity on them.

"Go get a breakfast ration. I'll listen for any trouble." The words are barely out of my mouth when they hurry toward the banquet hall. Before I turn back around to face the city, Jeremiah shuffles down the hall, his purple bow tied smartly around the collar of his tunic. He nods to me and then disappears into the room he's been using to draw Logan's map.

Boom.

A long scraping noise fills the air. Like a giant metal fingernail sliding across the cobblestones.

The debris is shifting. There's no way to tell how much longer it will take for the army to create a hole big enough to use, but we're leaving soon. Hopefully it won't matter.

Before I turn to tell Logan about the battering ram's progress, I take one more look at Baalboden. My eyes seek out the street where I was raised, just a little north of Lower Market. Splintered beams and solitary brick chimneys stretch toward the sky, but there's nothing else. No rooftops. No homes. Nothing but ashes and memories.

Boom. Scrape. Slide.

I wait for the loss of my father's laughter to hurt me. For the memory of Oliver's sticky buns and fairy tales to cut me to pieces, but I'm hollowed out inside.

Boom.

Turning away, I decide it's better this way. Easier. I can walk away from this if I don't let myself grieve for what I'm leaving behind.

The sense that something is wrong comes quietly. A tiny finger of fear skating over my skin. A whisper that I've missed something important. I stop chewing, strain to see deep into the fog-drenched ruins, and listen.

Silence.

The battering ram has fallen quiet.

I see flashes of red moving quickly through the foggy streets and swear.

The army is coming.

Racing up the steps, I slam the front door behind me. Pushing the metal bars into place, I lock the door and hope Carrington wastes plenty of time hunting through the rest of the city before they come so far north.

"Jeremiah, get out of there. The army is coming." I smack my fist against the closed door of his office as I race past.

At the end of the hall, I nearly collide with Willow as she leaps from the tiny stairway that leads up to the watchtower.

"Carrington—"

"They're coming straight for us," Willow says. "Not even bothering to search anywhere else. It's like your leader knew right where we'd be."

My pulse pounds, and my skin feels too tight. "Let's go."

Logan is helping Elias and Sylph roll up the last of the canvas shelters. He takes one look at my face and leaps to his feet, already shouting for quiet.

I take a deep breath and try to sound calm. We need these people to move down to the basement and into the tunnel without hysteria or panic. "Carrington is through the gate." I meet Logan's eyes and try to convey with my expression that there's more to the situation, but I needn't have bothered.

Willow says, "They're coming straight for the compound. Better get into that tunnel if you don't feel like being skewered by a sword."

Chaos erupts. People scream, shout, and scramble for the doorway, sometimes knocking each other down in the process. I glare at Willow. "Do you ever *not* say exactly what you're thinking?"

She shrugs as Quinn, Logan, Drake, Frankie, Nola, and Ian

hurry up to us. Logan starts spitting out orders the second he arrives.

"Ian, run ahead into the tunnel and tell Thom what's going on. Make sure they've surfaced. If they haven't, switch the angle of the machine and get it done. Nola, take Jodi, Sylph, and Smithson and get the injured into the medical wagon and then *go*."

As they leave, he looks at Drake. "Get these people organized into two lines and move them down the stairs and into the tunnel. Make sure they understand that they must be absolutely quiet. I'll be there in a minute with the device so we can keep the Cursed One at bay. Frankie, grab a few helpers, blindfold the animals, and lead them through."

"What can I do to help?" Quinn asks.

"I need to know that we got everybody out. Can you check the compound and send any stragglers to the basement? You'll have to move fast. Once the army reaches the compound, I want you in the tunnel."

Quinn nods, and Willow immediately says, "I'll go with him. It'll be faster with two people searching."

"Someone needs to know what's happening outside the basement while you get our people far enough into the tunnel to safely detonate the explosives," I say.

"I'm not leaving anyone outside the basement door. It would be a death sentence." Logan glares at me.

"Just until Quinn and Willow get back. And I'm not asking permission. I'm telling you where I'll be."

He grabs me and pulls me against him. "The second you see them, get to the tunnel." His kiss is rough and a little desperate. "I love you."

"I love you, too. Now go."

As soon as he's down the stairs, I race into the main hall. Maybe I can move some furniture and block the door. Buy us more time. Maybe I can give us more information on the enemy.

Maybe the Commander will lead the charge, and I'll get my chance to shoot him in the face.

I hurry into the room closest to the front door and glance out of the lone rectangle of glass beside me. The Carrington army is now pressed against the fence—a mass of red uniforms and sword hilts that flash beneath the sunlight in brilliant sparks of gold.

Four soldiers crank a chain on something that vaguely resembles an elongated catapult built to stand waist high on the average man. A thick log of metal, about the same diameter as a mature oak trunk, lies in the catapult's cradle. The log inches back with every rotation of the chain, and beneath the log, a spring coils tightly. In seconds, the soldiers have the log pulled as far back as it can go. One of them yells, and the two closest to the spring pull a metal pin out of each side of the frame, releasing the tension. The log swings forward with terrible speed and slams into the solid iron fence surrounding the compound.

The fence bends, and the shriek of metal tearing asunder fills the air. Another two or three assaults with the battering ram, and that section of the fence will collapse.

The Commander is nowhere in sight.

Forget barricading the door or gaining information. Those soldiers will be inside the building in minutes.

I run down the length of the hallway until I come to the banquet hall. Only a handful of people remain. Willow is ushering them toward the basement stairs.

"Do we have everyone?" I ask.

"Quinn is doing one last check. I'll find him before I go down."

"Don't take long," I say as a tremendous *thud* shakes the walls.

The army is at the door. I draw my knife and back toward the basement stairs, keeping my eyes on the far end of the hall as the front door begins to splinter. The metal reinforcement rods bow inward as the battering ram slams into it again.

"Hurry!" I yell as I hear Quinn's and Willow's footsteps pounding toward me. Any second now, that door will give, and we need to be hidden inside the basement before that happens.

A door about halfway down the hall cracks open, and Jeremiah steps out. He clutches a sheaf of paper in his arthritic fingers.

He's as good as dead.

"Run!" I scream as the main door flies off its hinges and careens down the hall.

CHAPTER ELEVEN

RACHEL

Jeremiah shuffles back, his eyes locked on the soldiers pouring through the entrance. I run toward him, holding my knife, blade out.

"Rachel!" someone yells behind me, but I don't look back. I can't.

Jeremiah presses his back to the wall and holds the papers against his chest like he can somehow protect them from the soldiers who race forward, swords drawn.

"Get back!" I lunge in front of Jeremiah and whip my arm up to block the first soldier as he swings his sword toward Jeremiah's head. The blow slams into my arm, and my knife feels tiny and insignificant clutched in my desperate fingers.

Another soldier leaps forward. I plant my right foot, lean back slightly, and snap my left leg into the air, kicking his windpipe with my boot. He drops to the floor, and as I dodge another blow from the soldier to my right, I bend to scoop up the fallen soldier's sword.

It's too heavy for me. Too long. I'm overbalanced, and I won't be able to fight with it for long without tiring, but it's better than going up against trained soldiers with nothing but my knife.

More soldiers rush into the building. Some converge on us, some kick open doors and start searching the rooms that line the hallway. We have to get to the basement stairs before they do, or we'll be cut off from the group. If that happens, Jeremiah and I are both dead.

"Move," I say to Jeremiah, who huddles behind me. He slides along the wall while I hold my stolen sword in front of me and wait for the next attack.

It doesn't take long.

One of the soldiers closest to me whistles, a sharp, piercing sound that hurts my eardrums, and every man within a five-yard radius instantly pivots toward me, swords drawn.

Not good.

"Jeremiah, get to the basement. Don't worry about me, just go," I say quietly. I can't take my eyes off the soldiers in front of me to see if the old man is obeying. The soldier who whistled tenses slightly, and I crouch, weapons steady. Obeying some silent signal, the closest row of soldiers—five? six?—rushes me.

The shock of metal clanging against metal reverberates through me, and I block. Duck. Spin and parry only to find another three swords advancing. My vision narrows down to the wall of uniforms in front of me. I slash with my knife, slicing into a soldier's neck. A line of brilliant red spills across his coat and splashes onto my hand.

The blood is warm and sticky, and for one awful second, it's Melkin's blood gushing over my palms to swallow me up in guilt.

That second is all the distraction the soldiers need.

They lunge at me from all sides. I don't know where Jeremiah is. I don't know where *anyone* is. I'm surrounded by soldiers, by the flashing teeth of swords, and it's all I can do to stay alive.

An arrow zings past me and the soldier to my right falls. Another arrow, and a soldier to my left falls as well. I dive to the floor and roll backward as arrows fly over me, mowing down the first line of soldiers.

A second wave of soldiers leaps across the bodies of their fallen comrades, and suddenly Quinn is there. Lashing out with his feet, his hands—tearing through the barrier surrounding me with methodical precision.

"Run!" he yells.

I shove myself to my feet. At the end of the hall, Willow is half-carrying Jeremiah, and they're almost to safety. If we sprint, we can make it before the soldiers cut us off. The heavy, too-long sword slows me down, so I fling it behind me and say, "Let's go."

Quinn grunts, a strange animal-like sound of pain. I whirl around to find a line of blood blossoming from a cut to his leg. The soldier who wounded him raises his sword for another blow, and I lunge forward, my knife braced for impact.

I slam into him, and my knife slides uselessly off his stomach. I forgot about the Dragonskin. I've knocked him off-balance, so his sword misses Quinn, but we're running out of time. Several more soldiers are pressing close behind this one. If any of them get past us, we'll be cut off from our only avenue of escape.

I can't wound his vital organs, but there's more than one way to stop a man. Quinn's foot lashes out and blocks another soldier's sword as it arcs toward me. The blade bites into his boots, and Quinn has to grab onto the wall behind him for balance.

Time to end this.

The soldier in front of me raises his sword arm, and I drop into a crouch seconds before he can impale me on the weapon. Diving forward, I flip in midair and slash at the back of his knees. Before his scream leaves his throat, I spin around and slice into the legs of the two soldiers behind him. Inner thigh. Major artery. Just like Dad taught me.

Quinn shoves the first soldier into the other two, and they fall. We have a few seconds before the next line of soldiers can climb over the bodies of their comrades, and I don't plan to waste them.

"Need help?" I ask, but Quinn is already half-limping, half-running for the open doorway at the end of the hall. I shove my knife into its sheath and follow him at a dead run.

"Get in, get in, get in," I say as I skid around the doorframe and launch myself onto the stairs. Willow slams the door behind us and bolts it. We race past Jeremiah just as Logan reaches the bottom of the steps.

"Carrington?" Logan asks.

"At our backs. We have seconds before they're through the door," I say.

"Thank you," Jeremiah says as he reaches me. His voice shakes. "I was working on the map. I didn't realize they could break down the door so fast, so—"

"You aren't safe, yet. None of us are," I say. "Get in the tunnel."

Above us, booted feet slam into the door and the hinges whine in protest.

"Get in the tunnel!" Logan yells, his voice rolling across the fifty yards that separate us from the mouth of the tunnel. The thirty or so people who still huddle uncertainly in front of the tunnel's mouth flinch. "I can protect you from the Cursed One, but I can't save you from Carrington if you're still in the basement when they come down those stairs."

The people start moving. Grabbing torches. Grabbing each other's hands. But they still aren't going fast enough. We race across the basement, herding stragglers and feeling the weight of Carrington's blades coming closer to our necks with every second that passes. Quinn helps Jeremiah into the tunnel, though with his limp I'm not sure he doesn't need some help himself. The rest of the people still refuse to go underground.

"You have to lead them," I say, and Logan shakes his head.

"I have to detonate the explosives." He gestures toward the string of black metal boxes he attached to the ceiling beams last week.

"We'll do that," Willow says. "Rachel's right. Those people are too afraid to go underground without you."

The door cracks, a loud pop of sound that echoes across the cavernous basement. Logan looks between the door and the tunnel and makes up his mind.

"Here." He thrusts a small copper oval into my hand. A raised lever rests in its center. "You need to be at least ten yards inside the tunnel before you detonate, or you could be buried." His voice is calm, but his face is white, and I understand. I wouldn't want to leave him behind to face an army with nothing but a battery-operated fuse box and a collection of the Commander's explosives for protection.

"We'll be inside the tunnel. Don't worry." I clutch the trigger with clammy hands, and he pulls me against him for a second. I breathe in the scent of him, holding it inside of me with the memory of Oliver's maple-raisin baking and Dad's leather cloak. Then he's gone. Disappearing into the tunnel, torch in hand. Calling out instructions and reassurances in his calm, logical, I've-always-got-a-plan voice.

The door at the opposite end of the room comes off its hinges, and soldiers run toward us.

"Ready?" Willow asks as the last Baalboden survivor hurries into the damp, cool darkness of the tunnel.

"Ready."

She grabs a torch, and we step off the stone floor and onto the dirt. Behind us, the chilling war cry of Carrington fills the air as the army rushes toward us. We run the ten yards Logan said would give us a margin of safety, and then I turn, lock eyes with a soldier who is mere steps away from entering the tunnel on our heels, and flip the lever.

For three excruciating seconds, nothing happens. The soldier reaches the entrance and lunges through. More are closing in. Willow drops to one knee and whips an arrow out of her quiver.

Then the ceiling explodes. Pillars of stone sway and grind against their moorings. Chunks of the floor above slam into the ground. The soldier inside the tunnel looks over his shoulder as the pillars tumble down and the compound collapses in a deafening roar. A cloud of gritty gray dust billows into the tunnel, coating his red uniform as Willow buries an arrow into his neck, and then the mouth of the tunnel crumbles and seals us off from what's left of the basement.

CHAPTER TWELVE

Thunder rumbles, low and ominous, as Willow and I climb out of the tunnel and find Quinn waiting for us, his face calm, but his fists clenched. When he sees us, his hands slowly uncurl and he takes a deep breath. Another crack of thunder rolls across the sky, and the air presses against us as if determined to hold us back. Thick swells of purple-gray clouds seem to touch the tips of the trees as we walk into the northern Wasteland and join the rest of the group.

"You made it," Quinn says, and those three words carry the weight of his fear with shaky fingers.

"Of course we made it," Willow says, her tone sharp, though she slides an arm around her brother's waist and leans against him briefly.

"I was about to go back for you."

"One injury isn't enough for you today?" She shoves her words at him.

"Willow, don't be mean," I say, and she glares at me.

"Please tell me you realize it isn't always up to you to rescue others," she says to Quinn, though she's looking at me.

"I didn't try to rescue you." His voice is as sharp as hers. "I was waiting for you. There's a difference between being worried about someone you love and underestimating their skills."

"Then make sure you know the difference between those you love and those you have no business worrying about."

He lets go of her and won't look at either of us.

Willow is still glaring at me. I shrug and turn away. I can't understand the hidden depths lurking within their conversations, and I don't want to. I have enough trouble navigating the hidden depths of my own words without worrying about anyone else's. Taking a few steps away from them, I scan the survivors who huddle within the Wasteland in near silence.

Logan stands at the front of the crowd with Ian near his side. Drake, Nola, Jodi, and Elias are each seated at the front of a wagon, reins in hand. The donkeys harnessed to the wagons look supremely unconcerned with the entire situation. Frankie and Thom bring up the rear riding the two horses we managed to save. The goats and sheep are attached to a long rope that is held at either end by one of the girls who are usually busy flirting with Ian. Logan catches my eye, and the intensity of his gaze makes my knees unsteady. I'm not sure how to interpret his expression. It's somewhere between I-thought-you-might-not-make-it-out-alive and I'm-about-to-kiss-you-senseless, and my cheeks feel warm as he slowly turns away and gives the order to move forward.

The recruits who attended sparring sessions fan out along the flanks of the group, weapons in hand. Quinn, Willow, and

100

I join them. The line of people stretches out, a long, winding snake with four wagons nestled in its belly. Two wagons carry supplies. Two carry the elderly, those still recovering from the injuries they sustained in Baalboden's fire, and the very young. Eloise is in one of those wagons, Melkin's unborn baby sheltered inside her body. I choose a place along the western flank, as far from her wagon as I can get without joining Frankie and Thom at the rear.

Ahead of me, the front of the line disappears into the Wasteland, following the faint outline of an old road now overgrown with grass and underbrush. Somewhere at my back, the ruins of Baalboden crouch behind the Wall. I no longer wait to feel the grief of leaving it all behind me. The silence within me absorbs the pain and gives me nothing in return.

Dark green moss clings to tree trunks and belly-crawls across the ground. Drifts of black and silver ash hug the underbrush briefly, only to skim the ground again with the next gust of wind. Once upon a time, those ashes were someone's home inside Baalboden. Someone's family. Now they're a formless monument to destruction, forever condemned to wander.

I touch the pouch hanging from my neck, the one Quinn gave me so I could carry some dirt from my father's grave. I've since added ashes from my home in Baalboden, and I squeeze the soft leather as if by hanging on to the dirt and ashes I carry, I can somehow find a connection to the girl I used to be. But just like my final glimpse of Baalboden, the remains of my former life leave me hollow inside. Letting go of the pouch, I slide my fingers up until I grasp the delicate pendant Logan gave to me.

The promise he spoke when he fastened the chain around

my neck echoes in my head: *I will always find you.* And he had. He'd built a tracking device into the battered copper cuff I wear around my arm. He'd blown up his cell in the Commander's dungeon, escaped beneath the Wall, and trekked across dangerous territory in the Wasteland just to find me. And he'd pushed past the shock and the damage to show me that as long as we love each other, we haven't lost everything.

I can't admit to him that even with his promises, even with his love, I still feel lost.

Thunder cracks again, a slap of sound that vibrates through my bones like a physical blow. I glance at the treetops piercing the bruised sky and wonder how far we'll get before the storm that's brewing unleashes its fury on us.

Ahead of me, Quinn bends to pull a handful of graceful, fernlike leaves from a scrubby-looking bush. Folding them in half, he packs them against the wound in his thigh and then pushes the torn edge of his pant leg against it to keep them in place.

Willow steps to my side and says, "Achillea plant. To stop the bleeding."

"If he'd been carrying a weapon, he might not be injured right now."

Her dark eyes snap with sudden fury. "If he hadn't met *you*, he wouldn't be injured right now."

"Excuse me?"

She whips her bow up to aim at my face, but I slap it aside with my Switch before she can position the arrow.

"Are you crazy?" I snap as people around us begin to stare. "What are you trying to prove?"

"Just seeing if your reactions are always poor, or if you only choke when it really counts." She tucks the arrow back into her quiver and slings the bow over her shoulder without once breaking eye contact with me.

I match her glare with one of my own. "My reactions are fine."

"You're impulsive, and you freeze at the sight of blood. That's a dangerous combination considering the kind of enemies we have." She gestures toward the tunnel now many yards behind us.

"I'm not—"

"You ran toward an army with nothing but your knife so you could try to save the life of an old man you don't even really care about."

"Jeremiah is one of ours." My voice shakes. "Maybe *you* could leave him behind, but I can't."

The wind whips her silver ear cuff, tugging at the black feather that brushes her shoulders. She keeps talking like I haven't said a word. "And then you hesitated. You wounded a man. You had the opportunity to shove him into the soldiers behind him and run for cover, but as soon as his blood hit your hands, you froze, and my brother had to rescue you. Again."

The angry words I want to fling at her shrivel up, and I look away. She isn't finished.

"I don't get it. The Rachel I first met would've taken out that man and the two beside him without even flinching. Now you rush into danger with no escape plan. No spine for doing what it takes to win. What happened?"

Anger is a sudden brilliant fire warming the emptiness inside of me. Turning, I spit my words in her face. "*What happened?*

You were there for most of it. My city is destroyed. Most of the people I knew are dead." I lean closer. "Melkin is dead. My father is *dead*."

The silence within me shivers as my words scrape against it. I imagine cracks across its surface, the terrible depths of grief and guilt buried beneath it a yawning mouth of unending darkness. I'm not ready to dive in. Not ready to be swept under when I have no safety rope to keep me tethered to my sanity.

Willow watches me, a challenge in her eyes. "Except for Quinn, all of the people I knew are lost to me now. And my father is dead, too. You don't see me hesitating when it comes to survival."

Her words sting, but I take a deep breath and try to sound calm. "I didn't know about your dad. I'm sorry he died."

"I'm not," she says. The coldness in her voice makes me wrap my cloak tighter around myself. "But that isn't the point. You need to figure yourself out, Rachel. Either you're going to help us fight our battles no matter what it takes, or you need to go ride in a wagon with the elderly."

"You never cared about my choices before. Why start now?"

"Because until I saw my brother shield you with his body, I had no idea your actions might hurt the one person I still love." She grips her bow with bloodless fingers. "He's saved you twice now. And this time it hurt him."

"I didn't ask to be saved. I don't need him to protect me."

"Try telling *him*. I can't convince him that you aren't his responsibility. So I'm talking to you instead." She leans closer. "Stop deliberately putting yourself in danger unless you're sure you won't choke. Start paying attention. You lost people you loved. Others did too. You killed a man. Others have too. You don't have the luxury of losing your edge, Rachel, because if you do anything—*anything*—that costs my brother his life, I will make you pay for it."

Turning on her heel, she grabs a low-hanging branch and vaults into the closest tree as the skies split wide open and streams of icy gray water plummet to the ground.

I turn my back on the ruins of Baalboden one final time, and start walking.

CHAPTER THIRTEEN

<u>LOGAN</u>

Ian walks beside me as I lead the group toward what I'm hoping will be a usable campsite for the night. According to Jeremiah, we have only another hour or so to walk before we get to a large rock that will shelter us from at least some of the elements.

Rain is a merciless companion as we struggle through the Wasteland. It pools on our shoulders, our hoods, and our boots, chilling us to the bone. It flattens the grass with quick-moving streams of mud and lashes stray twigs and leaves from the trees above us. It drastically reduces visibility.

It's the best travel companion I could've hoped for.

Highwaymen won't brave the storm, so we're safe from them for the moment. And the sudden streams that make walking difficult also wipe the land clean behind us, destroying all evidence of our passage. Unless the Commander is able to track our wristmark signals, he won't know which way we went once we reached the Wasteland.

We've traveled hard for most of the day and have seen no sign of the army at our backs. Even the rain can't dampen the relief I feel. A relief I see echoed on most of the faces around me. We're free of the Commander. Free of the threat of Rowansmark coming after us.

For the first time in three weeks, I feel like I can breathe.

It's a temporary reprieve. Once the storm passes, the water that wipes our tracks away will become mud that holds the proof of our journey in sharp relief. We have to put as much distance between us and our starting point as possible before then.

A tree in front of me shakes gently, and Quinn drops from a low branch and walks toward me. He's limping.

"Tree leaping instead of walking?" Ian asks beside me.

Quinn shrugs. "It's how I was trained to travel. Leaves fewer signs for a tracker to follow and offers better visibility. Even in the rain." He pulls a slim sheaf of papers from beneath his tunic and thrusts them at me. "Jeremiah's map. He says the terrain gets tricky in the next two hundred yards or so and wanted you to have this."

I roll up the papers and tuck them into an inner cloak pocket where they'll remain dry. "What happened to your leg?"

"Got sliced by a sword."

"How deep?"

He waves his hand in the air as if swatting away any concern I might feel. "It's superficial. I'll be fine in a day or two."

"What happened?"

"Jeremiah was in the hall when Carrington broke down the compound's door. Rachel went to rescue him. Willow and I helped."

"You'd be better able to protect yourself if you carried a sword of your own."

"That's not an option."

I swipe rain out of my eyes and look at him. His dark hair is plastered to his head, and his shoulders are hunched against the downpour, but his eyes are full of resolve.

"Do you need to ride in a wagon until the leg heals?"

He raises a brow. "I think you just insulted my manhood."

I smile. "I think you're right. Sorry about that."

Before he can leave, I reach out and clasp his shoulder. "Thank you. For bringing the map and for helping Rachel. Both with Jeremiah and with the Commander."

He holds my gaze for a moment and then says, "Happy to help."

"I hope you mean that, because I need to ask you for a favor. It's about Rachel." I pause, but I can't think of any way to ask for help protecting her that doesn't make it sound like I think less of her skills. I don't. I respect her tremendously. I also understand her, which means I know without a doubt that if the Commander is within reach again, every cautious word I've spoken, every careful plan we've constructed, will turn to ash in the flames of her need for vengeance.

"I'm always kept busy now," I say, gesturing toward the crowd behind us. "And while Rachel is very capable of taking care of herself in a fight, if the Commander shows up again . . . he hurt her." I push the memory of Rachel, broken and silent after Oliver's death, away from me. "If he's near her, I don't know what she might do."

"I know what she'll do," Ian says, grudging admiration in his voice. "She'll kill him. Probably while extracting as much pain from him as she can. You have to admire that kind of dedication."

"And what would be left of her when she finished?" Quinn asks. Ian looks away, and Quinn locks eyes with me. "She won't sacrifice herself on my watch."

"Thank you." The words are inadequate, but they're all I have.

As Quinn hoists himself into the closest tree again, Ian asks, "What's his story?"

"What do you mean?" I glance at the crowd behind me, their chins tucked down and their cloaks clutched close to their throats as they trudge through the rain. I can't see Rachel, though I know she's near the back of the line. The people walk slowly, mud sucking at their boots, and I bite back a surge of impatience. I want to prod everyone to move faster. To ignore the discomfort and do what it takes to survive.

"He's a Tree Person. Why is he with us? Why doesn't he carry a weapon when he's clearly been trained for battle?" Ian asks, and I face the trail again as it starts a gentle curve toward the northeast.

"He's with us because he chooses to be. And his reasons for not carrying a weapon are his own." The faint road we're traveling winds up a steep hill, which will impact the amount of time it will take to get to a place suitable for making camp. At this point, I'm worried we'll still be trying to travel at night. Without the ability to see roots, bushes, or holes in the path, we'd destroy a wagon or two for sure. I start calculating the distance we've traveled and the yardage we still need to cover. At our current rate of speed, and factoring in the weather—

"Okay." Ian holds up his hands as if to show he meant no harm. "So what are your plans once we reach Lankenshire?"

The mathematical equation in my head dissolves, and I say sharply, "I already discussed my plans at our group meeting yesterday."

"Fine. Don't tell me," Ian says, and something in his voice makes me study him closely. His fists are clenched, and the set of his mouth is mutinous.

"What's your problem?" I ask.

He bends with me to lift a fallen branch out of the path and toss it into the forest. It lands among the oak trees with a wet thud.

"I know what this is about. I'm not stupid." He tugs his cloak closer to his body and walks a little faster.

Gritting my teeth, I catch up to him. "I have no idea what you're talking about, Ian, and I have very little time or energy to try to figure it out. In case you haven't noticed, I have a group of scared, inexperienced travelers to lead through the Wasteland and a furious tyrant with an army at our backs. If you have an issue with me, either say it plainly or drop it."

"You don't trust me."

I stare at him like I'm questioning his sanity, and he says, "Now that you know my background, you don't trust me. You treat me differently."

He's wrong. I haven't had a second to even *think* about Ian since we had our conversation in the tunnel. I've been too busy trying to keep everyone safe from Carrington's swords. I'm about to tell him he's imagining things when I notice the tight line of his shoulders. The way his I-don't-really-care expression is plastered to his face like a shield.

How many times in my childhood did I look like that after I'd scrounged up the courage to beg a merchant for an odd job or a bit of spare food? It's the look of a boy expecting to be kicked but too proud to show you that it hurts.

Choosing my words with care, I say, "I'm sorry I gave you that impression, but I really haven't thought about your Brute Squad background since we discussed it. If you think my unwillingness to discuss what little I know of Quinn means I don't trust you, you're wrong."

"You talk to Drake, Thom, Frankie, Quinn, Willow, Nola, and Rachel about your plans. You listen to their opinions before you make decisions."

A headache is beginning to throb behind my eyes. Between Ian's ability to turn the girls in camp into giggling, starry-eyed creatures and his apparent need for my approval, I'm beginning to wish he hadn't volunteered for guard duty. It would be easier if he'd wanted to cook, or chop wood, or anything that didn't require direct contact with me.

"I volunteered to fight off Carrington at the gate so that you and Rachel could make it back inside because I believed you were different from the Commander. That you were a leader who would listen to your people, not just to the few who already agree with you."

His voice is quiet, but his words leave a mark.

Taking a deep breath, I say, "You've earned the right to speak your mind to me. But honestly, there's nothing new to share. My plan is to get us safely to Lankenshire, demonstrate that Rowansmark has deliberately built tech that can destroy any city-state whose leader opposes them, and then prove my words by telling them what happened to Baalboden."

We skirt a large puddle, and I glance behind me again. Not because I expect to see my people moving any faster, but because the tension that grips me insists I search the surrounding Wasteland for flashes of red-jacketed soldiers running toward us in the rain.

"Have you considered that you might be starting problems between Rowansmark and Lankenshire that don't need to exist?" Ian asks.

"What do you mean? I thought that of anyone here, you'd be happy to have a city-state ready to stand up to Rowansmark, since your father died there."

"I don't hold Rowansmark personally responsible for my father's death." There's a thread of ugly viciousness in his voice that promises retribution for the man he does blame. I can't help but be grateful to have another person in the group who truly understands the depths of the Commander's evil, and who knows that stopping him permanently is the only possible option.

He wipes at the streams of water that sluice over his cheekbones where his hood fails to cover him, and looks at me. "Lankenshire is a city of scholars. Healers. Most of them prefer books instead of swords." He says this like he can't fathom the absurdity of such a thing.

"And you know all of this . . . how?"

He rolls his eyes. "I apprenticed to take my father's place. Who do you think traveled with the Commander when he visited the other city-states? Regular guards? Please."

"So you've been to Lankenshire?"

He shakes his head. "My trip to Rowansmark was my first and only mission outside of Baalboden. My apprenticeship required a deeper study of each of the nine city-states. But every boy in the group knows Lankenshire is a city of scholars. We studied them in school."

Ah, school. Something as an outcast I was never allowed to attend. Not that it stopped me from learning. I have Oliver and Jared to thank for that, though I didn't have a chance to tell Jared. I never expected him to die in the Wasteland and leave Rachel and me alone. I have to hope that somehow he knew what he meant to me.

What he still means to me.

"My point is that Lankenshire won't be prepared for this. They can't stand up to Rowansmark—"

"No one can. Don't you see?" My voice is too loud, and I work to speak calmly. Ian has surprised me once again. Clearly, his Brute Squad training was incomplete if he's actually concerned about the welfare of a group of strangers. "If Rowansmark is the only city-state that can harness the Cursed One and use it at their whim, *no one* is safe. The only way to stand up to them is to inform the other leaders of the situation and then get busy building tech that can match theirs."

"So you really mean to do it? Copy their design and build weapons to match it? Give every single leader, regardless of his moral compass, a weapon of that magnitude?"

"I don't think I have a choice."

He's silent for a moment and then asks, "Can you build it fast enough to protect Lankenshire from both Carrington and Rowansmark?"

I have no idea. It depends on what tech supplies Lankenshire has. On how fast I can interpret the nuances of the device currently strapped to my chest. On how fast the Commander tracks us down.

Best Case Scenario: We reach Lankenshire safely, they listen to me and agree to an alliance, and I'm able to quickly duplicate the device.

Worst Case Scenario: We're caught before we reach the city-state, Lankenshire refuses to work with me, or the tech is beyond my skills.

Ian is watching me, his question still lingering in the air, and even though I know he wants to be taken in my confidence, I can't bear to put into words the thought of failing. As we crest the top of the hill and start down the other side, I meet his eyes and say with as much confidence as I can muster, "Yes. I can duplicate the tech in time to protect us all."

As the rain lets up and the late afternoon sun begins baking the ground we travel, I pull Jeremiah's map from my cloak pocket and begin planning tomorrow's route, hoping that somehow I can deliver on everything I've promised.

CHAPTER FOURTEEN

RACHEL

We make camp on the eastern edge of a small clearing. The rain stopped hours ago, but my cloak has yet to dry. Once we've erected our shelters and eaten a cold dinner—Logan refused to allow torches or cooking fires in case Carrington is following us already—I hang my cloak over the thick tree limb that props open the jagged canvas flap of the tent I share with Logan and crawl into my bedroll.

I expect to lie awake, listening for threats. Thinking about the Commander. Trying to figure out how to make a plan to separate him from Carrington's army so that I can honor Logan's wishes if possible.

But instead, the soft carpet of moss beneath my blanket cushions my body, and the sight of Logan hunched over his tech bag, muttering to himself while he tries to work by starlight, makes me feel safe. Before I know it, my eyelids drift closed, and I sink into the dark embrace of sleep.

Blood surrounds me. It stains the sky with viscous swirls of crimson and snakes down tree trunks to drip from leaves. Thick garnet drops cling to me. I raise my hands above my head to ward it off, but it flows over me in a river of rust. Sticky trails of heat bite into my skin and burrow toward the bone. Tilting my face up, I stare in horror. The blood has drained from the sky and abandoned the trees. Instead, it leaks from my fingertips and gushes from my palms, an unending tide that covers me from head to toe.

"*Guilty,*" it whispers, and Melkin lies beneath my blade, calling for his wife.

"*Alone,*" it says, and Dad turns to dust beneath the shining white cross on his grave.

"*Broken,*" it cries, and Oliver's cold hands grasp mine while the bloody wound in his neck pours and pours and pours.

Their voices waver, solidify, and then join together into one deafening stream of accusations. *Guilty, alone, broken. Guilty, alone, broken.*

Worms, pale and wriggling, pour from Dad's mouth, leak out of Melkin's eyes, and squirm in the gaping wound at Oliver's neck.

I scream and the crimson crawling over me slides past my lips and coats my tongue with bitterness. I gasp for air, but the blood is there instead. Tearing at my throat and plunging down to fill my chest, my stomach, and my lungs. I can't breathe.

I can't *breathe.*

"Shh," someone says.

Another scream gathers at the back of my throat and claws its way through the blood filling my mouth.

"It's all right," someone says.

I stretch my lips wide, seeking air that refuses to come. Something warm and heavy presses against my cheek. Jerking my head to the side, I snatch a quick breath of blood-tainted air.

"Rachel. Wake up."

My eyes fly open. A shadow looms over me, blotting out the faint light from the tent's doorway. The shadow's hand rests against my cheek, pressing close.

I whip my knife up and aim for the throat. The shadow twists, water-quick. Grabbing my wrist with its free hand, it slams my arm to the ground with enough force to knock my weapon loose.

I dig my heels in and wrench my body to the side. The shadow pins me and leans down.

"Shh, it's Logan," he says quietly against my ear.

It takes a moment for his words to penetrate the panic. My heart pounds against my chest, and my lungs are convinced I don't have enough air. Not nearly enough air.

"Rachel?"

Slowly, the scent of blood fades, and I exhale, forcing my muscles to relax beneath him.

He releases his grip on my wrist and slowly slides his hand over mine, tangling our fingers together. I press my palm to his, desperate to imprint his skin where seconds ago the slick heat of blood had poured.

"Are you okay?" he asks.

My body shakes, my teeth chattering like I've been left out in the cold for hours, but I say, "I'm fine."

It's a lie, and we both know it, but I can't bear to remember. I can't bear to strip myself down to nothing but the blood that haunts my dreams. If I let it into my waking hours, I might drown in it.

"You're shaking," he says, but what he means is, "You're lying."

"I'm cold."

He pulls me close, fits me against his side like a puzzle piece that was always meant to be there, and warmth seeps onto my skin.

"Rachel, please talk to me," he whispers, but the voices in my head are louder.

Guilty. Alone. Broken.

A chorus that sounds like the only truth I have left. I push it away from me with desperate strength. I refuse to feel it. I *refuse*. It sinks into the silence, but I still feel covered in blood and shame. Logan leans closer, his dark blue eyes filled with worry, and opens his mouth as if to ask me another question. I don't want to talk. I don't want to sift through the nightmare and find the reasons behind it. I just want it all to go away.

"What happened—"

I raise my head to kiss him, swallowing the rest of his words.

My lips are harsh. My hands grip his arms. Claw his shoulders. Pull him closer until I can't taste the blood. I can't suffocate from it. I can't hear Oliver, Dad, or Melkin whispering in my head.

This is what I need. This will make it better.

I wrap my leg around his, and he makes a tortured noise at the back of his throat. I kiss him hard enough to hurt—a tiny bite of pain against my lips that feels *real*.

"Rachel—"

He pulls away, and I follow him. Clinging. Desperate to bring him back.

"Wait," he says, his voice breathless. "Just wait a minute."

"Why?" I curl my fingers around the back of his neck and tug him toward me. "We're alone in our shelter. We can do whatever we want. There's no one here to stop us."

He closes his eyes for a moment, and then looks at me. I can't read his expression. "I'm stopping us."

I let go of the back of his neck and my hand falls to my side.

"It's not because I don't want . . . um . . ." He gives me a look that is apparently supposed to suffice for the rest of his sentence.

"Me?"

"Yes. I want you, Rachel." He lies back and wipes a hand over his face. "I really do. But I don't think this is about wanting something between the two of us. At least, not for you."

My teeth start chattering again. "Fine."

"No, it isn't *fine*. It is anything but fine."

I pull my blanket over my shoulders and wrap my arms around my chest. "Just forget it."

"I don't want to."

"Well, I do."

He's silent for a long moment. Long enough for me to realize my words might have hurt him. Long enough to feel regret.

"I'm sorry," I say, though I don't know how to put into words everything I'm sorry for.

He rolls onto his side, facing me. "When you kiss me, I want it to be because you're thinking of me. Because you really want *me*. Not because you're trying to distract me from something you don't want to talk about."

I look away. At the silver wash of moonlight seeping in through the entrance of our tent. At the tufts of springy grass our bedrolls don't cover. At anything but him.

"I didn't mean to use you. I didn't really think it through." I scrunch down into my blanket. "I just . . . I can't . . . I wanted something real. Something to make the stuff inside of my head fade away. And what we have is the most solid thing in my life, so . . ."

"I understand," he says softly.

"Do you?"

"I am kind of irresistible." He wiggles his brows at me.

I laugh, and the lingering tension leaves my body. He grins at me, a funny, lopsided smile that wraps around me like comfort. He scoots closer to me and runs his fingers through my hair, gently tugging at the knots he finds.

"I'm sorry," he says. "I just want to be here for you."

"I'm here for you, too," I say. "I'm not the only one who lost family."

Pain brackets his mouth and fans out from his eyes, and I slide my arm out of the blanket to press it against his chest. My fingers curve over the flesh and bone that shelter his heart. A heart strong enough to keep moving forward even when he's lost so much. Strong enough to lead even when he doesn't want to.

Strong enough to commit to me when I know I'm not an easy person to love.

"You could kiss me now," he says, his voice low.

I smile. "Could I?"

"Yes." He sounds breathless.

"Are you sure? Because I wouldn't want to overstep or—"

"Rachel—"

"—make you uncomfortable, or—"

"Just *kiss* me."

"—take advantage of poor helpless Logan."

He leans down and covers my mouth with his. This time, I kiss him not to forget or to drown anything out, but because he's Logan, and he's mine. And then he holds me close as sleep overtakes him. I lie beside him, clinging to his warmth and desperately trying to stay awake as long as possible so that I can savor this before I'm once again plunged into a world of blood, loss, and unbearable guilt.

CHAPTER FIFTEEN

RACHEL

Sunlight pours through the gap at our shelter's entrance as I stretch my back and shove my blanket to my knees. Logan is gone, and by the sounds of the camp outside my shelter, I can tell most people are up and moving around. My stomach grumbles as I yank my fingers through my hair and splash my face with water I saved from last night's ration.

When I've finished, I shake the dust off my trousers and then consider which tunic to wear. We were lucky to recover enough clothing to give everyone two changes of clothes.

We were less lucky in the recovery of laundry soap.

Either that or the girls who are desperate to catch the eye of one of our few available boys are hiding the soap for themselves. I seem to recall that a few of our sparring participants smelled suspiciously like a spring meadow.

I sniff the tunics, choose the cleanest, and decide to take Willow up on her offer to teach me how to make soap. Shoving my feet into my boots, I strap on my knife, lace up my travel pack, and exit the shelter.

The camp is busy. The older men and women beat dust out of clothing and then place them into travel packs or on blankets that will be filled with light supplies, tied off with rope, and carried over the shoulder. The younger ones sharpen weapons, tear down shelters, and load the wagons.

Hoping I'm still early enough to get a breakfast ration, I head toward the canteen wagon. When I get there, Adam, Elias, and Willow are packing up the last of the morning rations. Willow is laughing while Adam waves his hands around, telling a story in a voice free of the hostility I'm used to hearing from him. I beg a piece of oat bread and a healthy dollop of goat cheese from Elias, who stares at me like I'm up on the Claiming stage until I tell him if he can't find something better to do with his eyes, I'll remove them from his face.

Turning from Elias, who suddenly finds the task of packing up the food far more interesting than looking at me, I jump when Quinn suddenly appears next to me. My bread goes flying out of my hand and nearly slaps him in the face.

He leaps back and catches it before it hits the ground. "Throwing food at me?"

"You startled me." I grab my breakfast from him and take a bite.

"Next time I'll announce my intention to walk up to you at least three minutes before I actually arrive." His face is as stoic as ever, but a gleam of sly laughter lurks in his dark eyes.

Huh. Quinn has a sense of humor. Who knew?

"I think you'd look good in goat cheese. Might be an improvement." I poke his chest and take another bite.

His left brow climbs toward his hairline. "Did you just insult me?"

"Only if you disagree with my opinion."

He smiles slowly. "Do you have plans this morning?"

I shrug.

"I was hoping you could help me decide which weapons to assign to which trainees."

I look him up and down—battered leather pants, half-laced tunic, scuffed boots—and see no evidence of a weapon of his own. "And which weapon to assign to you, too, right?"

The laughter disappears from his eyes, and he starts walking toward the wagons. "I don't carry a weapon anymore. And I'm getting tired of making that clear to both you and Logan."

I hurry to catch up to him, stuffing the last of my breakfast in my mouth and swallowing quickly. "You need one. We have a lot of enemies—"

He turns on his heel and stops directly in my path. I nearly plow into him, and manage to sidestep just in time.

"No." His voice is cold, but something burns in his eyes.

"I know you're good. I saw it for myself when you fought Carrington outside the gate." I look away for a moment as I remember his promise to stay by my side and sacrifice himself with me so I could have my shot at the Commander. "But you'd be even better with a weapon." And by better, I mean safer.

"Do you really think I need a sword to destroy any threat that comes at me?"

I cross my arms and stare him down. "How should I know what you're capable of?"

"Because I told you."

It takes a moment to realize he means the conversation we had in the Wasteland when he told me he'd once killed a man he wasn't sure deserved it. "You told me you—" A woman walks by us, a large basket of dandelion greens cradled in her arms. I lower my voice. "You told me you killed a man, but that doesn't mean you can constantly fight trained predators without a weapon in your hand and expect to live." I gesture toward his leg. "You got cut the last time you fought. Next time, it could be much worse. You're good, Quinn, but not good enough to keep taking on armed soldiers and expect to survive. Be reasonable."

"I can do damage enough with my bare hands. I'm not changing my mind on this."

Oh, how cute. He thinks he can out-stubborn me.

"I'm not changing my mind, either," I say, my voice a harsh whisper between us. "We have enemies. Real enemies. And a bunch of untrained people who will probably panic and forget which end of the sword to grab if we're ever attacked. We need you to be able to help."

"You don't think I helped yesterday? And the day before?"

"You did. But how long could you have held out if they'd cornered you? It was only a matter of time." I blow a wayward strand of hair out of my face. "Look, Willow told me you don't like to even spar anymore, and now you've had to fight soldiers twice in two days. I get that it goes against your principles. I know I'm asking a lot, but—"

"But you know best?"

I jerk back as if he slapped me, but he isn't finished.

"You know what I need? You know better than me that I should change my decision to remain unarmed?"

I open my mouth. Close it. Feel heat stain my cheeks.

His expression softens a little. "If we're under attack, I'll help, Rachel. I won't let anyone down. But I'm not going to pick up a blade again, and nothing you say will change that."

The heat in my face gushes through my body, and I grip my Switch as I step closer to him. "So you'll just die, then? Just cling to your precious convictions and go up against men with swords to prove something to yourself? Fine. Go ahead. Die and be justified that you did it on your own terms. What do I care?"

I turn before he can see the tremble in my lips. Before the image of yet another person I care about bleeding to death in front of me can bring my breakfast up the back of my throat. I've walked five steps in the opposite direction when his hand descends on my shoulder.

I whirl and swing my Switch at him before I realize what I'm doing. He disappears. One second, he was standing before me, about to be hit with the weighted end of my weapon. The next, he's rolling across the grass and coming up to stand a yard to my left.

My fingers tremble as I grip my weapon, and sick horror crawls up the back of my throat. I could've hurt him. But stronger than the horror is the rage that begs me to take another swing at him. To change his mind, through force if necessary. To make him see that he can't make me care about him and then take risks like it's *nothing*.

"Want to take a swing at me?" he asks. "Will that cure the nightmares and let you feel alive again?"

I throw my Switch to the ground and charge, my fists flying toward his chest. He blocks the blow with effortless grace, faster than I expected. Faster than I've ever seen.

I swing again and again, but he parries every blow. His movements are controlled and powerful, and I realize he could hurt me. He could hurt me badly, and I'd never be able to stop it.

He catches my fist as I take one more halfhearted swing, his grip gentle. My lips are salty, and it takes a moment to realize I'm crying.

"Do you feel better?" he asks, and the compassion in his voice makes me want to hit him again.

I don't need his understanding and his sympathy. I just need to be left alone to pick up the pieces of my life, deliver the survivors to safety, and then kill the man who ruined me.

My tears dry slowly, and the rage disappears with them. The silence within me absorbs them both. Stepping back from Quinn, I wipe my hands on my pants and refuse to look at him.

"You don't have to worry about me." His voice is still gentle. "I can handle myself."

I want to hurt him for making me worry. For making me cry when I have to be strong. I want to, but he doesn't deserve it, and I've had enough of hurting those who haven't earned it to last me for the rest of my life.

I bend to pick up my Switch, and then say, "You've clearly been well trained."

He remains silent.

I meet his eyes, feeling raw inside at the way he watches me. "You're more than qualified to choose which trainee should carry which weapon. I have something else I have to do."

Without waiting for a response, I walk away. Across the clearing. Through the eastern edge of camp and deep into the shadowy depths of the Wasteland with its scrubby ferns and spongy moss, its reverent stillness and its well-kept secrets. I keep my head held high and my shoulders straight, though there's no one left to see it. I won't look weak and broken again. Not for Quinn. Not for anyone.

CHAPTER SIXTEEN

LOGAN

It's been four days since we left Baalboden behind, and there's still no sign of the Commander and his army. My steps feel lighter with every day that passes, even though whoever sabotaged the machine is still playing stupid pranks around camp. A bag of grain sliced open and spilled. A wagon canvas slashed. Petty things. I even found another note lying on my bedroll when I entered my tent one night. It said, *Justice requires sacrifice.* I refuse to allow some disgruntled prankster with a penchant for drama to get to me. Not when we're still enjoying the triumph of outwitting the Commander and breaking his control over us.

We've traveled northeast, following the broken outline of a road from the previous civilization. Thick weeds and clumps of grass shove their way through the faded gray stone, and monstrous tree roots reduce entire portions of the road to crumbled pieces. In some sections, the path disappears completely, overtaken by the ever-encroaching vegetation of the Wasteland.

Rachel walks beside me, twenty yards ahead of the group,

her cloak billowing in the stiff wind that plunges through the trees. Skinny maples and scattered evergreens creak beneath the onslaught.

While every step we take away from Baalboden and the Commander buoys me with a sense of freedom, the opposite seems to be true for Rachel. She grows more and more withdrawn—turned inward toward whatever thoughts haunt her until she realizes I'm watching her. Then she'll smile and talk and focus on the task at hand, but it's a thin mask that barely covers the truth.

I don't know what to do about it when she refuses to tell me what's bothering her.

Ian walks a few yards behind us, a girl on each arm. He talks to them as they walk, and the girls blush and giggle like he just offered to Claim them. I don't know how he does it. I have a hard enough time figuring out what to say to Rachel, and I've known her most of my life. The thought of carrying on a flirtatious conversation with two girls at once makes my stomach feel like I ingested an unstable element.

The rest of the group lags behind Ian and his girls by a good ten yards. I've asked Quinn and Willow to hunt for tonight's meal, and they've promised to catch up to us again by sundown. If I had my way, we'd travel without stopping until twilight, but most of the survivors won't make it another two hundred yards without a rest.

"We'll stop for lunch soon," I say to Rachel as another gust of wind slaps me in the face. "Jeremiah's map shows a large clearing of some sort about fifty yards after an old sign."

Rachel glances around us. "What old sign? There's nothing

out here but broken-down road and Wasteland."

As if to prove her wrong, several yards ahead something gleams copper and brown beneath the thick carpet of moss that covers the forest floor. I stride forward and crouch to pull moss and vines away from what looks like a narrow road made of two parallel metal bars nailed into rotting planks of wood. The corroded metal is rough beneath my fingers as I run my hand along it. The road bisects the path and disappears into the Wasteland, where vines and tree roots hide it from sight.

"It's a railroad track," Rachel says, shoving the toe of her boot against the metal bar I'm touching. "Dad showed me one on a trip once. He said the earlier civilization had giant wagons called trains that hitched together and ran on fuel instead of horses and donkeys. This was the road the trains used."

I stand slowly, my eyes still on the track. "Can you imagine being able to travel from city-state to city-state without walking? Of course, we'd have to build better roads. And we'd have to figure out a way to build trains that are quiet enough to escape the Cursed One's notice—or maybe equip the trains with the same sonic pulse that repels the beast. I bet I could—"

"Hey!" Rachel snaps her fingers in front of my face, and I realize the rest of the group has nearly caught up to us. "Before you decide to invent super-quiet trains with sonic weapons mounted on the front, maybe we should find that old sign and stop for lunch."

I grin. She smiles back, and the shadows momentarily lift from her eyes.

"You're right. Besides, I have enough inventions to worry about at the moment without adding another one to the mix."

"How's that going? Are we still going to be able to drop these people off at Lankenshire and then go hunt down the Commander?" She steps across the tracks, and I follow as the broken road beneath us curves through a sparse clump of trees.

"*If* Lankenshire makes an alliance with us—"

"Of course they will." She kicks a chunk of crumbled stone off the trail before it can snag a wagon wheel or trip an unwary traveler. "You'll have a replica of Rowansmark's device to offer them. They'd have to be pretty stupid to turn that down."

The Rowansmark tech is easy to use, but hard to duplicate. The internal wiring is a braided copper wire, sixteen gauge. The mechanisms that make up the levers are obviously handcrafted out of paper-thin silver. I don't have anything in our salvage wagon, or in the bag of tech supplies I recovered from the abandoned armory in Lower Market where I'd stashed a few backup plans, that's comparable to either the braided wire or the silver. And everything else I've tried has failed. Without the ability to duplicate the device, and with the worry that it will somehow malfunction when I need it most, I've settled for increasing the power in the booster I built for it, even though it now uses all but two of my remaining batteries. I may not be able to replicate Rowansmark's tech yet, but I can improve it.

All of which does nothing to help me broker an alliance with Lankenshire, because I have no intention of handing over the only working model.

"I still have some issues with the Rowansmark design," I say as we pass an evergreen whose top half has snapped off and balances haphazardly on the thin arms of the tree beside it. Placing my hand on the small of Rachel's back, I guide us both away from the tree and shout a warning back to the others as well. In wind like this, we don't want to take any chances.

"What about the device you're building to find the Commander?" she asks, and it's clear from the impatience in her voice that this is the only invention she truly cares about.

"It's coming along." Something else gleams beneath the thick greenery of the Wasteland. Something just off the path, about fifteen yards ahead of us.

"How can you be sure it works? Don't you need his individual wristmark signature? Not that we couldn't just search for the bright red Carrington uniforms, I guess."

"I have his signature." I quicken my pace as I see rusted metal poles, laced with vines, stabbing the ground like twin legs braced several yards apart. "I traded six fully functioning cloaking devices once to get it because I thought I might need it someday."

"And you just happened to have stashed it with your extra tech at the armory?"

I turn to face her as we reach the metal poles. Something large is bolted to the rods, about halfway up, but the vines obscure it.

"Memorized it." I tap my temple with my finger. "I didn't want to write it down and get caught with it in case the Commander ever had cause to search my house. Plus, I couldn't risk misplacing something so important."

She smiles, but her eyes are fierce. "I love that you always think five steps ahead."

"I seem to recall you once comparing my plans to an overly cautious grandmother crossing Central Square."

"Well, I was still mad at you for everything when I said that."

"And by 'everything' you mean my clumsy use of logic and

reason to turn you down when you told me you loved me on your fifteenth birthday?"

She winces. "Don't remind me. It's still humiliating."

I frown. "Why? You did nothing wrong."

A pink glow suffuses her cheeks. "I embarrassed myself. Throwing myself at my father's apprentice because I was so sure you felt the same. What an idiot." She refuses to look at me.

I wrap my arm around her waist and lean down until my lips are right beside her ear. Quietly, I say, "I used to feel like someone sucked all the oxygen out of the room whenever you came near me. I would sit at your father's dinner table, eating his food and discussing my job requirements, and I would have to force myself not to study the way the lamplight turned your hair into flames." My voice lowers. "You reminded me of fire—brilliant, warm, and strong. And every time you brushed against me, I felt like I'd swallowed some of that fire, and that if your father looked at me then he'd know it."

"Really?" Her voice is low and breathless.

"Really."

"You told me you didn't love me," she says, and there's a tiny note of hurt in her voice.

"I told you the truth. I didn't love you, then." My arm tightens around her waist. "But being near you was like waving my hand through a lit torch, hoping I might get burned just a little. I thought that was just the way a boy feels when he's near a girl. I didn't realize the feeling was specific to *you*."

She laughs and leans into me. "You also told me I'd get over you."

"I've been known to be wrong," I say, and kiss her before she can say anything else. She rolls her eyes, but kisses me back until Ian whistles appreciatively behind us.

Laughing, I step back from Rachel and turn to the vine-clad rectangle that looms above us. Grabbing a handful of thick, rubbery kudzu, I tug sharply and the entire curtain of vegetation begins slowly sliding to the left. Rachel wraps a few more vines around her hands and helps. In a few seconds, we can see most of the sign. White letters against a faded blue background say *Best Races in Town*. Just above the words, a brown horse with a rider on its back is pictured running like his life depends on it.

"This is it!" Jeremiah comes up beside us, his bent fingers clamped on his head to keep his hat securely in place. "This is the sign. The clearing is just past those trees." He points north, where the road beneath us wraps around a thick copse of black cherry trees whose white blossoms flutter in the wind.

"We'll stop there for lunch and sparring practice," I say as I let go of the kudzu and join Rachel in leading the group toward the clearing. We round the curve and find a large metal wheel, mounted upright as if trying to spin into the sky, resting near the center of a field of wildflowers, spring grass, and scrubby bushes with tiny berries clustered against their leaves. Kudzu climbs the wheel, wraps around its spindles and gears, and then plunges down the other side in a curtain of green.

I've never seen anything so strange and beautiful.

"What is that?" I ask.

"It's a Ferris wheel," Jeremiah says. "Folks used to ride them."

"Ride them where?" I look around the field for the rest of what must have been an enormous vehicle.

Jeremiah laughs a little. "It doesn't go anywhere. It spins.

You'd sit in one of the seats"—he points to large buckets in sun-faded colors that dangle from the inner edge of the circle—"and take a ride, round and round, until the ride operator stopped your cart at the top. Felt like you could see the whole world."

"Seems like a waste of time," Rachel says.

"Seems like a technological marvel." I walk closer to the wheel, skirting a thorny bush before it snags my cloak. Behind us, the wagons reach the field and Nola supervises the task of setting up for lunch.

"It was just something fun we did whenever a carnival came to town," Jeremiah says.

"What's a carnival?" Rachel asks.

"Well, now, used to be we'd have sort of a community holi-day once a year." He twists his hat in his hands. "The folks that ran the carnival would bring rides, like the Ferris wheel, and cook kettle corn and funnel cakes and pies—celebratory food like we'd have on Claiming Day."

"Where did the Claimings take place?" I ask as I glance around the field, looking for a fancy stage.

Jeremiah coughs. "No marriages at the carnival. No Claim-ings, period. Not in the old civilization. Men and women asked the person they loved to marry them, and then picked a date and a fancy location, and did it themselves. Claiming is something the Commander came up with."

Before I can reply to him, a shout goes up behind me. I spin on my heel and nearly get knocked flat on my back as Adam and Ian crash against me. Adam's face is flushed with rage, and he throws a punch straight for Ian's nose.

Ian blocks the blow and delivers one of his own, slamming

his fist into Adam's shoulder and spinning him directly into me. We hit the ground hard, and the thorny bush I'd been so careful to avoid earlier pierces my thigh with needle-sharp spindles.

I swear and push Adam off of me. Ian lunges forward, grabs Adam's tunic, and hauls him to his feet. Ian's eyes are murderous as he reaches for his sword.

"Hey! Stop!" I scramble to my feet, but Rachel is already shoving her way between them.

"What are you two idiots doing?" she snaps.

"He *hit* me." Adam spits blood onto the grass and glares at Ian while his fingers bunch into fists. He takes a step toward Ian, and Rachel smacks his chest with her Switch.

"Unless you want me to make you cry in front of everyone, you'd better calm down," she says.

"I hit you because you deserved it," Ian says, and every ounce of the charm he wears like a second skin is submerged beneath the cold brutality in his voice. "And if I ever hear you say something like that again, I'll take my sword to you."

"No one is going to take a sword to anyone unless we're facing Carrington or highwaymen," I say. "Both of you take a step back and calm down."

"Not before he apologizes," Ian says without once breaking eye contact with Adam.

"You owe *me* an apology," Adam says, and shoves against Rachel's restraining hand.

She braces herself. "Adam, I'm warning you—"

"No, you owe Logan an apology. You and that silent little creep." A vein in Ian's forehead throbs as he points behind me. I turn to see Elias standing a few yards away. When he meets my gaze, his blue eyes widen like he's just been caught pickpocketing a guard in Lower Market.

"I owe Logan nothing." Adam spits the words at Ian as if I'm not standing right beside him.

"You owe him your life," Rachel says, removing her hand from his chest and glaring at him like she's about to team up with Ian and take Adam down for the sake of my honor.

"Let's all just take a moment and calm down," I say, waving discreetly to Drake as he heads our way. He understands my request and changes course, gathering up those who hover near us with eager ears and shepherding all of them toward the canteen wagon parked at the edge of the field.

"He said you weren't worth following. That we should wait for the Commander to catch up to us and rejoin our true leader," Ian says, his fist still wrapped around the hilt of his sword, though he's made no move to pull it from its sheath.

"I said I didn't sign on to wander endlessly through the Wasteland at the whim of someone the Commander declared unfit for society."

"I declare *you* unfit for society." Ian raises his fists. "Every time I turn around, you're huddled with Elias discussing the good old days when the Commander used to tell you how to wipe your nose and how to use a fork and how to—"

"He's a great man!" Adam's voice rings out across the field, and I push a hand against his shoulder when he moves toward Ian again.

"He was a monster who deserved to lose his city and everyone in it."

"My family *died* that day." Adam lunges forward, shoving

past my restraining arm, and slams into Ian.

They hit the grass in a tangle of fists, feet, and limbs. Adam grabs the silver chain Ian wears around his neck and jerks it free, leaving a long red welt on the side of Ian's neck. Ian howls with fury and pounds his fists into Adam's face, shoulders, and back. I bend down, grab Adam's shoulders, and pull him off of Ian. Rachel crouches beside Ian as he rolls over and slaps the thick tufts of grass with his hand.

"I've got it," Rachel says as she hands Ian the chain, its little copper charm undamaged.

He takes it from her and rubs his thumb across the charm's surface.

"Nice piece of jewelry," Adam sneers, and I give his arms a sharp little shake.

Ian looks up, the sun gleaming off a thin trail of blood that leaks from a split in the corner of his lip. "My father made it. It's all I have left of him. The Commander saw to that."

The fight slowly drains from Adam, and I release his shoulders as I feel them slump. Rachel meets my gaze, and I nod as I read her expression. I can't let this situation with Adam go unaddressed any longer.

"I understand that you don't want me as your leader," I say quietly as a faint rumbling echoes out of the Wasteland to the south of us.

"You're nineteen! The same age as me. What qualifies you to tell me what to do?" Adam glares at me through eyes already starting to swell, courtesy of Ian's fists.

"The fact that I have a plan, I know how to put it into action, and the majority of those who survived Baalboden voted to put me in charge," I say, and Adam looks at the ground. "Why didn't you leave with the others who headed east to find the Commander? Why stay with me if you despise me so much?"

"Because I couldn't bear to leave my family behind." His voice is raw with grief and the kind of unspent rage that sometimes lashes out of Rachel. "How was I supposed to know you weren't planning to stay in Baalboden?"

I don't know what to say to that, and the rumbling is growing louder. It no longer sounds like it's coming from the south of us. Instead, it feels like it's in the ground beneath us. The dirt shakes, sending mild tremors through my legs. My muscles tense as Ian looks at Elias, who still waits a few yards away. We need to get off of this field. Now.

"What about you, Elias?" Ian asks as the people behind us begin clutching each other and backing away from the center of the field. "What's your problem with Logan's leadership?"

He shrugs. "I guess I just need proof that he can really protect us the way the Commander could."

The field shudders and sways, and the rumbling begins to sound like thunder beneath us.

"I think you're about to get a firsthand demonstration," Ian says as he lunges to his feet.

The rumbling becomes a muted roar, and a ripple shudders across the field, sending the metal Ferris wheel swaying in its berth.

"Get to the trees!" I yell as a crack begins to widen in the soil, and the Cursed One surges toward the surface.

CHAPTER SEVENTEEN

RACHEL

People scream and run toward the edges of the field as the guttural roar of the Cursed One thunders toward us from beneath our feet. I whirl around and yell, "Quiet!"

When most of them ignore me, Ian steps forward and bellows, "Silence or you die!"

People moan and whimper, clutching each other or falling to their knees as the ground heaves beneath our feet.

"Get them away from the epicenter," Logan says as he whips his tunic off and pulls at the rope that holds the Rowansmark device to his chest. The third button, the one that should send the Cursed One away from us, is still tied down, which means the device is malfunctioning again. If Logan's booster pack doesn't work, we're dead.

A glance at the ground shows the beginnings of a long, jagged crack right beside me.

"Listen to me!" I have to yell to be heard above the rumbling beneath us. "Run at least fifteen yards into the forest and climb a tree as high as you safely can. Once you get up there, stay silent at all costs. If there are children near you, help them into a tree as well. *Go!*"

People scatter, hurtling over bushes and scrambling to find trees to climb. To his credit, Elias races for the stragglers and helps them off the grass. In seconds, all that's left on the field are the four wagons. The sheep, goats, and donkeys tied to the wagons bellow their distress. The people in charge of driving the wagons are yanking at the reins and screaming at the donkeys to move, but panic has the beasts kicking at the traces and jerking forward in sharp movements that do nothing to help the wagons get rolling.

"Let's go!" I say. Logan and Ian ignore me, but Adam grabs my arm.

"The medical wagon still has people inside. The wagon behind it has the pregnant woman and at least five more who are too old to travel well. They can't run, much less climb."

The roar beneath us becomes a ferocious howl of rage as the crack widens beside me.

"Rachel, get out of here!" Logan yells as he braces his legs for balance. The device is clutched in his hand.

"Not without you," I say.

He leaps over the jagged gap that is steadily tearing the field asunder, and we all race for the wagons.

Before we're even halfway there, Frankie and Thom, still mounted on the horses they ride at the far end of our line of travelers each day, reach the wagons. Frankie leaps from his horse and thrusts the reins into Thom's hands. Then he rushes for the lead wagon, the one filled with the survivors who are still recovering from the injuries they sustained during Baalboden's destruction. The wagon's donkey struggles against the traces, desperate to be free. Frankie grabs its bridle and tries to quiet it before it attracts the Cursed One with its noise.

"Look out!" Thom cries as the ground heaves, throwing all of us to our knees.

I skid forward on my palms and roll into a crouch just in time to see the Cursed One explode out of the ground six yards from the edge of the field. The trees closest to the monster snap at their bases and tumble to the ground with a *crack-swoosh* that echoes across the forest. Just beyond the carnage, people huddle on the ground or cling to branches, their eyes wide with terror.

Behind us, the donkey yanks free of Frankie's hands and flees, dragging the medical wagon violently across the field. I glance back to see Thom spur his horse in pursuit, his hand still firmly wrapped around the reins of Frankie's horse.

The Cursed One looks like a giant, wingless dragon with a serpent's tail. It coils its huge body like a snake, muscles gleaming beneath black interlocking scales. Dirt, vines, and clumps of grass slide off the ridge of webbed spikes running down its back. Digging thick yellow claws into the ground, it pulls itself forward, puffs of smoke already leaking from its snout.

Ian crouches beside me. Adam shoves himself to his knees on my other side and says, "Holy—"

I slap my hand across his mouth, but it's too late. The beast swings its head toward us, milky yellow eyes staring at nothing while it sniffs the air. I hold my breath as sharp bits of rock dig into my knees.

Ten yards to our right, Logan steps forward with Rowans-mark's device in his hands. The flutelike gray metal object gleams dully, but bright copper wires coil around the gears and lead to a small box in his other hand.

I hope his modification is enough to give him control over the beast before it incinerates us where we stand.

Logan steps to the side, distancing himself from us as he circles the Cursed One.

A low rumble shudders through the creature as it pins us with its sightless eyes and creeps closer. Only fifteen yards separate it from Ian, Adam, Frankie, and me. The puffs of smoke coming from its snout turn into steady streams of gray-black as the terrible fire that burns in its belly rises up its throat.

Logan had better *hurry*.

We can't run without triggering an attack, but if we stay here much longer, it won't matter. We'll be dead either way.

Deep inside of me, the silence chills me to the core, and I wonder what it would be like to let the Cursed One burn it all away. All the memories. The nightmares. The yawning pit of loss that lurks within me, waiting for one tiny misstep to drag me under forever.

Maybe I would be free. Maybe in death, I would find the peace that eludes me here.

Or maybe the unfinished business between the Commander and me would haunt me beyond the grave.

The Cursed One claws its way toward us, snapping thick kudzu vines like twigs. Whatever Logan's doing with the device, it's not working.

"We have to move," Ian breathes softly. "It will most likely shoot a stream of fire straight in front of it. On the count of three, scatter to the sides and don't stop running."

It's as good a plan as any. I gather myself and get ready to leap to the left. Beside me Adam trembles, his breath grating harshly against the morning air. Behind us, Frankie says in a voice I can barely hear, "You three stay put. When it turns its head, *run*."

Before I can question him, he leaps past us and yells, "Over here, you misbegotten creature from hell!"

Frankie runs toward the monster, angling to the right as if determined to drive his sword into the beast's belly. The Cursed One snorts, jerks its head toward Frankie, and bellows.

A thick stream of red-gold fire spews out of its snout. Frankie dives beneath it, but flames grab hold of his tunic and his clothing ignites. He rolls across the grass, extinguishing the flames, while the beast gathers itself for another blast.

"Come on." Ian wraps his arms around my waist and scoops me up off the ground. As he pulls me toward the trees, I realize Adam is already there, waiting for us, his dark eyes full of horror as he stares at Frankie.

Frankie lies on his back, his clothes still smoking, staring up at the Cursed One with defiance written in every line of his body. The creature is ten yards away, but the sinuous coils of its body close the distance between them quickly. A guttural choking sound issues from the beast's throat, and the smoke in its nostrils turns gray-black again.

Frankie digs his fingers into the dirt and braces himself. I close my eyes, praying that Frankie dies quickly and that the pain is over in seconds. Praying that the monster leaves once he's satisfied his prey is dead. Praying that everyone else has the good sense to honor Frankie's sacrifice by remaining silent.

"No!" Logan's voice cracks through the air like a whip, and my eyes fly open. The Cursed One swings its face toward him instead of Frankie. Logan stands alone in the field with the ruined Ferris wheel thirty yards behind him. No trees for protection. No place to run.

No exit strategy except his own death.

Terror is a bright shaft of pain through my chest as Logan walks closer to the monster.

I jerk against Ian's arms, but he won't let me go.

The muscles beneath the beast's scales writhe as it gathers itself. Smoke pours out of its nostrils.

I slam my elbow into Ian's stomach and stomp on his instep with my boot. I have to save Logan. *I have to.* I can run onto the field and scream. The beast will come after me instead. I'll be far enough away from Ian and Adam to keep them safe. No one else will die.

No one else here deserves to die.

"Not going to happen," Ian says against my ear, his grip tightening as I struggle harder.

I grab his arm, drop my shoulder, and twist toward him in a move I've practiced a hundred times. A move designed to send him flying over my shoulder and onto his back.

Instead, he pivots gracefully and uses my own momentum to trap me.

"Like I said. Not going to happen. I don't think Logan would appreciate you sacrificing yourself for him, and I'm not going to be the one he blames for it." His eyes find mine for a moment and then flicker toward Logan, standing alone in the clearing, facing the Cursed One.

The monster howls, smoke gushing from its mouth.

"No!" I scream the word, straining against Ian's grip, all thoughts of protecting Adam and Ian forgotten as the beast claws the ground and lowers its snout toward Logan.

Logan presses a lever on the top of the small box in his hands, and it emits a strange buzzing noise. The third button on the device is still tied down.

My breath is a sob of panic and despair as the beast shudders, lashing the fallen trees with its tail and sending sprays of kindling into the air.

"Go back." Logan presses the lever again and raises his voice. "Go back!"

The Cursed One shakes itself, and its scales scrape together like metal rubbing against stone.

"Please," I whisper. Ian crushes me against him until I can hardly breathe, but when I look at him, he's staring at Logan with something like pain on his face.

Logan hits the button one more time, and the beast jerks backward. Coiling in on itself, it roars once more, strafing the ground in front of it with fire. The fallen trees burst into flame, hissing and popping, but the creature slithers over them, crushing them into splinters and extinguishing the fire. The earth trembles as the Cursed One dives back into the hole it created. Logan slowly lowers the device as the beast slips beneath the surface, its howl of rage fading as it tunnels down.

As the monster's cry disappears, people creep from the surrounding forest to stare.

Jeremiah shuffles away from the tree he hid behind, his purple bow askew and his hat crushed in his hands as his eyes lock on the device Logan holds. An expression somewhere between dread and fascination washes over his face. Frankie struggles to his feet and clenches his big fists while he looks at the slim piece of gray metal as well.

Even Adam, standing next to me with his lips pressed into a tight line, stares at the device with hunger in his eyes.

"So he does have it. And now he's proven himself to the doubters," Ian says against my hair. He still holds me too tightly for comfort, and now that Logan is safe, I have time to deal with Ian.

"Let go of me," I say. My voice shakes.

His grip eases. I step away from him as Adam leaves the shelter of the trees, calling for people to help him go find Thom and the wagon. Before I can rush to Logan's side, though, Ian grabs my arm.

I glare at him. "I'm getting really tired of you—"

"But why didn't he use it?" He sounds hurt and a little lost. His eyes are dark with the kind of pain that is rooted deep within me.

I stop trying to pull away. "What do you mean?"

"When the Commander used Carrington to attack us. When he was right *there*, easily in our reach, why didn't Logan call the Cursed One and end it?"

I meet his gaze for a long moment while I search for the right words. "Because Carrington soldiers were there, and Logan doesn't think they deserve to die because of the Commander. And because the last time we called the beast"—I swallow past the memories that choke me—"we couldn't control it. I'm sure he didn't want to risk our people again."

"But you would've," Ian says quietly, and my eyes snap to his. "You understand that Carrington chose its master, and that the soldiers are collateral damage. And if you had the opportunity to destroy the Commander, you wouldn't stop to worry about whether you could control the beast. You'd risk anything to punish him. Even your own life."

My skin tightens, my heart pounds, and the lie that I know should leave my lips—the one that will protect my secrets and keep up the pretense that I wouldn't sacrifice everything I have for a chance to hurt the Commander—refuses to come.

"I'm right, aren't I?" he asks, and this time I hear the desperate purpose that consumes him.

That consumes me.

Slowly, I nod.

"You'd go to any length to make the man responsible for your pain hurt, wouldn't you?"

"As long as it doesn't endanger the few people I love, yes."

"Even if it cost your own life."

"Yes."

We lock eyes for a long moment, and something unspoken shivers in the air between us. He smiles, the sharp angles of his face transforming.

"So we understand each other," he says.

"Apparently."

"Who knew I'd have common ground with the mouthy redhead?" He winks.

I roll my eyes. "Who knew I'd have common ground with the camp flirt?"

He laughs. "You might try a little flirting. It would soften your image."

"My image doesn't need softening."

"It does if you don't want your enemies to see you coming."

Now I'm the one who laughs. "It's a little late for that."

"But it's not too late to finish this. Anyone who abuses his power and betrays his people must be brought to justice. No matter what." He watches me carefully. "We could help each other."

It's on the tip of my tongue to tell him I don't need help taking down the Commander, but I swallow the words, because he's right. Two people working together toward a common goal are more effective than one.

Not that Logan isn't already committed to bringing the Commander to justice, but he has lines he won't cross. The only lines I won't cross are the ones that would hurt Logan, Quinn, Willow, or Sylph.

And Logan has just proven that using the device is no longer a threat to us.

"What do you say, Rachel? If we have the opportunity, should we destroy the man who ruined our lives? Even if it means taking the device from Logan and using it ourselves?" He extends his hand as people brush past us to hurry onto the ruined field, clutching each other and talking in breathless, hurried gasps.

It's just a backup plan. It doesn't mean I don't trust Logan. It doesn't mean I'm not going to fight by his side to deliver justice. It's just a piece of insurance in case something goes wrong.

In case Logan doesn't capitalize on the opportunity when it's in front of us.

I take his hand and shake it briefly. "If the Commander is in range, and Logan's plan doesn't work, you and I will kill the Commander."

"Whatever it takes."

I nod. "Whatever it takes."

He squeezes my hand briefly and then lets it go. I weave my way past clumps of people, climb over ruined trees, and fight to reach Logan's side, all while trying to shake the feeling that I've just done something that would disappoint the boy I love.

CHAPTER EIGHTEEN

LOGAN

I don't call for us to make camp for the night until it's nearly
twilight. I wanted to put significant distance between us and
the place of the Cursed One's attack in case the beast returns to
finish what it started. And I was looking for a location that could
shelter us from the relentless wind. Wind that drove rain into
our faces for most of the afternoon, and then whipped us dry as
the sun steadily disappeared into the western horizon.

I find what I'm looking for at the base of a rock outcropping
that blocks most of the wind and also seals off the western edge
of camp from possible intruders. Not that we've seen anyone in
the Wasteland since leaving Baalboden four days ago, but that
doesn't mean our luck will continue to hold.

Still, most of the survivors seem to feel like we've escaped the
worst of our journey unscathed. We outwitted the Commander
and left him far behind. We sent the Cursed One back to its lair
without losing a single life. A sense of giddy triumph envelops

the group. Children laugh and chase each other through the shelters while Jan, their assigned keeper, watches them with a light of hope in her eyes. A woman with wavy white hair and skin as wrinkled as a prune plays a violin she carried out of her home during the Cursed One's rampage. The tune is lively and the notes swirl through the air, causing toes to tap until a few of the men gather up the courage to ask some of the women to dance.

I smile a little as I watch them, but the elation they feel won't take root in me. I see too many worst case scenarios, too many ways the dangers of the Wasteland can still turn against us, to feel like celebrating.

The tall gray-white rock we're camped beside is easily as high as Baalboden's Wall. I feel better about our safety knowing that we have to keep watch in three directions instead of four, but the fact that most of my guards have no experience is a constant worry in the back of my mind.

So is the fact that Quinn and Willow have yet to return. That I don't know where the Commander is. And that I can't explain why the Cursed One attacked us today after nearly four days of safe travel. The fight between Ian and Adam wouldn't have generated enough noise to attract the beast, especially when I had the third button on the device tied down. It's a mystery, and that makes me nervous.

When Ian bows to a trio of girls and asks them all to dance with him at the same time, I shake my head and decide to work on the tech I'm building to track and destroy the Commander. Ducking inside my tent, I see a folded square of parchment on my bedroll and swear. I snatch it up and open it. The words *Payment is due* are scrawled across the parchment in thick, black letters.

I crumple the note in my fist and toss it to the corner of the tent. I have bigger things to worry about than whoever thinks it's funny to leave cryptic notes in my shelter. Still, my worry over the sudden appearance of the Cursed One today mixes with irritation over this latest note and leaves me feeling on edge. I shove the canvas flap of my tent aside and find Elias standing a few yards away. He stares at me as I stride toward him.

"Did you see anyone go into my shelter?" I ask.

He shakes his head.

"Did *you* go into my shelter?" My voice promises swift retribution for him if he did, and he shakes his head faster.

"Then what are you doing standing out here instead of hanging around the campfire with everyone else?"

A pretty brunette who looks about Rachel's age steps out of the tent beside Elias and joins him, her eyes glowing when he offers her his arm.

"Just waiting for Melanie," Elias says, and they turn away from me before I can say another word.

Forget working on the tech. The restless energy coursing through me won't let me sit quietly. I'll walk the perimeter of the camp instead. I haven't gone more than a few yards though, when Quinn and Willow, both carrying sacks of small game, step out of the trees.

"You're back," Frankie says, and he doesn't sound welcoming. His eyes slide past the two Tree People as if he can't see them. One more thing I'll deal with when all of the life-and-death issues in front of me are resolved.

Brushing past Frankie, I say, "Good to see you both. Find anything?"

Quinn shakes his head and hands me his bag of game. "Found rabbits, some birds, and a small pig. Enough to feed us tonight, at least. We checked for pursuers, but there wasn't any sign of Carrington. Either they're too far back for us to find on a one-day tracking excursion, or we lost them at Baalboden."

I turn to Willow, but she isn't looking at me. Instead, she marches up to Frankie, elbows him aside, and drops her bag of game beside the cooking fire Jodi and Adam are busy building. Grabbing a knife from a sheath strapped to her thigh, she whips a rabbit's body out of her bag, lays it on the ground, and skins it with quick, graceful movements.

"You're making a mess right next to where people need to eat," Frankie says.

Willow looks at him, her dark eyes glittering in the firelight. "If you can't handle what goes into preparing meals in the Wasteland, go back to Baalboden."

"I think he just means it's not very ladylike for a girl to do . . . that." A dark-haired girl who hangs on Ian's arm during the day drifts closer to the fire and looks at Willow like she sees something that needs to be washed.

Willow hands the rabbit to Adam and pulls out a squirrel. "I suppose it's not very ladylike to be rude to others, but you don't seem to have a problem with that."

The girl—Veronica? Vickie? Something with a *V*—folds her arms across her chest while my first-shift guards, boys who are almost all younger than me, crowd closer to the fire, waiting for their dinner rations before they take their posts.

"I wasn't being rude. I was pointing out—"

"You were rude," I say, my voice sharp. "And if this continues, I'll make a new camp rule. You only eat what you catch and skin and cook yourself. How would that suit you?"

The girl turns on her heel and walks away, but not before she says, "I suppose the Tree Girl doesn't have to worry about being a lady. It's not like she's going to find a man willing to Claim her."

Willow goes still, and her shoulders roll forward as if protecting herself from a blow. I'm about to go drag Veronica/Vickie back to the fire and force her to apologize or go hungry when Donny Miller, one of our first-shift guards, squats next to Willow and says, "I'd Claim you."

He's twelve if he's a day. Thirteen, maybe. But his voice is earnest, and Willow's shoulders straighten.

Another boy, closer to my age, says, "If I get to Claim a girl one day, I want one who knows how to hunt and fight like you do."

"Don't listen to her," Adam says as he crouches on her other side. His voice is both fierce and kind. I didn't realize he had this in him. I wonder what it would take to win him over to my side.

"She isn't half the girl you are, and she knows it." Adam rubs his palm against Willow's back for a second before looking at Quinn and dropping his hand.

Willow hands the squirrel to Adam and smiles. I've seen Willow smile before—quick, sassy grins and dangerous, I-dare-you-to-cross-me expressions—but this smile is slow and warm and a little shy.

"Adam's right," I say. Adam jerks his eyes to mine and stares.

"You're amazing and anyone with half a brain can see it. Hold your head high."

Willow gives me a saucy little grin and starts skinning the next animal. Adam holds my gaze and then slowly nods once, as if to acknowledge that in this one instance, we are both on the same side of the line.

The first-shift guards eat their rations and head to their posts. Adam, Jodi, and Willow extinguish the cooking fire and head to their shelters with everyone else. I join Rachel in our shelter and hold her as she falls asleep, but my brain won't let me relax. The Cursed One's arrival, Adam and Ian's fight, and the fact that I had no time to work on either piece of tech today keep me restlessly tossing and turning until I realize I'm going to wake Rachel if I don't find a way to settle.

Since sleep feels impossible, I decide to check the perimeter of the camp once more, even though I've already walked it six times. I grab for my boots, careful not to make too much noise. My fingers fumble with my laces as the damp night air seeps into my clothing. I wrap my cloak around my shoulders, and then listen for a moment.

Someone several yards south of me snores in loud, fitful bursts. Beyond the borders of our makeshift camp, the Wasteland hums with life. Crickets chirp, owls hoot, and the occasional animal rustles through the bushes.

Sliding my dagger into the sheath strapped to my left ankle, I leave the shelter. It's easy to slip away from camp in the middle of the night unnoticed. Too easy. I simply hug the shadows and choose my steps with care.

The first-shift guards are little more than kids themselves and terribly inexperienced, despite the fact that they've been training with Rachel, Quinn, and Willow for almost four weeks now. The oldest is eighteen. The youngest, Donny, the one who gallantly offered to Claim Willow, swears he's fifteen. He's lying, but I'm too desperate to argue. The older, more experienced guards spent all day patrolling the edges of our path as we traveled, digging wagon wheels out of mud, and generally wearing themselves out with what seemed like a hundred little things. I made the decision to let them sleep for a few hours before I call them up for the early-morning guard shift, because I know tomorrow they'll be wearing themselves out all over again.

Creeping along the back of our makeshift shelters, I step carefully to minimize the crunch of my boots against the springy undergrowth that spreads along the base of the rock like a moss-green apron. With every step, my mind restlessly chews at the problems facing me.

I need to calm down. I need to *think*. I need to distance myself from the camp for a few minutes and just breathe until my thoughts settle and I can see things clearly.

Every guard I've posted is under strict orders to raise hell if they see even a hint of movement. Better a false alarm than to be caught unaware. It worries me that I've moved past most of the shelters without alerting a single guard. Not that I want to be caught. But still . . . I'm trusting kids to keep us safe. *Kids*. Never mind that I'm only nineteen. I've been looking out for myself since the Commander killed my mother and branded me an outcast when I was only six. Most of these boys haven't faced anything worse than a tongue-lashing their entire lives.

I reach the eastern edge of camp and see Donny, Willow's

hopeful young suitor, slumped against the thick branch that holds up the final tent in this row. I can hear him snoring from five yards away. Barely suppressing a sigh, I crouch down and lay a hand on his shoulder.

"Wake up, Donny."

He jerks awake, flinging my hand off his shoulder as he sits up. He doesn't go for his knife. I rub the bridge of my nose and try for the most patient tone of voice I can muster. It's too much to expect that a handful of sparring sessions would take the place of the kind of training that gave Rachel and me our fighting instincts.

I keep my voice pitched low. "It's Logan. Where's your knife?"

"I'm sorry. I've only been asleep for a second." Faint traces of moonlight gleam silver and white against his shaggy brown hair, highlighting the cowlick that waves like a rebellious flag above his left temple. "I'm sorry, Logan."

"You said that. Now where is your knife?"

He fumbles around at his belt for a few seconds, and I realize his knife is trapped against his waist.

I lean closer and press my finger to his throat. "You're dead."

He swallows hard, his Adam's apple scraping against my finger. "I just thought . . . it seemed safer to—"

"Weapon always at the ready, Donny. Always. We don't want to lose you."

His cowlick waves earnestly as he nods his head. "Okay. Yes. Weapon ready."

I pat his shoulder. "Stay awake. You only have another two hours until shift change. We need you alert. Helps if you stand up."

He nods again and scrambles to his feet. "I won't let you down. I promise."

I smile as if I never had a doubt. "I know you won't."

"Where are you going?" he asks as I step past the camp's perimeter and toward the scraggly line of trees that press close to our little clearing on three sides.

"Just for a walk."

"In the Wasteland?" Uncertainty fills his voice. "There might be . . . things out there. Dangerous things."

"Yes," I say. "And I'm one of them."

"I'll come with you. Isn't safe to walk alone." He shoves his knife into his belt again.

"Weapon at the ready," I snap.

"Sorry! Sorry." He fumbles for the knife again.

I draw in a breath and remember how young he is. How innocent he was until the snowball effect of the Commander's treachery, Rachel's need for vengeance, and my thirst for justice conspired to rip his childhood from him in one fateful morning.

"I appreciate the offer. But I need you here. Alert. Someone has to watch over the camp. You're just the man for the job."

He straightens and holds the knife loosely, blade out, like he's ready. "I won't let you down."

"I know that. Keep that weapon out, Donny."

I leave him there, moonlight dancing in his shaggy hair and glinting along the edge of a blade I pray he'll never have to use, and let the shadows swallow me whole as I step into the forest.

The ground is still damp from the day's rain, and the musky scent of dirt, bark, and growing things envelopes me. I move south, breathing deeply and listening to the soft hoot of an owl and the high-pitched whirring of the cicadas that cling to the branches above me. Slowly, my thoughts settle into something logical and coherent.

I don't know why the Cursed One came after us today, but I can't attribute significance to it where none exists. The booster pack I built for the Rowansmark tech did its job. I have to be satisfied with that.

I can't convince Adam to let go of his grief and his anger when I understand the reasons behind them. I can only hope to show him that I have his best interest at heart. If he settles into my leadership, we won't have a problem. If he doesn't, I'll have to figure out an effective consequence that will demonstrate I mean business, but that won't alienate him further.

As for the final problem—I can't finish the invention I'm building to track the Commander, and I can't replicate the Rowansmark tech, without more supplies. I have to hope Lankenshire either has what I need or knows a way to get it.

Feeling settled and ready for sleep, I hurry through the forest and reach the edge of the tree line just before the guards are scheduled to change shifts. As I approach the camp, I see Donny, his cowlick glowing in the moonlight, slumped against the tree limb again.

I don't bother suppressing my sigh this time. Clearly, he's too young for nighttime guard duty. I don't know who will take his place, but I'll find someone. I can't risk the camp, and I can't risk Donny. If it comes down to it, I'd rather take the extra guard duty myself.

I reach Donny and squat in front of him. His knife is out, the blade facing me as he clutches it in his hand. Half the battle won.

Now if we can just find a way to keep him alert, he might make a decent guard after all.

The slight smile spreading across my face dies as a pungent, coppery scent fills my nose.

"Donny?" I reach out and grasp his shoulder. "Wake up."

He remains still. Dread pools in my stomach.

"Donny!" I shake him and watch in horror as his head tips back, revealing the thick crimson slice across the base of his neck.

CHAPTER NINETEEN

<u>RACHEL</u>

"Rachel, wake up!"

My eyes snap open, and I reach for my knife even as I recognize Quinn's voice. The dregs of another blood-filled dream cling to me as I roll over and realize Logan isn't beside me.

"What's wrong?" I ask, pushing myself off my bedroll and reaching for my cloak. "Where's Logan?"

"He's at the east edge of camp. Someone murdered the guards." His expression is stoic, but I'm learning to listen for the things he refuses to show, and I hear the horror in his words.

I stare at him for a second, and then I *move*. "What about the people within the camp? Are we surrounded? Is it Carrington?"

"Everyone else seems to be fine. No one's in the Wasteland close to camp. And I don't know if it's Carrington," he says as he follows me out of my tent. "Would the Commander quietly kill the guards and then pull back?"

I sidestep a bundle of supplies. "No. He'd attack with every soldier at his disposal." The wind tugs at my hair, and I yank the strands out of my face. "Highwaymen wouldn't do this either. They'd kill the guards, loot the camp, take some female prisoners, and then run into the Wasteland again. Are we sure no one—"

"No one is missing. No shelters look disturbed. Thom and I looked inside each of them."

I shake my head and lengthen my stride, my knife held steady in my hands. Let whoever killed our guards come for me next. I'll be ready.

We reach the east edge of camp a moment later. The metallic sweetness of drying blood blankets the air and creeps across my tongue. For one terrible moment, my nightmares blend with my waking life until I can barely tell the difference. I cup my hands around my mouth and nose before the smell makes me gag. Or worse, scream.

Logan has enough to worry about without adding me to his list.

He looks up as I approach. A single torch, staked to the ground beside the bodies, burns brightly, washing Logan's face in orange and gold. His lips are tight, his eyes hollowed out. I reach for him as he stands.

He leans into me as I wrap my arm around him.

"Someone murdered the boys I'd asked to stand guard." His voice is weary. "Just walked right up to them and slit their throats." He chokes on the last word and scrubs a hand over his eyes.

"I know." My words are gentle, at odds with the pounding of my heart. "It must be an enemy camped in the Wasteland. Someone . . ." Who? Who would benefit from killing our guards and leaving the rest of us alone?

"The Wasteland is empty," he says, and Quinn nods.

"How do you know?" I make the mistake of looking down and seeing a bloody smile carved into each boy's neck. My knees shake, and a strange buzzing fills my ears as I remember Oliver's blood pouring over my hands while I sat in silent impotence.

"Rachel?" Logan asks, pulling me away from the bodies. "Are you okay?"

It's just blood. Not Oliver. Not someone I had the chance to save. I swallow hard and force myself to look Logan in the eye. "I'm fine. Now, how do you know someone isn't surrounding the camp while we stand here talking?"

"Because Quinn and I walked around the entire perimeter. We went fifty yards into the Wasteland. It's empty."

I pull away from him. "You came to the camp to wake Quinn but didn't wake me too?"

"Quinn was already up. I met him while I was walking the southern section of camp. I'd already awakened Frankie and Thom so they could gather the second-shift guards and get into position."

"Wait. You knew a killer was out there, and you decided to go find them *by yourself*?" I stare at him.

"Would you rather have me take the few guards we have around the camp and leave our people totally unprotected?"

I snap my mouth shut before I say yes. Yes, I'd rather have Logan protected and alive than everyone else in our camp. It's selfish of me, I know that. But I've lost everyone else in my family. I can't stand the thought of losing him, too.

Instead, I say, "Next time you want to lecture me about

putting myself in danger without having an acceptable exit strategy, I want you to remember this."

A muscle along his jaw flexes. "It's not the same."

Shaking my head, I glance at the sky. At the faint violet rim that is slowly spreading along the eastern horizon. "It's almost dawn. These are first-shift guards. This happened several hours ago. Why didn't you get me?"

"You needed sleep," Quinn says.

I turn on him, and the fear that courses through me for Logan snaps out at Quinn instead.

"And what were *you* doing in the southern section of camp? That's a long way from your shelter."

"I was having trouble sleeping," Quinn says, and the quiet hurt in his voice makes me feel small inside. He crouches beside Donny's body, his dark eyes guarded. "I wander the Wasteland when I can't sleep. It helps to clear my head. You can check with Willow if you don't believe me."

"Why wouldn't I believe you?" I ask, though I already know his answer. Didn't I just question him like I thought he might have something to hide?

"Because someone killed these boys, and everyone else was sleeping except for me and Logan."

"Not everyone," Logan says, and the cold fury in his voice sends a shiver down my spine.

Placing his hand on Donny's head, Quinn tilts the boy's chin toward the sky and examines his neck in the flickering light of the torch.

I choke and look away.

"The killer used a short blade, easily hidden," he says. "The deepest part of the cut is on the left side of the neck where he first stabbed his victim. The wound then decreases in depth as the knife slides across the throat." He considers the other bodies for a moment. "Looks like the work of the same man on each boy."

Sweat beads my upper lip and covers my palms. I want to throw up. I *need* to throw up. I tilt my head back and drag in a shaky breath, trying not to think of bloody knives sliding across tender throats.

Logan presses a hand to the small of my back.

"Most people are right-handed," Logan says. "If a right-handed man attacked someone from the front, he'd swing his knife left to right for maximum speed and velocity. The wound would start on the right side of the victim's neck."

"So our killer might be left-handed." Quinn rises.

"Or he killed them from behind to avoid blood spatter on his clothing."

"He punctured the artery on the left and made a long clean slice to the artery on the right. That isn't easy. He knew exactly where to strike and how much pressure to exert so he wouldn't get caught up in the trachea, the ligaments, or the esophagus. He's done this before," Quinn says.

"Wouldn't it be hard to sneak up on them since they were all facing the Wasteland? Especially if he needed to get behind them before killing them?" I ask.

"I walked right up to Donny before he saw me," Logan says.

"But all eight of them?"

"Maybe he didn't have to sneak." Logan is wearing his I'm-three-facts-short-of-figuring-out-the-entire-thing face. "Maybe he just walked right up to them."

"And no one ran? No one screamed for help to alert the others?" I ask as Quinn moves toward us, his eyes on the pale pink sky.

Logan's voice is flat. "They wouldn't scream for help if they didn't realize he was an enemy."

"Someone we know?" Quinn asks, wiping the tips of his fingers on his pants. "No offense, but the list of potential professional killers born and raised in Baalboden begins and ends with the two of you. We're dealing with an expert here."

I don't want to know what was on his fingers. I refuse to look at the faint dark stains marring his pant leg. Instead, I step to the side and stare at the huge white rock rising just behind the camp while I gulp in deep breaths of damp morning air.

"Still, we have to look at every possibility. Are we absolutely sure every survivor in our camp was a citizen of Baalboden before the fires?" Logan asks, and a chill sinks into me. "When we blew up the gate and escaped the burning city, it was chaos. People running into the Wasteland, convinced the Cursed One could find them anywhere. People still staggering out of the city long after we thought everyone inside must be dead. How hard would it have been for someone to pretend to be one of us?"

"But why would anyone want to?" I ask.

Logan makes a rough sound. "I don't know. *I don't know.* I'm just looking at all of the possibilities and seeing which one, no matter how unimaginable, lines up with the facts."

"Wouldn't you recognize a stranger in the camp?" Quinn asks.

"No," I say. "Baalboden was a city-state of thousands. We

have only one hundred and—" I can't complete the number without subtracting the boys lined up on the ground beside us, and I don't know how to calculate their loss and still sound strong enough to face this. "We have a small group. Many of us had never met until the fires."

"Well, that just made this more difficult," Quinn says. "What if it isn't someone in the camp?"

"Then we're back to guessing who could possibly have something to gain by killing our first-shift guards and leaving the rest of us alone," Logan says.

My eyes stray to Donny's face. His cowlick dances in the morning breeze, and I suddenly find it impossible to swallow. I tear my gaze from him and look at the rock instead. Something mars its pale surface. I take two steps forward and strain to see as the sun slowly spills across the horizon behind me.

"Rachel and I discussed it briefly on our way here." Quinn's voice is calm, but I catch an undercurrent of darkness beneath it. He isn't as unaffected by these deaths as he'd like us to believe. "She said this isn't the Commander's style, and we both know highwaymen would have pillaged the camp."

I take one more step toward the rock as the darkness dissolves into the rosy gold light of dawn, and horror washes over me.

"Agreed. So either we have an unknown enemy lurking in the Wasteland, we have a stranger masquerading as a Baalboden survivor, or it truly was one of us." Logan's voice shakes with anger. "If it's one of us, these boys welcomed their killer because they thought he was a friend. No wonder he'd be worried about blood stains. Along with the wristmarks, we're about to personally check every inch of clothing in this camp."

"Logan." I push his name past lips that feel cold and stiff. "Look."

Logan and Quinn turn to face the rock, and we all stare at the message painted across the stone in huge, bloody letters.

Your debt is still unpaid. Who will be the next to atone for your crimes?

CHAPTER TWENTY

LOGAN

The funeral is over. Eight graves now lie at the base of the rock, far enough north to be out from under the killer's bloody message. I said words I hope sounded comforting even though the senselessness of it all scrapes me raw inside. Nola sang Baalboden's traditional mourning song, her voice breaking as tears flowed down her face. Flowers were gathered from bushes in the Wasteland and laid at the head of each grave.

The air of celebration that filled the camp last night has been replaced with shock and dread. People huddle in groups, holding on to each other as if afraid they might be next.

I'm afraid, too. That's why I called a meeting with those I know I can trust.

"It's possible the killer might be someone living in the camp," I say.

Silence, thick and unwieldy, greets this announcement. I've gathered Rachel, Quinn, Willow, Drake, Nola, Ian, and Frankie into a small clearing just inside the tree line on the south edge of camp. We lean against tree trunks and face each other in the sun-dappled gloom.

I trust Rachel, Willow, and Quinn implicitly. And because they once aided me when I was at the Commander's mercy, I trust Drake and Nola, too. Ian is here because he risked his life for mine, and because he trusted me with his secret. Frankie is here because he also risked his life for mine and because Drake swears that a streak of implacable loyalty lives beneath Frankie's hot temper. I trust Thom, too, but I'm using him to supervise as our people break camp. Frankie will fill Thom in on the details later.

"Where did you get that idea?" Drake asks, the creases in his forehead deepening as he frowns at me.

"Look around us." I fling my hand out to encompass the vast forest that surrounds us. "There's no one here. No Tree Villages. No city-states. No highwaymen camps. Nothing. Plus, the boys didn't put up a fight. Either they truly didn't have any warning, or they thought their killer was their friend." My throat closes over the last word, and I swallow hard. The thought that one of the survivors I've sheltered, fed, and protected might have betrayed us like this makes me sick.

"The killer might be one of us, and you didn't tell the others during the funeral?" Frankie asks, crossing his large, freckled arms over his chest while he stares at me with blatant disapproval on his face.

"No. I told them to be on guard, that we hadn't caught the murderer yet, but—"

"But they still think the person next to them is safe," Frankie says. "We have to *tell* them."

"And give away the one thing we might know about the killer?" Willow asks.

"I didn't ask your opinion, leaf lover."

Willow smiles slowly, and the air shivers beneath her dark gaze.

"She's right," I say, glaring at Frankie. "If the killer is one of us, the only advantage we have is that the killer doesn't realize we know."

"Are you sure we're looking for a man?" Willow asks, her slim hand gently tracing a pattern against the worn leather strap on the brace of arrows resting against her back.

"Did you see those wounds?" Drake shoves a hand through his dark silver-shot beard to mime slitting his own throat. "No way a woman would be strong enough to do that."

"I could," Willow says. Quinn makes a choked noise and shoots a glare at his sister. She rolls her eyes. "I'm not saying I *did*. I'm saying I could. We can't rule out a woman simply because the men in this group can't imagine the possibility." She nudges Rachel with her elbow. "We're just as capable of killing. Tell them, Rachel."

Rachel flinches.

"We believe you," I say quickly, and everyone's eyes slide past Rachel to land on me again. "But you're an exception. It's much more likely we're looking for a man, but"—I throw a palm up in Willow's direction before she can argue further—"we'll consider all our options."

"I don't agree that it has to be one of us," Quinn says quietly. "Those wounds were made by a professionally trained killer. We didn't have torches lit. It wouldn't have been hard for someone with experience to sneak up on the boys."

"Sneak up from where?" My voice rises. "We're in the middle of nowhere. We haven't seen any signs of civilization for days. Unless someone followed us all this time and just now decided to kill our guards, I don't see how that scenario makes sense."

The midmorning sun is a weak stream of gold that fills the small clearing with hazy light. Quinn's features blur, and I blink rapidly to push the fatigue away.

"Logan?" Drake asks, his mild brown eyes full of worry. "You all right?"

"Sorry. I haven't slept in over twenty-four hours." I scrub one hand over my face and slide the other on top of Rachel's. Her skin is cold. "Quinn can tell you why we think this was the work of a professional."

Quinn explains why the wounds point toward a right-handed man with training in how to kill. Then I say, "The murderer left us a message. If we can figure out what it means, we'll be one step closer to understanding who we're dealing with. The message said, '*Your debt is still unpaid. Who will be the next to atone for your crimes?*' I didn't say anything about this before, because I assumed it was a prank, but I've found similar notes in my tech bag back in Baalboden and then twice more since we left the city, including last night before dinner."

"Then it *has* to be one of us," Nola says. "The gate—"

"I found the one in my tech bag before we blew the gate. It could've been one of us, or a stranger could've crept into our camp while we were all busy sparring or scavenging. My point is that someone is committed to the idea that we have a debt to be paid. If we can figure that out, maybe we can find who did this."

"We don't owe anyone a debt," Frankie says, his lip curling around the words.

"Clearly, someone disagrees with you," Willow says.

"Shut your mouth."

"That's enough, Frankie," Drake says calmly. "We're all upset about this, but turning on each other won't help." He looks at me. "What possible crimes could we have committed that would cause someone to kill our guards and leave a message like that?"

Rachel lets go of my hand and begins ticking items off on her fingers. "We didn't run after the Commander and beg to be under his control again. We have the tech he wanted to steal from Rowansmark, and we know Rowansmark was committed to getting it back."

"How do you know that?" Ian asks.

"Because they posted a ridiculously high reward for my father's capture, and then once I'd recovered the tech, they came after us with trackers and a battalion of soldiers."

"And you escaped all of them?" He gives her an admiring look, but she doesn't seem to notice.

"We *killed* almost all of them. The ones we missed were too busy running for their lives through the Wasteland to bother with us again." Her voice is cold, as if the memory of being surrounded by a Rowansmark battalion while the Cursed One tunneled up beneath our feet is a thing of little consequence, but her fists are clenched hard enough to turn her fingers pale and bloodless. "The point is that both the Commander and Rowansmark have reason to believe we wronged them."

"If the Commander catches up to us, he isn't going to bother killing a few guards," Nola says. Her dusky skin glows beneath the sunlight, but her dark eyes are haunted. She slides her arm through Drake's and leans against her father. "He'll come straight for us and make an example out of us that no one will ever forget."

"Not if we make an example out of him first," Rachel says. "But I agree, this isn't the Commander. And I'm not sure it's one of us, either." She looks toward the camp as if she can still read the bloody letters slowly drying on the porous surface of the rock. "I think it's Rowansmark."

Frankie leans forward. "A battalion wouldn't—"

"Not a battalion. A tracker. Maybe more than one, though one would suffice. They have the skills to quietly murder eight guards without any of them raising an alarm." Rachel looks at me. "And I think the message is a twisted example of pain atonement."

"What's pain atonement?" Frankie stares her down.

"Rowansmark's system of consequences. Honor and loyalty mean everything to them. They don't even have a prison. If someone dishonors the city, their leader, or their family, they are immediately sentenced to pay for their crime with increments of pain atonement. If the accused can survive the punishment, honor is restored." She looks toward camp again and shudders. "If the accused can't survive, the debt is considered paid by death."

A hawk soars overhead, its piercing cry puncturing the silence that follows Rachel's words.

Quinn says, "What was done last night took skill, and the message does mention both a debt and the need for atonement."

"But to kill a few of us and then just disappear again?" Drake frowns. "That's a cat-and-mouse game. Why would a

Rowansmark tracker do that instead of going straight for Logan and Rachel to reclaim the stolen tech?"

Rachel says, "Maybe he doesn't know which of us has it. Maybe he really believes he has to punish us first. Or maybe—"

"Maybe he's got rocks for brains." Willow shrugs her arrow brace into place. "Doesn't really matter. All that matters is that this stops now."

"How are we going to stop someone when we have no idea who he is?" Ian asks.

"I don't know," I say quietly. "But the message makes it clear whoever did this thinks we still owe a debt. Which means he'll come after us again. We have to be ready."

"So you think a professionally trained Rowansmark killer might be hiding in plain sight among us?" Nola asks, her voice trembling a little.

I shake my head. "If it really is someone from Rowansmark, the theory that it's one of us becomes harder to support. We checked everyone's wristmarks before the funeral. They're all from Baalboden. We also checked clothing, but found no bloodstains. I think Rachel's right. It's a tracker, and he's disappeared back into the Wasteland. I don't know why he'd play with us like this, but we won't find him until he decides to come after us again."

"I could find him," Willow says. "And then I could kill him and put an end to this."

A muscle along Quinn's jaw clenches, but he doesn't say a word.

"You're a girl," Frankie says. "He's a trained killer. One decent confrontation with a Rowansmark tracker and you'd crack under the pressure."

"Want to have a confrontation with me and see if I crack?" Willow asks, her dark smile back in place.

"Enough, Frankie," I say. "We aren't living by the Commander's rules anymore. If Willow says she can find him, we're going to let her do it."

"I'm going with her," Quinn says.

"Okay. You two track the killer while we take the camp north." I pull Jeremiah's map out of my cloak pocket and unfold it. Using my index finger, I trace the route we're going to take. "We're going here, veering east after this large hill, and then we'll turn north again when we reach this point." I tap the map. "Jeremiah says it's a ruined city from the old civilization. Considering how slowly we have to travel, it should take us three or four days to get there. You should be able to catch up to us without a problem."

"If there's a tracker in the woods, we'll do our best to find him," Quinn says.

"And then we'll make him wish he'd never decided to slit the throats of those boys." Willow's voice shakes with fury, something I've never heard from her.

"You aren't even a Baalboden girl," Frankie says. "What do you care?"

She's on her feet and in his face before I even realize she's moving. Her fists clench her bow, and her dark eyes blaze. "Those boys were *kind* to me."

Frankie swallows and says nothing. For once. Nola lets go of Drake and steps forward to slide an arm around Willow's waist instead. Willow stiffens and glances sideways at Nola like a rabbit judging the best way to run from a predator.

"They *were* kind, weren't they?" Nola's voice breaks. She

doesn't seem to notice that Willow isn't sure what to do with her affection. "They adored you. Going after their murderer is the right thing to do."

Willow nods once, a sharp, choppy movement that sends her ear cuff swinging, and then she turns and walks into the forest without another word. Quinn meets Nola's eyes and mouths "thank you" before he silently follows his sister.

I'm about to give the rest of the group instructions for doubling the guard along our flanks as we travel when Thom runs up to us, his craggy face flushed and his fists clenched.

"Had two of the men up in the trees as lookouts." He pants heavily between his words. "Said they saw something. Went up the tree myself to have a look. Took my spyglass." He pats his cloak pocket.

"What is it?" My hand is already reaching for my sword.

"Carrington. Whole mess of red uniforms just pouring over the top of that hill we crossed late yesterday afternoon." Thom waves to the south of us. "At the rate they're traveling, they'll be here in less than three hours."

"Get everyone on the road. Whatever isn't already packed up gets left behind. Let's *go*."

We run through the trees and onto the campsite, where people stare at us with terror on their faces. Leaving Frankie and Thom in charge of making sure no one gets left behind, I race to the front of the line and start calculating how much distance I can put between our group and the approaching army in just three hours.

Any way I look at the scenario, the answer is the same: not enough.

CHAPTER TWENTY-ONE

RACHEL

We've been traveling hard for two days while the army at our backs slowly closes the distance between us. We've tripled the guard at night, and everyone carries a weapon during the day. I alternate between walking beside Logan and positioning myself by Sylph in the middle of the group. If Carrington attacks, I'm going to be in a place to defend the two people I love.

Last night, we camped beside a river and were nearly eaten alive by mosquitoes. This morning, Logan had us up at dawn and moving east while the early morning gloom was still clinging to the sky. It's going to take us another two days to get to the ruined city where we'll meet up with Quinn and Willow. I find myself worrying that they won't catch up. That they've been hurt or killed.

I don't want to add anyone else to the list of people I've lost. I've learned that death is an insatiable creature with greedy hands, and the people I love seem to be easy targets.

Which is why I've dedicated chunks of time every day to

tutoring Sylph, Jodi, Cassie, Mandy, and any other girl who wants to learn the art of surviving in the Wasteland. I teach them as we walk. We discuss which plants are edible, which are medicinal, and how to cover your tracks so your enemy can't find you. We hunt small game, skin it ourselves, and find hiding places in the dark underbelly of the forest's depths. We shoot arrows and hit our targets. We throw knives and hit those targets, too. And we know how to fatally injure a man who makes the grave mistake of underestimating us.

If the Commander catches up to us, I want the girls he tried so hard to keep under his thumb to be his worst nightmare.

"Chickweed," Sylph says, and tugs on my arm as she points to a thick bush on the side of the trail. The small oval leaves form a cross with a white flower in its center. "Am I right?"

"You're right." I smile as she bounces off the path and begins gathering handfuls of the edible plant. Jodi joins her, her blonde hair coiled on top of her head in a thick braid.

"And blueberries," Jodi says as the springy chickweed plant gives way to a tangle of berry-covered vines. "Right? Or are these pokeweed? I don't want to pick something poisonous."

"That's pokeweed. See the bright purple stem? That's how you tell the difference."

Sylph and Jodi return to my side, each carrying a cloth sack full of chickweed. I wrap my arm around Sylph's waist and give her a quick squeeze. "Lesson's over for today. I have something to discuss with Logan."

"Sounds serious." Jodi wiggles her brows at me.

"I think that's just Rachel for 'I need to go kiss my boy.'" Sylph laughs when I glare at her.

"She does like to lock lips with him every chance she gets, doesn't she?" Jodi laughs, too.

I reach up and pat them both on the head. "Poor things. If you had a boy who looked like Logan, you'd be kissing him every chance you had, too."

"I was right, you know," Sylph says.

"About what?"

"About Logan. I told you he was waiting for you." She grins.

I laugh. "Took him long enough to figure it out."

"So is he a good kisser?" She elbows me in the side and bounces a little as she waits for my answer.

"I don't . . . I mean, I've never been kissed by anyone else, so . . ."

"Well, how do his kisses make you feel?" Jodi frowns at me. "He doesn't drool on you, does he?"

"No, he doesn't drool. He just . . ." He just makes me feel almost whole. Almost better. Like if I could just get close enough to him, everything else would fade away and never come back. I lose myself for a moment in the thought of his callused fingers gently sliding over my back, his lips pressing urgently against mine, his breath quickening against my skin.

Sylph laughs and snaps her fingers in front of my eyes. I jerk my attention back to her and feel heat in my face.

"Well, I don't know what you were just thinking about, but I'm going to guess it means Logan knows what he's doing when he kisses you."

The heat in my face spreads down my neck. "Yes. He knows what he's doing. I only hope you can say the same about Smithson."

"Smithson is just as good a kisser—"

"Then why are you over here with us picking chickweed instead of kissing him?" I ask, and Sylph's dark eyes light with mischief. Without another word to us, she jogs to where Smithson walks, throws her arms around his neck, and kisses him. When she comes up for air, Smithson's cheeks are as bright as the pokeweed stems, and his expression is dazed.

"Your turn," Jodi says. I'm about to offer to stay with her so she won't have to walk alone, but she isn't looking at me. She's eyeing Ian with a speculative gleam in her eye. I silently wish her luck prying him away from the two girls who are currently admiring his biceps and giggling over his compliments and then head toward Logan.

The ground beneath me is spongy with the river's damp. My boots skid a little as I hurry past the wagons, intent on reaching Logan, who walks at the front of the line as usual. Even from here, I can see the weary line of his shoulders. The way he keeps rubbing his eyes like he can push the fatigue away for another hour. Another day.

When he isn't leading us through the Wasteland, he's giving orders and then double-checking that the orders have been followed. At night, when he should be resting in our shelter, he's either poring over the Rowansmark tech, trying to understand the device well enough to re-create it, or he's taking a shift of guard duty.

I, on the other hand, have walked the edges of the group by day, ready to fight off an attack that never comes, and have slept in the shelter by night because Logan keeps telling me he has the night-shift guard duty covered and doesn't need me.

I think it's because he's afraid I'll die next.

Hurrying past the wagons, I slip through a knot of men who talk in fierce undertones while they watch the forest around them. Adam walks a little ahead of them, his golden skin free of bruises for the moment, and his beautiful eyes full of the kind of darkness that lurks somewhere inside of me as well.

"Where's Willow?" he asks me quietly as I try to walk past him. "She's been gone for two days now."

I push a low-hanging branch out of my way and look at him. "She and Quinn had something to do."

He opens his mouth. Closes it. Stares at me like he just broke his only compass and has no idea how to find his bearings.

I sigh. Angry Adam I can handle. Adam pining after Willow leaves me fumbling for words. "She'll be back."

"When?"

"Soon." I start to move past him, and he touches my arm.

"Did she leave for good? Was it Frankie?" His voice rises. "Did she get tired of the people who treat her like an outsider but are more than willing to eat the food she hunts and let her stand guard over them while they sleep?"

I stare at him.

He leans toward me. "The girls treat her like competition. The men treat her like she's a baby playing at war. And the older women avoid her." His mouth is a tight line.

"I promise she plans to come back." My voice is quiet, and I scrub my hand against my heart as guilt prickles against my skin. I could ask myself why I've ignored the fact that Willow is being mistreated, but I already know the answer. I've been so caught up in my own pain, in looking strong during the day so that no one knows how fragile I feel at night, that I haven't really looked at anyone else.

And if I did look at someone else, it wouldn't be Willow. The girl who always seems so self-assured. The girl who threatened to hurt me if her brother lost his life because of me.

The girl who has fought beside me and *for* me since the day I met her.

"They think she's unnatural because she doesn't wear dresses and always carries her bow and arrows. Because she can hunt and fight," Adam says.

"I can hunt and fight too."

"But you're from Baalboden."

"Why does that matter? I hardly act like it."

"Your dad was well-respected. And some of them knew your mother." His voice gentles unexpectedly. "They think you bucked Baalboden traditions because you lost her at such a young age, and your father didn't know any better when he raised you."

I glare at him even though I know he isn't the real target. "My father raised me exactly how I needed to be raised. I'm not some lost soul acting out because I don't have a mother. I'm a fighter, both by nature and by training, and they should be *thanking* both Willow and me for being willing to stand between them and everyone who wants us dead."

His smile slowly transforms his face, and I find myself smiling back.

"I think I like you," he says.

My smile falters.

"No! Not like that." He holds up his hands as if to ward off the ridiculous assumption that he would ever be attracted to me.

My eyes narrow.

"Not that there's anything wrong with . . . I mean, you and Logan seem to have a pretty good thing going, and I'm not . . ." He meets my eyes, but I can't read his expression. "I just meant that I didn't like you before because you can be sort of cold. I thought you didn't care about us. But now I think maybe you're just really good at hiding it."

I don't know what to do with Adam-being-friendly. I'm far more used to Adam-being-angry. I hope he means what he says; I can't help but compare the earnest look on his face to the fierce anger that burned there just a few days ago. Maybe he's sincere. Maybe he's trying to come to terms with everything he's lost. Or maybe I'm not the only one who's really good at hiding things.

"I'll watch out for Willow when she returns," I say. My voice sounds odd. Shaky. I clear my throat. "And maybe part of the problem is that I'm not standing guard with her at night. I'm about to fix that."

Before he can say another word, I move away, trying desperately to shove the warmth of his sudden friendship away from me before it can linger and take root. Logan walks beside Ian, about twenty paces in front of the pack. The faint path we're taking follows the riverbed and then veers east into the forest. I catch up to Logan and Ian just as the road wraps around a corner and the river slips out of sight.

Logan smiles and holds out his hand for mine. Beneath his smile, I see the exhaustion that clouds his eyes and drains the color from his face. I take his hand and hold on tight.

"I'm taking your guard duty shift tonight."

His smile disappears. "No, you aren't."

"Yes, I am." I give him the look that used to make Oliver send me to my room for hours. "You're so tired you can barely function. If you keep pushing yourself this hard, you'll get sick. Or you'll make a mistake, and you know you're impossible to live with when you realize you've made a mistake."

Ian snorts out a little laugh, and I level him with my gaze. "*You're* impossible to live with, period, so don't start."

He shakes his head and smirks.

"Rachel, you need your sleep."

"And you don't? How much sleep have you had in the past few days?"

He looks away.

I rub my thumb across the back of his hand. "You know I'm right."

"I know you aren't going out there to stand guard while there's a chance the killer might come back." An edge of fear sharpens his words. "Plus, there's the army to worry about."

"Who is better qualified?" I ask, and he closes his eyes like I've hurt him.

"She has a point," Ian says, and Logan's eyes snap open.

"Stay out of this," he says.

"Logan, I can guard the camp. I can fight a professional killer—"

"I wouldn't be too sure of that," Ian says softly.

"I've had far more training and experience than anyone else in the camp except you," I say to Logan. "And there's Willow to think of."

Logan frowns. "What does this have to do with Willow?"

"Adam told me some people are mistreating her. Mocking

her or giving her the silent treatment because she's different from what Baalboden told us a girl was supposed to be. If they see that I'm like Willow, maybe they'll have to reconsider their ideas."

"Or maybe they'll just start mistreating you as well," Ian says.

"Maybe I don't care what they think of me," I snap at him.

He grins. "Maybe you don't."

"I'll put a stop to it," Logan says. "I've seen how Frankie treats them. How some of the others treat Willow. I'd hoped that if everyone spent enough time around the Runningbrooks, really got to know them, the prejudices would die. But I'll step in and make it stop."

"How?" I ask.

He rubs his temples. "By punishing Frankie or anyone else who disrespects them. Publicly."

"Good, we got that settled. Now tonight. Guard duty. Do you want me to take first shift or second?"

"Rachel, please."

I tug him closer to me and meet his gaze. "I know why you don't want me out there, and I understand it. But I'm a fighter, and this is my battle. You can't hide me in our shelter to keep me safe. It isn't fair to the others, and it isn't fair to me."

He stops suddenly and wraps his arms around me. Burying his face in my hair, he whispers, "I don't care about fair. I just don't want to lose you."

I lean into him and let his warmth press against my skin. "I know. But you need rest, and I'm a lot harder to kill than most of our guards. I'm not asking your permission, Logan. I'm simply asking if you'd prefer to sleep during the first or second shift."

His shoulders shake, and for a second I think he's lost his mind and is crying in front of Ian and everybody else, but when he pulls away from me, I see he's laughing. There's a note of despair under the laughter, but still, I smile back.

"You are the fiercest, most stubborn girl I've ever met." He makes it sound like a compliment. We start walking again before the rest of the group can catch up to us.

"You're pretty stubborn, yourself." I nudge him with my elbow, and see Ian roll his eyes.

"Not so stubborn that I can't see reason," Logan says. "You're right. I need sleep. And we need your instincts on the guard shift. I've delegated the task of assigning and rotating the guards to Ian during Quinn's absence. He can choose which shift you take."

I raise my brows and glance at Ian.

"First shift," he says.

"Fine."

"Don't screw it up." He winks at me.

I heft my Switch. "If your eyelid twitches one more time while you're looking at me, I'm going to remove it and feed it to the birds."

Logan wraps his arm around my shoulders and tucks me up against his side. His eyes are suddenly serious when he looks at me. "Be careful tonight."

It's on the tip of my tongue to tell him that I'm always careful, but even I don't have the audacity to lie like that. "I will," I say, and I mean it.

I will carefully stand guard, and if anyone tries to hurt

someone in the camp again, I will carefully spill their guts across the Wasteland floor and carefully wait for the vultures to feast on the remains.

For the first time since Melkin died beneath my blade, I don't mind the thought of having more blood on my hands.

CHAPTER TWENTY-TWO

LOGAN

When we finally climb to the top of a steep bluff and see the ruins of a large city laid out before us, I breathe a sigh of relief. It's taken six days instead of four to get here, despite the fact that I've pushed my people to their limits. I guess estimating distance on a hand-drawn map is harder than I realized.

I've spent those six days triple-checking our security, encouraging the group to move faster, and worrying that the Commander could catch up to us at any moment. His army is too large to move much faster than we can. Still, every day we catch glimpses of them behind us, on hilltops and ridges, and it seems like they're steadily closing the distance.

When I'm not worrying about the Commander, I'm busy trying to figure out who killed our boys. There've been no more deaths, either because of the increased security or because the killer is somewhere in the Wasteland being hunted by Quinn and Willow.

Or because he's simply waiting for his next opportunity.

The constant threat against us has caused a subtle shift in the dynamic of our group. Fewer complaints. More offers to help without being asked. And most surprisingly, instant obedience from the most rebellious survivor—Adam.

I fold Jeremiah's map and put it into my cloak pocket. I hope Quinn and Willow are already in the city, because with the Commander closing in behind us, we can't afford to wait for them. The sun is sinking toward the western skyline, and we need to be back on the road at dawn.

The ruined city laid out before me is a mess of charred, twisted hunks of metal and piles of broken brick. Thick trees dressed in spring blooms push their way out of windows. Wildflowers grow amid tumbles of debris. And what look like wide roads balanced on thick white pillars rise up from the ground and then drop away into nothing, their jagged edges draped with ivy.

A slim metal pole near the entrance of the city has a tattered, sun-bleached flag flapping in the wind.

"The stars and stripes," Jeremiah says beside me.

I turn to find that most of the group is lined up along the bluff staring at what remains of the city. "The what?" I ask him.

"Stars and stripes." He points to the flag. "You can't really see it anymore, but it had fifty white stars on a blue background in the upper left corner. One star for every state."

"There were fifty city-states?" a woman asks.

"No, there were fifty *states*," he says. "States were big territories with hundreds of cities inside their borders."

"Sounds crowded," Rachel says in the same tone she'd use when Jared made his infamous broccoli casserole for dinner and expected her to eat it.

Jeremiah laughs. "Oh, some of the cities were a bit crowded. Take this one. See that?" He points to the strange wide road that rises up on pillars. "That used to be an interstate overpass. We built roads over the top of other roads in some places just to allow everyone to get around."

"Fascinating," I say, but I'm already looking beyond what's left of the interstate to examine the city itself. Somewhere in its depths, I need to find shelter for my people tonight. Near the center of the city, a short distance from a large river, three buildings rise toward the sky in slender, towering masses of steel draped in moss and kudzu. I've never seen buildings so tall. The thought of living so far off the ground makes my stomach queasy. It's one thing to climb fifteen yards up a strong tree and rest in its cradle. It's another to be one hundred yards off the ground in a man-made tower of metal and glass.

I study the ground between us and the buildings. Even with nature trying hard to reclaim the land, I can still make out a faint grid of roads slicing the city into neat rectangles. One road, the one leading through the center of the city, is mostly clear.

We're two weeks away from Lankenshire. Three weeks from Hodenswald. I don't know how far it is to the other three north-eastern city-states, but it's apparent that Jeremiah's map has led us to the main artery used by highwaymen and couriers alike when traveling between the southern and northern territories. We're going to have to leave the main road if we ever hope to elude the Commander and his army. Tomorrow, I'm going to find another way to reach Lankenshire. One that will hopefully throw the Commander off our scent.

First, though, I need shelter for the night. A scan of the

buildings we could reasonably reach with the wagons without leaving an obvious trail shows limited options, however. We could travel through most of the main part of the city and hope one of the brick buildings near the north edge is intact enough to shelter us. We could split up and camp throughout the semi-destroyed shops that line the side streets to the west, but I'd feel better keeping us all together.

That leaves the ridiculously tall buildings, which seem to have survived the fires and destruction mostly intact. If we cover our tracks, and if the inside of the building is in decent shape, we could assign guard shifts high enough to have a panoramic view of the ruins, which would be to our advantage.

My stomach pitches at the thought of being trapped above the ground in a prison of steel and glass, but I give the order to move out. Several hours later, we're ensconced in the most stable of the three buildings, and we've covered our trail well enough that we'll see Carrington coming long before the army ever sees us.

My people are spread across the bottom three floors of the building. The animals and wagons are stashed on the main level. The living quarters are on floors two and three. The medical quarters and the rooms reserved for my inner circle are on floor five. The fourth floor smelled like dead rats, so we left it alone.

I've stationed guards at the stairwells of each occupied floor, just in case. The more experienced guards are posted on the ground level by the wagons and livestock. And, per his own request, I've sent Adam up the stairs to the roof, where he can watch for Quinn, Willow, Carrington, highwaymen, or anyone else we need to worry about.

We've yet to see any sign of Quinn and Willow, and tension coils inside of me. I told them we'd meet them here in four days. It's been six. I don't know what could've held them up, but we can't wait for them. The army will be inside the city limits tomorrow, and we have to be long gone. I have to hope they'll either show up tonight or be able to find our trail when they do arrive.

I refuse to contemplate any scenario in which Quinn and Willow fail to return to us at all.

With everyone settled for the night, I decide to work on perfecting the tech design for the Commander's tracking device. I've been chewing on an idea all day long, and now it's time to put it on parchment and see if it will work.

Frankie stands guard in the stairwell as I approach my floor. I clap my hand on his shoulder as I pass, and he nods a greeting. He surprised me the morning of the Cursed One's attack. He and Thom both. Not that I expected them to be cowards, but I also didn't expect them to risk everything without a second's hesitation and without needing to be told what to do. Thom kept up with the runaway wagon, gathered the reins, stopped the donkey, and calmed the frantic people trapped inside. Because of him, we didn't lose anything more valuable than a cracked wagon wheel, and we have several spares.

Frankie saved Rachel, Ian, and Adam. By leaping in front of them and distracting the beast, he'd given me the extra seconds I needed to finish connecting the device to the power booster. That power booster amplified the sonic pulse I was able to aim at the Cursed One and ensured my control over the creature.

After the tragedy in Baalboden, I'm not willing to risk our

lives by relying on unmodified Rowansmark tech again.

I'm nearly to the room I share with Rachel when a faint scratching sound from inside catches my attention.

In two strides I reach the door. Wrenching it open, I cross the threshold and stare. Jeremiah is hunched over my bedroll, his twisted, arthritic fingers digging through the outside pockets of my travel pack.

"What do you think you're doing?" I close the door behind me and walk across the room.

He jerks his hands away from my pack and struggles to stand. "I was looking for the map. Thought I'd add some more detail to it, seeing as how we're getting close to Lankenshire."

"You told me you'd finished the Lankenshire portion of the map before we left Baalboden."

"But what if Lankenshire turns us away? What if we need to go to Hodenswald or up to Brooksworth? I didn't finish those parts yet."

I stare at him in silence, my arms crossed over my chest. Maybe he was only looking for the map. Or maybe he was getting ready to leave me a note like the one I fished out of my tech bag in Baalboden.

"I'm sorry." He yanks his hat from his head and twists it beneath his fingers. "I shouldn't have been in here without your permission. I know that. I just didn't know where you were, and my old knees can't handle climbing up and down those stairs the way you young people can."

I push past him and grab my pack. Flipping it open, I search the contents. Nothing seems to be missing. And there isn't a cryptic note about debts to be paid either.

"I swear, I was just looking for the map," he says.

Maybe he's telling the truth. Maybe he isn't. But considering our current circumstances, giving him the benefit of the doubt isn't something I can afford to do.

"What else were you hoping to find?" My voice is calm, but my thoughts are racing. Now that I know he wasn't leaving a note, I have to consider other options. My pack has spare clothing, tech supplies waiting to be built into working inventions, and an extra dagger. The only item in my possession worth stealing is the Rowansmark device, and I wear that at all times. Not that I've made that public knowledge. Most of my people were busy running into the forest and climbing trees to avoid the Cursed One while I was unstrapping the tech from my chest. For all Jeremiah knows, I keep the device in my travel pack.

Was Jeremiah one of the survivors who advocated returning the device to Rowansmark and asking for their protection? Would he steal the device himself and try to broker his own deal?

Or have the unsolved murders of our eight boys and our theory that the message points to Rowansmark made me so paranoid that I'm looking for problems where none exist?

"I wasn't looking for anything else." His voice is quiet. Sincere. His pale eyes hold mine without wavering.

I watch him for a long moment, but he doesn't look away. Finally, I move past him, grab my cloak, and pull the map out of the inner pocket.

"Here," I say as I thrust it at him.

"I'll work on it some tonight," he says, and pushes his hat back on his head. "And again, I'm sorry, Logan. I should've waited for you, or sent one of the young ones looking."

I nod once, and he walks out of the room, the map curled inside his hands.

For his sake, I hope he was telling the truth. I'd hate for my first public punishment as leader of this group to be an execution.

CHAPTER TWENTY-THREE

LOGAN

With less than an hour until dark, I make my way to the long rectangle of a room at the end of the hall where Rachel is drilling our recruits on fighting techniques. Thick ivy clings to the windows. The sunlight that seeps past it is a sickly green-gold color that bathes the room in a verdant half-light. Rachel stands in the middle of the room, her sleeves rolled to her elbows, her Switch in hand, and her eyes locked on Ian's. A scattering of others—Jodi, Elias, Keegan, Cassie, Eric, and Thom—lean against the walls, watching Rachel and Ian spar.

Ian lunges forward, his practice stick whistling through the air.

Rachel blocks him and swings the weighted end of her Switch into his thigh. I wince in sympathy. I've been on the receiving end of that move a few times. It took every ounce of pride I had to walk without limping afterward.

"You can cry if you need to," Rachel says as she drives her

elbow into his stomach and then whips around to swing the Switch at his head.

He dives under the blow and slams into her, knocking them both to the ground.

"You first," he says as he tries to pin her to the floor by holding her arms down.

I sigh. This is going to get bloody, and Ian's wearing his best tunic.

Rachel goes limp and drops the Switch. Ian relaxes his grip for a second, tossing a quick grin toward his audience, and Rachel attacks. Bringing her knees up, she plants her boots on his chest and sends him skidding onto his back. Flipping into a crouch, she lunges for him before he can get to his feet.

She's got him. He's on his back, out of position, and she's dropping toward his chest. He'll be lucky if he can breathe without pain for the next hour once she lands.

But before Rachel can deliver, Ian scissors his legs and rolls to his left. Rachel lands where seconds before Ian was lying. With controlled, methodical movements—movements that speak to years of training—he lashes out and sweeps her legs out from under her, flips onto his stomach, and whips her arms into a submission hold.

Rachel swears, and both Jodi and Cassie applaud Ian's win. He grins.

The second he lets go of her, Rachel gets to her feet and shoves a finger into Ian's chest.

"Where did you learn how to do that?"

"You've been training us for over a month now," he says.

Her eyes narrow. "I never taught you how to do that. I don't even *know* how to do that."

He casts a quick, pleading glance my way, as if hoping I have some magic answer that will derail Rachel once she's on a roll. I'm not going to be the one to tell Rachel that Ian apprenticed to be on the Brute Squad. Not after what they did to her on the Claiming stage. Not after they were a party to Oliver's death. She'd tear him to pieces. I'm also not going to lie to cover Ian's mistake. I give him a little head shake. He's on his own.

He raises his hands slowly as if to placate her, and says, "You weren't our only teacher, remember?"

"Quinn taught you that?" she asks, and I can see she believes it's possible.

He's spared from answering when there's a commotion in the hall and Quinn himself strides through the door, Willow right behind him. Relief weakens my knees for a moment, and I steady myself with one hand on the wall beside me. I'd truly thought I'd have to leave them behind in the morning.

"You made it," I say, and Rachel rushes to my side.

"We're two days late. You shouldn't have waited," Quinn says, but he smiles at us both.

"We only arrived an hour ago, and plan to leave in the morning." I walk forward and clap him on the shoulder. "Did you find the killer?"

"We found his boot prints," Willow says. "Twice. He's following the group."

"Pretty sloppy for a tracker," Rachel says.

Willow smiles a little. "Not where these prints were. We had to move leaves and underbrush to find them. He'd done a good job of covering his tracks, but he made the terrain a little *too* perfect, and that's usually the sign of someone trying to be invisible."

"Could you see a maker's mark on the print?" I ask.

"Rowansmark," Quinn says. "He's good enough to hide from Willow and me. We doubled back, circled around, laid traps . . . everything we could think of, but he stayed a step ahead of us. He'll come after the group again. No one dedicates this much time and attention to hunting down prey without coming home with their prize."

Prey. A chill brushes across my skin.

"Well, we're safe for now. Rachel, Ian, and Adam checked every inch of this building before we allowed the group inside. We're alone here, there's only one entrance, and I've tripled the guards we normally use. No one is going to get inside this building tonight."

"I hate to tell you, but the tracker is the least of your worries." Willow grabs my arm and pulls me toward the stairwell at the end of the hall. "You have a bigger problem now. Come on."

My heart thuds painfully against my chest as we reach the stairwell and begin to climb. This ridiculous building has thirty-five floors. I cling to the railing and practically drag myself up each miserable step. The air in here is stale and dank, and clusters of moss cling to the cracks that spread across the walls. Sweat gathers at the small of my back, and I'm breathing way too fast, but I can't seem to control it.

Did the previous government outlaw the building of new homes or shops? I can't imagine any other valid reason for agreeing to stretch steel and glass toward the sky as if daring the wind to knock it over.

I'm panting, and my fingers feel numb when we finally reach the brown metal door that leads to the roof. It sticks. Quinn slams into it with his shoulder, and it reluctantly creaks open on hinges nearly immobile with rust and age. He walks onto the roof, followed by Willow, Rachel, and Ian. Thom, Cassie, Keegan, and Jodi stayed downstairs like the admirably sane people I know them to be.

Adam looks up as we walk onto the roof, and his eyes go straight to Willow. "You're back. I was getting worried."

She tugs on her braid and says, "You don't need to worry about me."

"No, but I did anyway," he says. Willow's cheeks turn a dusky pink, and her smile is a little shy.

Then she turns to me and says, "Coming out sometime today?" Before I can respond, she strides toward the edge of the roof.

I cling to the doorjamb, staring at the wide-open space before me. The rooftop is a faded gray stone riddled with cracks and holes. Rusted pipes stick out at irregular intervals, like some sort of ventilation system. A large, square metal box rests in the corner. Almost every available inch is covered with a clinging green vine or a carpet of moss. The edge of the roof is surrounded by a low railing that barely reaches Willow's waist.

That can't possibly be safe.

She waves me over, a sharp, impatient gesture, and I edge my way out of the doorway. The wind tugs and pushes, and only pride keeps me from dropping to my knees and crawling. I step over vines, slide across moss, and grimly calculate the trajectory necessary to slam into the railing instead of sailing over into thin air, should the capricious wind have its way with me.

When I reach Willow, I grab the railing with both fists and hold on as if my life depends on it. Which it probably does. Because no one was meant to be this far off the ground.

"Look." She points south. "No, *there*. A few degrees to the east."

I crane my neck and sweep the cityscape and beyond, manfully swallowing the need to whimper when I accidentally look too far down. "I don't see anything," I say in a voice that doesn't exactly shake, but doesn't do me any favors, either.

"That line of buildings to the south of us is in the way. We need to find a better angle. Come on," she says, and starts walking. The others follow her.

I stay put. I'm not walking across that death trap again unless I'm heading for the door. "I'll take the east side," I say, and creep along the railing by sliding my fists. No need to let go. No need to plummet thirty-five stories to my inglorious demise.

I scan piles of rubble with trees growing from their centers, broken metal spires leaning precariously over the remnants of roads, and random clusters of buildings that remain somewhat whole. My eyes are drawn to the edges of the Wasteland, steadily encroaching on the borders of the city. Nothing moves. Nothing is out of place.

But when I lift my eyes above the tree line, I see faint lines of smoke drifting up into the air from the bluff just beyond the city limits.

"Fire?" I ask, because apparently along with a shaking voice and a white-knuckle grip on the railing, I feel the need to humiliate myself by stating the obvious.

"Campfires," Willow says. "The army. That's what took us so long. We had to go west and circle back around to avoid them."

"Our lookouts have reported that the army has been getting closer every day," Ian says.

"If they get any closer, they'll be able to hear you snoring in your sleep," Willow says.

"I don't snore." Ian sounds offended.

"Right. And bunnies don't reproduce every time they look at each other, either."

"The army is right on top of us. I think the only reason they haven't already attacked is because they don't know exactly where we are." Quinn appears at my elbow. If he notices the death grip I have on the railing, he doesn't react.

Rachel's voice is fierce. "The Commander will send scouts. We should—"

"Oh, he sent scouts," Willow says. "Five of them. And they were doing a good job of searching the city. Unfortunately for them, all they managed to find was me."

"You killed them?" Ian asks.

"No. I invited them over for dinner." She smacks his shoulder. "The sun is almost down. By the time the Commander realizes his scouts aren't coming back, it will be too dark to send more. He can't risk us seeing torchlight, and they can't search these ruins without light."

"You scare me a little," Ian says, but his voice is full of admiration.

Adam steps closer to Willow. "She's good at everything she does."

Quinn clears his throat. "Maybe we should get back to the problem?"

"We can't travel at night," I say. "We need light as well. But we can leave at dawn, and—"

"They'll leave at dawn, too," Adam says. "And if they're that close already, there's no way we can outrun them. Not with children and elderly and the wagons."

"Which is why we're going to create a barrier between us," I say. "Something they can't cross."

Rachel meets my eyes, and her smile is cold and bright. "Fire."

I match her smile with one of my own. "Fire. And when the army finally gets past the blaze, we won't be where they expect, because we're leaving the main road behind."

"What are we waiting for?" Willow asks. "Let's go burn something down."

CHAPTER TWENTY-FOUR

RACHEL

As the sun disintegrates into ribbons of fire in the western sky, we huddle at the edge of the rooftop, scanning the southern entrance to the city while we make a plan.

"Those houses along the western edge look like they'd burn." Adam points toward a dilapidated row of homes that skirt the city limit.

"There's plenty of flammable debris through the side streets that lead to this building, too," Willow says.

"We'll create a firebreak behind those houses at the edge of the city." Logan's voice is calm, though he won't relinquish his grip on the guardrail that encircles the rooftop. "We'll go out in teams after dark. One team will create a twenty-yard perimeter behind the houses to keep the fire from spreading toward us. The other team will gather wood, dried grass, underbrush . . . anything that will burn. We'll spread the flammable materials in thirty-yard lines from the houses and into the Wasteland to help the fire head toward the bluff."

"And then we light it?" Adam asks as we turn toward the stairwell.

"No," Logan says. "We get a few hours of sleep, make sure we're ready to travel just before dawn, and *then* light it. We need to be ready to move the instant that fire catches, just in case. The flames and smoke will obscure the Commander's sight line, and he'll have to find another way through the city, because the whole main entrance will be on fire."

After a quick dinner, Logan and I divide up our nighttime volunteers. Logan takes those who will be working on the firebreak, mostly because he can't stand not to be in complete control of how much distance the team creates between the line of houses we're using to start the fire and the road that leads directly to our shelter. I take those who are gathering materials to create a sustained blaze large enough to both camouflage our movements and force the army to find another path. We leave Frankie and Eric in charge of guarding the entrance to our shelter and make sure every volunteer understands that we have to work in pairs and stay alert.

None of us have forgotten that we have a Rowansmark tracker out there waiting for the chance to kill again.

Ian, Thom, Jodi, Cassie, Derreck, Smithson, and Sylph are on my team. The row of houses perched at the southern edge of the main road are leaning against each other like unevenly stacked books just waiting for a strong wind to push them over. Jodi, Cassie, Smithson, and Derreck gather armloads of flammable debris from the team creating the firebreak and from the streets closest to the houses. Thom, Ian, Sylph, and I create trails for the fire to follow straight into the Wasteland and toward the army camped on the bluff above us.

Hours pass. We work in near silence as the stars slowly drift across the night sky. Occasionally, we hear snatches of loud conversation and laughter echoing down from the bluff, as if the soldiers are already celebrating a victory. As if they're so sure they can annihilate us.

Every word, every laugh, pours salt on a wound I don't know how to bandage. Somewhere up on that bluff, the man who ruined my life eats his dinner. Gives his orders. Stares at the dark ruins of this city and congratulates himself on winning the game.

As I drag another branch into place and sprinkle rough stalks of grass over it, I come to a decision. We wouldn't have to light this fire if the Commander was dead. We wouldn't have to flee toward Lankenshire like deer trying to outrun a hunter. We could find peace.

I could find peace.

It's not that far to the bluff. Without the group to slow me down, I can be there in an hour. Maybe less if I don't run into any guards. I'll scout out the army's camp, find where the Commander is staying, and then shoot him in the head with an arrow. The army might come after me then, but I'll have darkness on my side, and they'll never find me. Dropping the rest of the grass onto the branch, I turn and silently melt into the Wasteland.

"Going somewhere?"

I whip my knife out of its sheath before I realize the person standing just yards away from me is Ian. "Don't *do* that. I could've killed you." I fight to keep my voice down. If I can hear the army, they can hear me.

"You could've tried." He steps closer and the starlight gleams against the angles of his face. "What's the plan?"

"The plan?"

"For killing the Commander. That's where you were going, right?" He jerks his chin toward the bluff and says quietly, "I'm in. What's the plan?"

"I sneak up to the camp, look for the Commander, and shoot him with an arrow."

Ian is silent for a moment, and then he says in a fierce whisper, "That's a terrible plan. One girl and one arrow against an army of hundreds?"

"Who says I have just one arrow?"

He grabs my arm. "Normally, I like your kind of crazy. But this is our chance. Remember? We made a deal. We can't take down the Commander by sneaking into their camp. Don't you think every single soldier is on the lookout for a girl with red hair and a nasty look in her eyes?"

"That's the beauty of a bow and arrow." I shake my arm free. "You can shoot from a distance."

"And if you miss? Or if you can't find him without getting close enough to be seen? Or if he's out of range? Then what?"

I glare even though he can't see my expression. "You're starting to sound a lot like Logan. *What's your exit strategy, Rachel? What's your backup plan?*"

"Shh." Ian looks over his shoulder for a second. Then he says, "We already have our backup plan. We use the device. Logan proved that it works. We destroy the enemy, and then it's over."

"I don't have the device. Logan does. He wears it strapped to his chest, and he isn't going to just give it to us." I shove my knife back into its sheath. Time is slipping away from me. If I'm going to make it to the bluff, find the Commander, and hopefully shoot him where he sits, I have to leave now.

"And you can't think of a single thing you could do out here in the dark to get him to take it off? We need it, Rachel."

"What do you need?" Thom asks behind us.

I grit my teeth and bend to grab another branch as if all I have planned for the evening is the task of laying fuel for tomorrow's fire. "Nothing."

"Didn't sound like nothing to me."

"Do you make a habit of eavesdropping?" Ian asks, and there's an edge to his voice.

"If you hadn't been so focused on trying to convince Rachel to do something for you, you'd have heard me come up," Thom says. "We still need to work on the eastern fuel trails. Let's go."

"I'm going to finish up here. I'll be there in a few minutes," I say.

"No one's working alone. There's a tracker out here. Might be army scouts, too. We'll wait for you." Thom folds his big arms across his chest and watches us both.

Perfect. Now how am I supposed to get to the bluff? If I just leave, Thom will tell Logan in a heartbeat. I have no trouble envisioning what Logan would do with that piece of news.

I also have no trouble remembering the hurt in his eyes when he begged me not to sacrifice myself for revenge and leave him with no one.

The silence within me presses close, hungry for vengeance, but I make myself walk toward the city instead. Logan and I have a plan. And we have people to protect before we can put that plan in action. If I try for the Commander and fail, I'll be another tool the Commander can use to hurt Logan.

"Rachel?" Ian asks as I brush past him.

"You two can finish the eastern fuel line. I'm going to check in with Logan."

I leave them there without a backward glance, feeling emptier with every step I take away from the bluff.

CHAPTER TWENTY-FIVE

RACHEL

I find Logan inside the Wasteland inspecting one of the fuel lines. Quinn and Willow are with him.

"There you are," he says, and there's relief in his voice as he steps away from the others and moves toward me. "I sent the rest of your team back to the shelter, but couldn't find you, Ian, or Thom. I thought . . ."

When he doesn't finish his sentence, I say, "I know there's a tracker out here somewhere. I was careful."

He looks at me for a long moment, then says quietly, "I was more worried about the fact that the Commander is so close. I thought you'd be tempted to do something . . . unplanned. I'm sorry I misjudged you."

For a moment, I consider lying to him, but I can't stomach the thought. Quinn and Willow leave to inspect the next fuel line, and I'm grateful for the privacy.

"You didn't misjudge me. I was about to sneak up to the bluff, look for the Commander, and shoot an arrow in his eye."

He makes a strangled noise in the back of his throat and starts pacing. "You were . . . that's just . . ." He draws in a deep, slow breath, as if he needs the time to find the words missing from his sentences.

"We could still get him. He's so close. We could use the device with your booster pack attached. We already know it works—"

"Absolutely not." He stops pacing and faces me.

"Logan, he's *right there*." I gesture toward the distant bluff, with its cheerful campfires and snatches of laughter drifting on the wind. "Every soldier with him would kill us without hesitation if they had the chance. Why can't we do the same? We have the advantage. We could use the Cursed One and finish this."

His voice is fierce. "Last time we called the beast it wouldn't touch the Commander because of the necklace he wears. Instead, it destroyed our city. I refuse to take a chance with our lives again. We have a plan. I have an invention that will find him and *kill* him, Rachel. I just need a few more supplies to finish building it."

"I thought you were building a tracking device. How would that kill him?"

"It's basic science. I can't believe I didn't think of it before. The tracking device sends out a sound wave, which is essentially an oscillation of pressure traveling through an acceptable medium at various frequencies—"

"You're losing me."

"The tracker sends out a sound wave, searching for a specific signal. The Commander's, in this case. For the tracker to find the signal, there has to be a receiver at the other end. Something to accept and translate the sound wave. The tracking device's signal is strong enough to ping off of the receiver and bounce back to the original tech." His words tumble over each other in his eureka!-I-just-invented-something-epic! voice. "But what if the signal was stronger? What if I could increase the sound wave to something the receiver couldn't accept?"

"You mean you think you can overpower the Commander's wristmark receiver? I don't want to dump cold water on your enthusiasm, but what good would that do? Wouldn't it just break the receiver and leave us with no way to track him at all?"

"I'm not just going to break the receiver. I'm going to obliterate it. Use sound as a weapon."

"Explode his receiver?"

"Yes."

"In his wrist."

"Yes."

"Next to his artery." My breath quickens as something brilliant and sharp surges through me.

"Exactly."

I throw my arms around him. "You're a genius. I don't tell you that often enough, but you really are."

His voice is quiet. "We agreed to a plan. I told you I could build something we could use after we delivered these people safely to Lankenshire. Why didn't you trust me? Why go off on your own?"

"I didn't go." My voice sounds small. "Ian stopped me at first, but then I thought about what you asked of me back in Baalboden. How you didn't want me to risk myself without an exit strategy because if I die, you'll have no one. I decided not to go, but a big part of me still wishes I had."

He wraps his arms around me and pulls me to his chest. "You don't have to face him alone."

"I don't care if I face him alone. I just want this to be over. I want him to suffer and die. I want to stop running for our lives. I want to stop seeing . . ." Melkin's dark eyes, burning with fury as I drive my knife into his chest. Oliver's neck bleeding and bleeding. The white cross on my father's grave.

"Stop seeing what?" His voice is gentle, but he holds me like he's afraid I'll disappear if he lets go.

I tell myself I want to shatter the deafening silence inside of me and *feel*, but I know I'm lying. I can't wait to shove the guilt and grief away from me. Can't wait to take a breath without suffocating on the blood of everyone I've lost. I flinch away from truth and into the silence.

The comfort it offers is cold and empty. A barren tomb cutting me off from the rest of the world. I should be clawing at the sides, screaming my lungs out, and fighting to escape.

Fighting to live.

I dig my fingers into Logan's cloak and breathe. The air smells of musky tree bark, rich, dark earth, and the faint sweetness of the flowering sweetshrubs that dot the landscape.

"Please talk to me," Logan says quietly, and something heavy lies in his voice. "Tell me what's hurting you."

I step back and my heart thuds against my chest.

"It has something to do with your nightmares, doesn't it?" He reaches out and traces my cheek with his finger. "What do you dream about, Rachel?"

Blood. Pouring endlessly. Those I've lost. Those I've taken. Guilt writhing through me like a poisonous snake, killing me slowly from the inside out.

He's silent for a moment, and then he says quietly, "Don't you trust me?"

"Of course I do." I do. I just don't trust myself. I can hold myself together during the day. I can take charge of what needs to be done; I can say the words everyone seems to want to hear; and I can pretend real feelings live inside of me instead of the vast wall of silence. But I can't pretend at night. I can't hold myself together when everything the silence keeps from me floods into my mind and brings me to my knees.

If I put words to it, if I let it cut me like I deserve, how will I ever keep the two parts of me separate again?

"If you trust me, then let me in. Please. I want to help you, but how can I when I don't know what you're facing?" Hurt crouches inside his words.

I swallow the automatic protest that rises to my lips. Once upon a time, I told Oliver everything. Told Dad almost everything. And I'd like to think if my mother had lived, I'd have shared almost everything with her, too. Maybe that's what love is. Giving others the power to hurt you and trusting that they'll use it to heal you instead.

Stepping forward, he cups my face in his calloused palms and says, "I know you aren't okay. How could you be? I'm not okay, either. But hiding from it isn't going to solve it."

Something hot and painful throbs inside my chest. "Nothing's going to solve it, Logan. I can't . . ."

"You can't what?"

"I can't be strong enough to face this"—I gesture toward the bluff behind us and hope he knows that I mean everything.

Oliver. Dad. The Commander. *Everything*—"if I start talking about my nightmares. And you need me to be strong. Everyone needs me to be strong. Falling apart isn't an option."

"Who says you're going to fall apart?" He leans closer. "You're the strongest person I know. Most would've quit trying by now, but not you. Trusting me with whatever is hurting you won't break you, Rachel."

He's wrong. If I trust him with it, I have to also trust myself. I'd have to drag what lives in the shadows out into the light and hope I survive what I see.

And if I look my darkness in the face and it overwhelms me, how will I find the strength to get back on my feet again?

He rubs his thumb across my cheekbone. "It's hard to face talking about things that hurt. But I think if we're going to survive this together, we have to."

"How come I'm the only one who has to talk about the hard stuff? You said you aren't okay, either."

"Fair enough. I'll go first." He lets go of me and pushes his hand through his hair. The silence between us lengthens until he laughs, a sharp, bitter sound. "You're right. It's a lot harder to talk about stuff like this than I gave you credit for."

"Stuff like what?"

A shout goes up from the bluff, followed by more laughter. Behind us, the city is silent.

Logan tilts his head back and stares at the sky. "I think I might be to blame for the Rowansmark tracker killing our boys." His voice sounds weary. Like this is a familiar thought he can hardly stand to face again.

"How could you possibly be to blame?"

"What if the message the killer left for us was meant for *me*? The first message was in my tech bag. What if the debt that needs to be paid is mine? What if I'm . . ." He swallows hard. "What if my choices are responsible for the deaths of those boys?"

I fist my hands on my hips. "Who put that stupid idea into your head?"

He shakes his head and doesn't speak.

An owl hoots somewhere above us, and something scurries through the underbrush at our feet.

I step closer to Logan and put every ounce of conviction I possess into my voice. "You aren't responsible."

"I am if this really is a tracker delivering Rowansmark's sentence of pain atonement. I kept the device—"

"I gave you the device in the first place. If you're responsible, then so am I. So is Quinn, for keeping it safe for me instead of bringing it back to Rowansmark. In fact, while we're busy writing fairy tales, my dad is responsible too, for bringing it out of Rowansmark in the first place." I tap my foot against the ground while I wait for him to see reason. "Anyone who could slit the throats of innocent boys is a twisted, depraved lunatic. I don't care what his sick justification was. If you take a life, you and you alone are responsible for that choice. If you can't see that then you aren't half as smart as I've always thought you were."

He reaches out, takes my hand, and pulls me against him. His hands tangle in my hair, and he leans toward my mouth. "Do you know one of the things I love most about you?"

"No." My voice is a faint breath of air.

His fingers slide down my back. "You are incapable of being tactful to spare someone's feelings."

My heart sinks a little. "That doesn't sound like a compliment."

"I've spent my life as an outcast." His voice is quiet. Steady. "I walked into stores and people started whispering. I'd enter a crowd and see parents shoo their children away from me like I'd contracted some terrible disease no one else wanted to catch. Yet all the while, those same people would smile to my face. I never knew if the friendliness I saw in someone's eyes was real until I met you."

"Well, those other people were obviously idiots."

He tilts my head back and leans closer. "I always know where I stand with you. Even when you were angry with me, you never bothered trying to hide it. You are exactly who you seem to be, and I wouldn't have it any other way."

His kiss is gentle, and much too short. When he leans back, he says, "I shared what was bothering me, and it helped. Ready to do the same?"

My throat tightens, and I swallow hard. "I dream of Dad and Oliver." And Melkin. And blood, but I can't find the words to paint that picture. "I see them die. Over and over. Or they come to me already dead." My voice sinks into a whisper. "Nothing feels right inside of me since I lost them. Since *we* lost them."

He wraps his arms around me and pulls me against him. "I'm sorry." Warmth from his mouth whispers across mine as his lips brush against me. "I love you, Rachel."

I wrap my arms around him and stretch up on my tiptoes. "I love you, too." I kiss him until the forest seems to spin around me, and I can't tell which of us is holding the other up.

A faint crunch, like a boot stepping on the rocky forest soil, echoes behind us. The whispery hiss of someone drawing in a ragged breath crawls across the air and raises the hair on my arms.

CHAPTER TWENTY-SIX

RACHEL

Grabbing our weapons, we turn back-to-back, and face the shadowed forest around us. I raise my knife and crouch. Forcing myself to control my breathing, I listen intently. Behind me, Logan is quiet too as we wait for the Wasteland to give up its secrets.

A scout from the army? The tracker?

Something scrapes against a tree to the left of me. I adjust my grip on my knife and get ready. If someone attacks us, we won't see him coming before he's almost on top of us. I'll have only seconds to assess the threat and remove it.

Blood on my hands. Pouring from my palms. Rushing down my throat to choke me with my guilt.

I bite my cheek hard, and use the pain to banish the memory of my nightmares.

Another faint sound floats toward us. This time from the right. Either two people are out there, or someone knows how to move quickly in near silence.

Logan whispers, "When I say go, we drop to the ground and crawl beneath those bushes. Put your back to the tree."

I can just make out the cluster of shrubs he's talking about. They're a good six yards away, but if we can dive underneath them and keep our backs to the huge oak tree beside them, we'll only have to defend possible attacks from one direction. Plus, it will force whoever is out there to hunt for us, which will hopefully give us the advantage of hearing little telltale sounds that will give away his position before he attacks.

"Ready . . . set . . ."

There's a thud, and Logan lands heavily on the ground, groaning in pain. A jagged chunk of stone the size of my palm hits the forest floor beside him.

I lunge for Logan, searching for wounds with my left hand while my right holds my knife steady. "Are you hurt?" I whisper, even though I know he must be or we'd both be crawling beneath the bushes right now.

The sticky warmth flowing from the back of his head answers my question before he can open his mouth. He's bleeding, hit by a stone thrown by an opponent we can't see. An opponent who could even now be coming in for the kill. We're exposed, and every second I spend trying to figure out how this happened is another second I give our attacker to close in on us.

"What direction did it come from?" I ask against his ear.

"West," he breathes, and struggles to roll over.

Transferring my knife to my left hand, I grab the stone, slick with Logan's blood, and jump to my feet. Spinning to the west, I pull my arm back and throw the rock with all the strength I've got.

It slams into a distant tree with a resounding thud. I'm already on the ground grabbing a fistful of Logan's tunic and pulling him toward the bushes, hoping the small distraction I caused will buy us enough time to get to safety. Logan pushes my hand away and gets to his knees.

"I can make it. You go first." His voice is slurred.

Right. Why don't I leave the boy I love lying injured and disoriented on the forest floor and get myself to safety instead?

"Don't be an idiot," I say, and reach down to tug him forward.

Someone laughs—an ugly sound of vicious amusement. A man. Behind us and to the west.

"Pay your debt," he says in a harsh whisper that lingers in the air and sets my heart pounding with fury.

It's the Rowansmark tracker. It has to be.

My hands shake as I let go of Logan's tunic and grab my knife again. Cowards deserve to be punished. Especially ones who throw rocks instead of finding the backbone to fight an opponent face-to-face.

And *especially* ones who kill innocent boys and then leave cryptic messages about debts and atonement written in blood.

"Crawl," I whisper to Logan. "Fast. I'll buy you some time."

"What are you doing?" Logan asks. "The bushes—"

I lunge to my feet and raise my voice, "You filthy, miserable, no-good coward! Get out here and face me like a man."

Logan grabs my ankle and hisses his words. "Get down. Stop making yourself a target."

"Crawl."

I raise my voice and keep my arms up around my face in

case the killer decides to throw another rock. "You're a coward without honor. Too afraid of us to do anything but throw rocks."

Anger gushes through me, fueled by the memory of eight boys carved up like slaughtered sheep. "I'll make you beg for mercy, but there won't be any. Not for you. Not after what you've done. Do you hear me?"

Something feral claws at my throat—a wild, furious need to rip the tracker apart. To make him pay. To scream and scream and scream until all the broken pieces inside of me soften into something that no longer cuts into me every time I sleep.

My knife is a silver-sharp slice of diamond beneath the glistening light of the moon. I stab the air in front of me as if I can kill the thing that hurts me even though it's buried so deep inside, I no longer know how to find it.

"Rachel!" Logan drives the point of his sword into the ground. Using the weapon as a crutch, he pulls himself to his feet. He leans precariously to one side, and I swear as I wrap an arm around his waist and anchor him to my side. "The tracker will follow your voice—"

"Let him." My knife is still raised, my body shaking with the need to punish someone for the fear, the blood, and the injustice of it all. "We'll kill him."

A shadowy blur moves in the corner of my eye. I whip my head to the right, but I can't see far in the dark. Logan tries to lift his sword, but the movement nearly pitches him to his knees.

"Rachel! Logan!" Quinn's voice echoes through the night. "Where are you?"

I grab Logan's tunic and hold him steady. "Here!" I call out, and scan the area again, my knife ready.

"Need help—" Logan says, his shoulders slumping.

"Hold on. Quinn's on his way. If anyone attacks, he and I will take care of it. But no one is going to attack"—I raise my voice—"because cowards who throw rocks in the dark don't have the guts to attack face-to-face."

The only sound that greets this pronouncement is the soft slap of Quinn's boots against the dirt. Seconds later, he whistles, and I call out our location.

When he reaches us, he says, "I heard you yelling from thirty yards away. Are you deliberately putting yourself in danger?" He sounds angry.

"Sort of. Logan's hurt. The tracker threw a rock and hit him in the head. Help me get him back to camp."

"How do you know it was the tracker?" Quinn asks.

"Because he said something about our debt needing to be paid. It was all very dramatic and cowardly."

Logan says something that sounds like he's missing most of his teeth and has a bee sting on his tongue.

I take more of his weight and say, "He wants to know where Willow is."

"She was escorting Thom and Ian back to the shelter. I was coming to find you two so we could all go back together."

Logan mumbles something else.

Quinn snakes an arm around Logan's other side. "He doesn't sound good. Let's make this quick."

We're quiet as we navigate the forest, climb over the fuel line, and head down the main road into the city. It takes twenty minutes to get to the shelter, and I keep glancing over my shoulder, looking for any sign that the tracker is following us. When we reach the building we're using for shelter, Frankie steps away from the door and says, "Who's there?"

"Rachel, Logan, and Quinn," I say. "Logan's hurt. The tracker threw a rock at him. Double the guard on this door tonight. We need to make sure he doesn't try to kill anyone in their sleep."

"You hear that, boy?" Frankie asks. Eric steps to his side, his dark hair nothing but a smudge beneath the starlit sky. "Go wake four people instead of two and have them take over this post."

It takes less than five minutes for Eric to return with four new guards. We wait at the entrance with Frankie, our eyes constantly scanning the street, looking for threats.

When the new guards are informed of the situation and are in position, we start toward our room, and Frankie says, "Where's Logan hurt?"

"Took a rock to the head," Logan says, his words sounding clearer than they did a few minutes ago.

"Good thing they went after your head. Anywhere else, and they might've done some damage," Frankie says.

Logan laughs and then hisses in a breath. I don't laugh. I don't see anything funny about the situation at all. The tracker is still with us. Still focused on hurting us.

Most troubling of all, he's focused on hurting Logan.

It takes time to navigate the stairs and reach our room. Willow is waiting in the hall.

She holds our door open and peers at the dark trail of blood slowly sliding down Logan's face. "It's a good look for you, but I wouldn't recommend repeating it."

He tries to smile, but moans instead as we lower him onto his bedroll.

I hurry to the corner of the room where I keep the rest of my water ration waiting to help me freshen up in the morning. Tearing a strip from one of my blankets, I dunk it in the water and press it against Logan's cut. By the time I'm done cleaning the cut, Drake, Nola, and Adam are hovering in the doorway, concern evident on their faces.

"So what happened?" Frankie asks.

I tell them. When I'm done, Drake says, "You're sure it was a tracker?"

"We're sure a tracker is following the camp," Quinn says. "If he's the one who killed the boys and left messages for Logan, it makes sense that he'd attack Logan."

Frankie's small eyes focus on Quinn. "How'd you manage to be close enough to come to Logan's rescue?"

"I'd just finished checking the fuel lines and was looking for Logan and Rachel so we could come back to the shelter."

"Weren't you also out alone in the forest the night the boys were killed?" Frankie slowly crosses his bearlike arms and stares at Quinn.

"He walks the forest almost every night," Willow says as she takes a step toward Frankie. "What's it to you?"

"I'll tell you what I think." Frankie's voice shakes with anger.

"Oh, yes, please do," Willow says.

"I think it's a mistake not to say that the most obvious suspect is standing right there." Frankie points at Quinn.

"My brother isn't the killer." Willow whips her bow up to aim an arrow at Frankie's throat. Her voice is cold and cruel. "He has moral qualms about taking another's life. I, on the other hand, have none."

"Willow, put it down," I say. Willow ignores me. "Frankie, Quinn didn't do this. I'm sure of it."

"All I know is we got ourselves a leaf lover who's good enough to fight off Carrington soldiers even though he wasn't carrying a weapon. He admits that he was out walking alone the night the boys were killed. We all know those boys wouldn't have suspected a thing if he walked up to them while they were standing guard." Frankie's eyes bore into Quinn's. "And then he left camp for nearly a week, and we had peace. Now first night after he's back, we got problems again, and we have to take his word that there's a Rowansmark tracker out there."

Willow's fingers are white where they bend around her bow. Her arrow is steady. I don't know how to convince her to lower her weapon. Willow does what she wants. Besides, if Frankie had said terrible things about Logan, I'd want him to pay for his words, too.

"It's okay, Willow," Quinn says quietly, and she slowly lowers the bow.

"I don't believe Quinn would kill anyone." Logan's words are slurred, but his voice is as unforgiving as the floor beneath our feet. "And, Frankie, that's the third time you've used the derogatory term 'leaf lover' toward Quinn and Willow. Do it again, and I'll chain you to the supply wagon for a week."

His lip curls. "You defend these strangers? Over your own people?"

"Quinn and Willow are my friends. They've acted with honor and courage for the entire time I've known them. In fact, they've treated me far better than most of my *own* people, and I'm not going to forget it."

Frankie backs toward the hall. "Fine. But I've got my eye on you." He looks at Quinn.

Willow moves restlessly, but Quinn stills her with a glance. Meeting Frankie's gaze, he says, "As you wish." His stoic exterior is firmly in place. "Now Willow and I are going to get some rest. We have a fire to start just before dawn."

Without another word, he brushes past everyone and leaves. Willow stalks past Frankie, muttering something about gutting him like a fish, and disappears after her brother.

"We should all get some sleep," I say, and those who remain take the hint.

As they leave, I wrap my arms around Logan and help him lie on his bedroll. Almost before his head touches the blankets, his eyes close and his breathing slows as sleep takes him.

For the first time since the tracker attacked us, I let myself think about Logan's words to me. About trusting him. About facing what lives in my nightmares and believing I'm strong enough to come out whole on the other side.

Maybe I am strong enough. Maybe the things that crouch behind my inner silence wouldn't hurt me if I drag them into the light.

Or maybe my secret horrors would cling to me with bloody fingers and destroy what's left of me.

It doesn't matter. We have a tracker to catch. People to keep safe. And the Commander to destroy. Compared to that, one girl's nightmares are a thing of little consequence.

CHAPTER TWENTY-SEVEN

LOGAN

I wake at dawn to a splitting headache. Shadowy half-light seeps in past the mossy window, turning everything around me into hazy, indistinct shapes.

Or maybe taking a rock to the head did that.

Trying to get up sends shooting pain into my eye sockets and makes my stomach pitch. I lie still, breathing deeply for a moment, and then slowly roll to my side.

Rachel is asleep, slumped against the wall beside me, her knife clutched in her hand. Since I didn't wake to screams, she either had a peaceful night, or she stayed up until sheer exhaustion kept her from dreaming. Judging by the faint dark smudges beneath her eyes, I'm betting on the latter.

It's time to get the camp up and moving. We need to light the fire before the army starts moving off the bluff.

My head pounds, a sick throbbing that increases as I push myself to my knees. I move my feet underneath me until I'm crouching over my blanket, cradling my head in my hands. The bandage that Rachel tied over the cut feels like it's stuck to the back of my skull. Dried blood, probably. I'll need to dunk my head in some water to get it off.

The thought of it makes me want to lie down again.

Instead, I hold still and breathe deeply, hoping the throbbing in my head will lessen. If I can't get this pain under control, I'll be in no shape to lead us into the Wasteland.

I let go of my head and press my palms to the ground. Surely, if I move slowly enough, I can stand up. The contents of our room lurch sideways as I push myself off the floor and instantly crash back down onto my hands and knees. I look at Rachel, but she's still sound asleep, her knife gleaming against the dark brown of her cloak.

I'm going to need some leverage to get myself on my feet. Moving cautiously, I crawl toward the doorway, my eyes on the sturdy table that hugs the wall beside the entrance. The rug that covers the floor is brittle and seems to crumble beneath my fingers as I lean on my hands.

I'm nearly there when something sharp gouges my palm. Looking down, I see a slender gray piece of metal, about the length of my index finger. One end is fluted, its slim edges now covered in blood from the shallow cut on my hand. The other end looks like a miniature spear, its needle tip buried in the rug beside my travel pack.

It's a dart. Made from the same metal as the Rowansmark tech I wear strapped across my chest. A small white cloth is pinned to the floor beneath it.

My chest feels like a slab of steel is crushing me as the implications hit home.

The tracker was in our room.

Which means he got inside the building. Which means the four people who stood guard over the main entrance last night are probably dead.

My fingers shake as I grasp the dart and yank it free. The pressure in my chest joins the throbbing in my head as I unfold the cloth and stare at the letters penned in delicate swirls of drying blood.

The marked will die to pay your debt.

I swear viciously and crumple the cloth in my fist. Rachel jerks to attention and comes to her feet, her knife gripped tightly.

"What is it? What's wrong?" she asks.

"This." I toss the cloth to her and pick up the dart instead. Definitely the same material as the device. If I had any doubt left within me that I'm dealing with a Rowansmark tracker, it's gone now.

I drop the dart and press my fingers to my eyes in the futile hope that somehow if I just push hard enough, the pain will go away.

"Where was this?" Rachel asks. Her voice crashes into my head and doubles the pain.

"Here." I gesture toward the floor and immediately regret it when the movement sends brilliant white sparks through my brain.

Her words are furious, but I hear the thin thread of fear beneath them. "He was *in here.* When?"

"I don't know, but I'm afraid the guards we had at the building's entrance must be dead. We have to go check, and then get our people out of this place before he does anything else."

"It says the marked *will* die. That means it hasn't happened yet. If we can figure out what he means or how he intends to do it, we can stop him," Rachel says. "Let's go."

"Yes," I say, though with every sound crashing around inside of my head like it's trying to crack my skull, I'm not in any shape to figure out how to stand up on my own, much less how to out-think a killer.

She slides her knife into its sheath and wraps her arm around me. I lean heavily on her while I stagger to my feet. The ground dips and sways, and I close my eyes until the world around me settles. Then we slowly make our way toward the door.

"The marked will die," I say as we reach the doorway. "I wonder what kind of mark he means?"

Rachel shoves the door open and we step out into the hallway. A few people walk out of their rooms, travel packs slung over their shoulders, but we barely spare them a glance. We're too busy staring at the row of doorways stretching along the corridor.

Scattered throughout the hall are doors marked with a bloody X.

CHAPTER TWENTY-EIGHT

RACHEL

My stomach feels like it's caving in as I stare at the red Xs marking random doors. I glance behind me, but our door is unblemished. I don't want to take another step. Don't want to open the marked doors and see what lies inside.

Logan swears quietly, his hand gripping my arm like I'm the only thing keeping him upright.

Fear is ice in my veins, keeping me rooted to the spot as I frantically scan the row of doors until I find the one I'm looking for.

The one Sylph jokingly calls her honeymoon cottage.

A giant X slashes across the door like a knife wound.

A small, hurt sound escapes the back of my throat, and I move. Half-dragging Logan with me, I stumble down the hall, past a marked door on my right, and another on the left.

Sylph can't be dead. She *can't*.

The X is still wet, blood gleaming faintly against the dark brown wood. I reach for the doorknob, and stop, my hand hovering just beneath a streak of crimson.

"Open it, Rachel." Logan's voice is calm, but I hear the dread underneath.

"I can't." What if she's dead—another piece of my childhood brutally ripped away from me? Will I see her face when I close my eyes at night? Will her blood pour over my hands while she tells me I should've saved her?

He reaches past me and turns the knob. Sylph and Smithson lie on a blanket, another blanket covering them. I can't see if she's breathing. I can't see if there's blood.

Logan shuts the door behind us and grabs the doorjamb as I let go of him and rush to Sylph. I fall to my knees beside her, and grab her shoulders.

"Sylph!"

Her eyes fly open. So do Smithson's. And I suddenly realize Sylph's shoulders are bare.

So are Smithson's.

"Oh!" I let go of her.

"What's going on?" Sylph asks, shoving a hand through her tousled black curls. The blanket slips.

"Ah!" I yell, and turn around to block Logan's view. Smithson beats me to it by sitting up and yanking the blanket up to Sylph's chin.

"What are you *doing* in here?" Smithson asks. His chest is covered in curly brown hair, and I can't even look at him. Or at Sylph. Or at Logan.

I should just close my eyes and hope nobody notices while I crawl out of the room.

"There was a note. And then we saw the X. And I thought you were dead." I find Sylph's eyes and hold her gaze. "I thought you were dead."

A frown pinches her brow, and she starts to sit up.

"No, no," I say, even though she's clutching the blanket to her neck.

"Stay down," Smithson says.

She throws him a look of affectionate exasperation. "It's just Rachel."

"It isn't just Rachel," he says, and Logan clears his throat behind me.

"I can step out for a minute," he says.

And leave me alone with a naked Smithson and a naked Sylph? Over my dead body.

"No!" I say, and everyone stares at me. "I mean, um, maybe we should both leave. Because clearly they aren't dead. And they need some . . . they need a minute."

Sylph's hand joins mine, and I feel new calluses on her palm. I stare at our hands, her golden fingers curved around my pale ones, and the relief I feel threatens to choke me. I clutch her hand too tight for comfort, but I can't bear to let her go.

"Why did you think I was dead? What X?" she asks.

I shake my head. The lump in my throat isn't going to let me talk. Plus, I'm busy not noticing that no one close to me is wearing clothing.

"The tracker got into the building last night. He left a note for me in our room," Logan says, and the strain in his voice might be due to the subject matter, or he might be busy not noticing the general lack of clothing as well. "It said that the marked will die."

"What does that mean?" Smithson asks, and reaches behind him for his tunic.

"We aren't sure, but when we left our room, we saw several doors marked with an X." Logan clears his throat again as Smithson reaches for his pants. "Maybe you should join me over here, Rachel."

"Good idea," I say, but Sylph won't let me go. She tugs my hand closer to her, and I meet her eyes.

"Our door was marked, wasn't it?" she asks.

"Yes."

Her breathing quickens, but her voice is calm as she says, "Well, the message lied. We're fine."

"Maybe it didn't lie. It said 'the marked *will* die.' That's in the future. Maybe we've been selected as the next target," Smithson says, and I look at him with new respect.

He flaps his pants at me, and I whip my head around to stare at the other side of the room while he finishes dressing.

"Maybe that's it," Logan says. "We'll need to take down the names of those whose doors were marked and keep a careful watch on them."

"Good plan," Smithson says. "Now get out of our room so my wife can get dressed."

I give Sylph's hand one last squeeze and gently disentangle our fingers. "I'm glad you aren't dead," I say, and my voice breaks.

Her smile is gentle. "I'm glad you aren't either."

"Come on, Rachel," Logan says, and then he lets go of the

doorjamb and nearly pitches to his knees. Smithson lunges forward and catches him.

"Sorry," Logan says as I hurry to his side. "Took a rock to the head last night. Still a little dizzy."

"Who did that to you?" Smithson's voice promises retribution, and the burgeoning respect I feel for him doubles.

"The same person who put a bloody X on your door," I say.

Logan pushes his fingers against his temples as Smithson holds him up on one side and I support him on the other.

"Has he had any medical attention?" Sylph asks.

"Not yet," I say. "We have to go check on last night's guards, get the group ready to leave, and light the fire. Then he can visit the medical wagon."

"I'll ride in the wagon and get the medicine ready for him," she says.

"And I'll stay with you," Smithson says to her, his eyes on the door as if he can see through to the bloody X on the other side.

"Thanks," I say, tightening my hold on Logan. "We'll see you once we get away from this city."

I help Logan back into the hall. People leave their rooms and stare in fear at the crimson Xs sprinkled throughout the rows.

Quinn joins me on Logan's other side, and together we weave our way through the terrified people, afraid that we'll discover that every guard we posted during last night's second shift is dead.

CHAPTER TWENTY-NINE

<u>RACHEL</u>

People roll up blankets, fasten travel packs, and jostle each other as they maneuver into the hallway and instantly add their voices to the tumult when they see the Xs on the doors. We push our way toward the stairwell while people fling frantic questions at our backs.

What happened?

Who did this?

Is anyone hurt?

I don't have any answers for them, but since Logan looks like he's about to pass out, and Quinn would rather eat dirt than speak up when a crowd is watching him, it's up to me to respond.

Quinn dabs his finger in the blood of an X marking the door closest to the end of the hall and then rubs his finger and thumb together.

"Is it human blood?" I ask.

He shrugs. "I can't tell." He gazes down the long corridor.

"But this took a lot of blood. Unless whoever did this bled someone dry, my guess is he caught a few rabbits in the Wasteland and drained them."

The people around us keep calling out questions and dire predictions. I have to put a stop to it so we can check on the guards and then get out of the city before the army arrives. Raising my voice to be heard above the commotion around me, I say, "We aren't sure what happened, yet, but—"

Is this some kind of sick joke?

Is it the Commander?

A woman with her graying dark hair pulled back in a bun bumps into Quinn as she hoists her travel pack over her shoulders, and he almost loses his grip on Logan. Two young boys race down the hall and nearly knock me over as they try to slide past me to get to the stairs. Their faces are full of fear—wide eyes and pale skin.

"Hey, where do you think you're going?" I ask, but they aren't listening. No one is listening. They're too busy shouting, moving around, and panicking. Irritation surges through me, and I grit my teeth as yet another person yells a question in our direction but won't stop talking long enough to hear the answer. Lifting my thumb and pointer finger to my lips, I give a piercing whistle, just the way Dad taught me.

A sudden silence falls over the hallway, and I raise my voice to fill it as Drake hurries to my side. "We don't have time to panic over this. Get your bags and go line up downstairs the way you were told to last night."

"But who did—"

"Quiet." I glare at a thin man with knobby shoulders who

stops midquestion when he sees my expression. "We will figure out who did this and what it all means, but right now we have to light our fire and get out of here before the Commander and his army kill us where we stand. So get your things, get downstairs, and don't lag behind, because the fire goes up in ten minutes, no matter what."

Turning on my heel, I shove the stairwell door open and help Logan through it. Behind us, people scurry to obey me. Drake follows Quinn, Logan, and me downstairs. None of us say a word. I don't know what they're thinking, but I'm busy swallowing past the oily sickness that rises up the back of my throat when I imagine what we'll find at the building's entrance.

The stairs are slick where patches of moss cling to the steps, and I keep a tight grip on Logan's tunic as we descend. The door leading to the first floor is covered with coppery rust that flakes off on my cloak when I slam my shoulder into the door to get it open. The room beyond is a large square with an impossibly high ceiling, more panes of glass in one wall than in my entire house in Baalboden, and thick curtains of bright green kudzu clinging to everything in sight.

The wagons and livestock take up the middle of the room. I can't see beyond them to the front door to check on our guards, and the dread that tightens around my throat won't let me yell out their names.

I can't bear to find them dead. Cassie. Sam. Derreck. Pauline. I can't bear to move around the wagons and see them lying cold and silent. I can't, but in the last two months, I've done a lot of things I didn't think I could bear. I can make myself do one more.

"I'm going to check on the guards," I say, and my voice sounds too thin. "You two help Logan."

Drake takes over supporting Logan's left side, and I hurry forward, crushing kudzu and thorny weeds into the moldy remains of the rug that once covered the floor. The goats are tied to the back of the wagon closest to the stairwell. They flock to me as I make my way around the edge of the wagon. I nudge their heads away from me with trembling fingers, and clear the wagon.

The faint light of dawn seeps through the wall of windows in shades of green and gray. There's a hush inside the building, as if the outside world couldn't possibly penetrate its thick walls.

I know better. Someone got in. Marked our doors. Left us a message. And probably murdered our guards.

My eyes sweep the entrance slowly, expecting to see bodies lying on the floor. Instead, I see Cassie and Pauline standing side by side inside the doorway while Derreck and Sam pace the length of the windowed wall, their eyes trained outside to catch sight of any approaching threats.

They're *alive*.

The relief that makes my limbs feel like they're filled with water quickly gives way to anxiety as the implications hit me. If they're alive, and this is the only entrance to the building, then whoever marked our doors last night was already inside. The only people inside the building are the Baalboden survivors.

Which means we might have a traitor in our midst.

My heart slams against my rib cage, and my hand closes over my knife hilt before I've even finished the thought. Skidding on mold and rubbery vines, I close the distance between the wagons and the door.

"Did you leave your post any time after I took Logan upstairs last night?" I ask. All four turn to stare at me. My voices rises. "Did you leave your post? Fall asleep? Hear a noise and leave the door unattended for a few seconds while you investigated?"

Sam raises his hands as if to calm me down and says, "We've been in front of this door for the past four hours. No one fell asleep or left the post. Why?"

Drake, Logan, and Quinn catch up to us, and I turn to them. "They've been here all night. No one fell asleep."

"We checked the building thoroughly yesterday," Drake says, and the creases in his face seem to deepen. "No one was here."

"And we know the tracker Willow and I followed was outside last night, because he attacked Logan," Quinn says.

Logan's face is white as he says, "Then it's one of us. Whoever marked the doors and left me that message had to be one of us."

"If the message matched the others you found, then either someone in our camp is working with Rowansmark, or the fact that a tracker is following us is a coincidence and has nothing to do with the messages or the killings." Quinn's voice is calm, but he grips Logan's arm tightly, and his dark eyes sweep the room with careful precision.

My fingers no longer tremble as I grip my Switch and turn to survey the survivors who are climbing over the vines and circling the wagons in our wake. The fierce anger that wells up in me spills over into my voice. "It's no coincidence. The only people outside of the building when the rock was thrown last night were you, Willow, Thom, and Ian. It was a man's voice I heard. Thom and Ian were heading back to the shelter together, and we know it wasn't you. That leaves the tracker. And the words he said match the stupid messages we've been getting, so I think Logan's right." I have to swallow hard to get the next words out. "One of our group is working with Rowansmark."

I'm already striding toward the group milling around the wagons before I finish my sentence. One of the people we've protected is a wolf prowling among the sheep. I'm not about to let that go unaddressed.

Giving another piercing whistle, I grab the handle on the side of the supply wagon and vault into the driver's seat. Planting my boots firmly on the seat, I rap my Switch sharply against the wood beneath me and glare at the few who dare to continue speaking until they fall quiet.

"We have a problem." I draw the words out, filling them with every shred of the anger and betrayal that rushes through me.

"Yeah, someone got into the building and marked some of our doors last night," the knobby-shouldered man who questioned me in the hall speaks up. One hand is wrapped around a donkey's bridle, and the other is clenched around the strap of his travel pack.

"Yes, someone marked the doors." I slowly scan the crowd, making eye contact and daring one of them to look away. To fidget. To give me any reason to doubt. "But the real problem is that no one breached the entrance last night. We're the only people inside this building."

Murmured conversation instantly explodes across the room, and I yell, "Quiet! We don't have time to debate this. One of you is working with the Rowansmark tracker who showed up outside our camp when our guards were murdered." I slam the end of my Switch onto the wagon seat, and the people nearby jump. "If you've betrayed us, if you've taken part in the atrocity that cost those boys their lives, do yourself a favor and stay behind. Or better yet, crawl off and *die*, because when we figure out who you are, there will be no mercy."

My voice shakes, a too-frail vessel for the fury that blisters through me. I raise my Switch like the formidable weapon it is. "There will be *no* mercy. You will pay for your crimes with your life. It won't be quick. It won't be easy." My breath rasps against my throat, tearing its way to freedom in sharp gasps while the memory of eight boys with bloody necks rises up to choke me.

"You're a coward." My voice fills the room. "A spineless dog who does his dirty work under the cover of night because you're too scared to show your true face. Well, I'm not afraid of you." I lean toward the crowd, and my teeth peel back from my lips in a snarl as I spit the words at them. "I'm not afraid of you, but *you* should be very afraid of *me*. You should look over your shoulder every minute of every day and wonder when I'm coming for you. You should tremble when you close your eyes because one of these nights, you'll awaken with my blade against your throat, and there will be nothing you can do to stop me."

Someone climbs into the wagon beside me, but I don't turn. I don't look away from the wide-eyed, terrified expressions facing me. "I know what you're capable of, you filthy coward. But you have no idea what I can do. What I've already done."

Melkin's eyes haunt my memory, and I clamp my lips shut before my truth pours out into the green-gray air and condemns me.

"Good job," Logan says for my ears only as he wraps an arm around me. When his warmth presses against me, I realize I'm shaking. "You made them understand."

I look at the silent crowd who faces us and realize he's right. They know they're prey, and that someone close to them might betray them. They'll be on their guard. And the one who marked the doors last night knows his days are numbered. I meet Logan's eyes and find the same furious sense of betrayal in him that exists within me.

"We're going to find whoever marked those doors," he says.

"Yes, we are. But first, we need to light that fire and get out of the city before the army reaches us."

He nods, and sways sharply to the left. I grab his tunic and face the crowd again.

"Frankie and Thom will light the fire. They have horses and can catch up to us once the blaze is burning. Jodi, Eric, and Lila will oversee getting the wagons and livestock out of the building. The rest of you get into your assigned positions. We're leaving this city, and the Commander's army, behind."

I raise my Switch into the air again. "And if you're the one who betrayed us, find a dark hole to hide in and stay behind. Because I promise you, if you leave this city with us, you're as good as dead."

The crowd moves quickly, casting furtive glances at each other and talking in hushed bursts. In five minutes, we have the wagons lined up on the main road leading out of the city. The survivors flank the wagons in their assigned positions, though Willow and Adam will be leading us until Logan's had medical treatment and can once again walk in front.

In the dim light of dawn, we can see movement on the distant bluff. The army is coming for us, but they won't reach us. Not today. Thom and Frankie mount their horses and head toward the fuel lines we built last night. The rest of us start walking north through the ruins. Minutes later, a shout goes up from behind us, and I turn to see a sheet of brilliant orange and red flames devouring the row of houses at the edge of the city. Black smoke gushes into the air and spreads across the sky as the fire eats through the dry tinder we left for it, greedily devouring the fuel lines, and then explodes into terrifying life in the Wasteland itself.

The fire is a voracious beast consuming everything in front of it. Trees flicker gold and orange against the dawn sky as flames slide over trunks, race across branches, and then leap for the next tree. Suddenly the bluff is alive with frantic motion as hundreds of soldiers realize death is coming for them unless they get out of the way.

We're free of the Commander and his army, at least for the moment. But we've exchanged one threat for another, and as we make our way out of the city, I slowly study the expressions of those around me. Looking for secrets. Searching for guilt.

Hunting for a killer.

CHAPTER THIRTY

LOGAN

I sit on the bench in the medical wagon, holding the canvas flap out of the way so that I can watch the smoke-drenched ruins disappear in our wake. There's no sign of the Commander and his army, though Thom and Frankie said they saw significant movement on the bluff as they were lighting the fire.

If we're lucky, by the time the Commander and his troops get around the blaze, we'll be well off the main path to Lankenshire, our trail will be hidden, and he won't be able to find us.

Just in case we aren't lucky, I've been busy trying to think of every worst case scenario and at least two solutions to each. The constant throbbing pain in my head that multiplies with every bump of the wagon wheels makes thinking clearly almost impossible. When we hit another bump, I let go of the canvas flap and grab my aching head instead.

Rachel, who sits opposite me where she can watch for signs of the army's pursuit, huffs out a little breath and says, "We're clear of the city now. No one is following us. Either let Sylph treat you, or I'll do it myself." The worry in her voice softens the sharpness of her words.

I make myself smile at her, and then turn to Sylph, who sits with Smithson beside an open crate of medical supplies.

"Open your mouth, please," Sylph says. I obey her and grimace as she sprinkles a pinch of bitter white powder onto my tongue. "There. That should help the headache. Now let's take a look at this cut."

Sylph's fingers are much gentler than Rachel's. She treats my cut like a new friend she's just getting to know while Rachel treats wounds like challenges that must be overcome through sheer strength and tenacity. Still, even with Sylph's gentleness, brilliant shards of pain jab at my skull like they're trying to drill through the bone.

I sit still while she pats antiseptic on the wound and carefully cuts a small strip of bandage to protect the area from germs. Smithson moves to the bench opposite me, his eyes constantly seeking his wife like he's afraid if he turns his back she might disappear.

I know the feeling—my eyes are trained on Rachel as she crouches by the wagon's entrance watching the road. She's already left me once to tell Drake to write down the names of everyone in a marked room. As soon as I'm finished in here, she'll resume guard duty along the western flank, and I'll take my place in the lead. After that, we'll be focused on staying ahead of the Commander, keeping our people safe from the predatory elements in the Wasteland, and catching whoever left the message in our room last night.

My hand reaches for the gray metallic object that pinned

today's message to our floor, and I worry its smooth surface with my fingers as I pull it from my pocket.

I don't want to let Rachel out of my sight, not when I know one of our own has betrayed us, but of everyone in camp, she's one of the most capable of handling herself against a killer.

Besides, the coward only attacks at night.

"It's a shallow cut. No stitches required. You were lucky," Sylph says.

"I would've stitched him up last night if he'd needed it," Rachel says.

Sylph's smile is quick and bright. "I'd have given half a day's food ration to see that."

Rachel sounds offended. "I can stitch up a cut. I sat through the same Basic Medical class in Life Skills as you did."

"Yes, but I paid attention." Sylph's voice is warm. "You spent every minute in Life Skills pretending you were somewhere else."

"Well, maybe if they'd taught us something worth knowing instead of wasting our time with how to sew a pretty dress or set a fancy table, I would've had more incentive. Besides, I did well in Basic Medical."

"Mr. Phillips said you had the worst bedside manner he'd ever seen."

Rachel rolls her eyes. "I just have a low tolerance for whining."

I laugh, and the pain in my head is nothing but a faint twinge now. The powder has done its job.

"I can put more salve on this if you'd like. Maybe it won't scar quite so . . . badly." Sylph's cool fingers brush lightly against my neck, tracing the edges of the brand the Commander burned into my skin while I was at his mercy in the dungeon. It's still healing, and the new skin feels tight and itchy.

"Don't worry about it. There's nothing you can do to make it look like anything less than the Commander's Brute Squad insignia," I say. And because both Sylph and Smithson look uncomfortable, I laugh a little. "Is it really that bad? Do I need to wear a scarf for life?"

Smithson's brown eyes meet mine for a long moment. "It's a good reminder of why we follow you instead of him."

Now I'm the one who's uncomfortable. I look at my hands, and wait quietly for Sylph to finish checking the burn.

She pats my shoulder. "All done. Do you want some pain medicine to keep with you in case the headache comes back, or do you want to find the medical wagon when you need more?"

"I'll take some with me."

She measures a few pinches of powder into a pouch and hands it to me.

"Thank you," I say, and capture her gaze with mine. Once upon a time, she was the talkative, energetic girl whose heart was big enough to love Rachel, sharp edges and all, even when she could never fully understand the inner chambers of Rachel's spirit. Now grief and loss have carved away the innocence and left wisdom in its place. I'm grateful that the size of her heart remains unchanged.

She smiles, her green eyes lighting with true pleasure. "You're welcome. You've done so much for us. It's nice to be able to do something for you."

I don't know what to do with her words, so I smile a little and head toward the wagon's exit. Time to get us off the main road to Lankenshire.

Best Case Scenario: I continue to elude the Commander, get our people to safety, and catch the killer before the body count rises.

Worst Case Scenario: I fail.

I step out of the wagon as the path dips down between two chunks of moss-covered stone. I don't know if I can catch the killer. I don't know if I can keep everyone alive as we travel through the Wasteland. And I don't know if I can convince Lankenshire to form an alliance with us.

But I do know that I'm prepared to lay my life on the line to make it happen. These people may have ignored me or mistreated me when we were all living in fear of the Commander's vicious reprisals, but now they look at me with respect and trust. I refuse to be unworthy of either.

CHAPTER THIRTY-ONE

RACHEL

Logan pushes us hard for four hours before calling a halt for lunch. We left the main road to Lankenshire two hours ago. Quinn, Willow, Ian, and I doubled back and did everything we could to disguise our trail and lay false ones instead. Hopefully by the time the army reaches the place where we left the road, we'll be too far out of range for any of the guards to track us with our wristmarks.

We've seen no sign of the army behind us, but everyone is jumpy. Looking over their shoulders. Losing their tempers. Clutching their loved ones close. We may have left the Commander on the other side of the fire we set, but all one hundred forty-five survivors are still traveling with us, which means the person working with the Rowansmark tracker is still in our midst.

I take my lunch ration of rabbit meat wrapped in dandelion leaves and find Logan sitting next to Drake beneath the shade of a large walnut tree. He smiles when he sees me, but there are shadows in his eyes that have nothing to do with the pain in his head, and he won't hold my gaze. Drake's shoulders are slumped, and he keeps tugging on his beard, something he only does when he's worried.

I toss my cloak onto the ground and sit beside Logan. "What's going on?"

Logan holds the gray metallic object he found with this morning's message. His thumb rubs across the fluted edge as if he thinks he can figure out who put it in our room if only he presses hard enough.

Without looking at me, he says, "According to the map, we should reach the river that separates us from the northern city-states by nightfall. Maybe sooner. I just hope I can find a way to get us across before the Commander realizes he's lost us and starts looking for where we left the main road. If he's using a tracking device, it won't take him long to figure out we aren't where he thought we'd be."

I wait for him to say more, but he doesn't. Neither does Drake. And both of them won't stop looking at the metallic object in Logan's hand. Finally, I say, "Okay, what's *really* going on?"

Logan rubs the piece of metal. "We need to talk about what happened this morning."

I sit up straighter. "Yes, we do. We need a plan. We have to catch this person before he has a chance to kill again."

Drake tugs on his beard, and Logan's jaw clenches.

"What? What did I say?" I look from one to the other.

Logan holds up the gray object. "See this edge?" His thumb presses against the fluted end again. "There's a hole here and the tube is hollow inside. The other edge is as sharp as a needle." His eyes meet mine, and the pain in them makes it suddenly harder to breathe. "I think this is a conduit for poison."

The ground beneath me remains steady. The birds above me still chatter and squawk. All around me people eat their lunch rations and huddle in small groups. Everything is the same, and nothing is the same. My hands start to shake and my pulse feels heavy and uneven as it slams against my skin.

"The message said the marked *will* die. We think the killer poisoned the people in the marked rooms. He could've taken a syringe from the medical wagon. If someone is sleeping heavily enough, a little prick against the skin isn't enough to bring them fully awake," Drake says. His words rake across the silence inside of me, and I wrap my arms around my stomach as I stare at Logan.

"Sylph was in a marked room." My voice is a desperate, haunted thing, and Logan looks as if I've struck him.

"I know." He reaches for me, but I can't bend into his embrace. I can't let him comfort me, because I won't need comforting. Sylph will be okay. We'll find the antidote. Better yet, we'll find the killer and force him to give us an antidote. She'll be fine. Everyone will be fine.

"We won't know for sure unless people start getting sick," Drake says.

"We can't wait for that." Logan shoves the dart into his cloak pocket and takes out the packet of pain medicine Sylph gave him earlier.

While he measures out a dose for his headache, I scan the little clearing we're using for our lunch break and find Sylph laughing with Jodi and Cassie, her arms wrapped around them both. My heart twists painfully inside my chest, and I have to look away before my eyes start to sting.

I turn to Logan. "The message said the marked *will* die. That's in the future. Maybe he was warning us. Maybe it hasn't happened yet."

He takes my hand in his. I imagine I can still feel the cold imprint of Rowansmark's dart on his skin. "I hope so. But we need to keep a close eye on everyone who was in a marked room last night. And we need to start looking for anyone in the group who could have loyalty to Rowansmark."

"The real problem here is that Baalboden was a city-state of thousands, and there's only a handful of us left." Drake scratches his leg with fingernails that have tiny half-moons of dirt beneath them. "Many of us didn't know each other before the fires. We're just taking everyone's word that they lived in Baalboden, because why else would they be here?"

"We can start by checking again to make sure everyone in the group has a Baalboden wristmark. It was chaotic before the funeral. We could've missed someone," I say. "Anyone besides Quinn and Willow who doesn't have one—"

"Will be arrested." Logan gets to his feet and reaches down for me. "And then questioned."

"Forget questioning. I want whoever did this to be *dead*."

Logan's eyes are grim. "Oh, he will be. But not before he gives us the answers we need."

Drake stands. "I'll go line everybody up."

In minutes, the entire camp stands in two rows facing each other. Drake and Thom walk down one row, checking each survivor's right wrist for the distinctive tattooed ridges of Baalboden's mark. Logan and I take the other row.

"Right arm, please," I say to a man nearly as old as Oliver. He raises his hand, and I slide his tunic sleeve down his arm. His skin sags away from his bones, and the wristmark has faded over time, but it's there. I rub my thumb over it, searching for any signs that it could be fake, but the ridges are right where they should be and the ink is a permanent stain on his forearm. The ridges in his mark are longer than mine. Skinnier, too. Each mark is different, so that a guard's Identidisc can bounce sound off of the mark and come back with a sound signature unique to that citizen.

Logan stands beside me, checking Jan's wristmark. I move past him to check the next person, and we quickly fall into a rhythm.

Cassie. Ian. Elias. Geraldine. Susan. Nick. So far everyone in my line has a wristmark. Logan is checking the wristmark of a woman whose brown skin gleams like a polished jewel beneath the midday sun. I step around him and discover that Sylph and Smithson are next in line.

"Right arm, please," I say to Sylph. She smiles at me and lays her hand in mine. I lift our hands in the air, and her sleeve slides to her elbow. I gasp. A deep purple bruise blossoms like rotting fruit along the underside of her arm.

"What happened?" Abandoning any effort to check her wristmark, I grab her arm as she starts to pull it down. "Who did this to you?"

The bruise is easily the size of my palm, and its center is black. Whoever hurt her *meant* to hurt her. With a bruise like this, she's lucky her arm didn't break. Fury gushes through me, sharp and vicious.

My eyes find Smithson, and I arrow my rage at him, as if I can flay him to pieces with nothing but my glare.

But he isn't looking at me. Instead, he's staring at Sylph's arm, worry in every line of his face. "What happened?"

Sylph pulls her wrist free of my grip and examines the bruise. "I guess this is from hitting my arm when I got our lunch ration. I slipped in some mud and fell against the wagon. I must have fallen harder than I realized." She sounds puzzled, but not upset.

Poison.

The air is suddenly too thick to breathe. I've known Sylph for most of my life. I've never seen her bruise easily. Sickness crawls up the back of my throat as I make myself ask, "Any other bruises? Do you feel sick? Tired?"

She shrugs and smiles at us both. "I'm fine! I feel fine. I didn't realize I hit my arm that hard. That's all. Honest. Stop worrying. Both of you. I'm not used to roughing it, but I'll toughen up. We all will. Now shouldn't you be checking my wristmark to make sure I'm really from Baalboden?"

My fingers rub gently across her wrist, though I don't need to check. Sylph is a bright, laughing presence in most of my childhood memories. I can't think of my life in Baalboden without thinking of her. And I refuse to consider a life outside of Baalboden without her.

Smithson thrusts his arm at me, lets me verify his wristmark, and then carefully wraps his arm around Sylph as if she's made of glass. She laughs and leans into him, but I meet Smithson's gaze above her head and know the worry burning in his eyes also burns in mine.

Only he doesn't realize how much he truly has to fear.

Unlike Logan, I'm not brave enough to put it into words. Because maybe Logan's wrong. Maybe Sylph really did hit her arm too hard against the wagon. Maybe the knowledge that someone out there is ruthlessly determined to torture us is messing with my head.

Besides, if bruising were a symptom of poison, wouldn't Smithson be bruised too? The X was over both of them. Holding on to that thin comfort, I continue down the row, checking every survivor with dogged determination.

All of them have a Baalboden wristmark. So do the survivors in Thom and Frankie's row. We're no closer to figuring out which one of us is working with Rowansmark. As Logan calls for us to start moving again, I slowly scan the faces of the survivors who walk past me.

One of them is a traitor. One of them might have poisoned Sylph. All I need is a sign, a single glimmer of guilt or treachery, and whoever painted a bloody X on her door is mine.

Ignoring the tiny voice whispering that I was once sure of Melkin's guilt, and now I don't know how to live with myself, I heft my Switch and take my place along the western flank.

CHAPTER THIRTY-TWO

<u>RACHEL</u>

We camp on a small rise beside a wide river. The air smells of muddy soil, fresh grass, and moldy wood. Logan wastes no time ordering his team to create a perimeter—wagons, children, and those too old or frail to easily defend themselves are in the middle. Those marginally able to fight are circled around them. And then those of us who've been trained take up our posts at the outer edge.

There's a new tension in the camp. Partially because we've seen signs that someone else regularly travels on this faded, poorly maintained path, and the possibility of running into highwaymen or unsympathetic envoys from other city-states is a clear danger. And partially because we're no closer to catching the killer, and the strain of wondering which of us is a traitor wears us down.

I'm stationed with two of our newer guards on the southern edge of camp. Logan has a guard with him as well and is ten yards away. He watches me with worry and regret in his eyes, and I know it's because he can't stop the poison when he has no idea what was used.

I suppose I should find the energy to comfort him, or at least to tell him I know this isn't his fault, but the dread that has filled me since I saw Sylph's bruise seeps into my bones, and I can't find any words.

I give the men standing guard with me the first watch, and close my eyes, not intending to actually fall asleep. The Wasteland's nighttime noises crowd around me. Owls hooting. Things rustling through the underbrush. The far-off howl of a wolf pouring out his misery to the unfeeling moon.

The howl climbs through the sky and wraps around me as I sink into a dream. It feels like I'm the one crying, I'm the one putting inarticulate sound to the things that haunt me. I don't see clouds gathering over the face of the moon, but suddenly rain streaks from the skies in relentless streams. It strafes the canopy of leaves above me, skids down bark, and pools in the mud beneath me. I get up and try to walk—I *have* to walk—but my feet refuse to move.

Looking down, I see the mud is bubbling around my boots, a seething mass that defies gravity and slides viscous tentacles over my ankles, searching for skin.

Whipping my knife from its sheath, I beat at the mud with the flat of my blade.

It can't touch my skin. It *can't*. Something terrible will happen if it does.

The rain plummets down. The mud bubbles and slurps and grows until the toes of my boots disappear beneath the writhing mass.

The flat of my blade isn't helping. I flip it around and crouch. The tip of my knife gleams silver beneath the water, and I plunge it into one questing tentacle as it slides over the lip of my boot and onto my skin.

Pain flashes, a brilliant light that explodes behind my eyes and rips a scream from my throat.

The knife is useless. The mud burrows in, and the ground beneath me becomes a crimson sea of blood crawling over my feet.

I bruise where the tentacle meets my skin—a decaying blossom filled with agony. Abandoning my knife, I rip at the crimson threads with my fingers.

"No, Rachel," Melkin whispers. *"You deserve this."*

His face rises from the seething pool of blood at my feet, and bubbles escape his gaping mouth.

"No," I say.

"You're broken. This is what happens when you're broken," Oliver says gently, and Melkin's face melts into Oliver's full cheeks and dark eyes.

"Please. Don't," I say, but another tentacle reaches my skin and sinks into my veins. Another bruise spreads, the pain twisting inside of me like a living thing.

"Look around," Dad says, his gray eyes shining out of Oliver's face. *"You're alone now."*

I stand up and try to run.

"Rachel!" Dad yells my name, but I don't look down. I don't look at his ruined face hovering over Oliver's while their blood slides over my skin, leaving a trail of agony in its wake.

"Rachel!" A hand shakes my shoulder, and the blood disappears. Noises rush in—shouts, the rasp of a sword leaving its sheath—and my eyes fly open.

Logan looms over me. "Wake up. We're under attack."

He whirls away and lunges forward as a man nearly twice his size lumbers out of the trees, a pair of mismatched swords in his fists. The man's clothing is a collection of bits and pieces of cloth from the old civilization patched and stitched into a haphazard outfit that is specifically geared toward surviving outdoors—tough fabric, thick lining beneath the tunic, and heavy rawhide coverings strapped around his legs.

A highwayman.

Two more men explode out of the woods on his heels, their expressions feral and hungry in the wash of moonlight.

My knife is already in my hand as I jump to my feet. Beside me, the men Logan and I recruited to stand guard with us are waving their weapons in the air like they can scare off our attackers if they flash enough silver.

I bend down and snatch my Switch from the ground. The highwaymen are too big and too well armed for knife work. I need to keep my distance.

More men pour out of the tree line and the sounds of battle fill the air—hoarse cries of fury, the clash of metal, and the solid thunk of a body hitting the ground. I sheath my knife and release the blade on my Switch as two of the highwaymen race toward me.

The guards sharing my post step in front of me as if to protect me.

"Get back!" I shove my way through them. "Stay behind me. When I knock them to the ground, you finish them, do you understand?"

I can't wait to see if they agree with my strategy. The highwaymen are converging on me. I widen my grip, plant my left foot, and whirl out of the path of one and directly into the second. Slamming my Switch into his stomach, I dive out from under his feet before he can finish swinging his sword at me. His momentum carries him past me, and I slash the tendons behind his knees with my blade.

I'm already on my feet as he falls to the ground screaming. The second man is attacking one of my fellow guards with a curved blade that flashes like quicksilver beneath the stars.

"Get the one who's down!" I yell to the other guard as I sprint toward the fight and launch myself at the highwayman swinging the blade.

The weighted end of my Switch smacks into his shin, knocking him off-balance. He whips toward me, his weapon slicing with terrible speed. I slam the middle of the Switch against the hilt of his sword, blocking his blow. Breathing in heavy pants, he sizes me up.

"A girl?" He sounds amused and interested in a way that makes my skin crawl. "This is going to be fun."

He's bigger than me. Stronger, too. He leans his weight against the Switch, and the sword slowly edges toward my face.

I let my arms tremble a bit as I quickly assess his weaknesses. I'm not going to choke this time. No one is going to have to rescue me.

And no one is going to get the chance to rescue him.

A smile smears his face with malice and his rancid breath fills my nose as he chuckles. "Give up now, sweet thing, and I won't kill you."

"I can't say the same." I go limp and drop to the ground. The sudden lack of resistance causes him to stumble forward a single step.

That single step is all I need.

Dropping my Switch, I snatch my knife and lunge to my feet, burying my weapon in his sternum as I stand.

He deflates slowly, and I shove him away as he crumples. My knife glistens beneath the moonlight, and I shudder, but I can't stop to count the cost of adding more blood to the overwhelming tide I've already shed.

"Logan!" I yell his name as I run toward the place I last saw him.

"Here," he says, and I find him crouched beside Keegan, who is moaning in pain. A quick glance around shows all is nearly quiet again.

Two of the intruders are attacking Adam and Ian. I take a step forward, already sizing up the situation to see where I could make the most impact, when Adam just comes undone. Screaming, he dives at one of the men, his weapon flashing. It's like watching a tornado—all fury and strength and very little finesse. Not that he needs it. The intruder is motivated by greed. Adam is fueled by loss and a desperate need to make someone pay for it. It's over in seconds. When I see Ian can handle the second one, I scan the rest of the meadow.

One highwayman peels away from the camp and runs toward the tree line. The soft *thwing* of an arrow disturbs the air, and he falls to the ground. It's almost frightening how accurate Willow's aim is even in the dark. The other highwaymen appear to be dead or wounded. No one is fighting. No one is looting. We won.

We *won*.

I crouch beside Logan. "We did it. The camp arrangement worked. We held our perimeter. The new guards got a taste of experience." I look around again, afraid we might have sustained losses that will destroy this small moment of hope. "I don't know how many wounded we have, but we did it, Logan. We defended ourselves."

His hand finds mine and squeezes. "We did it." His voice holds wonder and weary satisfaction.

Neither of us points out the obvious: This was a small group of highwaymen. Twenty at the most by the looks of things. Defeating twenty highwaymen is a far cry from defeating the Commander's army, but still, it's a victory. We'll take every victory we can get.

CHAPTER THIRTY-THREE

RACHEL

We killed twenty-three highwaymen. Two of our inexperienced recruits died, and five others are injured seriously enough to need medical attention.

The loss of two of our own hurts, but even through the pain of more death, the people stand a little taller, and I imagine the spark I see in their eyes is a tiny glimmer of hope.

I help Logan carry Keegan, the guard with the stab wound in his leg, to the medical wagon. Blood pours from his wound, and he shivers uncontrollably. Sylph meets us at the wagon's entrance, her dark curls thrust into a messy bun, her sleeves rolled up.

Another bruise spreads across her left wrist like an indigo stain.

"Your wrist!" I say.

She shakes her head. "One of the injured was thrashing around. It's nothing. Let's get him into the torchlight."

I meet Logan's eyes, my stomach clenching. This much bruising isn't normal. Not for Sylph. Not for anyone.

"Rachel!" Sylph says. "Help me with him."

I shake off my unease as best as I can and follow her. There's no room in the wagon for another patient, so we stretch him out on the ground. Thom drives a torch into the soil beside Keegan. The heat of the flames licks against our skin.

"I need to seal up the camp's perimeter again," Logan says softly.

"Go. We've got this." I wave him away and something wet flies off of my fingers.

I look down. My hands are slick with Keegan's blood. My throat closes as I frantically clean my hands on the grass beside me.

"Press on this," Sylph says as she shoves a folded cloth against the wound.

I lean forward and press, gulping back nausea as the image of Keegan blurs and becomes Oliver lying beneath my hands, his blood pouring out in a thick, hot river.

This isn't Oliver.

I'm not in a wagon.

I'm not at the Commander's mercy.

"Press harder." There's an edge of worry in Sylph's voice, and when I focus on Keegan again, I see why.

The cloth is soaked through, and still his blood gushes.

"Nola!" Sylph's voice rings across the space between Keegan and the wagon. In seconds, Nola is by our side staring at the wound.

"Maybe the sword cut his artery?" she asks.

I shake my head and try to ignore the wet, slick heat of his blood against my skin. "This is nowhere near an artery. I know because my dad taught me exactly where to slash a man's leg to make him bleed out so I could get away."

Sylph shoots me a look that manages to be both horrified and impressed.

"I don't know. It should be slowing." Nola reaches down and pulls the cloth away from the wound, and we stare in silence at the shallow cut, right across the meat of his calf, and the unending flow of thin, orange-red blood that runs out of him like water.

"Blood shouldn't be that thin," I say quietly, though a glance at Keegan's white face tells me he's too far into shock to understand what we're saying anymore. "And it shouldn't flow this fast."

"Pressing harder isn't stopping it. We need to cauterize." Sylph reaches for the torch. "Give me your knife, Rachel."

I hand it to her, and she thrusts the blade into the flame until it glows red along the edges.

"Hold him still," she says. Nola grabs his shoulders, and I lie across his thighs, pressing down as hard as I can. Sylph bends swiftly and presses the flat side of the blade to the wound.

His flesh sizzles and burns, filling the air with a sickly sweet smell. I turn my face into the grass at Keegan's waist and gag. He doesn't jerk away from the knife. He doesn't scream. He just lies on the ground trembling, his skin waxy and white.

I climb off of his thighs and look at the wound. The flesh is seared shut, an angry red welt of puckered skin. The blood no longer leaks out of him like a stream, but I don't think it matters. His eyes roll back in his head, and his entire body shudders. And then he sighs, a long puff of air that hisses from his lungs before they go still.

"No!" Nola rips at his tunic, yanking the laces until she has his chest bare. She presses her hands to his heart and pumps up and down. Up and down. Up and down. Leaning forward, she blows air into his mouth, listens for a heartbeat, then starts the process all over again.

I don't know how long she tries. Long enough for Keegan's too-thin blood to soak into the ground like it was never there. Long enough for others to bring two more injured recruits to the wagon.

Long enough for me to notice the ugly bouquet of purple-black bruises spreading along Keegan's stomach and chest like flowers crushed beneath someone's careless heel.

Sylph finally leans in and gently pulls Nola off Keegan, whispering reassurances as Nola cries against her shoulder.

I have no reassurances to offer. No condolences. Nothing but the terrible fear gnawing away at my chest as I stare at the fresh bruise circling Sylph's wrist and wonder if Keegan woke up yesterday morning beneath a bloody X.

CHAPTER THIRTY-FOUR

LOGAN

The day dawns bright and beautiful. Somehow that makes our current situation feel so much worse. I didn't sleep much after the attack. Just caught a few light naps in between circling the camp, checking on the medical wagon, and worrying about Keegan's death and what it might mean for the rest of us.

The list of names I took from Drake in the wee hours of the morning is a leaden weight in my hand. Nineteen names, including Keegan's. The last time I checked the medical wagon, five of those nineteen were dead. Two of them bled out almost instantly after receiving light wounds in last night's battle. The other three complained of exhaustion and pain and then eventually bled out through their noses, gums, and eyes.

Each of them had deep purple bruises all over their bodies.

Bruises like the ones on Sylph.

I don't know what kind of poison causes blood to refuse to clot, but I'm racking my brains to come up with an antidote. A plant. A mineral. Surely *something* in this neglected wilderness we're stranded in can cause blood to clot.

I have to find an antidote before Sylph gets worse. Before any of the remaining fourteen get worse. So far, the ones who died without an injury to speed the process have all been older than fifty. I'm hoping the younger names on the list can fight the effects of the poison for a while longer, but the reality is that I have no idea how much time they have left. And no idea how to help them.

A few of the older men work quietly to divide up the last of our food rations for breakfast as I pass the supply wagon. We'll need to hunt today. And we'll need to bury our dead.

We also need to leave the meadow behind and push forward. Staying in one place before we've reached Lankenshire is suicide.

I reach the medical wagon and find Sylph asleep on a blanket inside. Rachel sits beside her.

"How is she?" I ask quietly. Three others injured in last night's attack are sleeping in the wagon bed as well. The medical supplies have been stacked against the back wall or shoved under side benches to make room.

Rachel meets my gaze, and I shiver at the bleakness in her eyes. "She's tired. And her stomach hurts." Her voice is like an empty room swept clean of any sign of life.

Something hot and thick burns in my throat, choking off my air. Sylph is going to die if I can't figure out a way to fix this.

"Where's Smithson?" Rachel asks, and her pale fingers gently trace a pattern against Sylph's hand. "He should be here."

"I sent one of the recruits to call him to the medical wagon. He was on guard duty all night, and I didn't realize she was already . . ." My words fade as Sylph moans and opens her eyes.

"Rachel?"

"I'm here," Rachel says, and reaches up to comb stray curls from Sylph's forehead.

"I think I'm sick," she says.

Rachel makes a tiny choked noise. I step forward, and fumble for something to say that will comfort Sylph without lying to her. I can't think of anything.

"Yes, you're sick." I can hardly hold her gaze—this girl with a heart big enough to take in a sharp-tongued, independent girl and an orphaned, outcast boy. This girl who deserves so much better than to bleed to death in the middle of nowhere.

She lifts the neckline of her tunic and stares at herself. Then she lowers the neckline and swallows audibly. "I'm sick like Keegan was sick, aren't I? Was he marked, too?"

I nod, and work hard to get my lips to form words that will give her hope. Comfort. *Something*. But words won't come. Maybe they don't exist. Not for this.

"Smithson?" she asks, and her voice is already threaded through with exhaustion.

"He's on his way," Rachel says just as Smithson pulls the flap aside and climbs into the wagon. He takes one look at Sylph and nearly shoves me to the ground in his effort to reach her side.

"What's wrong with her?" he asks, his hands hovering over her bruised arms and sweat-slicked face as if he just needs to find where the sickness started so he can fix it.

"Are you sick too?" she asks, her fingers trembling as she reaches for him.

He shakes his head and catches her fingers in his hand. "I'm fine. Shh." He brushes her palm against his lips. "I'm fine. Let's worry about helping you get better."

Rachel's shoulders bow as if an impossible weight has just landed on them, and she curls toward her knees.

"I'm not going to get better," Sylph says softly, and tears trace a glistening path down her cheeks.

"Of course you are." Smithson looks at Rachel. "Tell her, Rachel. Tell her she's going to get better."

Rachel shivers and slowly lowers herself to the wagon bed until she's lying pressed against Sylph's side.

Smithson looks at me, his expression frantic. "She's going to get better."

I make myself meet his gaze. "I think she's been poisoned."

"By whom?" The veins on his neck bulge.

"By the same man who marked your door. Five of the nineteen who were in marked rooms died last night. Their symptoms started out just like hers." My voice shakes, and I wonder if he can hear the regret I don't know how to say. If he knows the guilt I feel for failing to protect them. "Do you have bruises too?"

He shakes his head and looks from me to Sylph, whose eyes are closed again. "How much time does she have?" He chokes on the words. "How much?"

"I don't know. The others eventually bled . . ." I don't want to finish the sentence. Don't want to paint an image in his head of Sylph bleeding out while we all hover in helpless anguish by her side.

"If it's poison, there has to be an antidote." His agony is a palpable force, barely contained by the flimsy walls of the wagon. I can hardly stand beneath the heat of his stare. "Find the antidote, Logan. Please."

The pressure of feeling responsible for outwitting the Commander, catching a killer, and safely delivering my people to Lankenshire doubles as his words sink in and take root.

Find the antidote. How? I don't even know what kind of poison was used, much less where to begin looking for an antidote. But I can't tell him that. I can't rip his last shred of hope away from him.

"I'll try," I say, and put as much confidence into the words as I can muster. It isn't much, and I know he hears it, but he nods and turns back to Sylph.

Rachel lies still beside her friend, staring at Sylph's face as if she can hold back the poison by the force of her gaze. I leave the wagon without saying another word.

Quinn waits for me outside, his dark eyes shadowed. "What happened?" He gestures toward the row of bodies lined up under a long sheet of canvas. "We didn't sustain this many serious injuries last night."

I press my fingertips to my eyes as the beginning of a headache throbs against my skull. "Those people were all in marked rooms yesterday morning. They all appear to have been poisoned."

"Does anyone else have symptoms?"

I nod. I don't know how many of the other names on my list are already bruising. Already bleeding from the inside out, though they don't know it yet. I don't know which of them will die next. Lee Ann Blair? Heather Palmquist? Paul Lusk?

"What are the symptoms? Logan!" Quinn snaps, and I open my eyes. "What are the symptoms? If we know what kind of poison we're dealing with, we might be able to save them."

"Exhaustion. Abdominal pain. Unexplained bruising. And eventually, they bleed—"

"Through the eyes, nose, and mouth?" he asks.

"Or even faster if they've been cut. The blood is too thin and won't clot." I look at the list in my hand. Scott Godsey. Hanna Burkes. Lila Toshiko. I know these people. I care about them. I can't just let them die.

"Castor seeds," Quinn says, and the tone of finality in his voice raises the hairs on the back of my neck.

"Castor seeds?"

"The seeds of the castor plant are poisonous. If you swallow them unbroken, you have a chance. But if someone crushes the seeds, mixes it with a liquid, and injects it into your bloodstream, you die."

I shake my head. "No. There has to be something. The blood just needs to clot. We have to find a plant. A seed. Something around here has to help."

He wraps a hand around my shoulder and squeezes. "There is no antidote, Logan."

"There must be—"

"Castor seed poison doesn't cause the blood to thin. It causes it to *clot*. Inside all of their bodies, their blood is clotting, blocking their veins, growing bigger. Injuring their organs. Breaking down the tissue. Their bodies throw so much effort into clotting that the blood in their extremities grows thin and can't clot at all. That's when they start bleeding out."

I stare at him in horror, my heart thundering in my ears.

"You can't give them something to clot the blood without killing them faster. And you can't give them something to thin the blood without causing hemorrhages from their mouth, nose, and eyes."

I can't speak. Can barely breathe. I throw off his arm.

"I'm sorry, Logan."

"Maybe you're wrong," I say, because he has to be. He *has* to be.

"I'm not."

"Maybe you are. Who made you an expert in poisons, anyway? You could be wrong."

His expression looks carved in stone. "Willow and I are both experts in the many, many ways a person can be killed. Our father saw to that."

"It can't be castor seeds. It can't . . . Sylph is sick, Quinn. She's in there"—I gesture toward the medical wagon—"with bruises all over her body, and I have to save her. I can't let Rachel lose anyone else. Do you hear me? I have to save her!" My voice is raw and desperate, and already the bitterness of grief is spilling into me, because I look at Quinn's face, and I know.

I can't save her.

I can't save any of them.

And they're all dead because the Commander wanted power. Because Jared gave us the device. Because we brought it back to Baalboden instead of returning it to Rowansmark.

Because of me.

Did I really think I could lead these people and prove my worthiness to them? The dregs of my belief taste like ashes on the back of my tongue as the soft sound of Smithson calling Sylph's name in broken tones pierces the morning air.

CHAPTER THIRTY-FIVE

LOGAN

The lazy hum of bumblebees fills the air as I climb through patches of spring grass sprinkled with wildflowers on my way to the lip of land above the river. The camp at my back is a whirlwind of activity as some pack canvas, blankets, and torches back into the supply wagon while others work with Nola and Drake to reconfigure those riding in the other wagons so we can accommodate the newly sick among us.

Three more people on my list have symptoms. Word has spread that those dying from bruises and bleeding gums were all marked. Everywhere I go, people watch me. Whispering. Wondering what I will do to keep them safe. Wondering how I can force our group to travel with so many sick and so many more destined to fall prey to the symptoms.

The soil beneath me gives a little as I walk. Bending down, I press my fingers into its cool, dark depths. Gusts of air rise from the river and roll over the edge of the meadow. The water smells like a musty, dirt-floored basement with leaky walls. The ground around me is covered in a light film of residual moisture.

We can bury our dead here. The damp soil will make for easy digging. Plus, the profusion of flowers makes this spot pretty, and that means something. We might be barely clinging to survival. We might be running low on hope and optimism. But we can still give our dead the dignity of a proper burial.

The thought that we might have more dead to bury when we set up camp this evening makes me ache down to my bones. But beneath the regret and the guilt, a steady flame of anger burns within me.

When I catch the man who did this, I'm going to punish him in ways that will be remembered long after his body has turned to dust. No one in the beleaguered group at my back will doubt that I fought for them. That I was worthy of the trust they placed in me.

Dusting the soil off of my fingers, I stand and continue on toward the drop-off above the river. The highwaymen won't get a burial. We can't afford the time or energy to dig a grave for twenty-three men who wanted nothing more than to murder us and steal everything we own.

I've already sent Quinn, Thom, and Frankie to scope out the forest for the highwaymen's belongings. With no city-state nearby and no known highwaymen camps to resupply them, I'm positive they weren't just wandering around with nothing but weapons and the shirts on their backs. We could use some fresh supplies.

I reach the edge of the meadow and gaze into the river below. The water is a murky green, nearly the same color as the cypress needles that cover many of the trees in the surrounding forest.

The morning sun ricochets off of the rippling current, igniting tiny shards of brilliance that make my headache worse.

I raise my face, staring north at the line where the thick green forest meets the clear blue sky. The sky is the same color as Rachel's eyes. I can't bear to look at it. If I do, I'll have to remember how small she looked huddled next to her best friend, willing her not to die.

A movement along the river bank catches my eye, and I stare as Willow surfaces, flips her braid out of her face, and tugs a long cylinder made of silver wire out of the water. The cylinder is easily the length of a wagon bed and is full of fish.

It's a fish trap, and an expertly crafted one at that. And it isn't ours. Which means either the highwaymen dropped it in the river yesterday, intending to use the catch today, or another group of people live near here.

A Tree Village, maybe? I hope so. Of all the possibilities, they're the only ones who aren't likely to try to rob us or kill us on sight.

Willow is struggling to haul the trap up the slippery riverbank. I start looking around for the path she used to get down to the water. In a moment, I see it—a narrow trail is carved into the side of the bluff, paved with flat stones that line up end to end.

Man-made. Just like the trap. If these fish belong to anyone but the dead highwaymen, their owner could return at any time. I doubt we'd get a warm reception as we lunched on a pile of stolen fish.

Not that I'm about to return them to the water. Not with so many people needing to be fed.

I carefully navigate my way down the path, sliding

uncomfortably close to the edge a few times as my boots hit a stone slick with damp. The ground is spongy and strewn with rocks. Thick river birch trees line the bank, their branches arching out over the water. The current moves quickly, and I give Willow credit for being a strong swimmer. Most people who stepped foot in this water would wash up on the shore hundreds of yards downstream before they ever knew what hit them.

Which is unfortunate, because I need to get my people across this river.

Approaching Willow, I see the fish trap is about three yards long, and a generous assortment of carp, perch, and trout flop around inside, their gills heaving. I knew Willow was a formidable girl, but being able to drag a full fish trap through a swift-moving current just raised formidable to a whole new level.

I'm grateful she's on my side.

"Nice," I say as I bend down to lift one side of the trap. It's ridiculously heavy. I grunt with the effort.

"Watch yourself," she says. "Might be easier just to roll it."

I shoot her a look. "I'm honor-bound not to struggle with this since you just retrieved it all by yourself. Please do me the courtesy of pretending this is hard for you as well."

She rolls her eyes. "It was a lot lighter in the water. Roll it, honor boy. I'm not lifting this."

We shove the cylinder over the muddy bank. It catches on stones and tree roots and in general does its best to defeat our efforts, but eventually we get it to the base of the path.

"Now what?" she asks.

"I'll walk up the path backward and pull while you push."

"Do me a favor and try not to back right over the edge."

"I'll do my best," I say.

She takes a moment to wring some water from her tunic. The sun slides over the silver ear cuff she wears and dies when it hits the black feather dangling limply against her shoulder.

"What's the feather for?" I ask.

Her dark eyes are unreadable. "For my first kill."

A chill raises the hair on the back of my neck. "How old were you?"

"Eight. If we're done talking about me, let's—"

"Wait a minute." I hold my hands up. "You killed someone when you were eight? That seems . . . that's very . . . why?"

She fists her hands on her hips. "You could say it was my initiation into the family business."

"Willow. You were just a child." Horror fills my voice, and she gives herself a little shake and bends toward the trap.

"Not quite enough fish here to comfortably feed the entire group, but I think I saw another trap farther south." Her voice is calm, but I hear the finality in it. She won't discuss her childhood, and given what I know now, I can't blame her.

Between this conversation and Quinn's revelation about his father teaching his children every possible way to kill someone, I now regret ever giving Quinn a hard time about refusing to carry a weapon.

"Let's get this up to the meadow and let Nola figure out if she wants to cook it now or transport it raw, and we can go get the other trap." I keep the lingering horror out of my voice, and swallow the pity as well. Willow wouldn't appreciate either.

"She'd better cook it now. Few things are worse than the smell of a dead fish," she says. We start pushing and pulling the trap up the trail, and she looks at me. "Forgot to tell you there's a bridge just south of here."

I stop pulling. "A bridge? A fully intact bridge?"

She shrugs. "It looked intact to me, but I didn't swim close enough to get a good look."

A bridge. I have a way to get my people across the river. And thanks to the jars of glycerin and acid I took with me out of Baalboden after blowing up the gate, I have a way to destroy that bridge and cut off any efforts to track us further.

For the first time in weeks, I feel a tiny shred of hope.

CHAPTER THIRTY-SIX

RACHEL

Logan conducts a funeral service on the rise of land at the north end of the meadow. The morning chill still clings to the air, and a somber mood lies over us like a blanket. I leave Sylph resting peacefully in the wagon with Smithson by her side and join the crowd of mourners. I tell Smithson I feel I should be present for the burial, and that's partially true.

But really I need a few minutes away from the sight of Sylph's slow deterioration and Smithson's increasing desperation before the silent wall within me threatens to crack. I can't grieve yet. Not while she's still alive. Maybe not at all. If I let the depth of what she means to me hurt me, every other ghost that haunts me will demand its due, and how will I ever survive that?

So I stand at the edges of the crowd, letting Logan's voice wash over me without leaving a single word behind, and tell myself that the scars that harden the surface of my heart are necessary for survival.

When Drake takes over to supervise the actual burial, Logan

works his way around the side of the field until he's standing beside me. He wraps an arm around my waist, and I lean against him as the first shovel bites into the ground. We stand in silence as those who loved the ones we lost say their words, pick their flowers, and find their own way to let go of one more dream.

When the crowd begins to disperse under Drake's orders to help Nola cook the fish Willow caught, pack up the rest of the supplies, and be ready to move out in an hour, I look at Logan.

"This poison . . . there must be an antidote. We just need to figure out what we're dealing with, right?" Deep down, though, I already know the answer. If there were an antidote, if Logan knew how to stop this, he wouldn't be standing still doing nothing. But I have to ask. I have to know I tried everything to save her.

His jaw clenches. "It's castor seed poison. And according to Quinn, there is no antidote."

A weak spurt of anger warms me. "How does Quinn know about poisons? You're the scientist. If there's an antidote, you can figure it out."

"Quinn and Willow both know a frightening amount about poisons and weapons and every other way to kill someone." His voice is quiet, but still I glance around to make sure no one in Frankie's small circle of friends overheard. The last thing we need to deal with is more suspicion aimed at the Running-brooks. None of Frankie's friends are nearby. There's only Ian, rolling up a few yards of canvas, and Elias, slowly packing his travel bag while he watches us like he'd love to know what we're talking about.

Logan turns me around to face him. His eyes burn into mine.

"Rachel, I'm sorry. If I could think of anything—*anything*—to try, I would. But I don't know how to save her." His voice is nothing but a whisper now. "I'm sorry."

The hurt stabbing through me throbs once or twice and then fades into the bleak silence. I don't try to get it back. Sylph is going to die. There's nothing I can do to stop it. One more person stripped from me. One more ghost to haunt me while I sleep.

Feeling nothing but icy emptiness is better than sliding into the gaping pit of loss and destruction lurking somewhere inside of me. If I feel nothing, I can function. I can go back and face her. I can be strong for Smithson.

I can keep going.

"Rachel?" Logan asks, his hand reaching for me as if to offer comfort.

I step back. I don't need comfort. Comfort doesn't solve anything. Tears don't either. I just need to put one foot in front of the other and pretend I can handle this. If I pretend long enough, maybe it will become real.

Logan's hand falls to his side, and I read the guilt and regret on his face as easily as if he'd said the words aloud. He feels responsible. He thinks I blame him. I should do something. Say something. Find a way to ease his mind and heart.

I should, but any softness that once existed in me has disappeared.

Before either of us can say another word, Quinn runs up to us. "Found the highwaymen's campsite just west of here. They had two wagons full of supplies."

"Where are they?" Logan asks.

"Over there." Quinn points, and I turn to see two new

wagons, each pulled by a sturdy-looking horse, resting at the southern edge of the meadow. "One of the wagons has blankets and bedrolls inside. The other is full of weapons, jars of fruit, sacks of jerky, bolts of cloth, and boots. Looks like they'd just come from a successful trading mission. Which makes finding *these* very suspicious."

He holds out his hand, and we stare at the pile of silver coins spread across his palm. On one side is a bold, raised *C*.

"They traded with Carrington," I say, and hunch my shoulders as an itch of awareness prickles the hair on the back of my neck. "They're too close to the northern city-states for a trading mission with the actual city-state of Carrington. Highwaymen don't travel that far."

"Which means they most likely traded with the army," Logan says.

"The army would've been fully provisioned before they marched on Baalboden," Quinn says. "And the highwaymen's wagons are full, so whatever they traded, it wasn't food, weapons, or cloth. I don't like it. I sent Frankie and Thom south to search for signs of anyone else close to us. I have a bad feeling about this. What did the highwaymen have that was valuable enough for the Commander to buy?"

The itch on the back of my neck becomes a terrible need to get out of the open. Get the people into the Wasteland.

Run.

"Information," Logan says, and he's already moving. "They traded information about other routes to the northern city-states, and they must've done it yesterday, which means the army has had enough time to catch up to us. We're in trouble. Let's go."

A shout goes up from the eastern edge of the meadow. We spin toward the noise and stare as Frankie and Thom thunder out of the forest, their horses galloping at top speed. Frankie locks eyes with us and yells, "Move, move, move! The army is coming!"

"South! Go south! Find the bridge." Logan waves at Frankie to take the lead, and as the horse races past us, Logan yells to the crowd of survivors who stand frozen in horror, packs on their backs, food in their hands. "Follow Frankie. Men carry the children. Guards, grab your weapons. Get those wagons moving." When everyone just stares at him for a heartbeat, he screams, *"Run!"*

The crowd breaks. Men grab children and race south into the tree line. Women hike up their skirts and follow. Nola, Jodi, Drake, and Elias climb into wagon seats and slap the reins to get the animals moving. Quinn and Willow run to the highwaymen's wagons, leap aboard, and reach back to haul slower-moving people into the wagon beds before sending the horses careening into the forest.

"I'm going in the medical wagon," I say as I run south beside Logan. "I'll kill anyone who tries to get inside."

"Be safe," he says, and leaps for one of the supply wagons.

I've nearly reached the wagon when Ian runs up to me. His eyes are lit with a wild light as he grabs my arm.

"This is it. This is our chance. The Commander is in range."

The medical wagon bounces over a rock, and Sylph's cry of pain scrapes my heart raw.

"Move," I say, and try to step around him.

"Rachel, we need the device. We can end this." His grip hurts my arm.

"Logan has the device, and he's in another wagon. Go talk to him if you—"

"We had a deal." Ian's voice is furious, but I don't care. The entire field is in chaos, the Commander isn't in front of us yet, and Sylph needs me. I'm not going to spend the last moments of her life trying to con Logan out of the device when I should be helping get everyone to safety.

I wrench my arm free and shove Ian aside. Before he can say another word, I grab the back of the medical wagon and jump onto the step as our people scramble into the trees while in the distance, a line of Carrington soldiers breaks out of the eastern forest and races toward us.

CHAPTER THIRTY-SEVEN

LOGAN

The meadow quickly empties as wagons and people rush into the trees. I crawl into the back of the supply wagon and focus on my plan as we rumble our way into the forest.

Frankie returns to tell me the bridge is thirty yards away and that people are already crossing it. His horse pants heavily as he gives me his report, and then he wheels south again to shepherd the people in the right direction.

Thirty yards away. Thirty yards of thick trees, rock-strewn ground, and dense underbrush. We're never going to make it.

We *have* to make it.

The consequences for failure are unthinkable.

I just need to buy us enough time to get every man, woman, child, and wagon over that bridge. I pray the bridge is strong enough to support our weight as we cross. We don't have any other options.

Jodi is driving the supply wagon I'm in. The wheels bounce over roots and bushes, flinging me to the side, and threatening to toss her off the driver's bench entirely. She hangs on to the reins with fierce determination as I yank the crates I need out from under the bench. Prying their lids loose, I do a quick count.

Fifteen jars of acid. Sixteen of glycerin.

More than enough to blow up a bridge.

Perfect.

"Stop the wagon!" I call to Jodi, and to her credit, she obeys without hesitation. Scooping up a jar of each substance, I leap from the wagon and wave Thom on when he whips his horse toward me. "Go to the bridge. Get everyone across. I'll be there soon."

"If you're going to face down that army by yourself, you'll need some help. I'm staying." His voice brooks no argument, but he isn't going to sway me.

"Thom, go. I'll be right behind you, I promise." A flash of Carrington red winks between the trees. They're gaining on us. I look around quickly. At least forty people still haven't managed twenty yards, much less thirty. I meet Thom's gaze. "Save these people, Thom. I need them out of here or I can't buy us the time we need. Save them. Please."

He nods and reaches down to haul a struggling woman onto his horse. As he moves to help others, calling out encouragement and instructions, I turn to face Carrington's army and find Jodi standing beside me, a jar of acid in one hand and a jar of glycerin in the other.

"Get in the wagon," I say sharply. "There'll be flying debris. I need you safe."

She tightens her grip on the jars and sizes up the soldiers racing toward us. "Do I throw them at the same time?"

"Jodi—"

"At the same time?" Her voice trembles, but her hands are steady, and with the first line of soldiers less than fifteen yards from us, I don't have time to talk her out of her foolish courage.

"No, throw one and then the other. High and to the left. The jars have to shatter against the same spot on a tree trunk. Choose the biggest tree you can reach."

She nods, and I take a deep breath. The soldiers are ten yards away. It's time. "Now!"

I whip my arm back, aim for the right, and throw the jar of glycerin as hard as I can. It arcs up, falls swiftly, and shatters against the trunk of a red maple. I hurl the acid after it, just as Jodi's second jar slams into the same cypress trunk she'd already coated with glycerin.

The cypress explodes in a shower of splinters, branches, and shards of bark the size of my arm. Seconds later, the maple explodes as well, and both trees topple to the ground. A handful of soldiers are crushed beneath the trunks. Still more are bleeding from gaping wounds to their heads, arms, and legs.

None of those who bleed are injured in their vital organs. The Dragonskin they wear sees to that. Still, the path we cut through the forest has been obliterated, and uninjured soldiers must waste precious seconds running around the debris.

We can't afford to let those seconds go to waste.

"Drive." I grab Jodi's tiny waist and toss her onto the driver's bench. Then I vault into the wagon bed and scoop up two more jars. As the wagon bounces its way across the forest floor, I brace myself against the wall and watch for my opportunity.

The soldiers are pouring over the debris, stepping on their

dead and injured if they must. Already, less than ten yards separate us. "Tell me when we reach the bridge," I yell to Jodi.

The man closest to the wagon meets my gaze and draws his sword.

I heft my jars.

Four more soldiers hurtle out of the trees, intent on flanking us.

I need a little more time. Just a little more time to get safely onto the bridge.

Five more men close in from the other side. All I see in front of me is a sea of red military jackets and drawn swords.

"Bridge!" Jodi calls back.

"Are there any stragglers?"

Two others join the ranks of those closing in on us. Six yards separate us.

Five.

"All clear," Jodi says. "We're the last ones. Should we cross it?"

"Get the wagon onto the bridge and then stop."

The wagon lurches onto a wooden bridge that lists to the left. The boards are the color of fig pudding and feel slippery and soft beneath the metal wagon wheels. Jodi yanks the reins sharply, and we come to a stop. The bridge sways in a jerky, sickening rhythm that fills my head with visions of my people tumbling to their deaths in the river below.

Carrington's front line is two yards from the bridge.

From us.

A long, flat rock juts out of the ground in front of the entrance to the bridge. I leap from the wagon, aim, and throw both jars at the same time. They smash against the stone and explode in a shower of glass, dirt, and slivers of rock, leaving a deep crater where the rock used to be. The force of the blast throws me against the wagon, and I dive underneath it as debris rains down. The soldiers closest to the explosion are thrown onto their backs, their skin riddled with cuts. The soldiers behind them now have to climb over the injured and carefully skirt the crater without falling off the sheer face of the drop to the river below.

I've bought us all the time I can. It will have to be enough.

"Go," I say to Jodi as I leap onto the wagon step and peer around the canvas to assess the scene before me.

The bridge is a narrow strip of wooden planks held in place by iron pillars that arch over the top of us like a naked canopy. Rust covers every inch of iron and eats through some of the pillars until the metal curls away from its moorings like it longs to reach the water below. Two wagons are still carefully negotiating the swaying planks. Their wheels bite into the rotting wood, making it sag dangerously. Here and there, a board has snapped in half, leaving gaping holes and forcing the wagons to the far side of the bridge, where they slide precariously close to the edge. At least fifty people still struggle to get across—gripping the rusty pillars, skirting the holes, and in general moving slowly enough that Carrington's soldiers will run them through with a sword before they ever have to worry about drowning.

"Move!" I scream to them. "Go faster or you'll die."

Some of them pick up their pace. Some of them don't. Their heavy packs, their exhaustion, or sheer, abject terror keep them crawling along the bridge at a snail's pace.

I'm not going to lose them. Any of them.

We're one third of the way across. Carrington soldiers are

skirting the crater and carefully climbing onto the bridge. I leap from the wagon's step and reach for the first straggler.

"Get in," I say, and half scoop, half shove a woman with gray hair and stooped shoulders into the wagon. The next two stragglers get unceremoniously tossed into the wagon as well.

I glance behind me and see a line of red-jacketed soldiers coming for us, walking two abreast. The bridge jerks and shudders beneath their momentum, but they don't hesitate.

"Faster," I say to Jodi, and race ahead of her to help a man struggling to carry two toddlers. As soon as the wagon pulls abreast of us, we dump the children inside and the man hurries to pick up a woman who clings to a rusty pillar streaked with black.

I look back. Carrington's men have reached the one-third mark. We're now a little more than halfway across. We're never going to make it.

Hoofbeats slam against the planks, and I turn to see Thom riding toward me, his broad face filled with determination. Instantly, I come to a decision. I'd wanted to toss jars of acid and glycerin out of the back of the wagon as we sped to safety, blowing up a chunk of the bridge in our wake. But there are too many people between me and the other side, and the bridge is already too unstable to risk blowing up any part of it before all of my people are on solid ground again.

Jodi and the man who was carrying the toddlers can get most of the remaining people into the wagon. Thom can shepherd the rest across.

I'll wait here with my jars and my sword and hold Carrington off as long as possible. If I soak the boards with glycerin, it will only take one jar of acid to destroy this section of the bridge. I'm a strong swimmer. If I don't get injured by flying debris or crushed by metal pillars, I have a chance to survive this.

"Keep going," I say to Jodi. "Pick up anyone you can fit into the wagon and get to safety."

"What about you?" she asks.

"I'm going to stop Carrington."

I grab three jars of glycerin and one of acid, and then move away from the wagon. The lead soldiers are less than fifteen yards away from me. I unscrew the first jar of glycerin and spill its contents on the boards at my feet while the unsteady creaking of Jodi's wagon wheels fades into the distance.

I'm spilling the contents of the second glycerin jar when Thom reaches me.

"I'll do that." His feet thud against the planks as he dismounts. "Give me the jars."

I shake my head and unscrew the third. Carrington is closing in on the one-half mark. The shudders running through the bridge's frame are slowing them down, but still they'll be on me in another minute.

"Make sure all of our people get to solid ground," I say. "Yell to me when the bridge is clear."

"And then what? You die?" he asks.

"Hopefully not, but it's a possibility." The contents of the third jar arc through the air and splash onto the planks a few yards in front of me.

I need a wide base for this explosion.

Thom grabs the fourth jar from my hands, and unscrews the lid.

"Thom, please. Get on the horse. Get everyone off the bridge."

"Get on the horse yourself. I'm doing this." His voice is calm.

"No, you aren't. I'm a strong swimmer."

"Don't figure I'll need to know how to swim," Thom says, and the finality in his voice stops me dead.

Carrington reaches the halfway mark and the bridge dips and sways, sending a few of them into the pillars and nearly bringing me to my knees. Thom grabs my cloak and holds me upright. I stare at him, at the pale sheen to his skin, the dilated pupils in his brown eyes, and I realize he means to die.

For me.

"They're almost here. We don't have time to argue. You aren't sacrificing yourself for me, Thom. I have a good chance of surviving. Please—"

"You have almost no chance of surviving, and the group needs you."

The insistent slap of Carrington boots against the planks comes closer. Thom upends the fourth jar of glycerin and coats the planks behind him.

A sense of sick desperation wells up within me. "The group needs us both. Go back, Thom. *Please.*"

He meets my eyes, and pulls the sleeve of his tunic up to his elbow. A bouquet of purple-black bruises mottles the underside of his arm.

"I'm a walking dead man, Logan. Let me die with dignity. I want my life to count for something bigger than myself."

"Thom," I whisper. My throat closes, and my eyes burn.

This quiet, hardworking man deserves better than this. I hold his gaze for another few seconds as gratitude and regret twist through me until I can't tell the difference, and then hand him the jar of acid. "Your life already counts for something bigger than yourself. I couldn't have come this far without you. You're a hero. Even before you blow up this bridge, you're a hero."

Grief is a tight band across my chest, and I clasp Thom's shoulder as Carrington's soldiers reach the glycerin-soaked planks. Then I lunge for the horse, pull myself into the saddle, and hammer the first soldier with the hilt of my sword.

His partner attacks, sword flashing. I parry, thrust, block, and stab. The horse dances in place, the bridge shudders and moans, and over my shoulder, I see the last of the Baalboden survivors reach solid ground.

I spur the horse into the next two soldiers, hacking and chopping with my sword to build a perimeter around Thom.

"Logan, go," Thom says. "Go!"

He holds the open jar of acid above his head. The planks around him are a glycerin-soaked bomb waiting for a spark. I kick another soldier into the men behind him, and whip the horse around.

Thom meets my eyes and nods.

I can hardly speak around the grief that suffocates me. "Thank you," I say, and spur the horse into a gallop toward the end of the bridge.

Ahead of me, solid ground is less than ten yards away.

Behind me, Thom's voice rises in a tremendous roar of fury.

"For Baalboden!" he yells.

I twist in my saddle and see him throw the acid onto the planks at his feet. There's a split second of silence as the liquid splashes through the air, and then the bridge explodes, sending a hail of wood, metal, and bodies to the river below.

CHAPTER THIRTY-EIGHT

LOGAN

"**N**o!" Frankie spurs his horse forward and meets me as my mount leaps onto solid ground. I duck against the horse's flank as chunks of debris slice into the surrounding trees. A hole the size of two wagons lined up end to end rips the bridge in two. The shorter piece, the one closest to us, remains solid. The longer piece, bereft of support and filled with soldiers, twists slowly in the air as if at any moment, it might rip free of the few pillars that still hold it in place.

Huge freckled hands reach for me and haul me out of the saddle.

"He doesn't know how to swim. Do you hear me?" Frankie shakes me like I weigh nothing. "He doesn't know how to swim."

Letting go of me, he rushes to the edge of the drop-off and stares into the pile of wreckage and bodies littering the river below. "Thom!" he screams. "Thomas Kocevar, you get out of that water. You raise your head right now. Thom!"

A flash of golden skin runs by us, and suddenly Willow soars off the cliff's edge. Jackknifing in midair, she splits the water between a slab of iron and a body dressed in red. Seconds later, the unsteady portion of the bridge rips free of its moorings with an earsplitting shriek of metal on metal and tumbles into the water below.

"Willow!" Quinn rushes to my side at the cliff's edge, and we scan the river. "Willow!"

Bodies flail in the water, but all of them are wearing red. Another kind of red is spreading in an ever-widening circle from the epicenter of the bridge's fall. The current tugs at the wash of crimson and slowly pushes it downstream until everywhere we look the water runs red with the blood of its victims.

Willow doesn't surface. Neither does Thom.

"She's a strong swimmer," I say. "Give her more time. She'll be okay."

But time passes, and she still doesn't surface. Two Carrington soldiers haul themselves out of the water and flop onto the bank on our side. A handful do the same on the opposite bank.

Willow is nowhere to be found.

Quinn makes a strangled noise in his throat, grabs Frankie's cloak, and throws him against a tree. Frankie raises his meaty arms, but Quinn plows a fist into his stomach and then pins him to the tree trunk with his forearm across Frankie's throat.

"Are you satisfied now?" Quinn yells. "Are you?"

Frankie's face turns red, and his lips move, but nothing comes out. I grab Quinn's shoulder.

"Let him go, Quinn."

Quinn ignores me and leans closer to Frankie. His dark eyes are cold and furious. "From the moment we joined your group, you've done nothing but degrade us and cast false accusations at us. Do you know why Willow jumped into the river? To prove you wrong."

Frankie gurgles, and his lips begin turning blue. He punches and kicks at Quinn, but Quinn parries the blows with swift, graceful movements, never once releasing Frankie's throat. It's like watching a cat toy with a mouse already half-dead.

"Quinn, you're killing him. Let him go," I say.

"She jumped in to prove you wrong. Not because she cares what you think of her, but because she cares what you think of *me*." His voice is calm. Deadly. The voice of a predator who knows his prey is helpless. "Your opinion isn't worth her life. *You* aren't worth her life."

"Quinn!" I slam into Quinn from the side, knocking his arm away from Frankie's throat. Frankie falls to the ground, gasping and choking. Quinn snarls at me and lunges toward Frankie again.

I jump in front of Frankie, and Quinn plows into me. We hit the dirt. I grab Quinn's tunic with both hands before he can get back up again.

"Stop!" I say, and Quinn looks at me—really looks at me—for the first time since Willow dove into the water.

"He dishonored her." He spits the words in Frankie's direction.

"Yes, he did. But Willow rose above it. For you. Because she admires who you've become. It was her way of defending your honor. Honor you're about to destroy by killing Frankie."

Quinn stares at me, his breath heaving. "I wasn't . . ." He stares at Frankie, who is rubbing his hands against his throat and coughing in harsh gasps.

"You were killing him," I say quietly.

"Yes." Quinn's voice is quiet.

"I'm sorry about Willow."

A flicker of pain lights Quinn's eyes, and then his customary emotionless mask slides back into place. Wordlessly, he rises and turns away from me. Away from Frankie.

"Logan!" Jodi is on her hands and knees, leaning out over the drop-off, her feet digging into the soil to help her keep her balance. She's pointing at something below.

I scramble to her side and peer over the edge.

Willow is slowly climbing out of the water, blood pouring from a gash in her back. Some of the pressure squeezing my chest eases. I whip my head around and say, "Quinn, she's alive. We need to help her." Then I jump to my feet and race to the supply wagon for the length of rope I have stashed inside.

Quinn is at the edge when I return. His jaw is clenched, his hands fisted as he watches his sister pull herself onto the riverbank. I loop one end of the rope around a sturdy tree trunk and lash it tight. All around us, survivors cluster at the edge of the drop-off. Some call encouragement down to Willow. Others stare in mute shock at the bridge's wreckage, and the long line of red-jacketed soldiers standing at the edge of the opposite tree line, their swords gleaming like a row of wicked teeth.

"I'm going down to get her," Quinn says, and I don't argue. If Willow were my sister, I'd be the one going down, too. He quickly fashions a harness and then slowly lets out the slack as he lowers himself over the edge.

Several more Carrington soldiers have now climbed out of

the river's swift current on our side of the bank. Three of them lie panting and bleeding on the rocky bank. A fourth starts moving toward Willow, who huddles on her hands and knees, blood pouring onto the sand beneath her.

A faint *thwing* disturbs the air, and an arrow flies past me and buries itself in the soldier's neck. He staggers, reaches up to grab the arrow, and falls backward into the river. Three more arrows fly, and all of the injured soldiers stop moving.

I turn and see Rachel standing behind me holding Willow's bow, her eyes bleak.

"Did I miss any?" she asks.

I scan the riverbank, but the only bodies washing ashore now are already dead. "No, you got them all."

She lowers the bow and comes to stand beside me. Together, we watch Quinn work his way down the side of the embankment.

"Thom is dead," I say, and the words burn my tongue like acid. "He insisted on staying behind to blow up the bridge instead of me, even though—"

"You were going to stay behind and blow up the bridge?" Her voice is as bleak as her eyes.

I look at her. "I wanted to toss the jars out of the wagon as we left the bridge, but there were too many people still trying to get across. I had to send the wagon ahead of me to help get everyone to safety."

She meets my eyes, but I can't figure out what she's thinking.

"Thom sacrificed himself. He was poisoned. Bruises already on his arms. And he insisted on staying instead." I want her to understand. To see that someone had to do it. Someone had to cut us off from the Carrington army or we'd have died like sheep penned in for slaughter.

"You were going to blow yourself up with the bridge?"

"I was hoping not to. I was going to get as far away from the glycerin as I could before throwing the acid, and then dive over the side before the explosion hit so that I had a chance of swimming to the shore."

Her gaze drifts past mine and lingers on the sea of wreckage floating in the crimson-streaked water. "You wouldn't have survived."

She's right, but the terrible emptiness in her voice keeps me from admitting it. I put my arms around her, but she remains stiff and unyielding. It's like holding a stone to my chest. Leaning down, I press my mouth against her ear and say, "They would've destroyed us, Rachel. Someone had to stop them. I didn't want it to be me, but sometimes we just have to do what comes next."

Below us, Quinn wraps his arms around his sister and gently slides her onto his back. She clings to his shoulders and wraps her legs around his waist. Her braid is undone, and her dark hair covers her face as she leans her head against Quinn's shoulder. I let go of Rachel and reach for the rope in case Quinn needs help pulling them both up to the tree line.

"Sylph is going to die," Rachel says, and I shiver at the aching void behind her words. "You're all I have left. How can I live with the fear that every time I turn my back, you might be sacrificing yourself for the rest of us?"

I dig my heels into the soil and brace my arms against the rope as Quinn begins to climb.

"Like you sacrificed yourself to save Jeremiah when

Carrington broke into the compound?"

She doesn't respond.

"Do you want me to promise you that I'll never risk my life again?" I ask. "Because that isn't the kind of life we have, Rachel. I wish it was, but it isn't."

She still says nothing. I look at her, but she's staring beyond me, her skin dead white against the brilliant flame of her hair, her eyes filled with cold fury. Turning, I follow her gaze and see the Commander standing at the distant edge of the ruined bridge, his sword flashing in the morning sunlight and his dark eyes boring into mine. Slowly he raises his arm until his sword is pointing straight at me. A row of archers stands along the embankment, their arrows nocked.

"Give me the tech, and I'll stop hunting you," the Commander yells, cutting his words into sharp, precise pieces.

Rachel whips the bow up and lets an arrow fly. It sails toward the Commander, but falls short, landing just shy of the opposite bank.

"He's too far away to kill," I say.

She says nothing.

As Quinn and Willow clamber onto the embankment, surrounded by hands reaching to help them up, to untie the rope, and to whisk Willow away to the medical wagon, I step to the side. I want an unobstructed view of the man who's ruined my life and the lives of so many others in his relentless quest for power. Then I whip my sword from its sheath, raise it in the air above me, and lower it until the tip is aimed at the Commander's vicious, brutal heart.

"You will never get the device from me." I fling the words at him, and then motion my people to move back into the trees.

"I will never stop hunting you." His voice echoes across the water. "Do you hear me, Logan McEntire? I will spend every waking minute of my life hunting you down like the dog you are. And when I catch up to you, I will slaughter you and everyone who follows you. Man, woman, and child."

"Not if I kill you first." Before he can reply, I turn on my heel and walk away.

He can't get to me. Yet. The ruined bridge made sure of that. But he'll keep coming, and I'll be ready. I'll train my people. I'll build every weapon I've ever designed. I'll make alliances of my own. And on the inevitable day when we finally confront each other face-to-face, I'll destroy him.

CHAPTER THIRTY-NINE

RACHEL

The medical wagon creaks and sways as it rumbles across the faint path leading north through the tree line. The river is a constant presence on our left. The tangled greenery of the Wasteland presses against our right.

I have to keep reminding myself that I'm not at the Commander's mercy. Oliver isn't dying in front of me. No guard waits to undress me and scrub me clean of blood.

Still, the four walls of the wagon want to close in on me, and I struggle to breathe past the rapid beating of my heart.

Willow lies in the wagon bed along with Sylph on a thick pile of canvas covered with a blanket. The others recovering from injuries have been transferred to the highwayman wagon that also carries blankets and bedrolls.

Quinn sits beside Willow, alternating between checking her brow for fever and lifting the edge of her tunic to examine the neat row of stitches he sewed into her skin to close the cut she sustained in the river. She sleeps now courtesy of a pinch of pain medicine, though earlier Quinn had his hands full keeping her from leaving the wagon to resume guard duty.

Smithson sits beside Sylph, his face pale and his eyes red. He holds her hand and leans down to whisper to her every few minutes.

I sit between Sylph and Willow and ache for a miracle. For inspiration. For something more to do than to sit here waiting for my best friend to die.

I don't know how to do this without losing myself. I don't know how to pretend to be strong for everyone else when I have no strength left.

Sylph moans and opens her eyes. "Stomach hurts," she says, and Smithson rushes to comfort her with words and touches and all the things I don't know how to do.

Guilty.

Alone.

Broken.

I want to fight the voices that whisper to me, but their words sound like the only truth I have left.

Something brushes against my hand, and I look down to see Sylph's fingers fluttering against mine. Gently, I wrap our hands together the way we used to when we'd lie beneath the stars in her backyard, giggling over our secrets while we ate the sticky buns Oliver always sent with me when I'd spend the night at Sylph's.

I can't remember our childhood without seeing Oliver's dark eyes lit with joy when we tumbled into his stall, begging for treats. Dad scooping us both onto his shoulders and pretending he would forget to duck on his way into our house. Pieces of home that I took for granted would always be there, but I was wrong. All the people I love leave. First Oliver, then Dad, and now Sylph—the girl who loved everyone with equal energy but spent extra love on me. The girl who wanted nothing more than to be Claimed and settle down to a quiet life full of children and laughter.

Instead, she lost her family, her home, and soon will lose her life for reasons that feel far away from me now. Because I wanted revenge? Because the Commander wanted power? Because someone from Rowansmark wants to punish us for crimes unknown?

The reasons don't matter. Only the results.

"Jeffrey Morrow." Sylph's voice is faint. I look down and find her green eyes watching me. "Remember?"

"I remember."

"Who is Jeffrey Morrow?" Smithson asks. His words sound stretched thin and tired, as if the effort it took to speak used them up before they left his lips.

"Boy . . . Rachel." Sylph draws a ragged breath and I lean forward, but she keeps speaking. "Beat up."

"His dad was the Commander's chief physician. He was a year younger than us, so you probably never had him in any of your classes," I say to Smithson, though I don't take my eyes off of Sylph. "He thought because his dad was so rich, he was better than the rest of us. He used to follow Sylph and me through Lower Market and call us names."

"Pushed me," Sylph says.

"Yes." I smooth the curls off her forehead and wince at the heat blazing on her skin. "We were in the alley behind Oliver's tent playing one day, and he snuck up on us and pushed Sylph down."

"And you did something about that," Smithson says in his stretched-thin voice.

I nod, and reach for the damp cloth resting in a bucket of water at my feet. "I chased him. Caught him after only half a block. And then—"

"Punched . . . face." Sylph smiles. "Bloody nose . . . crying . . . like a . . . girl."

I dab her face with the cloth and wish things were still simple enough that punching the right boy in the nose would fix it all.

"He told his dad I'd hit him, but when his dad came to Oliver's tent to confront me, Sylph said she'd done it," I say, and crumple the cloth in my fist. "Her father wouldn't let her come to Oliver's tent for a month."

"Brave." Sylph's eyes lock on mine.

"Yes, you were. You still are," I say.

"*You.*" She pushes the word at me. "Brave . . . always . . . braver . . . than anyone."

I'm not brave. Not anymore. I'm a broken girl too terrified of losing herself to name her fears and fight against them. But I can't tell her that. I can't stop pretending strength when she needs me. I swallow the words with all their jagged edges, and lean down to kiss her feverish cheek.

The wagon lurches to the left as someone jumps onto the back step. I look up as Frankie eases his large frame through the canvas flap and carefully makes his way toward us. His face is pale, and his eyes are swollen.

Quinn goes still, his fingers freezing in the act of checking

Willow's brow for fever. "What are you doing in here?" he asks.

Frankie looks at Sylph, and then turns his attention to Willow. He clears his throat, and then says quietly, "I owe you two an apology."

A muscle along Quinn's jaw leaps, but he says nothing.

"Is she awake? Can she hear me?" Frankie asks. "I can come back if this is a bad time."

Quinn is silent for a moment, then he gently taps Willow's cheek. "Wake up, Willow."

Her eyes flutter, and then slowly open. She frowns at Quinn. "Why is my head all fuzzy? What did you give me?"

"Something to help you rest."

"Don't do it again. It's bad enough when I have to see one of you hovering over me. Seeing two of you is more than I should have to deal with." She flashes a quick grin at her brother, but is instantly sober again when he doesn't respond in kind.

"What's going on?" she asks, and struggles to sit up. Swearing, she grabs her lower back and glares at Quinn as if it's his fault she's wounded.

"Please don't try to get up yet," Frankie says.

Willow looks past Quinn, her gaze sweeping the rest of the wagon before coming to rest on Frankie. "Why are you here?"

"I came to apologize." His voice is rough with emotion. "I've been hard on you. Both of you. Never did understand someone who'd choose to live in the trees instead of the safety of a city-state. Figured you were nothing better than highwaymen."

Willow's brow arches toward her hairline. "I'm a whole lot better than a highwayman."

Frankie crouches down beside her, keeping plenty of distance between himself and Quinn. "Thom was my best friend. Been my friend for over forty years." His voice thickens, and he clears his throat sharply. "He was dead as soon as that bridge exploded. I knew it. You knew it. Everybody knew it." He looks at his boots. "You didn't have to try. You didn't have to risk yourself like that, but you did it without a second thought."

Raising his head, he faces her. "I wouldn't have done the same for you or your brother. You knew that, too. I don't know how to thank you."

"I didn't do it for your gratitude."

"No, you didn't. But you've earned it anyway. If you ever need anything—anything at all—you ask me, and I'll do it."

Willow stares in silence for a moment, and then looks toward her brother. Quinn shifts his position and faces Frankie.

"Willow and I both thank you. And I owe you an apology as well," Quinn says.

Frankie holds up a hand, palm out. "Didn't appreciate being near choked to death, but I understand why you were angry."

"It's no excuse for losing control like that," Quinn says.

Frankie offers his hand, and Quinn shakes it without hesitation.

As Frankie carefully makes his way out of the wagon, I turn back to Sylph and have to bite my tongue to keep from crying out. Smithson leans over her, his wide palms tangled in her hair. She looks at him, pink tears slowly sliding down her face, while blood pours from her nose.

CHAPTER FORTY

RACHEL

"Oh, Sylph." I breathe her name out and the pain rushes in. A knot in my chest sends bright shards of hurt into my veins with every heartbeat. My hands shake as I grab another rag and try to capture the blood as it spills out of her nostrils, curves around her lips, and streams toward her jaw.

"Please," Smithson whispers, and Sylph tries to smile.

The rag can't contain the blood. It gushes from Sylph and coats my hands.

Blood pouring from the sky. Puddling at my feet. Biting into my skin.

A shudder works its way up my spine, and I barely keep myself from screaming.

I can't stay here, confined in this wagon while another person I love bleeds to death in front of me. I can't stay here, confronted with my impotence and helplessness. I *can't*, but somehow I have to. Sylph deserves to be surrounded by those who love her.

The shudder seizes my arms, my legs, and my teeth, shaking

me with merciless fingers until I drop the rag and wrap my arms around myself to keep from flying into a million little pieces.

"It's okay. It's okay." Smithson chants the words softly, rocking back and forth while Sylph grows pale and begins to tremble.

I slowly slide onto the wagon bed and curve my body next to hers the way we used to when we'd spend the night gossiping about our dreams. Hers were simple and sweet. She wanted a home of her own with blue curtains and white walls. Children and family dinners. A husband who wanted nothing more than what she could bring to him.

My dreams were bold and bright and impossible to articulate beneath the shadow of Baalboden's Wall. I wanted freedom. A place to live where I could wear what I wanted, say what I wanted, and challenge everyone as my equal. A crusade to lead if that was what my freedom cost.

My dreams are simple now. I don't want to change the world. I don't want to save it either.

I just want to save Sylph.

Wiping my hand clean on the blanket beneath me, I lace my fingers through hers and squeeze gently.

She doesn't squeeze back.

"Sylph. Please." Smithson chokes on a sob and leans down to press his cheek against hers. "I love you."

Her hand is cold in mine, and her body shakes as I stretch until I can rest my mouth next to her ear. "Thank you," I say, and swallow against the suffocating grief that stuffs my throat with cotton, "for everything. You loved me when no one else my age would. You accepted me. You stood up for me. You're brave and kind, and I will spend the rest of my life missing you."

Her lips move, but no sound comes out. I don't need to hear the words, though. I know Sylph would spend her dying breath telling us she loves us.

"I love you, too," I say, and stay pressed against her. With every faint beat of her heart, my pulse pounds harder. Faster. It feels like a metal vise is slowly squeezing my chest until I have to fight for every breath.

She moans, and I whisper, "Shh, it's all right," but it isn't. I'm a liar, and every tiny, shaky rise of her chest proves me wrong. Slowly, so slowly I almost believe she's simply holding her breath, she sighs and goes still. Silent.

An anguished cry rips past Smithson's lips, and he gathers her to his chest. The empty space beside me grows cool, and the blood soaks into the blanket. I sit up, shoving myself away from it.

"Rachel?" Quinn asks softly, but I can't look at him. At any of them.

I only have eyes for Sylph.

Crawling across the wagon bed, I brush her hair from her face as Smithson rocks her back and forth. Her green eyes stare at nothing. Her skin looks like candle wax. The Sylph I knew is gone.

No spark in her eyes. No laugh hovering just behind her words. No love spilling out of a heart that refused to turn anyone away.

A bubble of panic swells inside me, pushing against my chest. My breath tears its way out of my lungs, and my head spins.

She's gone.

Nothing I can do will bring her back.

The space in my heart reserved just for her is an aching void that threatens to slice into the silence and spill the blood of everyone I've lost, and I can't let it hurt me. I can't let it break me.

Scrambling away from Smithson, I slam into the wagon bench behind me.

"Rachel, wait." Quinn holds a hand out to me, but I'm already up. Already moving. I grab the edge of the wagon's entrance, rip the canvas aside, and leap for the ground.

The people walking behind the wagon shout as I roll across the forest floor, but I claw my way to my feet and start running. I shove the helping hands away from me, duck beneath the outstretched arm of the recruit guarding this edge of the line, and race into the trees.

Faster.

Stray branches whip my skin. Underbrush tangles around my ankles, threatening to bring me down. I dig my fingers into tree trunks for balance and push myself on.

Faster.

My breath burns my throat, my vision blurs, and something roars inside my head. The image of Sylph's waxy skin and lifeless eyes slams into the wall of silence, and I shudder as a dark, terrible grief tries to rise to the surface.

Faster.

I can outrun this. I can push myself hard enough to leave it all behind. If I no longer see it, it doesn't have to be real. It isn't real.

It isn't.

My feet slam into the forest floor. A branch tangles in my hair, and I rip it free. I don't need to cry. I don't need to feel. I don't need anything but to run until I leave behind the gaping wounds that carve my spirit into something I no longer recognize.

Something wraps around me from behind, and I tumble to the ground. Twisting, I punch and kick, but every move I make is easily parried until suddenly I find myself held close, tucked up under someone's chin.

"Where are you running to?" Quinn asks quietly.

My breath sobs in and out of my lungs. The longer I sit still, the faster the grief will catch up to me. "Let me go."

"And let you fall headlong into the river?"

I lift my head and see a sheer drop just six yards from us. I shrug.

"Do you want to die?" he asks as if he really wants to know.

Do I? It would be easier. I could fade into silence and all the broken pieces in me wouldn't matter anymore. I wouldn't have to grieve, or think, or desperately stuff everything I can't stand to face into the silence.

But Logan would grieve. And if Dad, Oliver, and Sylph are waiting for me on the other side, they'd be disappointed in me. I'd be disappointed in me. I'm not a quitter.

I slowly shake my head. No, I don't want to die.

"Why aren't you crying for Sylph?"

"Tears don't bring people back." Pain stabs from my chest to my fingertips.

"Tears aren't for the people we've lost. They're for us. So we can remember, and celebrate, and miss them, and feel human," he says.

Feel human. I push away from him, and he lets me go. If

allowing everything that wants to hurt me to rise to the surface and destroy me is what it takes to feel human again, then I'd rather feel nothing at all.

The silence greedily absorbs the shock of Sylph's death until the dark, fathomless void consumes me—a stranger pressing against my skin from the inside out. I don't feel human. I don't feel grief, or pain, or fear.

I don't feel anything at all.

Slowly, I climb to my feet and find Logan standing behind us. His eyes flicker from Quinn to me, and then he walks forward and opens his arms. I step into his embrace, but his touch is only skin deep. Inside me, the Rachel I once knew is gone.

CHAPTER FORTY-ONE

LOGAN

It's been ten days since Thom blew up the bridge, and we left the Commander and his borrowed army on the western side of the river. Black oaks, shagbark hickories, and the occasional cluster of pine trees mingle with the cypress and maple. Long slabs of gray-white rock rise out of the ground for yards at a time before submerging themselves in the soil once more. Every now and then we come across the sagging, ivy-covered hulk of a long-forgotten house perched at the edge of the river's steep embankment.

Why anyone would want to live near the constant musty-dirt smell of the water and the swarms of mosquitoes and gnats that fill the air at twilight is a mystery to me.

Most of my time has been spent working with Jeremiah to flesh out the map so that it includes the other three northern city-states in case Lankenshire won't reach an alliance with me, and perfecting my understanding of the Rowansmark tech so that I can replicate it once I have the right wire and metal at my disposal.

Using supplies I found in the highwaymen's wagons, I've nearly completed the device I can use to track and kill the Commander. We'll see which of us manages to put the other one down like a dog.

I like my odds.

I've also held two more funerals to bury those who were poisoned. Of the nineteen names on my list, ten are dead, including Sylph. Thom was poisoned as well, though he wasn't on my list. I don't know why the killer would go after Thom without marking his room, but Thom seems to be the only victim who didn't wake up with a bloody X on his door. The other nine who were in marked rooms show no signs of sickness. The killer deliberately separated families and friends by poisoning only one person per shelter. Knowing they aren't about to die, however, does nothing to comfort those who remain.

It does nothing to comfort me, either. I'm grateful I won't be losing any more of my people to poison, but I feel like I'm walking with the blade of an axe poised at the back of my neck. It's not a matter of *if* it will fall, but when.

When the killer will strike again.

When the Commander will catch up with us.

I skirt the wide trunk of a black oak tree and take a long look at myself. I've never had an easy life. I understood loss and fear before I was old enough to learn how to read. I knew what it felt like to fight for survival because survival was all I had left. I accepted that any respect I might earn from others, I must first earn from myself. And I overcame it all by refusing to allow my circumstances to dictate my intelligence, my courage, or my choices.

Those are valuable lessons to remember now. I might be walking with an axe against my neck, but I'm not going to fall to my knees and make it easy to take me down. To take any of us down.

The faint outline of a plan is taking shape in my head as the sun melts across the western tree line, and I start looking for a place to make camp. We're still a day's journey from Lankenshire. The path we've followed along the river is narrow, but fairly defined—worn down by regular trade missions or courier visits.

Drake walks beside me. "What's the plan?" he asks.

I know he means the plan for making camp, but I have another answer for him. I'm not used to talking through my plans with anyone except Rachel. But in the aftermath of Sylph's death, Rachel is a pale, silent shadow of herself, and while I'm not exactly sure how to fix it, I'm positive discussing worst case scenarios with her isn't the answer.

"I need solutions to our problems." The ground begins to rise, and ahead of us the path disappears down the other side of the hill we're climbing. "To do that, I need to see every problem clearly."

"Finding a permanent shelter, whether it's with Lankenshire or somewhere else, seems like it should be a priority," he says, huffing a little as the incline strains our legs. Behind us, the rest of the survivors climb in weary silence. Only the creak and groan of the wagon wheels and the faint shuffle of boots against the forest floor gives away their presence.

Even though Drake and I are at least ten yards ahead of the rest, I pitch my voice low. "Yes, that's a priority. But the real reason we need shelter so badly is because we have human threats after us. Remove the threats, and finding a place to live isn't as urgent."

A crisp breeze tangles in the leaves above us, and Drake pulls his cloak close. "How're you planning on removing the threats?"

"I'm nearly finished designing a piece of tech that will wipe out the Commander. If I take him out of the equation, the army will stop chasing us. The more immediate problem is that we still don't know which one of us poisoned our people, and we have no idea how or when he'll strike again."

"We've checked everyone's wristmarks and searched through every scrap of personal belongings. We didn't find any evidence linking anyone in camp to Rowansmark."

"I know." My fingers skim the rough skin of a branch as I push it out of my way. "But someone who is skilled enough to kill like a professional isn't going to be stupid enough to leave obvious clues lying around for us to find."

Drake skirts a half-submerged rock. "Willow could question everyone. One at a time. I'm willing to bet it wouldn't take her long to figure out every single secret any of us have to hide."

I shake my head. "I'm not going to torture one hundred thirty-two innocent people on the slim hope that I can catch one man. Or woman. Whichever. Besides, even though I know Willow would be willing to interrogate everyone, what would that cost her?"

"So what will you do?"

"I'll give the killer what he wants." My voice is as hard as the stone peeking out of the ground beneath our feet. "I'll publicly offer to exchange the device for his promise to leave the rest of us alone."

Drake tugs on his beard. "If you do that and then don't keep your word, more of us will die."

"Oh, I'll keep my word. I'll give him the device. And I'll make sure that the instant he takes it from me, he's dead."

"How will you manage that? He'll be expecting a trap."

"Then I'll have to make sure to devise something that takes him completely by surprise."

We reach the crest of the hill and stop.

Far in the distance, the white-gray stone of Lankenshire gleams in the fiery light of the setting sun. We've nearly made it. One more night of making camp. Building a perimeter. Watching for threats both without and within. One more night and then hopefully I can convince Lankenshire to help us.

Being so close to my goal lifts a bit of the pressure from my chest. I stare at the distant city-state and take a deep breath. Just one more day and I can deliver on my promise to get us to Lankenshire. I'm afraid to let the relief creep in yet, but it hovers at the edge of my mind, offering a small sense of peace.

Behind us, people shuffle to a stop. Some of them approach the top of the hill and gape at the sight of Lankenshire perched in the distance like a beacon of salvation.

"One more night," I say, raising my voice so that those around me can hear. "We'll arrive at Lankenshire tomorrow. Tonight, we'll camp there." I gesture to my left.

The patch of land I'm pointing to is twice the size of the meadow we camped in before. Once upon a time, it may have been a farm or a dairy. Now it's a huge expanse of high grass and collapsing barns. It gives us enough space to establish a perimeter so that we'll see any threats from the forest long before they reach us. I have no doubt that the Commander worked quickly to find another way across the river. At some point, he'll catch up to us again. I just pray it isn't tonight.

We follow the path down the side of the hill and then branch out toward the field. The wagons bounce roughly over the uneven ground, and we have to slow to a crawl to accommodate them.

Once we reach the grassland, I give the order to set up camp with the wagons and the weakest among us in the center, and the others arranged in circles around them until our strongest and most capable surround the camp, armed and watchful.

Then, because twilight is still nothing more than a smudge of gray in the early evening sky, I allow for a cooking fire to be lit so that Nola and Jodi can roast the pigs and rabbits Frankie and Willow caught during the day's walk.

Frankie is a different man in the wake of Thom's death. Subdued, introspective, and allied with Willow—something I would've sworn to be impossible two weeks ago. Having all of my inner circle at peace with one another eases the weight I carry, but I'd trade it all for Thom's life in a heartbeat.

I pace through the camp while food is passed from person to person and conversations slowly flutter to life around me. Eloise sits with her back against a wagon wheel and eats with one hand pressed firmly against her bulging stomach. One of the older women who also rides in the wagon during the day sits next to her, talking softly and occasionally reaching out to pat Eloise's belly.

I'm glad Eloise has a friend. She looked like a lost little bird even before receiving the news that her husband had died in the Wasteland. I'm also glad I chose to tell her nothing more than that he'd died trying to bring the device back to the Commander, and that Rachel finished the job for him. It's the truth, if you take out the fact that Melkin tried to kill Rachel to get the device, and she took his life instead. And I did remove those facts. Because her husband died trying to save her life. Even if his methods were questionable, his love wasn't, and she should be able to cling to that. Plus, Rachel doesn't need Eloise to haunt her during the day the way Melkin does at night.

Moving on, I pass Adam kicking dirt onto the cooking fire to douse the flames for Nola and Jodi. The anger he harbors still simmers just beneath the surface, but he seems to have accepted my leadership now and is trying to make the best of it.

Or he's learned how to lie, and I should keep a closer eye on him.

The people clustered throughout the field have become as familiar to me as the back of my hand. I can't remember all of their names yet, but I know their faces. I know which ones will leap to lend a hand without being asked, and which ones will barely wait for my eyes to open in the morning before they bring questions and complaints my way. I know which ones are still in shock over losing their loved ones and their home. Which ones are angry at the Commander, the killer, or both. Which ones are angry at me. The sound of their voices, the shape of their thoughts, and the increasing trust they throw at my feet have become the fabric of my days.

So when I walk through the camp, nodding to this girl or clapping a hand on the shoulder of that man, I'm doing more than making my way toward the guard post I assigned to myself and Rachel. I'm looking in their eyes. Letting them look in mine. Reassuring them that I know them, I see them, and that they matter.

I'm more than halfway between the center of camp and the outskirts when something tingles across the back of my neck. A sense that something I just saw is somehow . . . *wrong*.

Trying to make it look like I'm simply acknowledging another greeting called out to me, I turn and slowly scan the area I just crossed.

Eloise and her friend still sit against the wagon wheel.

Adam has joined Nola and Jodi for dinner.

A scattering of children play tag around clusters of seated adults.

Jeremiah and a few of the older men sit in a tight circle, heads together, playing checkers.

Behind them, close to the edge of the field, a man with black hair and olive skin stands beside the far corner of the aging barn, watching the camp.

He isn't one of ours.

My hand is already reaching for my sword when the man meets my eyes for half a second before turning and slipping into the woods.

He's wearing the uniform of a Rowansmark tracker.

CHAPTER FORTY-TWO

RACHEL

"Stop!" Logan yells, and runs toward the southern tree line.

"Logan?" Frankie asks, already running toward him even before he knows what's wrong.

"Rowansmark tracker!" Logan tosses the words over his shoulder as he plunges into the forest.

I leap up to follow them when the concussive *boom* of an explosion tears across the field. Before I can turn to see what happened, another *boom* sends me to my knees. The explosions sound like thick rocks being torn apart. I skid forward on my palms, and a sheet of yellow-white flame blazes to life from the ground three yards to my left.

One second, there was nothing but grass and a flat, white stone I nearly tripped over when I took my place at the guard station assigned to me. The next second, the force of the explosion knocks me to the ground as a wave of voracious heat rolls through the air, sucking out the oxygen and leaving the exposed skin on my face and neck feeling crisp and tender.

Dense, white smoke pours out of the flames, and I cough in harsh, hacking sobs as I crawl toward the next guard post. Behind me, another explosion rocks the field, and another sheet of pale flame leaps for the sky.

People scream. Run toward the wagons or toward the forest. Fall down and crawl while others run past them.

It's chaos. And chaos kills.

I struggle to my feet as another explosion rips through the air, this one closer to the tree line. Those running toward the forest skid to a halt and look around wildly for another plan. Before they can move, another piece of the ground bursts into flames, right beneath the feet of an older man I recognize as one who'd taken to sitting by Jeremiah every evening to play checkers.

He screams, a long, high wail of agony that tapers off into silence as his body twists away from the fire and falls to the grass in a smoldering heap.

A woman next to him leans over and vomits while another man grabs her around the waist and pulls her away.

I rush toward Drake, who stands ten yards from me at the next guard station. Another small slab of white rock, about the size of a loaf of bread, is hidden in the long grass. It catches my foot, and I fly into the air before slamming down onto the ground a yard from the stone.

The fall saves my life.

Behind me, the slab of stone sizzles for a second and then bursts into flame with a terrifying explosion of sound and heat. I press my face into the grass and start crawling as a thick cloud of white smoke pours from the fire. The smoke is bitter and leaves an acrid taste in my mouth.

Someone snatches the back of my cloak and drags me forward. My eyes are streaming as I look at Logan's furious expression.

"He did this," he says, and I know he means the man he chased into the woods. "We have to get everyone away from the fires."

"It's the stones." My voice is hoarse from the smoke, and I cough until I taste blood.

Another explosion. Another sheet of flames. This time to the south of us, putting another obstacle between our people and the trees. The fire licks at the grass and begins to spread.

"What stones?" he asks as he hauls me upright and looks around to assess the situation.

"The white stones. I just tripped over one, and a few seconds later, it exploded."

Logan frowns and stares at the collection of fires burning with brilliant white-gold flames. "Light flames. Tremendous heat. Thick smoke that smells like . . ." He sniffs the air.

"Garlic," I say, because the taste is scorched onto the back of my tongue.

He locks eyes with me. "It's white phosphorous. We have to get everyone off this field *now*."

"White phosphorous?" I jog at his side as he hurries toward Drake, who is busy shouting instructions and rallying people to him.

"Made by chemically altering phosphorous. Spontaneously combusts when it comes in contact with oxygen. He must've coated the phosphorous with something that would eventually let the oxygen through. Don't get burned, whatever you do. The phosphorous keeps burning you until either you starve the wound of oxygen or you die."

We reach Drake. Behind him, a thick white stone rests on the grass.

"Get back!" Logan shoves Drake away from the stone as it sizzles and then explodes.

By this point, no fewer than ten fires burn. The thick, noxious white smoke billows out, forming an impenetrable haze, and lines of flame snake away from their source like veins of brilliant gold spreading across the field.

Logan begins yelling instructions to Drake, Frankie, Ian, Willow, and Quinn. He wants Drake to recruit five others and drive the wagons back to the path we took to get to the field. Anyone close to the wagons can ride inside as long as no white stones lie in wait beneath the wheels, ready to turn the last of our resources into ash. The rest of us are to take quadrants of the field, shepherd the people there past any phosphorous, and meet at the path as well.

Controlling over one hundred panicked people isn't going to be easy. I scan my quadrant, which stretches from the western edge of the forest to where I stand now. People race away from the tree line, which is almost completely obscured by smoke. Some rush toward the wagons. Others flee back toward the path we took to get here. They can't go south or west because the fires burning along those edges completely cut us off.

Another stone comes to life, this time to the east, like another link in a bracelet of fire. Another board in a white-gold fence.

A fence.

"Logan, look!" I grab his arm before he can leave my side and point at the semicircle of fire. "We're being fenced in."

He swears, and yells to those closest to him, "Go north!" He points. "We'll regroup a hundred yards up the path." Then he looks at me. "I have to go redirect Drake and make sure the others know where to go."

What he's really saying is that he has to leave me alone and doesn't want to do it. I don't want to see him face danger without me by his side, either, but we don't have a choice.

"Don't worry. I'll get my people there. Be safe," I say, and race toward the group of terrified people milling around my quadrant, unsure where they should go.

The first trio I reach is a man and a woman who support a boy about my age. Burns cover his left leg, and he moans in pain.

"Get back on the path beside the river. Go north. Fast," I say. "The fires are closing in around us. Once you get there, smother those wounds, or they'll just keep burning."

I don't wait to see if they comply.

I run toward a man and his little girl who are doubled over coughing and choking. He presses his daughter to his chest, trying to shelter her from the worst of the smoke, while his eyes stream and his breath tears its way out of his lungs in harsh gasps.

As I close in on them, I see a white stone resting on the ground beside the little girl.

"Get back. Get back!" I scream, but the smoke curls into their lungs and steals their breath. Even if he could hear me, he can't move.

I'm less than two yards away. The stone starts to sizzle as I close in. I'll never make it in time. Digging my toes into the ground, I bend my knees and leap forward, arms straight out.

My hands collide with the child, sending her flying backward, and I slam into the father as the stone beside us roars to life. Pain—searing, vicious pain unlike any I've ever felt—blazes a trail of agony down my right forearm. I scream and belly crawl away from the terrible heat that reaches for me. Ripping the remains of my sleeve away from my arm, I see a fiery trail of phosphorous eating through my skin and turning it black.

The man beside me snatches up his daughter and stares at my arm. "Water," he croaks from a throat ruined by coughing, and looks around as if he can magically make water appear when none exists.

The pain is a white light blazing up my arm, digging into my shoulder, and setting my teeth on edge. I can barely think. Barely breathe.

Not water. I don't need water. I need . . . something else.

The man hacks and chokes, and I realize the little girl is barely breathing. I have to get up. Have to move. Have to save us.

Another scream rips its way past my clenched teeth as I struggle to stand. There are more people in this quadrant. More lives to rescue. And I didn't come all this way and survive every awful thing that's happened in the last few months so I could die on a field at the whim of a madman.

"Go." I wave my left arm north. "Get out of the smoke before you die."

"You need help," he says.

"Your daughter needs it more than me. Go."

He obeys me, and I hold my right arm against my stomach as I stumble into the smoke, looking for more survivors. The pain is as sharp as a shard of glass slicing through my arm. I cover my

mouth and nose with my cloak and try to ignore it. Every movement jars me, and I suck in little gasps of pain with each step.

More explosions sound in the distance, but the roar of the
flames near me and the thick cushion of noxious smoke nearly
drown out everything but the sobbing moans of pain escaping
my lips as I walk.

I find the next group of people by walking straight into a
man who's created a chain of survivors, linked by holding hands.
All of them cover their faces with their cloaks. I can't tell who
they are, but it doesn't matter. We have to get off of this field
before we all die.

"We're going north. Any others in this area?" I ask, and tiny
pinpricks of light dance at the edge of my vision.

"Not that I could see," the man at the head of the line says.
His voice is muffled by his cloak.

I try to turn away. Try to lead us north, but the pain is consuming me. My knees wobble and refuse to hold me as my head
fills with buzzing, like a swarm of bees is trapped inside my
brain.

As I slide toward the ground, he reaches out and catches me.
Pulling me close to him, he tips my head onto his shoulder.

I can't feel my tongue. Or my fingers. My arm, though, is one
continuous shriek of agony.

"Are you hurt?"

My head lolls back, and the world swims around me, a confusion of smoke, white-gold flame, and a pair of familiar eyes
staring into mine.

"Logan?" I ask, though I know I'm wrong.

"Shh." He presses a finger against my lips so hard my teeth

cut into my lip, and my mouth fills with the metallic tang of blood. His hand slides down my right arm until he comes to the burned flesh. "Pain is such a useful thing. It corrects us when we're wrong. It shapes our character. It teaches us that we're alive." He grabs my wound with rough fingers and squeezes.

I scream, an unrelenting wail of agony, and he snarls at me. "Don't you feel alive?"

My scream dissolves into choked gasps. He leans down to whisper next to my ear. "Judge and be judged, Rachel."

Someone shouts, and he lets go of me. I try to stand. To find my equilibrium. But the buzzing in my head spreads down my body, and I tumble to the ground as everything goes dark.

CHAPTER FORTY-THREE

LOGAN

I don't know how many survived the fires. It's too dark to count heads, and I'm more concerned with getting those who are still alive as far from the burning field as possible. The path leading back up the hill is completely closed off to us. Not that I want to backtrack when we could have Carrington on our heels. With the field destroyed, our only option is to travel toward Lankenshire and hope to find another place to stop.

I'm not leading them, though. I've handed that job over to Drake. I can't concentrate on the territory we're approaching until I know for sure if Rachel and the others in her western quadrant have joined the group. We left before they could catch up with us, and every second of not knowing stretches my nerves to the breaking point.

Striding quickly past clumps of silent survivors, I check faces and look for that confident I'm-about-to-teach-the-world-a-lesson attitude that marks her movements as surely as her red hair marks her appearance.

She isn't here.

I reach the wagons and hop on the back step of the first one. Pulling the canvas aside, I say, "Is Rachel in here?"

"No," a timid voice answers me.

Eloise? It doesn't matter. All that matters is Rachel.

The next two wagons are full of the elderly, the injured, and those desperate to catch their breath after inhaling too much smoke. Rachel isn't there either. But in the fourth wagon, a man answers me, his voice hoarse.

"She saved our lives. Me and my little girl. And she got burned. It looked . . . bad."

A fierce pain stabs my chest, and I clench my hands around the wagon's frame to keep from shaking the information out of him. "Where is she now?"

"I don't know. She told me to go north, and then kept looking for more people. It was really smoky there. Really bad. I don't know if she—"

I leap from the wagon before he can say something I don't want to hear.

Rapidly working my way through the rest of the crowd, I pray that I'll see her. That she made it out.

She isn't here.

I can't breathe. Can't make a plan. Can't *think*.

She isn't dead. She can't be. She'll walk out of the field at any moment. She'll race to catch up to the group. And she'll glare at me for doubting her survival skills.

Please.

Please let that happen.

I pass Frankie on his horse at the end of the group without sparing him a glance.

"Where're you going?" he asks.

"To get Rachel."

The field is a blaze of dancing white-gold light whispering in and out of the thick white smoke that chokes off my view of the other flames—the crimson and orange ones that have spread from the phosphorous and become regular fire greedily consuming the long grass and heading steadily into the forest.

Another reason why we can't turn back up the hill. Who knows how fast and how far this fire will spread through the Wasteland?

"I'll help," Frankie says.

It never occurs to me to turn him down. To ask him to guard my people's backs as they flee. I'm about to enter a blazing inferno, thick with smoke, to search for one girl. I need all the help I can get.

Before we go more than five steps toward the field, shadows move inside the smoke at the northern edge.

"There!" I say, and Frankie spurs his horse forward.

In seconds, the first in a long line of people crawls out of the smoke on hands and knees.

She did it. She gathered them all up and crawled her way across the field with them. I race to the leader of the group, throw back the hood, and frown as a man with brown hair and a short beard coughs hard enough to choke. I recognize him. Clint, I think. Usually walks in the middle of the pack as we travel.

"Rachel?" I ask, but he's coughing too hard to answer me.

More people crawl out, coughing and gagging. Disoriented and faint. None of them is Rachel.

The relief I felt at the sight of these survivors turns to bitter dregs as the last person crawls to freedom, and it isn't her.

"Take them north, Frankie," I say, and cover my nose and mouth with my cloak. Dropping to my knees, I crawl onto the field.

My world narrows down to the roar of flames, the searing heat that batters me from all sides, and the suffocating waves of smoke that want to steal my breath and leave me with nothing.

I slide one hand over the grass, searching for obstructions, and with the other hold my cloak to my face. Finding nothing in my way, I crawl forward a yard and repeat the process. On my third attempt, my hand slaps something.

Some*one*.

I lunge forward as the person digs elbows into the ground and slowly moves toward the edge of the field. Pressing my cheek to the dirt, I look into the person's face, lit by the flickering light of the flames that are closing in on us from three sides.

It's Quinn.

Before I can react, I see that one of his hands is firmly grasping a pale arm he has looped around his neck. He struggles to move forward again, and I reach for the person lying across his back.

Rachel.

I know it's her even before I see her face. The shape of her body is as familiar to me as my own thoughts. Relief gushes through me. Pushing myself up into a crouch, I take her from

340

Quinn's back. My hands shake as I hold her close. But on the heels of that relief, fear slides through me.

She's too still. Too unresponsive. And I can't take the time to see if she's breathing. Quinn is already crawling out of the smoke, coughing like his lungs are overflowing with soot. The flames are close enough that their heat stings my exposed skin. The newly healed brand on my neck aches in sharp, jagged pulses.

I lower my face to the ground again, cover my nose firmly, and draw in as deep a breath as I can manage. Then I stand, cradle Rachel in my arms, and run.

I nearly stumble over Quinn as I clear the smoke and flames. Leaning down, I pull him to his feet, but before I can figure out how to help him back to the group and carry Rachel at the same time, Frankie arrives and reaches for Rachel.

"I'll carry her back on the horse and get Nola to take a look at her. You help him."

I gently lift Rachel onto the horse. She lies over the front of his saddle with her hair hanging down below her fingers on one side and her feet hanging down on the other. I grab her arm and press against her wrist.

Her pulse flutters against my fingers.

The stone in my chest eases.

Frankie kicks his horse into a gallop, and I support Quinn with my left hand so I can carry a sword in my right. We make slow, steady progress as we listen intently for sounds of pursuit. I hope the tracker who set the fire comes for us. I can't wait to punish him for his lengthy list of crimes.

Best Case Scenario: I catch him tonight and teach him a thing or two about pain atonement before he dies.

Worst Case Scenario: He goes free for a little longer, and we remain in danger until I build the tech it will take to eradicate him.

The Commander isn't the only person with a unique sonar signal I can manipulate. Every Rowansmark tracker has an incendiary device rigged to an anatomical trigger in his chest. Surely I can figure out how to set it off from a distance.

No matter which scenario is true, those who've hurt us are dead.

CHAPTER FORTY-FOUR

LOGAN

We take shelter about a hundred fifty yards away from the fires. There aren't any convenient open spaces, but I'm done with open spaces for the night. Instead, I wedge us between a stone outcropping and the steep incline that leads to the river. No one can come at us from the east or the west, and I have so many guards posted at the north and south entrances of our camp, even a tracker will have trouble getting through.

Leaving Drake and Frankie in charge, I climb into one of the wagons Nola is using to treat the injured. Rachel lies silent and pale, and the burned skin on her right forearm makes my stomach queasy. A line of blackened skin peels away from a jagged split down the underside of her arm. The rest of her forearm is a deep, crisp pink.

Six others, including Quinn, sit or lie about the wagon with burns eating into their skin. We need to deprive the wounds of oxygen to stop the white phosphorous from burning down to the bone, and then we can figure out how to treat them.

I have to swallow hard before I can speak. "Their wounds will keep burning until we cover them. Come with me."

Nola follows me out of the wagon, and I quickly scan those around us to find others who can help. "You two"—I point to a woman with broad shoulders and a man who stands with his fists clenched like he needs something productive to do—"get to the canteen and bring back four buckets of water."

Pointing toward a pair of middle-aged men who look strong, I say, "Get four buckets from the highwayman supply wagon and bring them back here full of dirt." When they frown and look at me like I've lost my mind, I snap, "Get moving or so help me, I'll punish you in ways you've never dreamed."

I refuse to consider the idea that the words coming out of my mouth sound like the Commander. He punished to keep his people too scared of him to consider rebelling. I'm trying to save lives.

That has to count for something.

Turning to Nola, I say, "Mix the dirt into mud and pack it onto the burns. Then wrap a wet rag around it. Keep it damp. When daylight comes, we'll flush the wounds and make sure all the phosphorus is gone, and then figure out where to go from there."

Seeing that everyone is doing my bidding, I jump back into the wagon. Quinn leans against the wall beside the doorway, his head tipped back as he breathes in harsh pants. Rachel lies beside him, her chest rising and falling in jerky movements. I can't look at her arm.

I settle on her other side and glance around the wagon's

interior. Six others lie on the floor, on the benches, or sit propped against the far wall. Most are moaning in pain. A few are still coughing in painful bursts. None of them are looking at us.

"Thank you," I say to Quinn, and my voice shakes as those two small words struggle to carry the weight of my gratitude.

He coughs, then wheezes, "A man."

My jaw throbs as I clench my teeth. "A tracker, yes. He dropped those fire bombs in the field. Probably did it while we were organizing ourselves and cooking our dinner."

Bitterness eats at me like poison. I should've seen him. I should've noticed him walking the perimeter, planting destruction stone by stone. If I had, Rachel wouldn't be lying here beside me, barely breathing, her arm a mess of still-burning flesh.

"Not the tracker. Too . . . tall. Another man . . . had her. Baalboden cloak. Couldn't . . . see his face."

I go absolutely still as his words sink in. "He had Rachel? Are you sure?"

He nods. "Had . . . all of them. Lined up." He coughs and presses his hands to his forehead like his head wants to come apart. "Trapping Rachel's injured arm and hurting her. I found them . . . by following her screams."

Everything inside of me trembles as fury spills out of my chest, courses through my veins, and consumes me.

I was right all along. Someone in our group has been helping Rowansmark. I have no idea why one of the Baalboden survivors would turn against his own people in favor of a Rowansmark pain atonement vendetta, and I don't care.

I will *kill* him. I will flay the skin from his bones in tiny little pieces. Hold his head underwater until he nearly drowns, and then revive him just to do it all over again. Pour white phosphorous over his body and watch while he screams the way he caused Rachel to scream.

"Logan?" a voice asks right behind my ear.

I whip toward the doorway, my fist rising, and stop when I see Willow. Slowly lowering my fist, I get to my feet and climb out of the wagon.

The night sky is split in two. To my left, brilliant chips of silvery light twinkle and glow. To my right, a billowing cloud of smoke spreads across the horizon, obscuring all but the bright licks of orange flame cavorting in the depths of the hell we just left.

Willow pokes her head into the wagon, says a few words to her brother, and then comes to stand beside me. Her eyes glow, feral and dangerous, beneath the starlight. I meet her gaze with something feral and dangerous of my own and feel connected. A well of deep, unwavering rage forges a link between us that cannot be broken until we see the killers dead at our feet.

"Our assumption about one of us working with Rowansmark was right. Quinn said—"

"He told me," she says. "There's another message. A large piece of paper lying under a regular white stone. Right in the middle of the path."

"Did you read it?"

"I didn't touch it."

"Good. We're leaving it right where it is." My voice is cold. "We're done playing Rowansmark's games. From this point forward, if they want my attention, they're going to have to give me the message face-to-face."

"And then we kill them," Willow says in a voice as dark as the sky above us.

"Then we kill them."

Her smile is a vicious baring of teeth.

"I'm sorry Quinn got hurt. I'm grateful he saved Rachel and the rest of those trapped in the western quadrant, but I'm sorry he's suffering as a result."

She looks at me. "I warned Rachel that if she did anything to cost my brother his life, I'd make her pay for it."

"She didn't do this. I sent her out there." I sent her straight into the hands of the killer. The thought is like a splinter in my brain. I can't leave it alone.

"And Quinn followed her because he's determined to protect her. I know." Her voice sounds weary. "I tried to talk him out of it weeks ago, but he wouldn't listen. And it doesn't matter if you sent her or if she chose to go. If there's danger involved, Rachel will be right in the middle of it. I wanted her to know about Quinn's . . . determination . . . so she'd think about the cost of her actions."

"This isn't Rachel's fault. If you want to be mad at anyone, be mad at me. Or better yet, be mad at the killer who put us in this position in the first place."

"Oh, I know exactly where to put the blame for all of this," she says softly. "And I'm better suited than most at killing some-one in ways that will leave him begging for death before I end it. But Quinn would've followed Rachel into the smoke no matter who sent her there. Haven't you figured that out by now?"

She moves away, and I let her go, her words ringing in my ears as the memory of Quinn holding Rachel close to him after Sylph died burns my throat like acid.

CHAPTER FORTY-FIVE

LOGAN

Lankenshire sits atop a steep rise of land like a glittering white crown made of stone. A long stretch of ground between the Wasteland and the city's wall has been cultivated into evenly plowed fields with newly sprouted plants poking up from the rich soil. A path paved in dusty, white-gray rock leads between the fields and to the city's gate.

We've made it. Three weeks of staying one step ahead of the Commander, battling highwaymen and the Cursed One, and trying to protect ourselves from a Rowansmark vendetta—all to reach this city. I began the journey with a small group of experienced fighters who were desperately trying to train others on the basics of survival, but I'm walking into Lankenshire with a remnant of battle-scarred, capable people who can handle anything our enemies throw at us.

I'm also walking into Lankenshire with a killer in our midst, but I'd like to keep that a secret until I have a plan in place to catch him.

We arrive at Lankenshire's ornately scrolled iron gate a few hours after dawn. The city's wall is made of thick-cut white stone with flecks of silvery gray that glitter beneath the morning sun. Several soldiers in dark green uniforms stand at attention behind the iron bars, watching as we travel the path that bisects the fields.

Rachel is still unconscious. Quinn lapses in and out of unconsciousness as well, as do two of the others. One boy's leg is burned so badly, I'm sure it will have to be amputated. Another woman might lose her hand.

None of those wounds are treatable while we're camped out in the Wasteland. I need to get my people inside the safety of Lankenshire and into their medical building as fast as possible. Which means I can't tell Lankenshire the entire truth.

Not yet.

If they knew we might harbor a killer in our midst, we have both the army of Carrington and a contingent of Baalboden guards, led by the Commander, on our trail, and we've incurred the wrath of Rowansmark, we'd be turned away before I ever had the chance to make my case for an alliance.

If we're turned away, people will die.

Rachel might die, and I can't stand to imagine my life without her in it.

So as we approach the gates, I instruct Drake to let me do the talking and come up with a story that is completely true . . . without telling the whole truth. Guilt snaps at me, but I shove it aside. I have promises to keep to the survivors of Baalboden. I've made no promises to Lankenshire yet.

Just inside the entrance, a man wearing gold bars on the front left pocket of his uniform steps forward. "What business do you have with Lankenshire?" he asks as he stares at our group like he's never seen a crowd of smoke-scorched weary souls standing outside his gate. His voice is cautious but friendly enough.

"We're from Baalboden, and we were in a fire last night. I have several seriously injured people, some of our elderly are suffering from smoke inhalation, and I have a pregnant woman due to give birth any day. We'd like to respectfully request lodging and medical attention. I can offer payment."

Once I have the right supplies to replicate the device, that is. Until then the three elected leaders who govern Lankenshire—known as the triumvirate—will have to take me at my word.

"What are folks from Baalboden doing so far north?" He peers past me as if searching for someone. "Where's your leader?"

I clear my throat, and the man's gaze latches onto me again. "We're all that's left of Baalboden. The Cursed One destroyed it almost six weeks ago. I'd planned to negotiate a possible asylum for my people here, but last night's fire changed those plans temporarily."

"Baalboden's *gone*?" His eyes widen, and he glances over his shoulder as if the Cursed One might suddenly appear and light his city on fire, too.

"Please," I say as I step closer to the gate. "Some of my people will die if they don't get medical attention."

He tugs at the hem of his jacket. "I can't offer you long-term asylum. That has to come from the triumvirate. But I should be able to offer your people a brief stay in the hospital while our leaders set aside a time to meet with you and hear your case. Let me check with my commanding officer."

He hurries into the city, leaving the two soldiers who were with him to stand and stare at us while we wait. It isn't long before he's back, along with several other men in green uniforms and six people, both women and men, dressed all in white.

"I brought doctors," the gate guard says. "And my commanding officer." He snatches a thick gold key from a chain around his neck and unlocks the gate. "You're welcome to stay in the hospital while your people recover. The triumvirate is being told of your presence and will request a meeting with you as soon as you are not as concerned with the immediate care and treatment of your people."

"We'll take your animals and wagons, if you like," one of the other uniformed men says. "We can spread them out between several local farmers and care for them until you need them again."

"Thank you," I say. My voice can't encompass the relief that fills me. I set out to find a safe asylum for my people, and I've done it. Now I just need to catch a killer, outwit the Commander, and warn the other city-states about Rowansmark's tech.

The doctors surround the medical wagon, and in seconds, it's whisked off toward the hospital. The rest of us follow slowly on foot, led by Coleman Pritchard, the man in charge of Lankenshire's security.

Coleman points out the local sights as we walk. The greenhouse beside the city's best pub. The museum that is solely dedicated to restoring and displaying artifacts from the previous civilization. The central irrigation system that makes it possible to raise crops, even if the rainfall won't cooperate.

I try to act interested and respond in all the right places, but I keep scanning the faces that peek out of buildings as we walk the glittering stone road that winds through Lankenshire's business district like a loose spiral.

I keep looking for the tracker.

"Did anyone else enter Lankenshire today?" I ask when Coleman takes a break from explaining the newly installed gas streetlamps and switches to discussing the sizable mercantile that sells the best pickled okra in all of the nine city-states.

"Not yet," Coleman says as the road curves gently to the right. "Are you expecting someone else? Do you have missing people?"

"No. I just wondered how often people visit."

Coleman points to the hospital, a solid four-story structure that gleams in the same pale glittery stone as the roads beneath us. "Here we are! Elim is our head nurse. She'll make arrangements to allow your uninjured to lodge here as well while you wait for everyone to heal. I'm sure your people will appreciate the warm beds and the opportunity to shower."

He looks over his shoulder at my people, and I follow his gaze. Dirty, soot-stained faces and torn clothing greet my perusal.

"Perhaps I can ask our Charity Committee if we have any spare clothing as well," Coleman says.

"That might be a good idea," I say.

"There's Elim now. I'll leave you in her hands, and see about setting up a meeting with the triumvirate. And about getting you some clothes."

Before I can thank him again, he's gone, and Elim, a slim, capable-looking woman with the same beautiful olive skin and almond-shaped eyes as Adam, walks toward us. I'm about to greet her when a flash of movement behind her catches my eye.

I freeze, and my pulse races. I could've sworn I just saw a man in the hospital lobby wearing the brown-and-green uniform of a Rowansmark tracker. Craning my head so I can see around Elim, I sweep the lobby, a spacious room done in calming green and white, but can't see anything out of place.

"Everything okay?" Elim asks me.

I look at the lobby again, but all I see are doctors, our seriously wounded, and a nurse or two. I haven't slept since the night before last, and I'm running on nothing but worry and adrenaline. I can't trust my judgment, but I'm also not willing to take any chances.

"I'd like all of my people to be on the same floor, if possible. I understand that means you'll need to put several people per room, but we prefer it that way." I smile at her and hope she doesn't ask me why I don't want my people spread all over the building.

I really don't want to have to explain that I need guards stationed, and that one of the citizens I'm guarding is a traitor who deserves to die. Or that I'm worried a tracker might attack us if we're separated.

"Of course," Elim says. Her smile is warm. "Please come inside, and I'll make arrangements. Let me just check with the doctors to see which floor they prefer to have the most critical patients on."

We follow her into the hospital, which smells of soap and illness, and I take the opportunity to wander through the lobby, checking every chair and every corner, and looking down every hall.

I don't see a tracker, but that doesn't mean we're safe.

Lankenshire was the only possible destination in the area. It wouldn't take a genius to figure out that's where we were heading. The tracker could've come inside the city's wall last night after setting the fires that killed some of my people.

I'm going to take all the necessary precautions to protect my people as if an attack is imminent. And hope that once the triumvirate hears my case against the Commander and Rowansmark, and sees what I have to offer in exchange for an alliance, they'll help protect my people, too.

Until then I'm going to plant myself next to Rachel's bedside and work day and night on the tech I need to bring down our enemies.

CHAPTER FORTY-SIX

RACHEL

Awareness creeps through me as if a thick fog is slowly lifting from my thoughts. I'm lying on my back, and something soft cushions me. I feel . . . disconnected. Like my brain and my body aren't talking to each other yet.

"Almost three days," a voice says somewhere above me.

Someone else replies, but I don't catch the words. My head is heavy with sleep and something else. Something that dulls my thoughts and makes it impossible to lift my eyelids.

I feel like I'm floating underwater beneath my skin.

". . . not normal, is it?" the same voice asks. It sounds familiar, but holding on to the voice long enough to put a name to it takes more effort than I can give.

My thoughts spin away from me, but it's not unpleasant. I don't have to think or remember or make any decisions. I just have to lie here.

I should float underwater more often.

". . . both exposed to the smoke for longer than anyone else," a different voice says. This voice is higher than the other. Calmer. A woman.

I don't think I know her.

The woman says, "They breathed in a great deal of smoke, Logan, but look. Quinn woke up several times today and his breathing has improved. He'll be walking around by tomorrow."

"What about Rachel?" Logan asks.

Logan. My thoughts spin faster until pieces of memory fly through my head in rapid disorder.

A little girl by a white stone. Familiar eyes. Thick billows of noxious smoke rushing down my throat and burning my lungs.

Burning.

White-gold flames. Explosions. *Pain.*

As soon as I think the word, I realize a dull throbbing reverberates through my right arm, from my shoulder to my fingertips. Trying to move my arm gives the pain a set of vicious teeth.

I moan and my eyes flutter open. The room I'm in tilts and wobbles, and I close my eyes again before the motion makes me sick to my stomach.

"Rachel?" Logan asks, and calloused fingers stroke my cheek.

I try opening my mouth to answer, but my lips feel sewn shut.

"Here," the woman says, "give her some water."

The woman is a stranger. But the hand belongs to Logan. The room—I have no idea how I came to be inside a room instead of a wagon, but my mushy brain refuses to tackle this conundrum.

Something cold presses against my lips, and water trickles over them and into my mouth. It feels like my throat is the size of a small canyon when I first swallow, but the second and third swallows are easier. After five swallows, the cup is removed from my mouth, and I risk opening my eyes again.

The room remains unfocused. A wash of soft green and white. I turn my head, and a blurry Logan crouches beside me.

"I can't see you," I say, and my voice sounds like that time I caught bronchitis from Sally Revis, who coughed right in my face during Social Etiquette class.

"Are you . . ." Logan's clothes rustle, and when he speaks again it sounds like he's stepped away from my side. "Is she blind?"

"My ears work. You don't have to talk about me like I'm not here," I say, and he crouches back down.

"I'm sorry. I'm just worried. It's been . . . you've been asleep. For days. And it's fine if you're blind! I mean, it isn't fine. Of course it isn't, but it doesn't matter to me. I love you just the same—"

"You babble when I make you nervous."

The woman laughs. "Want more water?"

"Yes." I drink a few more sips and risk opening my eyes again. Still blurry, but it's getting better. "I'm not blind, Logan. Just having a hard time focusing my eyes. Where are we?"

Instead of answering, he leans down and presses his forehead to my chest. His hand tangles itself in my hair, and his breathing sounds unsteady.

"I'll give you two some time alone," the woman says, and leaves the room.

"What did she give me to make my brain feel so disconnected?" I ask.

"Pain medicine. I thought you were going to die." He lifts his face, and every sleepless hour he's endured while waiting for me to wake up is carved into his expression. "I thought I'd lost you."

His voice breaks, and he lays his face against me again. I should comfort him. Say something soft and understanding. Reach for him, because I know my touch soothes his ragged edges.

I should, but suddenly, I don't know how. I'm not just disconnected from my body. I'm cut off from my emotions, too. I'd forgotten the price I'd paid to be free of the terrible pain of Sylph's death.

Not a real person.

Not anymore.

I didn't realize my choice would also cut me off from Logan.

But I don't have to feel soft and warm inside to offer comfort. I know what's expected of me. I can mimic the emotions.

I can't lift my left arm to embrace him because he's pinning it to my side with his chest. And trying to lift my right arm sends sharp spikes of pain up my shoulder and into my jaw. I hiss in a breath, and Logan lifts his head again.

"I can't move my arm," I say. Only after the words are out do I remember I was going to offer him sympathy and softness.

His eyes shift toward my arm, and then back to my face. "You were burned. Do you remember?"

The white stone. The little girl. And pain like nothing I've ever felt burrowing down below my skin like it wanted to light my bones on fire.

"I remember. How many did we lose?"

"Seventeen." The loss of those seventeen lies heavy in his voice.

I push with my left hand, trying to sit up. He leans forward to help me.

"Take it slow. You've been lying down for three days."

The agony of those three days lies heavy in his voice, too, and I don't know what to say. He gently fluffs the pillows I was lying on and arranges them behind my back.

Wait.

Pillows?

"Where are we?" I look around the room again, and this time most of the details are clear. The floor is covered in a beautiful white rug that fills every corner of the room. The walls are the green of pistachios, and sunlight pours in from a window framed with starched white curtains.

Four beds line the walls, two on each side. I'm sitting on a bed with a comfortable mattress beneath me and thick white blankets covering me. Directly across from me, Quinn sleeps on a similar bed. The other two beds are empty.

"We're in Lankenshire," Logan says. "They've offered us temporary asylum while our injured heal. I'm hoping I can convince them to make the asylum permanent once they hear my case against both Rowansmark and the Commander."

"But the killer . . ." Familiar eyes. Cruel laughter. "He had me."

"Pain is such a useful thing. Don't you feel alive?"

"Rachel, I'm sorry," Logan says, and the raw grief in his voice scrapes against the silence within me. I flinch and look down at my bandaged arm. What will I find when I peel back those layers? Ruined flesh? Destroyed muscle? An arm that will refuse to hold another weapon?

"Are you listening?" Logan asks. I jerk my gaze up toward him and then let it skitter away before he can see that I don't know what to do with his apologies or his grief.

"Of course I am," I say, and hope he doesn't ask me to repeat anything he's just said.

"Quinn found you. The killer had you by the arm . . ." He swallows. "Quinn found you—and the others in the western quadrant—by following your screams."

Fury, sharp and lethal, lives beneath his regret. I used to understand that. Respond to that. I used to *be* that. Now I can't find my regret. I can't work up any anger. I can't do anything but stare at the boy lying in the bed across from me and wonder if he'll die, too. If I'll have to add his face to the list of those who tear my throat raw every night while I scream the things I no longer allow myself to think about during the day.

The silence between me and Logan has gone on for too long. I feel the prickle of his unease even before I see it in his face. I should be saying something. Offering something. Acting like the horror, rage, and pain he feels are mirrored inside me as well.

"I'm okay," I say, though we both know that can't possibly be true. I look back at Quinn, at the rise and fall of his chest, and wish he would wake up.

Logan follows my gaze and says quietly, "He saved your life. You were already unconscious when he reached you. He crawled across the entire field with you on his back."

When I don't say anything, Logan turns my face toward his. "Rachel, something's wrong. What is it?"

I try to dredge up concern. Fear. *Anything* that will make it look like I still know how to feel something when I should.

The effort exhausts me.

"Are you worried about the killer?" he asks. "Grieving Sylph? Upset that Quinn is taking a while to recover?"

I nod. Yes. All of those. And none of them. Not really. A girl who isn't quite real anymore can't worry or grieve or feel upset.

"I can't make losing Sylph any easier on you, though I wish I could." His fingers gently run through my hair. "And Quinn breathed in a lot of smoke, just like you, but he's gaining strength quickly. As for the killer, we'll catch him. Even if we don't know what he looks like."

What he looks like. I raise my face and stare into Logan's dark blue eyes. "His eyes reminded me of you," I say.

A little line digs in between his brows. "Is there anyone in camp whose eyes have reminded you of me before the fires?"

I scroll through a mental list of the Baalboden survivors and shake my head. "I don't think so. But maybe that's because on the night of the fire, all I could see were his eyes. Maybe if the rest of his face is visible, the resemblance disappears. Or maybe I was delirious from pain, and we should throw out everything I just said."

"I don't think we should discount anything. Even in a crisis, you know how to keep your head and pay attention to details. We'll discuss it more when you feel stronger. For now, I'm just grateful that you're getting better. I don't ever want to come so close to losing you again." He holds my gaze for a moment, and I can see the uncertainty growing in his eyes as I fail to respond.

I can't bear to tell him that a part of me wishes I wasn't going to get better. That I could join Sylph, Oliver, and Dad and find peace.

"Rachel? Is something—"

"I'm tired." My voice sounds too abrupt, and I make an attempt to soften it. To smile a little, because he needs it. "I'll be okay. I'm just so tired."

He leans forward and kisses me gently. "I need to make the rounds now and check on some things. Nola and a few of the others are working our medical rooms in shifts, but the woman you just met is Elim. She's the Lankenshire nurse in charge of this wing of the hospital. If you need something, just call out. Someone will hear you."

I nod.

"I love you," he says as he leaves. His voice is distant, as if a host of worst case scenarios are begging for his attention and somehow one of those makes him wonder if loving me is still worth it.

I can't blame him. I'm broken in ways I have no strength to fix, and even though he doesn't know the cause, he feels the results. The cost of my choice to push my pain away from me lies between us like a mountain neither of us knows how to climb.

"Pain. It teaches us that we're alive. Don't you feel alive?"

The killer's voice echoes inside my head as I slowly pull my right arm onto my lap. I don't feel alive. I feel like a shell walking around with something else beneath my skin. I can't access the pain that sliced my heart to ribbons, but maybe I don't need to. Maybe *any* pain will give me relief from the terrible void that lives within me.

Slowly, I unwind the bandage that covers my burned arm until the final, sticky layer peels away. I stare at the jagged line of blackened, split flesh that stretches from my inner elbow nearly to my wrist. The damaged skin is several layers deep, and beneath it, where fresh skin is trying to grow, thin pearls of blood glisten.

Maybe the killer told the truth. Maybe pain, any pain, makes us feel alive.

I grit my teeth and reach forward with my left hand until my fingers find the broken seam along my forearm. And then I press down, as hard as I can, and do my best to prove the killer right.

CHAPTER FORTY-SEVEN

LOGAN

I lean against the wall outside Rachel's room for a long moment, eyes closed, my body vibrating with the need to *fix it*. Fix whatever is eating at Rachel that keeps her from letting me in. Fix the fact that we've been in Lankenshire for three days, and I'm no closer to figuring out which of my people is working with Rowansmark.

I can't fix either problem without more information, and I have no way of getting that at the moment. I can, however, keep working on backup plans in case the triumvirate turns down my petition for an alliance.

One backup plan involves making sure I no longer have the Rowansmark tech on my body, and that it's hidden where no one, not even the traitor in our midst, will think to look. To accomplish that, I need help.

I find Willow on the roof of the hospital, crouched beside the slim silver rail that circles the building. She slowly scans the glittering city streets below, and I close the door softly behind me before joining her.

"No trouble walking across this rooftop?" she asks as I approach.

"Why would I have trouble?"

She laughs. "Last time you were on a rooftop, I thought we'd have to pry your hands off the railing with the point of a sword and carry you back to safety."

I make an effort to sound as dignified as possible. "That building was clearly an unsafe height. Not to mention that it had been abandoned for fifty years. And the kudzu covering it could've compromised the stability of the structure."

"Whatever you say." She tosses a quick wink at me and looks back at the street.

I crouch beside her and follow her gaze. "Are you looking for something in particular?"

"I came out here because the hospital smells like sick people and because I don't like being inside. But I stayed up here because I think something's wrong inside Lankenshire." She holds herself very still as she examines the street below us.

The flash of a man in a green-and-brown uniform moving through the hospital lobby rises in my memory, and I lean a little closer to the rail. The hospital is located halfway up a hill that rises just outside the main business hub of the city. From the roof, we can see a significant slice of the streets and buildings below us.

For a few minutes, we watch people move through the streets. Some stop to chat with a friend. Some hurry from one location to another. Some simply wander outside their place of business, look around, and go back in.

"Do you see it?" Willow asks as yet another shopkeeper steps out of her door, looks quickly up and down the street, and then lifts her gaze to study the buildings around hers.

"I see it." The people who stop to chat cast frequent glances at the rooflines around them, and put their heads close together when they talk. The ones who walk alone move like they don't want to be caught out in the open. And the shopkeepers seem far more interested in what's going on in other shops than in their own. The sanctuary I thought I'd gained for my people suddenly feels like a rock precariously balanced on the edge of a slippery cliff. "They're scared of something. Any idea what's making them so nervous?"

"Not yet. But I can go walk the streets and see if I can figure it out." She moves to stand, and I place my hand on her arm to stop her.

"Actually, I was hoping you could do me a favor."

"Need help walking back to the door?"

I roll my eyes. "You're hilarious. No, I need to hide the Rowansmark device before either Lankenshire or the killer tries to steal it or coerce me into giving it up."

She cranes her neck and looks at the streets again. "Not sure I'd hide it anywhere inside this city."

"I don't plan to. I need someone to take it into the Wasteland and hide it."

"I'm your girl." She reaches for the device as I pull it out from under my tunic. I hold on to it, and she looks at me.

"Willow, if things go badly for us here and Rowansmark figures out I gave it to you to hide, they'll torture you until you give up the location. I know I'm putting you in danger, and I don't ask it of you lightly."

Her smile makes me shiver. "I don't break easily."

"I know. I'm asking you to do this because you're smart, strong, and more than a little scary. And because you're one of the few people left whom I can trust completely." I wrap the device in a length of cloth I took from one of the hospital's supply closets. "You'll be seen if you try to leave through the main gate. There might be another way out of the city if—"

"Already found it." She starts toward the door, her long, dark braid swinging against her back.

"You already . . . when?" I follow her.

"I told you. The hospital stinks, and I don't like to stay inside. I've already explored most of the city." The door closes behind us, and she lowers her voice. "There's a cave underneath Lankenshire. It's a huge system of tunnels and caverns. I can get out that way."

"Be safe." I wrap an arm around her waist for a moment, and she stares at me like I've aimed an arrow at her face.

"We aren't the hugging type," she says, though she doesn't pull away.

"Maybe not." I smile. "But I wanted you to remember that someone besides Quinn cares about what happens to you."

One corner of her lip tugs upward, as if trying to smile. "Save the mushy stuff for Rachel. Just keep Quinn safe until I get back."

Without another word, she heads down the stairs, the device hidden beneath her tunic.

With one backup plan in motion, it's time for me to address

the second. If Lankenshire doesn't accept my offer of an alliance, or if whatever has the citizens so nervous makes staying here unwise, I need to have a travel route to the next city-state ready. To do that, I need Jeremiah.

Jeremiah spends most of his time on the ground floor of the Museum of Historical Artifacts, which is two blocks south of the hospital. He's been working with Lankenshire's head mapmaker, Darius, to complete a detailed map of the entire Wasteland. I've yet to meet Darius in person, but Jeremiah comes to dinner every night full of exciting city-state details like the type of quarry stone used for flooring in Brooksworth and the delicate bloom- ing vines specific to Schoensville. Sprinkled in among these details are plenty of "Darius says . . ." and "Darius thinks . . ."

I exit the hospital and quickly travel the two blocks between me and the museum. If the citizens of Lankenshire don't want to be caught outdoors alone, then neither do I. The museum is a humble square of a building painted blue and white. I pull open the bright blue door and enter a cool, dim interior. A woman with a short cap of brown hair cupping her elegant face points me down a back hallway and tells me to keep walking until I reach the last doorway on the right.

A row of candlelit sconces illuminates a colorful mural along the left side of the hallway. I glance at it as I walk and realize I'm looking at a city that resembles the ruins we left behind two weeks ago, except that this city is in pristine condition. Tall, shiny buildings, elegant bridges stretching over land and water, and splashes of color that give the entire picture an air of move- ment and life.

I can't imagine living in a city like that—so many people

packed into one place. So many buildings built much taller than they should be.

The next panel shows the Cursed One exploding out of the ground, spewing fire and reducing the vibrant city to a blackened, smoking carcass in just two panels. The ruins remind me of Baalboden.

Reaching out, I trace my fingers along the rough paint strokes while grief aches inside of me. So much loss. So much devastation. How many times will we rebuild only to be torn down again by the creature who lives beneath us?

Moving away from that panel, I pass more scenes of destruction. Fire raging through neighborhoods. Roads collapsing. Constant attacks from the Cursed Ones—sometime three or four surfacing at the same time.

The pictures of destruction disappear and in their place is a group of young men, all in military uniform. At their center, set apart from the rest, stands a young version of Commander Jason Chase. I'd recognize him anywhere, though his face is unscarred in this painting. His chin is tilted up like he welcomes the challenge of saving his world, and his eyes look calm and ready. In his hands, he holds what looks like an incendiary device and a remote trigger.

The next panel shows the Commander leading his team into the bowels of the earth, down the original mine shaft that opened the barrier between those who lived above the earth and the creatures that dwelt at its heart. The bomb is still in his hands. Courage is still on his face.

I reach the second-to-last panel and stop to stare for a long moment. Gone is the courage, the calm. Instead, the team is in chaos. A few stand firm, weapons drawn as the lone surviving Cursed One attacks. The rest of the team flee in panic, following the terrified retreat of their leader, whose face is nearly torn in two—as if he got swiped by the Cursed One's long talons. The Commander climbs the tunnel, the bomb still clutched in his hand, blood flowing over his military uniform, and the fear in his eyes is so sharp, I reach my hand out as if by touching the mural, I can somehow understand what I'm seeing.

Didn't he detonate the bomb? Didn't he at least try to remove the threat and save the world? We were raised in Baalboden on stories of the Commander's heroism in a time when heroes were in short supply.

Apparently, someone else has a different version of events.

The final panel shows the nine remaining team members—those who fled the beast's lair—standing in a semicircle, surrounded by the destruction of their world. Each of the nine wears an expression of regret and shame, but already the shame on the Commander's face is hardening into brutal anger, as if daring the survivors to dispute his claim of heroism and pay the consequences.

I wonder if regret over his cowardice still lives somewhere beneath his viciousness. No wonder he refuses to allow anyone to contradict him. No wonder he needs absolute power like the rest of us need air. Without it, he's just a man who dressed up like a hero only to discover he was a coward at heart.

The conference room is an elegant oval with a huge slab of cherry wood polished to a gleam and surrounded by chairs. Jeremiah is ensconced at the table, a plethora of parchment and quills spread out in front of him, while beside him a short, thin man who resembles a toothpick with a shock of red hair growing wild carefully pens a line on a piece of parchment.

"Mind if I interrupt?" I ask as I step into the room and close the door behind me. It's easy to make my voice sound calm and confident. It's much harder to banish the sight of the Commander's cowardice and its larger implications for our world from my mind.

"Come in, come in." Jeremiah waves me forward. Darius keeps his eyes on his parchment, his lip caught between his teeth as he concentrates. "I've been mapping out what I remember of the northern territory back before Brooksworth refused to allow the Commander to visit. It's been, what, two decades? My memories of this area are hazy, but Darius was able to fill in the details." Jeremiah holds up two sheets of parchment as if to show me his progress.

"How's your progress on Hodenswald and Chelmingford?" I ask. "I need detailed maps to all of the northern city-states."

"Planning on leaving us so soon?" Darius asks. Setting his quill carefully on its blotter, he looks up at me.

"Darius Griffin, meet our leader, Logan McEntire," Jeremiah says.

Darius's eyes widen. "Logan McEntire? Son of Marcus and Julia McEntire in Rowansmark?"

I stare at him. "No, Logan McEntire from Baalboden."

He slowly rises from his chair, his eyes never leaving my face. "Oh, I have no doubt you're from Baalboden *now*. But we both know you were born in Rowansmark."

CHAPTER FORTY-EIGHT

LOGAN

"*We both know you were born in Rowansmark.*" Darius's words linger in the air between us, and I frown. "You're mistaken. Now about Hodenswald and Chelmingford—"

"It's uncanny," Darius says, leaning forward as if he wants a closer look at me. "You have Marcus's eyes, but everything else looks like Julia."

"I don't think you heard me." I take a step back as Darius comes around the table. "I'm from Baalboden."

He stops a yard from me and slowly sizes me up. "How old are you?"

I'm getting very impatient with this whole thing. "Nineteen. Now about the maps—"

"It has to be him." He turns to Jeremiah, who looks as confused as I feel. "He looks like Julia, he has the same name, and he's nineteen. Why didn't you tell me you knew the lost McEntire boy?"

"Don't know what you're talking about," Jeremiah says, but

now he's examining my face like it's the first time he's seen it.

"That makes two of us," I say.

"You really don't know, do you?" Darius asks.

I stare him down. "I know exactly who I am. You're the one who seems to be having difficulty."

"I just thought . . . I didn't realize it would be kept a secret from you." Darius frowns at Jeremiah, who just keeps staring at me. "I lived in Rowansmark for a five-year scholarship exchange when I was fifteen. I was apprenticed to various scholars within the Rowansmark government so that our city-states could share knowledge and culture with each other. I remember the McEntire incident like it was yesterday."

Jeremiah slowly shakes his head, but I don't like the expression in his pale green eyes. It's a cross between dread and worry, and a finger of unease skates up my spine.

"What McEntire incident?" I ask.

"Commander Chase from Baalboden was in town for his annual state visit, and things were already tense because he and James Rowan didn't like each other much. There were areas of the Division for Technological Advancement that literally went into a lockdown while the Commander was visiting because James Rowan was afraid of spies and treason. A day after the Baalboden people left, it was reported that Marcus McEntire's newborn son had disappeared. Marcus claimed that the boy died, but he couldn't produce a body. Said he'd already buried the boy. Everyone suspected that the Commander took the baby as a way to gain access to the Division for Technological Advancement, since Marcus ran the entire operation. But when years passed and nothing happened, people forgot about it or decided maybe Marcus was telling the truth. Maybe little Logan died."

I look at Jeremiah. "This is a coincidence. I was born and raised in Baalboden. My father died before I was born. Tell him."

He takes a deep breath and says, "I can see the resemblance, but as far as I know Logan is right—he's from Baalboden."

Darius snorts. "Look at his *eyes*. Those are Marcus's eyes, and you know it. He's the right age, has the right name, and is the spitting image of his mother except for having his father's eyes. I don't believe in coincidences." He turns to me. "Who raised you?"

The world tilts beneath my feet, and I grab the back of the nearest chair to steady myself. "My mother. She told me my father died. She was already pregnant, and he died. She wasn't a liar."

"She wasn't your mother, either." Darius shakes his head, and I can't tear my gaze away from his shock of red hair, which quivers with his every movement.

My pulse is a deafening hammer pounding at my head. "This is ridiculous."

"Nineteen years ago, the Commander took his annual trip to Rowansmark. I wasn't head groom yet, so I stayed behind. But that year, my job changed." Jeremiah looks in my eyes. "That year, the Commander returned home, accused the few who'd accompanied him on the trip of treason, and executed them immediately. That's how I became head groom."

"It's not like executing people without cause is something the Commander never did. It doesn't mean he was trying to cover up a kidnapping," I say, because someone has to reach for logic and reason. "My mother—"

"Your mother had recently lost her husband and hadn't been assigned a new Protector yet. She'd been grieving inside her home for several months, unseen by all but the older neighbor who checked on her sometimes and brought her food. When she reappeared, she had you. Everyone assumed she'd been in confinement due to pregnancy. But I don't know, Logan." Jeremiah's eyes lock on mine. "I never had cause to think about it before now, but you *do* look a lot like Julia McEntire. She used to make it a point to visit the Baalboden staff when the Commander visited Rowansmark. At least she did for a few years. I never knew why she bothered, but maybe she was looking for you. You're the right age, the right name . . . plus the Commander always treated you like you didn't belong in his city. Darius is right. That's too big of a coincidence."

Something hot and vicious scrapes my thoughts, begging me to call him a liar. Demanding that I make him stop. That I keep the few precious memories I have of my mother—the only mother I ever knew—sacred. Untouched by this . . . travesty.

This truth.

The Commander's last words, hurled at me as he took the fake Rowansmark technology from my hands and sentenced me to death, ring with unforgiving clarity in my memory. *"You've outlived your usefulness to me. To all of Baalboden. It's been nineteen years of waiting for my investment to pay off, and I can't wait to rid my city of the stench of you."*

No wonder I was ostracized for a crime I didn't commit. Treated like a pariah. Like I alone was unworthy of Baalboden's protection. To the Commander, I was nothing but an investment. An interloper he couldn't wait to be rid of.

"Why?" The word falls into the space between us, fraught with betrayal.

The sympathy on Jeremiah's face is like salt on a wound. My mother, with her infectious laughter and her single-minded dedication to keeping me safe, even if it meant risking her life. My mother, whose necklace I'd passed on to Rachel as a symbol that she was now my family.

My mother, the liar. The grand pretender building a life with a child she had no right to call her own.

"Why let me keep my real name?" I have to push the words past my lips.

Jeremiah shrugs. "Your mother's surname was Billings, but she told everyone McEntire was your middle name, and that's all we ever heard you called. I guess after she died, and you spent years as an outcast, none of us remembered to attach Billings to the end of your name anymore."

"And why did being Logan McEntire of Rowansmark make me worth kidnapping?"

Darius says, "Marcus is a senior member of Rowansmark's military council and heads the Division for Technological Advancement. He's a brilliant scientist. Second to none."

"Logan is brilliant, too," Jeremiah says quickly.

I turn away. I don't want to hear myself compared to this man I feel nothing for.

"Nineteen years ago, Marcus was working on an invention that would call and control the creature you call the Cursed One. Once completed, the invention would give James Rowan unbridled power, something the Commander could never allow," Darius says.

I grab a quill from the table. Crushing it in my hand, I let its sharp edge press against my skin as something in me, some final piece that survived the heartbreak of my mother's death, the terrible loss of Oliver and Jared, and the horror of watching Baalboden burn, shatters.

"Marcus was a loyal man living in a city-state that values patriotism and self-sacrifice above all else," Darius says. "Bribery wouldn't work. Threats against his life wouldn't either. He'd fall on his sword in the grand Rowansmark tradition before dishonoring his leader by giving the technology to Baalboden."

"So the Commander found his weakness." My voice is a liar steadfastly refusing to reveal the wreckage beneath my skin. I'm not my mother's son. Not my father's either. Not really. I'm the ultimate pawn in a game that started long before I was born.

"We all figured the Commander struck a deal—your life in exchange for the completed invention. It's not like Marcus could go to James Rowan for help. In Rowansmark, loyalty and patriotism to the city-state come before individual lives. James Rowan wouldn't have attacked Baalboden to rescue you, and he would've immediately removed Marcus from the Division of Technological Advancement, thereby ensuring Marcus could never betray his city by trading technology for you—"

"He had to agree." I know what it's like to have my back against the wall because the Commander holds all the cards. A single, tenuous thread of connection unravels out of the tapestry of lies I was fed as a boy and stretches toward the man who spent nineteen years working on an invention meant to ransom my life.

"No wonder our people are being murdered in some twisted

example of Rowansmark pain atonement," Jeremiah says, and I silently curse him as Darius's eyes grow large. That's not a piece of information I wanted Lankenshire to have. "Remember that huge bounty Rowansmark put on Jared Adams because they thought he stole something from them?"

"Kind of hard to forget something like that when I'm in love with his daughter." I draw myself up and stand straight and tall, like finding out my entire life was a lie means nothing to me.

"I assume Marcus gave the device to Jared thinking the Commander would then let you return home. But obviously James Rowan learned that the device was missing. That would be a stain on Marcus's honor. He could only remove the stain by returning the device and then surviving his pain atonement."

"You're suggesting that my"—I can't bring myself to call him my father—"that Marcus is the one who slit our guards' throats, started the fires, and poisoned our people. . . ." I shake my head. "Why? Why work so hard to save me only to turn around and try to destroy me? It makes no sense."

"Maybe to him it does," Darius says. The avid interest in his voice turns my stomach. This might be an interesting family drama to him, but this is my *life* lying in pieces all around me.

Jeremiah speaks slowly, as if feeling his way carefully through each thought. "He must have dedicated himself to ransoming you, his son. Nine years after the Commander took you, we heard that your mother had committed suicide. He must have dreamed of a life with you. Introducing you to Rowansmark society. Telling others the glorious tale of how he defeated the Commander at his own game and rescued his son at the same time. I'm sure he was tracking the device. It's what you would do, isn't it?"

I nod.

"But then Jared didn't deliver the package. And someone in the Department for Technological Advancement realized the device was missing. Marcus must have thought all was lost. Rowansmark would recover the package and the Commander would make good on his threat and kill you for Marcus's failure."

"Only Rachel and I got to the device first," I say, and my heart thuds heavily against my rib cage as I realize the truth. Somewhere along the journey back to Baalboden, my father must've caught up to us and watched us from the shadows. The knowledge is a violation—a forcible unveiling of moments I thought were mine alone.

"And the first thing you did with the invention was bring it back to the Commander." Jeremiah's voice holds no condemnation, but I flinch anyway.

"We never planned to give it to him! We built a fake. We wanted to destroy the Commander's hold on Baalboden."

"But from the outside, it must've looked like you'd been raised to be the Commander's son instead of Marcus's. And a Rowansmark man wouldn't question signs of absolute loyalty and patriotism."

I stare at Jeremiah as sick horror crawls up the back of my throat. "And you think my father is the kind of man who would use that assumption as an excuse to murder innocent people?"

"No, and I don't think it's your father who's doing it. Not directly. I'd recognize him if I saw him, and he isn't here."

"So all we really know is that someone from Baalboden is helping someone from Rowansmark deliver a sentence of pain atonement against me. Which is exactly what we knew before I walked into the room. We're back at the beginning," I say. Without any additional information, everything we're discussing is speculation anyway. I need facts. Plausible theories. I need to look every single Baalboden survivor in the eye and search for a flicker of secret knowledge that shouldn't be there.

And I need to find a way to accept the fact that the heartbreaking loss and destruction we've suffered over the last six weeks is truly because of who I am and what I've done. I don't know how to wrap my mind around that without it crushing me, but I must.

But first, I need Rachel. With the foundation I've always depended on suddenly cracking beneath my feet, I can't think of anywhere else I'd rather be than by her side. She might not be able to make any more sense of this than I can, but her blunt honesty and absolute love for me will go a long way toward leading me to solid ground again.

"I need those maps," I say. "Tonight."

Turning on my heel, I leave the room before either of them can say a word.

CHAPTER FORTY-NINE

RACHEL

I press the fingernails of my left hand against my right forearm. Thin white crescents on blackened crimson. Somewhere beneath this wound—beneath my skin—redemption flows. I just have to dig deep enough to find it.

My hands shake. My fingertips are colorless and cold.

Guilty.

Alone.

Broken.

I strain to feel it. The weight of my crimes. My heartbreak. I want to reverse my choice—take back the part of me that made me human—but I've pushed the grief so far away from me, I no longer know how to find it. All that's left inside of me is silence, dense and absolute. A poison that promised peace but delivered hell. It fills all my secret spaces and pushes at my skin until something, somewhere, has to give.

Gripping the wound with shaking fingers, I slowly slide my nails against the jagged seam of broken flesh. A thin line of crimson wells up. The pain hits a second later, sharp and sting-ing, and I'm *grateful*.

Finally.

Something real. A tiny piece of the hurt I should be feeling. A small slice of the punishment I know I deserve.

The blood beads together, swells, and plummets down my arm and off my fingertips in shining red drops.

A harsh sob tears through me, choking me with its ferocity, and I slash another line of crimson into the wound.

The pain crawls up my arm, and my tears slide off my face to mingle with my blood on the soft white blanket covering me.

I can feel this. Why can I stand to feel *this*—this small, petty thing—but I can't stand to feel the loss of Dad and Oliver? The horror of killing Melkin? The still-gaping wound of Sylph's death?

I scratch at my arm, and pain is a fire-breathing monster underneath my skin, but it isn't enough. Not even close. The hurt is too small. The blood offered isn't nearly what I owe.

The killer was wrong. Pain hasn't made me feel alive. It's proven that nothing I do will ever be enough to unbreak all the shattered pieces of the girl I once thought I'd be. I bleed and bleed, but still the blood of those I've lost is stronger.

And already the first scratch is congealing. Hardening.

Healing.

How dare my arm heal when I can't? I scratch at it again, opening it wider. Digging deeper. The sobs racking my chest are heaving, desperate things tangled up with words—meaningless half sounds that flay the air but fail to give voice to the awful, consuming silence that refuses to let me go.

"Oh, Rachel." Quinn climbs out of his bed on unsteady legs, moves to my side, and swiftly wraps his arms around me.

I reach for my wounded arm again.

"Stop." Quinn's voice is firm. "Rachel, stop."

But I can't stop. If I do, the hurt will subside. The skin will knit itself back together. And I'll be a prisoner to the silence again.

Quinn's fingers grip my left elbow and squeeze. There's a sharp pain as a nerve is pinched, and then a buzzing, like a swarm of mosquitos trapped beneath my skin, races down my arm.

My suddenly numb fingers fall to the bloody blanket. Useless.

I turn on him, my right fist covered in blood, and punch his chest, his stomach, anything I can reach. My blows are weak; the burned muscle refuses to lend me any strength. He absorbs it without complaint while I pant and sob and push words at him as if by hurting him I will somehow feel better.

"Let go. Let. Me. *Go*." I choke on my tears, and try to twist away from him.

"If you stop hurting yourself."

"I can't. Don't you see that? It's all I have left." My chest aches as I gulp down air only to have it tear its way to freedom in a wail of anguish.

"No, it isn't." His voice is quiet as he reaches past me to grab a tin of salve. "You have Logan. Us. And most importantly, you have yourself."

I sob quietly as he smears the clear aloe over my wound. It turns pink where it mixes with my blood. The pain throbs, but the sharp spikes are already fading.

Soon, I'll be left with nothing but silence again.

"I don't have myself," I whisper, too desperate to let shame seal the words inside of me. "Not anymore. I'm lost. I'm broken, and I can't fix it."

He remains quiet while he carefully bandages my arm, and I realize his fingers are shaking, his breathing is harsh, and he looks pale. He inhaled too much smoke saving my life to be out of bed fighting to save it again.

"You may have lost your way, but *you*"—he points to my heart—"aren't lost. You're still in there. And you have everything you need to heal. You just have to find the courage to do it."

"Sit down, Quinn, before you fall down."

I pull my knees up to my chest, and he eases himself onto the middle of my cot and sits cross-legged, facing me.

"I don't like to tell my story," he says. The words are full of pain. The kind of pain I know runs deep beneath my silence. "But I think you need to hear it. Will you listen?"

He waits for my answer, his dark eyes watching me with a strange mix of dread and compassion. I nod.

Leaning his forearms on his knees, he splays his large hands over the white blanket, careful to avoid the blood I left behind. "My village is different from other Tree Villages. When we were formed in the aftermath of the Cursed Ones, the founders had to decide on a system of government. They chose to assign duties to each family based on that family's skill set. So someone who was good at baking would then become the baker, and someone who was good at farming would be in charge of growing the wheat. Make sense?"

"Yes."

"Whatever job your family was assigned, that was your family's job for the duration of your life in the village. If you were a schoolteacher, then you trained your children to be schoolteachers. If you were a leader, then you trained your children to be leaders. No one was allowed to switch jobs. Our leaders decided this would help our society run without conflict. From birth, every child knew his place and had no aspirations for anything different. And only those specifically trained to be experts in a field would be doing that job."

"I guess that makes sense."

He looks at his hands as though he can see something I can't. "Our family was in charge of protecting the village from outside threats."

"That makes sense, too."

His hair slides along his cheek as he raises his face to look at me. "Why?"

"Because you and Willow are scary good at fighting, weapons, and basic survival."

He laughs, but it sounds like it hurts him. "Scary good. Yes, we are that. My father was a boy when the previous civilization was destroyed. He was only fifteen when he joined the village. He couldn't farm, couldn't build, and couldn't fix things. He was good at only one thing: killing people."

I don't know what to say to this. Quinn's long fingers clench handfuls of blanket.

"He taught us only to be good at killing people, Rachel. That's all we knew. We hunted humans like you hunt animals. Learned their weaknesses and how to exploit them. How to extract every possible ounce of pain if we needed information from them."

He falls silent, and the cords on his neck stand out. I reach across the blanket and cover his hands with mine. "You can't help who gave birth to you. You can't blame yourself for what he taught you, or what he expected from you."

He looks at me. "No, I can't. And I don't. But that doesn't make the memories easier to face. Every time I killed, it took another piece of me until I was afraid I'd have nothing left. I didn't take joy or pride in it like he did. And he saw that in me. He called it cowardice."

My lip curls. "He's a fool. I call it courage."

He turns his hands over and laces his fingers through mine. "Your father called it courage, too. I'd started to stand up to my father. Started killing people quickly even when he wanted them tortured. Started refusing to search for highwaymen or trackers to kill unless they were actually threatening the village."

"And he punished you?"

"He punished Willow. He gave her the duties he'd formerly given to me. He expected her to stalk and hunt and torture and glory in it. And she . . ."

"She did," I say, because I can see it's true. Willow wouldn't back down, especially if she thought that by doing what was expected of her she could somehow save her brother pain.

"She did." His eyes are steady as he looks at me. "And then we captured Jared, and I refused to kill him. I knocked my father unconscious and took Jared to the leaders so they could detain him while we tried to decide if he was a legitimate threat. And Jared was . . . kind." His hands squeeze mine. "He was kind, Rachel. He didn't see Willow and me as monsters like the rest of the village did. He treated us with respect, and my father couldn't stand it."

I know what's coming, and a slick, icy dread fills my stomach.

"He turned Willow loose. Ordered her to kill Jared, and make it truly awful, or I would pay the price." He pauses and then says quietly, "And so I killed my father."

The breath I don't realize I'm holding explodes from me in a rush. I'd thought he was going to tell me he killed my father to spare Willow. But instead, he'd sacrificed another piece of himself to save both his sister and a man he barely knew.

"Quinn . . ."

"I didn't tell you that so you could feel sorry for me. I told you because I know what it's like to make choices that leave you with nothing. I know how it feels to be so broken you think nothing will ever make it right."

He leans forward. "Rachel, I know the pain scares you. It should, because healing is so much harder than being hurt in the first place. But you will never get better until you stop running and start looking things in the eye. Until you give the things that hurt you the label they deserve, feel the way they make you feel, and then let the pieces slowly settle until you can breathe again."

I shiver beneath the intensity of his gaze. "I don't know how to do that."

"Start small. Pick up one piece of it, look it in the eye, and let yourself feel it. You won't break, Rachel. You'll heal."

I shake my head. There's so much. Where do I start?

He rubs his fingers lightly across my knuckles, and waits until I meet his eyes. "Sylph is dead, Rachel. She's gone. You didn't get enough time with her, and that isn't fair. You loved her, and now she's gone."

My body trembles as his words slam against the silence within me, leaving a spiderweb of cracks in their wake. "No," I say, as though by protesting, I can push the truth away from me.

"Yes. This is true, and you won't be whole again until you learn how to live with the truth, even when it hurts. Sylph is dead."

Grief surges out of the silence, hot and sharp and utterly devastating. It wraps around my chest, crushes the air from my lungs, and sinks into every inch of me. I open my mouth to give voice to the horrible keening locked deep inside of me, but the air won't come. I'm choking on the memories. On the way her eyes lit up over every little thing. On the smile she gave to everyone else and the smile she reserved just for me.

"*Oh.*" Air rushes past my lips, and the grief becomes a creature of terrible strength determined to turn me inside out as tears pour down my face, and I sob her name.

His arms wrap around me as I cry and cry and cry. He doesn't tell me it's okay. He doesn't try to calm me down. He just holds me and lets me cry.

When the knife-sharp edge of the grief eases into a dull ache, I find I can touch Sylph's face in my memory without falling to pieces. It hurts, and maybe it always will, but by letting what she meant to me fill me up and spill me over, I find that a few of my ragged edges are a little smoother. A little less scary.

Quinn pats my back, and I realize I'm nearly in his lap with my face pressed to his chest, and I have no idea how long I've been there. I push away and wiggle back to the top of the cot, and someone clears his throat in the doorway. We glance over and Logan is there, looking like he did when he stood on the Claiming stage beside me, forced to give permission for another man to take me as his wife.

I open my mouth to explain, but he doesn't even look at me as he says, "Quinn, a word please?" and then walks out of the room.

CHAPTER FIFTY

LOGAN

I cross the hall, yank open a door, and barely contain myself while Quinn slowly walks in. Slamming the door shut behind him, I stalk to the other side of the room, where I have a better chance of keeping my fists off of him. I'm still reeling from the shock of learning who I really am, still wondering which of the people I'd come to trust and love knew the truth about me and which were in the dark, and I'm in no mood to keep my temper.

"Logan, that wasn't what it looked like," he says, but his voice is unsteady. Vulnerable. Very un-Quinn.

I think he's lying.

I think the fascination he's had with Rachel from the moment he laid eyes on her in the Wasteland has grown until . . . until what? Until he took advantage of her in her current state of distress? Distress she won't even talk to me about?

Maybe he didn't take advantage. Maybe she chose to go to

him because somehow she can no longer talk to me.

I turn to face him. "I don't know how to feel about you right now."

His brow rises, but he remains quiet.

"On the one hand, I'm incredibly grateful to you for saving Rachel's life. It almost cost you your own. I don't know how to repay that." I realize I'm advancing on him, and make myself stop halfway across the room. "On the other hand, I want to kill you."

"You're welcome. And please don't."

I wheel toward the closest wall and drive my fist into it. "How could you?"

"As I said before, it wasn't what it looked like." His voice is stronger now.

"She was in your lap. Your arms were around her." Which is closer than I've been to her in days.

"How long were you standing there?" he asks.

"Long enough."

He sounds like he's coming closer. Which is a truly, spectacularly bad idea. I don't care if he's an expert in self-defense. I will destroy him.

"Logan, how long?"

"I don't know. Twenty seconds? Thirty? Long enough." I turn to face him, and vaguely realize blood is dripping from my knuckles. "I thought you had honor, Quinn."

He looks like I've struck him. I don't give him time to respond.

"Why do you think I asked you to help me protect her in the first place?" I ask.

"Because you figured out I know how to fight."

"Because of the way you *look* at her." My voice rises. "Because you're always ready to step in. To fight. For *her*."

"Wait a minute—"

"You love her. I get it. And because you do, you're the perfect person to protect her. But if you think you can just . . ." I choke on the words. On the image of Quinn's arms wrapped around Rachel while she snuggles against his chest. "I respect you. Don't make me have to hurt you."

His mouth drops open. "You think I'm in love with *Rachel*?"

I stare at him for a moment as the anger slowly fizzles and confusion takes its place. "Well, I did until you just said her name like that."

"Her father traded his life for mine. He *gave* himself so that Willow and I could live." He leans forward. "You don't know how to repay me for saving Rachel's life, and I lived. How do you repay someone who dies for you? What kind of price can you put on that sacrifice?"

My anger drains away completely. "You think you owe Jared."

"I know I do. And Rachel meant everything to him. What better way to pay my debt than to keep his ridiculously head-strong daughter alive and well?"

"She is ridiculously headstrong, isn't she?" A weary smile tugs at my lips. The rest of my life might be an ugly lie, but I can trust Rachel to be exactly who she's always been.

He rolls his eyes. "I care about Rachel, but you have to admit she's unbelievably stubborn. Bossy. Never listens. Never! Keeping up with her is a full-time job. There'll be no rest for the man who chooses to spend his life loving her."

I feel a little lighter. "I'll sleep when I'm dead."

"I want to explain what you saw. I think it's important that you understand."

"Yeah, I'm still wondering what the girl I love was doing in *your* lap."

"The short answer is I was there, and you weren't."

Now I'm the one who feels like I just got punched. "In case you haven't noticed, I have one hundred fifteen people to take care of and a killer to catch."

He raises his hands as if to placate me, and I notice they're shaking. He should be in bed, but we are going to finish this conversation outside of Rachel's hearing.

"I wasn't criticizing." His hands lower. "The long answer is I woke up to see her falling to pieces. She was . . . hurting herself. Rebandage her wound if you want to see what I mean. She needed to be stopped. And she needed someone to confront her with the truth so she could stop running away from it and feel it. So I did. And the little piece that you saw was her seeking comfort after the first storm of grief had passed. It could just as easily have been your lap. I was just *there*."

I'm silent as I absorb this. As I see the depths to which Rachel has sunk. It hurts that she didn't trust me enough to tell me how dark things were inside her head. Then again, maybe trusting me isn't the issue. Maybe Quinn's right, and she was too afraid of her grief to ever speak of it aloud.

And maybe I've been too focused on the things I need to fix, the scenarios I need to be prepared for, to really see how much Rachel needs me.

How much I need her as well. As soon as possible, I want to get her alone and have a long talk about my past, her past, and how we move forward from here.

"Come on, let's get you back to bed," I say, and wrap an arm around Quinn's shoulders to support him. We move carefully out into the hall. Rachel is kneeling beside her bed as if she'd tried to follow us but lacked the strength. I smile at her, help Quinn lie back on his cot, and then move to her side.

"Can I help you up?" I ask softly, and now that I'm paying attention, I see the wild ravages of her grief still etched onto her face.

"Don't be mad at Quinn," she says as I scoop her up and lay her carefully on the bed. Her white blanket is covered with a large patch of drying blood. The sight pierces my heart, but I don't say anything about it as I strip the blanket away and reach for a fresh one.

"I'm not mad at him," I say, and smooth another blanket over her. My fingers itch to unwind the bandage she wears so I can see what she's done to herself. What she's been driven to. But I can't bring her secrets to light until I unburden a few of my own.

"I want to have a long talk with you," I say. She glances at her bandaged arm, and her lips tremble. I reach out and rub my thumb along her cheek. "I've learned some things about my past, and about who might be hunting us, and I need you to help me figure it all out."

Her voice is husky, as if the storm of grief that took her left her throat raw. "I need to talk to you, too."

The tension gripping me eases a fraction. "Good. But first, you look like you need rest. I'll be back soon." Bending down, I kiss her gently. "I love you, Rachel."

"I love you, too."

Holding those words close, I leave her room and start looking for Drake, Frankie, Nola, and Ian. If we have someone targeting us because of my past, it's only fair that those I've come to love and trust know exactly what's going on. Plus, they need to know what Willow and I observed while we were on the hospital's roof, and that if we need to escape whatever is brewing inside Lankenshire, there are tunnels beneath the city that will help us do that.

Best Case Scenario: The tension in Lankenshire doesn't put us in danger, the triumvirate agrees to an alliance with me, and the next time the killer makes a move, the triple security we've instituted stops him in his tracks.

Worst Case Scenario: We're caught in the crossfires of Lankenshire's current unrest, the triumvirate throws us out of the city once they learn we've brought along danger of our own, and the killer somehow manages to hurt us again.

The answer to all of them is to have backup plans for every backup plan. Heading down the hallway toward Drake's room, I start working on exactly that.

CHAPTER FIFTY-ONE

RACHEL

There's something strange about the look in Logan's eyes, but I don't have time to dwell on it. The second he leaves the room, Elim hurries in with her arm wrapped around Eloise.

"Don't worry, dear," Elim says. "We have a bed available for you right here. Now just breathe, slow and steady, and the pain will ease again."

Eloise doubles over and moans. Her pale skin glistens with sweat. Elim rubs her back in small, soothing motions, and then deftly transfers her patient into the bed beside mine.

The room seems infinitely smaller than it did a second ago. The air is harder to breathe. And the part of my soul reserved for the guilt I feel over Melkin's death burns as Eloise turns her head and stares at me.

Can she see her husband's blood on my hands? Can she look through me and find him crouched in the corner of my mind, his dark eyes accusing me of ripping his family to pieces?

Bile rises up the back of my throat, and I turn away when

Elim says, "Why don't you come sit by her and hold her hand? She could use a friend right now."

"Quinn?" I cast a panicked look across the room, but Quinn is already pulling his blanket up over his head.

"Not a chance," he says, his voice muffled by his bedding.

My fist grips my blanket with white knuckles. I could pretend I hadn't heard Elim. I could lie and say I'm not strong enough to sit up yet. I could, but just like grieving Sylph, feeling guilty for Melkin is mine. I can't run from it unless I want to lose myself.

The white carpet is soft beneath my feet as I shuffle toward Eloise, pausing to lean against the wall when the room does a slow, sickening spin. I breathe in through my nose and wait for my head to settle, and then I lower myself to Eloise's bedside.

She groans and clutches her belly. Elim reaches out to smooth Eloise's hair from her forehead with one hand while her other presses against Eloise's abdomen.

"Contractions are nice and strong. I bet you're feeling this one, aren't you?" She smiles at Eloise.

Sudden pain shoots up my right arm, and I jerk my hand out of Eloise's viselike grip. She pants, her face turning red, the tendons on her neck standing out like ropes as she hunches her shoulders, and then she slowly deflates back onto the mattress. Her thin hand flutters over mine.

"I'm sorry," she says in her timid, caged-bird voice. "Forgot your injury. I wasn't thinking."

The burning guilt in my soul spreads through my veins until I am turning into ash from the inside out. She can't apologize to me. Not for anything. Not when I'm to blame for the grief and loneliness in her eyes. Not when her husband will never know his child because of *me*.

Another contraction seizes her, and she arches her back and cries out. Her hand reaches, grasping for the man who loved her. I look at Elim and then at the exit.

"I don't know what to do," I say.

"Just talk her through the contractions and help her stay calm," Elim says as she arranges herself between Eloise's legs.

I look at the ceiling and take another deep breath. "I'm not suited . . . you really need someone else in here."

"No time," Elim says in the same tone of voice my father used when he pushed me to my limits as we sparred. "Do you want to hold her hand and help calm her down—"

"No."

"—or do you want to catch the baby?"

"What? *No*. I . . . isn't there another option?"

"Rachel, the baby is coming. Another few contractions will do it. Either hold her hand and coach her to push or get down here and guide the baby out."

Guide the baby *out*? Absolutely not. I shudder, and Eloise comes off the bed again, her cries of agony filling the room. "Fine. I'll hold her hand."

"And coach her. Calm her down."

"I'm not good at calming people down," I mutter, but I let Eloise's grasping hand find mine. I swallow the scream of pain that wants to tear out of me as her fingers squeeze the burned flesh at my wrist, and tell myself it's no better than I deserve. One small piece of penance I can offer to Melkin.

When Eloise collapses against the blankets again, her eyes find my arm, and she whispers, "Your wrist. I'm sorry."

"Please." I choke the words out. "Don't. Don't ever apologize to me."

Her weary gaze meets mine, and the hopelessness in her face hammers against my silence. Tears sting my eyes, and as the next contraction starts, I lean down and say, "Take a deep breath and hold it. There. Now push. You're strong enough for this, Eloise. You've been through hell, but soon you'll meet your child. You'll see proof that Melkin loved you, and that you aren't alone."

She sobs as the contraction eases, and her fingers refuse to let go of me. "Why did he have to die? You were there. Can't you tell me?"

A stone is lodged in my throat. Holding back my words. My tears. The truth I owe her. I make myself meet her eyes and swallow past the stone. Truth is what will make me better. I don't know if truth will make Eloise better, too, but I can't stomach another lie.

I'm finished with running from the things I've done. I help Eloise settle back against the blankets again, and say quietly, "Melkin died because I killed him."

She lies there, stunned and silent, as Elim murmurs something about seeing the baby's head and one more push.

"Did he try to kill you, then?" she asks, and the pain in her voice isn't for me. It's for Melkin. For her husband, who wasn't a killer but who was backed into a corner by his leader. Forced to do the unthinkable or lose everything that mattered to him.

"I don't . . . I thought he was. He needed the device, and I wouldn't give it to him. I didn't want the Commander to have that much power. But my reasons don't matter, Eloise. What matters is that I regretted it the moment I did it. I've regretted it every day since. If I could go back and do things differently, I would." My voice breaks, and I clench my teeth against the pain as Eloise rises off the bed and screams like a warrior while Elim yells encouragement.

Seconds later, there's a wet splotchy sound, and Elim coos gently. Eloise and I grip each other's hands and stare at Elim as she briskly rubs a clean cloth over the messy bundle lying in her lap.

"A girl," Elim says, and beams at us both while the baby sucks in a tiny breath and cries. "Let me finish cleaning her up, and you can hold her."

Eloise eases back against the bed and smiles while tears stream from her eyes. I try to disentangle our fingers, but she clings to me.

"I don't know how to feel about you," she says, "but I don't hate you. Logan was right. Melkin was dead the minute he left for that mission. Anyone who knew about the device was dead. The Commander never meant to leave any survivors."

I shake my head. No, the Commander never meant to leave any survivors, but his knife wasn't buried in Melkin's chest.

Her fingers squeeze mine. "I hate *him*. I blame *him*."

"But *I* did it," I say, because the truth needs to be clearly seen. By both of us.

Her eyes find mine, and they burn with a passion that feels as familiar to me as breathing. "Yes, you did. And if you hadn't, my Melkin would've died at the hands of the Commander. Or he would be sitting here instead of you, his mind and spirit broken because he had the blood of an innocent girl on his hands. There are no winners here, but none of this would've happened without the Commander."

Her words taste like truth, and I let them linger. Let the darkness in Melkin's eyes match the burning fires in Eloise's and consider that maybe—maybe—the accusation I see isn't mine to carry alone.

"Here you go," Elim says, and tucks a tiny, red-faced creature, tightly wrapped in a little yellow blanket, against Eloise's chest. I move out of the way so Elim can help Eloise sit up and lean against the far wall. She doesn't even look at us. Every part of her being is focused on looking deep into her daughter's eyes.

As Elim bustles about cleaning the bed and hauling the dirty linens away, I settle down beside Eloise and stare at the baby. Her lips are pink, puckered things, and she turns her face toward her mother as if she recognizes Eloise's voice.

"Want to hold her?" Eloise asks me.

Before I can respond, she lifts the baby into my arms, careful to position her on my left side so that my injury remains untouched. I clutch the tiny thing and pray I don't break her.

"I'm going to name her Melli. He'd like that," Eloise says, and there's peace in her voice.

"Melli," I say softly, and the baby looks at me with unfocused eyes. One tiny fist creeps out of the swaddling and flails. I stroke her hand with my finger, and tears slide down my face and onto the blanket. The guilt burning through me like a live coal sinks slowly beneath the cleansing tide of grief that pours out of the silence and engulfs me. It *hurts*, but it's real.

"I'm sorry," I say, gasping for air around the sobs that shake me. That tear through me until I think there will be nothing left of me when it's over. "I'm so sorry. You deserve to know your daddy. He should be here now instead of me, but he isn't, and I'm sorry."

Melli watches me, her fist bumping against my finger, and I cry until the tears are gone. Until the blood on my hands means less than the baby I now hold. The grief subsides, and in its place is a small fragment of hope.

I can't bring Melkin back. I can't make a different choice, and somehow, I'm going to have to find a way to live with that. I'm not sure how to learn to trust myself again, but maybe I don't have to be so afraid of the fierce instincts that live inside of me. Maybe I have those instincts because while I can't nurture like Nola, or love everyone like Sylph, or fall easily into motherhood like Eloise, I can do something none of the other girls raised in Baalboden can do.

I can fight.

CHAPTER FIFTY-TWO

LOGAN

After talking with Drake, I ask him to find Nola and bring her up to speed. I want to tell Frankie and Ian myself. Willow should be back soon, too, and she'll need an update. But first, I want to talk to Rachel. I return to her room, and stop when I see Quinn hiding under his blankets, Rachel's tear-stained face, and Eloise sleeping with a baby—*her* baby—cradled beside her.

I open my mouth to say something, but I never get the chance.

"Logan? Logan McEntire?"

A tall man with thinning blond hair and pale blue eyes strides into the room.

"Yes?"

"Maxwell Stallings, member of the triumvirate."

I step toward the man. "I'm pleased to meet you."

Maxwell's pale eyes bore into mine. "Why didn't you tell us you were actually from Rowansmark?"

Before I can answer, Darius and Jeremiah hurry in behind him, followed by two women I recognize as Clarissa Vaughn and

Portia Rodriguez, the other members of Lankenshire's triumvirate, who greeted me yesterday in the hospital and assured me they would wait to hold a formal meeting until after my people were out of medical danger. Willow walks in right behind them, nods briefly to me as if to tell me the device is now safely hidden, and then goes to stand beside her brother's bed. Frankie and Adam crowd in through the doorway as well, just in time to hear Maxwell say, "We're waiting for an explanation." Both Frankie and Adam look ready to start a fight.

"We aren't from Rowansmark," Rachel says. Her voice is still weak, still husky from smoke inhalation, but she manages to pack in every ounce of Rachel attitude she possesses. "We're from Baalboden. Look at our cloaks. Our boots. And then draw the logical conclusion instead of coming in here spewing foolishness."

"I didn't say all of you are from Rowansmark. I said *he* is from Rowansmark." Maxwell points at me.

Frankie laughs, a short bark of disbelief. Adam's lip curls. Willow tosses her braid behind her back and runs her hands down her bow.

They're not here to start a fight. They're here to defend my honor.

They may not want to defend me for very long once they realize the truth. If not for my past, none of our people would've died. If not for my choice to keep the device, Rowansmark would never have levied a sentence of pain atonement against us.

Against *me*.

"You're crazy." Rachel pushes against her pillows, wincing as she struggles to sit up straighter. "I've known him all of my life.

All of it. Are you going to tell me I'm from Rowansmark, too?"

Maxwell glares at Rachel, but Clarissa, a tall woman with dark hair cut close to her scalp and a delicate web of wrinkles spreading from the corners of her eyes, grabs Darius's arm and pulls him forward.

"Tell us what you know," she says in a voice that crackles with the kind of authority people rarely question.

Darius refuses to look at anything but the carpet. Jeremiah stands close to him, fury written in every crease of his face.

"Logan came to the museum to talk to Jeremiah and me while we were working on maps. I recognized his name, saw the similarity between him and the Rowansmark McEntires, and realized that he's the lost McEntire boy."

Frankie steps forward. "I'm sure McEntire is a common name. Probably every city-state has several families—"

"What do you mean by 'the lost McEntire boy'?" Clarissa asks.

The tension inside the room swells until I don't think the four walls can contain it as Darius explains that I was kidnapped during one of the Commander's visits, and that he recognized me as soon as I walked in the door. When he's finished, Rachel attacks.

"That's absurd." She shoves at the blankets covering her like she wants to stand up. "I knew his mother. I knew him. I *know* him."

"I think he's right, Rachel," I say quietly, because I can't stand to have every detail of my past dragged out of the mouth of a stranger. She stops pulling at her blankets and looks at me like I just suggested combining acid with sulfide salts and then drinking the mixture for breakfast. "It explains why I was always treated like an outsider. It explains why the Commander told me I was a nineteen-year investment that he couldn't wait to be rid of."

I try the words out for the first time, and find that they fit, sharp edges and all. "I was born in Rowansmark to Marcus and Julia McEntire. I was then kidnapped by the Commander when I was a few days old and was brought to live in Baalboden. All of my life, I've believed I was Baalboden born, but I wasn't."

There's a moment of tense silence, and then Adam shrugs. "So what? He was born in Rowansmark but was raised in Baalboden. I don't see how that's a problem."

"He's been Baalboden for all but five days of his life," Frankie says, his huge hands slowly clenching into fists and then relaxing. "He's ours."

I'm grateful that they'd jump to my defense so quickly, but the knowledge that the rest of the story is going to rip that defense to shreds makes me feel sick inside.

"Why were you kidnapped?" Rachel asks. Her voice is as cold as her expression. I can't tell what she's thinking, but I should've known she'd be the one to realize that the most important detail was the one I hadn't explained.

Darius clears his throat. "Because his father—"

"Let the boy tell his own story," Jeremiah snaps.

I take a deep breath and force myself to say, "Darius told me earlier that Marcus McEntire is a senior member of the military council in Rowansmark, and is also the head of the Division for Technological Advancement. He was working on designing tech that could call and control the Cursed One. Apparently when the Commander found out about it, he kidnapped me to use me as leverage over Marcus. The plan was to exchange my life for the completed invention."

"But you never left Baalboden," Frankie says.

"Because the invention took nineteen years to complete. In that time, Julia committed suicide. Marcus had lost both his son and his wife. When he finally finished the device, he gave it to Baalboden's courier—Jared Adams." I look at Rachel as I say her father's name, but she's no longer looking at me. Instead, she's cradling her injured arm and picking at the bandage with her fingers.

"But Jared refused to return the device to the Commander because he knew what it was," Quinn says from his bed behind me. "He hid it at his safe house and continued the journey home, prepared to lie to his leader in order to keep the Commander from having the power to destroy everyone who opposed him."

"You knew about me?" I ask.

He shakes his head. "I only know what Jared told me when we caught him traveling too close to the village. He was looking for a way to destroy the tech. He worried there was a tracking device on it that would make burying it only a temporary solution."

"Where is the device now?" Clarissa asks.

I don't glance at Willow as I say, "I have it." This is really not the way I'd hoped to reveal the key to leveraging an alliance with Lankenshire. "Rachel retrieved it from Quinn and Willow, who were keeping it safe after Jared was killed."

"Why not tell us?" Frankie sounds puzzled, but not yet upset. "We all knew about the device. We all knew Rowansmark wanted it back, and most of us agreed with you that we couldn't return it without jeopardizing the rest of the city-states. Why not just tell us the truth?"

"I only learned it an hour ago. I'd planned to tell each of you." My voice sounds thick and unsteady. I clear my throat and say, "I wanted to speak with you individually and give you time to get used to the idea."

Willow snorts. "Get used to what? You're Logan. Who cares where you were born?"

"His father does." Rachel's voice is calm, though her eyes burn into mine, and I can see that she understands my past has ripped her loved ones from her, one terrible loss at a time.

I straighten my shoulders like that will somehow help me bear the pain of their response, and say, "Yes, I think he does. I think . . . *we* think"—I gesture toward Darius—"that Marcus is in trouble with James Rowan and has to return the device to restore his honor. We also think that because I took the tech back to Baalboden, Marcus might assume I'm loyal to the Commander instead of to him, and that makes me as guilty as the Commander under Rowansmark's laws."

I can't decide where to look. At Rachel, whose best friend paid for my father's vendetta with her life? At Frankie, who lost his closest friend as well? At Adam, who lost his entire family in the fires that I now suspect were caused by trackers overriding our device and controlling the Cursed One?

How can I look at any of them when my choices have cost all of us so much? It's cowardly of me, but I can't stand to see their faith in me die. Instead, I stare straight into Clarissa's brown eyes.

"As a senior member of the military council, Marcus has the power to use trackers for his own benefit. I believe he sent a tracker after the device. We saw signs of a tracker in the Wasteland after eight of our guards were murdered one night. I also believe that the tracker was tasked with punishing me for keeping the stolen tech."

"Pain atonement." Rachel breathes the words like they hurt.

"Yes." I clench my fists.

"He killed our boys. Poisoned our people. Poisoned *Thom*," Frankie says.

"Yes. And he clearly has someone within our camp working with him," I say. "Though I can't figure out why someone from Baalboden would be sympathetic to Rowansmark."

When no one speaks, I say, "I'm sorry. I know it's not nearly enough, but I'm sorry. We lost our city, our families, and our friends. We've been terrorized as we traveled across the Wasteland. And all of it is because of me." My voice breaks. "I'm so sorry."

Clarissa opens her mouth to speak, but Willow beats her to it.

"Oh, I wouldn't go taking all the credit on this one, Logan."

"But all of it is because I didn't return the device."

"Why didn't you?" Clarissa asks, and there's something sharp in her tone that demands the absolute truth.

"Two reasons. First, because the Commander is a brutal, cruel man who abuses his power. His people have paid the price of his actions with their lives for too long. I wanted to use the device to finish him."

"And the second reason?"

I speak with more conviction than I have since the moment

they entered the room. "Because no city-state should have the ability to obliterate the other city-states. I wanted to show you and the rest of the northern city-states what Rowansmark could do, so that you'd be prepared. And then I wanted to offer you a replica of the device so that if Rowansmark ever attacked you, you could turn the tables and remain safe."

She holds herself very still and then turns to look at Portia and Maxwell. A look passes between them, fraught with meaning, and then she turns back to me. "Are you able to replicate this device?"

I take a deep breath and look her straight in the eye. "Yes. I need some specific supplies to complete the replica, but I understand the tech. Not only do I understand it, I can improve it. I can make a device with a more powerful signal than Rowansmark's."

Maxwell and Portia exchange a swift glance, but Clarissa doesn't look away from me. Instead, she says, "You asked for our hospitality, for our help, and we gave it to you freely. You neglected to tell us you'd brought a killer inside of our walls. Especially one intent on killing people associated with you."

"He should go." Portia speaks for the first time, her voice soft but unyielding. She pushes her glasses up the bridge of her nose and says, "If we cast him out, the killer will have to follow."

"You aren't throwing Logan out into the Wasteland." Adam steps to my side.

"If we decide—"

"Forget what you decide. He's one of ours. If he leaves, we all leave." Frankie moves between me and the members of the triumvirate.

My throat closes as Quinn hauls himself out of bed on shaky legs and stands beside Frankie to form a wall between me and those who want to cast me out.

"But he brought this on you," Portia says. "He brought death and destruction. We can't afford to risk the same." There's an undercurrent of fear in her voice. Willow casts a quick glance my way, and I give a slight nod. We aren't just talking about the risk of one tracker whose sole focus is on me. Whatever Portia fears, she thinks our problems will make the problems already existing inside Lankenshire worse.

"Don't be an idiot," Rachel says, and the fierce conviction in her voice warms me like nothing else. "It wasn't Logan's decision to steal from Rowansmark. That was the Commander. And if you think returning the device to Rowansmark and just *hoping* that they never decide to use it is a good move, then you're too shortsighted to be leaders."

Portia's mouth snaps shut, and she looks at Clarissa.

"You're acting like Logan killed our people. He didn't. Some sick freak of a tracker did that for reasons that make sense to no one but him and Logan's father," Adam says, and places a hand on my shoulder. "Logan has fought for us. Guarded us. Rescued us time and again."

There's an ache in my chest that is slowly spreading. I thought once the others understood how much my past and my choices had cost them, that they'd be angry with me. Unable to look me in the eye. Instead, they're standing by me in a united front. I've badly underestimated my people.

My friends.

"We have the safety of our own people to think of." Maxwell

looks over his shoulder as if expecting a killer to walk through the door at any moment.

"Maybe if we put him in the dungeon it will satisfy the tracker and keep him from killing again," Portia says.

Frankie's shoulders bunch as he raises his fists. Willow whips an arrow out of her quiver and aims it at Portia.

"Take one step toward Logan, and you get to be the first one to die," she says.

Clarissa raises her hand in a placating gesture. "There will be no violence." She locks eyes with Willow for a long moment. It's clear that she expects Willow to cave and lower her bow.

It's equally clear that Willow is prepared to outstare her for as long as it takes.

Clarissa finally lowers her hand and says, "Portia, I thank you for your suggestion, but I'd like to offer an additional opinion on the matter if I may."

Portia nods, and I get the feeling that Clarissa's question was mostly a show of politeness. I doubt anyone in Lankenshire says no to her very often.

"It seems to me that we are discussing taking action based on fear, instead of stepping back to look at the bigger picture. I don't believe placating a murderer by imprisoning an innocent man is the kind of careful, just approach Lankenshire is known for," she says.

"I appreciate your thoughts, Clarissa," Portia says. "But we can't let Logan McEntire and the others remain within our city when we know there's a killer on the loose among them. We owe our people a safe, stable environment. We owe these people nothing."

"They are people in need, Portia." Clarissa's voice is as hard as the floor beneath us. "The humanity in us requires that we take steps to help them if at all possible."

"But—"

"Besides"—Clarissa lowers her voice and steps toward me—"we need that device."

"In exchange for my freedom, and for offering my people shelter, I'll build a replica of the Rowansmark device, along with a power booster so that any attempt to override your controls will be thwarted."

The triumvirate exchange a look I can't decipher, and put their heads together to discuss my offer too quietly for me to hear.

Finally, Clarissa meets my gaze. "You're absolutely sure your power booster defeats any override attempts?"

"I am."

"Who else knows you can build this?"

"Just my inner circle of friends and advisors."

Portia says quietly, "If Rowansmark found out—"

"They won't." Clarissa's voice is crisp, though she speaks softly. "We keep the knowledge contained to the three of us and Logan's inner circle. If we give him a workspace in the council building itself, we should be able to keep this a secret from our Rowansmark keepers."

Time feels like it's slowing down while my heart is speeding up. Willow raises her bow again, and Frankie reaches for his sword while Rachel swears and tries to get out of bed.

My hand grips my sword hilt as I ask, "What do you mean,

your Rowansmark keepers? If you're in bed with Rowansmark, we're leaving. Now."

"We aren't in bed with them by choice. None of the city-states are." Maxwell's words are forceful, but there's fear in his eyes.

Clarissa straightens her back. "You aren't the first to bring us news of Rowansmark's ability to call and control the *tanniyn*." It sounds like she says "ta-neen."

"The *tanniyn*?" Rachel asks. "Do you mean the Cursed One?"

"Such a silly name," Portia says. "*Tanniyn* is a Hebrew word that means dragon or serpent. Because the creatures who roam the Wasteland are both dragon and serpent, our early scholars felt it an appropriate classification for the beast. I believe most, if not all, of the other city-states agreed with our scholars and use that classification as well."

"We didn't," Rachel says. "But then, keeping his people undereducated and superstitious sounds like something the Commander would do."

"We called it the Cursed One because that's the term Jared used," Quinn says. "In our village, we just called it the beast."

I look at Clarissa. "Who told you about Rowansmark's ability to call and control the Cursed . . . the *tanniyn*?"

"Rowansmark itself." Her mouth is grim. "They showed up here a month ago. Gave us a very convincing demonstration. Overrode the sonar signal all the leaders use to keep the beast at bay." She taps the thick silver chain she wears around her neck. "Then they explained to us that they were now our watchdogs. They would keep the *tanniyn* from attacking as long as we paid a hefty protection fee each year. They left some trackers behind as their eyes and ears. If it looks like we're considering rebellion against Rowansmark, the trackers will call the *tanniyn* and destroy us all."

"Not if I build you a device that can overpower theirs." I hold out my hand. "I will give you tech capable of freeing you from Rowansmark's tyranny in exchange for an alliance with my people. With *me*."

She turns to look at Maxwell and Portia for a long moment. I'm not sure how to interpret their expressions, but Clarissa doesn't share my difficulty. She turns to face me and takes my hand.

"We are allies." Her grip is firm. "We will give you a workspace in the council building under the guise of allowing you to borrow our library to research the city-states north of us. That should help keep the trackers from becoming suspicious. Make a list of supplies you need and meet us there in one hour. Elim can show you where it is."

Without another word, Maxwell, Clarissa, and Portia turn and leave the room. The second they reach the hall, Willow says, "Close the door. We don't need an audience for what I'm about to tell you."

CHAPTER FIFTY-THREE

LOGAN

"I've got good news and bad news. Which do you want first?" Willow asks as Adam shuts the door behind the Lankenshire triumvirate.

"The good news," I say, and hope she knows better than to admit that I gave her the task of hiding the device in the Wasteland. It's not that I don't trust everyone in the room. It's that the fewer people who know about it, the less likely it is that Rowansmark trackers can torture my people and discover the truth.

"I caught the tracker who was on the field when the fires were set. Or at least a tracker who looked just like him."

"Where?" I ask, as Rachel, Quinn, Frankie, and Adam lean forward, their eyes riveted on Willow.

"About forty yards into the eastern Wasteland. He must have thought any chance of being caught was gone now that we were inside the city wall." She shrugs. "He thought wrong."

"What were you doing out in the Wasteland?" Quinn asks, his voice just as raw and raspy as Rachel's.

"Hunting." Her eyes gleam. "And I found what I was looking for."

With the tracker in custody, perhaps I can get some answers of my own. Not that a tracker will give me information of his own volition. I'll have to get my hands dirty, maybe do a few things that until a month ago I'd have sworn I'd never do, but I will have answers. Whoever is masquerading as a loyal Baalboden survivor is going to be caught and punished.

"What's the bad news?" I ask, and Willow purses her lips like she's just sucked on a lemon.

"He didn't survive."

"What didn't he survive?" Frankie frowns at her.

She shrugs. "Me. He found it necessary to try to kill me after I'd already defeated him. I defended myself, and now he's dead."

I swallow the harsh tang of disappointment, and force myself to say, "It's okay. At least you removed that threat. Now we just have to figure out which of our people knows about my past and—"

"Oh, I don't think we're looking for one of your people." Willow's dark eyes find mine, and something feral lies in their depths. "The tracker had a wristmark on his right arm. It looked identical to the ones everyone in camp wears."

"Rowansmark trackers don't have wristmarks," Rachel says.

"Well, this one did." Willow fists her hands on her hips as if daring us to call her a liar.

I feel sick. Unsteady. My blood roars through me, and I have to grab the end of Rachel's bed to hold myself upright as the final pieces fall into place.

"No wonder we couldn't find the traitor in our camp. He had

a wristmark. He'd studied Baalboden. He knew just enough to masquerade as one of us, and we never questioned it because he looked the part." I can't stand still. Not when so much fury fuels me. Right under my nose this entire time. A tracker. Sneaking into my tent and leaving messages. Slitting throats. Poisoning us and then watching us burn. I stalk across the room and wheel back around to see the rage that burns in me reflected on every face I see.

"I know you said to leave the last message in the middle of the road, but it's a clue. After seeing the wristmark on that tracker, I figured we needed all the clues we could get," Willow says as she thrusts a piece of parchment at me.

It hasn't survived the night very well. It's stained with damp, and the ink is smudged in several places. I wish I could go back and reverse my decision to leave it where it lay, but wishing won't solve the problem.

"Spread it out," I say, and pull the small table beside Rachel's bed over to me. "Let's see what we've got."

Willow lays the parchment on the table's surface and secures two opposing corners by placing a mug on one and a jar of salve on the other. I peer at the words scrawled across the page and try to force it all to make sense.

Traitors d erve to ie. You h ve b n dged.

"The first sentence is obviously 'Traitors deserve to die.' Not quite sure about the end of the second sentence, though." Adam taps the parchment lightly.

"Traitors deserve to die. You"—I draw my finger in a line beneath the other words and go for the obvious—"have been . . . what? You have been—"

"Judged?" Adam asks.

"Sounds like the same pile of self-righteous idiocy he's been saying all along." Willow waves her hands in the air with more drama than I realized she possessed. "Your debt is unpaid! Traitors deserve to die! You've been judged!" She looks at me. "Wait until we catch him. Then I'll show him what it's like to be judged."

"Judge and be judged." Rachel's voice shakes as she struggles to sit up.

A finger of ice slides over my skin. I've heard those words before. Where? When?

"What are you saying?" Adam asks her.

"The killer. When he had me during the fires. He said . . ." Her fingernails scratch lightly at the bandage on her arm. I reach across the bed and take her hand in mine.

"He isn't going to hurt you again," I say.

"He is if he gets the chance," Willow says.

"Does it ever occur to you not to say whatever comes into your head?" I ask.

She shrugs. "Tell me I'm lying."

Lying. The killer's been lying to me all along. Maybe instead of concentrating on trying to find him by what we know of his past, we need to focus on what actions he took to make his lie seem like the truth to me.

I rub my thumb across Rachel's knuckles and say, "The killer needed us to trust him. Accept him. The best liars use as much truth as possible. He'd have a convincing story. One that could explain away anything we might find worrisome."

"He'd make sure his actions gained your trust as well," Quinn says from across the room. "He'd confide in you. Fight for you.

Maybe make it seem like he'd risked his life for you, because who would believe the person determined to destroy you would be willing to die for you?"

"Maybe he'd find a way to have an alibi during the murders— or something we'd believe to be an alibi—to deflect suspicion," Adam says.

"Judge and be judged." My blood hammers through my veins, and my breathing scrapes my lungs in harsh bursts. I remember where I've heard that phrase before.

"Logan?" Rachel leans forward. "Are you okay?"

"He said it was something his father used to say." I look at her, but I'm not seeing her. I'm seeing the boy who fought better than he should've been able to fight and explained it away with a convincing story about his former occupation. I'm seeing the boy who argued that it was morally wrong to give the Rowansmark device to any other city-state.

I'm seeing the boy who looked me in the eye as we stood in the tunnel beneath the Commander's compound and told me he wouldn't rest until the man he held responsible for his father's death was punished. I'd assumed he meant the Commander.

Now I realize he meant *me*.

"It's Ian," I say, and Rachel's face goes white. "He told me he could fight because he'd been apprenticed to the Brute Squad, but that was a lie. He also said his father was loyal to the Com- mander and that it cost him his life. I think he was telling the truth about his father dying. Everything Ian's done . . . this was personal to him. If James Rowan punished Marcus for his treachery, and Marcus didn't survive his pain atonement, that would be enough to push his son over the edge." I don't say that this makes Ian my brother. I don't have to. I can see the horrified realization on everyone's face.

Ian, with his easy charm and his courage against Carrington. Ian, with his false loyalty and his dedication to no cause but his own desperate need for revenge.

Ian, with his knife to Donny's throat. With his syringe full of poison in Sylph's room. With his hands on Rachel.

"I'm going to kill him." I let go of Rachel's hand and stand. "I'm going to find him and kill him." My eyes meet Willow's dark, feral gaze. "And I'm going to make it hurt."

She smiles. "Let's go."

CHAPTER FIFTY-FOUR

RACHEL

"You can't go without a plan," I say, but what I mean is they can't go without *me*.

"I have a plan: Kill Ian," Logan says. In his voice I hear the furious need to avenge Donny, Sylph, Thom, and the others who died under his watch because of his brother.

Because of Ian.

The boy who saved me from the Cursed One so he could gain my trust. So he could forge an alliance with me behind Logan's back. So he could try to use me to get his hands on the device.

Nobody uses me and gets away with it.

"I'm coming too," I say, and push the blanket off myself with my left arm.

"You're not going anywhere," Logan says.

"Logan, he killed Sylph. I'm going with you." I give him a don't-bother-arguing look and grasp the little table beside the bed so I can stand without falling.

"You're in no condition to go anywhere," Quinn says, and I glare at him.

"Neither are you, but that isn't stopping you, is it?" I ask as Quinn sits on the side of his bed, pulling on his boots with shaky fingers.

Logan mutters something under his breath, and Willow says, "You're both insane. Get back in bed."

Quinn meets her eyes. "No."

Willow shakes her head and looks away.

"Neither of you should come with us. You've been injured, and you're still weak. You don't even have a weapon in case he tries to hurt you," Logan says.

I pull a pair of pants on under the loose tunic I'm wearing. "So give me a knife, and let's go."

"You are so predictable," Logan says. "How are you going to use a weapon? Your right arm is injured."

"Nothing wrong with my left."

"You can barely stand."

"Which will make my facade of weakness even more convincing," I say. "You aren't going to stop me. If you leave me behind, I'll follow you anyway."

Logan closes his eyes for a moment, and then says, "You can come because I don't see any other option. But Willow and I are the ones who will capture him."

"And me," Adam says.

"And me. For Thom. For all of us." Fury and grief breathe power into Frankie's words.

"That's fine. I'll be your backup plan," I say.

"He knows you're weak from your injuries. He'll exploit that if he has the chance," Logan says.

"I certainly hope he tries."

"I refuse to bring either of you if you aren't protected by more than your instincts."

"Where are the weapons?" Quinn asks.

"Are you planning to carry one?"

He shakes his head. "Rachel needs one. I can find her something easily concealed. Seems to me you, Willow, and Adam need to check this floor. Ask around. See if anyone knows where Ian is before we rush through the city looking like a mob ready to burn someone at the stake. Wouldn't hurt to have a few more people with us when we find him."

Logan nods and points to the right. "Our cache of weaponry is four doors down. We'll canvas this floor, get some help, and return for you in just a few minutes. Be ready."

Quinn leaves to find a weapon for me, and I bite my lip as agony radiates along my arm while I try to button my pants. The pain still feels sharp and real, but I try not to let it comfort me.

My teeth scrape against a swollen nub on the inside of my mouth, and I remember Ian crushing my lips against my teeth as he said, *"Shh."*

I'll show him what happens to someone who shushes me.

By the time Quinn returns, I've managed to untangle most of my hair and am hunting for my boots. My hair smells like lemongrass, and so does my skin. Clearly, somebody washed me while I was unconscious. I sincerely hope that somebody wasn't Logan.

My body flushes with heat at the thought, and I shake it away. I have a killer to destroy. I can think about romance later.

My head feels heavy and off-kilter, and every breath I take burns against my lungs as if the smoke I inhaled still lives deep inside me.

"Which one do you want?" Quinn asks.

I look up as he tosses a silvery metal vest, as thin as a layer of silk, onto the cot beside me and holds out his hands. On the left, a small dagger with a double-edged blade barely fills his entire hand. On the right he holds the knife I've carried since the day we discovered the cache of weapons in the Commander's compound.

I stare at the blades and my mouth goes dry.

Guilty.

Melkin's tormented gaze mocks me as his blood pours over my hands. I start shoving it away, but stop before I can seal up the cracks in the silence that still crouches inside of me. I don't want to go back to feeling disconnected from myself. I'm a long way from better, but to refuse to face this now would be to unravel the tiny bit of healing I've managed to find.

"I thought the dagger would be better since you'll be using your left hand, and it's your weaker—what's wrong?"

I shake my head and draw in a deep breath. I've carried a knife for the duration of this journey, and it hasn't made me sick with fear. I see no reason to feel this way now, but still I stare at the dull gleam of the blade and tremble.

Quinn's hands slowly close over the weapons, and he lowers them. "You don't have to choose one."

"Yes, I do." I do. Because I'm not going to confront that monster without a way to bring him down.

But if I kill him, if his blood covers my hands, will it break me like killing Melkin broke me?

"You have other choices, Rachel."

"Like what? Like facing down a professional killer with nothing but my bare left hand?"

"Yes, if you'd rather. You could trust your survival instincts and trust in our ability to take Ian down as a group. It's up to you."

My fingers trace the outline of the bandage on my right arm as Melkin's face floats to the surface of my mind again. I press lightly and the instant bite of pain distracts me from his accusing eyes.

"It's not about trusting myself or anyone else to get me out alive. I'm not afraid to die," I say.

Quinn tosses the blades onto the cot and gently pulls my fingers away from my wound. "What are you afraid of, then?"

"He needs to die. Someone like this—someone who could do the things he's done and take pleasure in them—needs to die. If I'm close enough to him to deliver justice, then I need to be able to do it."

"Do you think you'll hesitate?"

"No. I know I won't." I glance at my hands as if I can still see the crimson evidence of my guilt slowly drying on my skin. "But maybe I should. After the Commander killed Oliver and then imprisoned Logan, I was driven by a need to seek justice. But after finding my father's grave, I wanted nothing more than revenge. Melkin got in my way."

I look at Quinn. "He got in my way. He didn't know how broken I was. He didn't realize what the Commander had done to me, and I didn't hesitate. I killed him."

Something dark and painful seeps out of the silence, but I can't succumb to it. Not when we have a killer to catch. I also can't bear to shove it away from me, because it's mine.

It's mine, and it's time to stop acting like it isn't.

"You don't carry a weapon anymore," I say. "Why not?"

He considers me before he answers. "Because I was raised to *be* a weapon. Not carrying one reminds me every minute of every day that I broke from that path, and that I'm never going back. But"—he holds up a finger as if he can already see the thoughts inside my head—"I told you once that I'd found answers, but that I didn't think they'd work for anyone else."

"Why isn't refusing to carry a weapon my answer, too?"

"Because you weren't raised to be a weapon, Rachel. You were raised to be a warrior. There's a difference. If you lay down your weapons, you'd be doing it out of fear, rather than out of knowledge." He smiles, and it warms his entire face. "You aren't a coward. Far from it. And the people most qualified to carry weapons are those who understand the consequences of using them."

"And if I can't stand to have more blood on my hands?"

"Maybe you need to take some time to really consider exactly how much blood is truly yours, and how much of that guilt belongs to others."

"Ready?" Logan asks as he walks through the doorway.

"Ready." I reach down and palm my knife without allowing myself to think about Melkin. Later, when I'm not about to face a killer, I'll think about Quinn's words. Right now I'm going to try my best to be the warrior they all think I am.

"Dragonskin?" Logan asks, pointing at the thin silvery vest lying on the cot behind me.

"There were several vests in the weapons room. I'm guessing a few of the guards no longer feel the need to wear them since we're inside Lankenshire?" Quinn reaches for the Dragonskin.

"The guards wore the vests to protect against a Carrington attack," Logan says. "We all realize they don't protect us against Ian, because he knows we're wearing them."

"Except we aren't," Adam says. "We stopped once we got inside Lankenshire because metal next to your skin isn't very comfortable. Ian wouldn't expect us to have Dragonskin on again."

"Vests for everyone, then," Logan says.

"Including you," I say to Quinn. He smiles and goes to join Willow and Frankie in the hall outside the room.

"Okay"—Logan looks at me—"let's get this on you."

My eyes dart between Logan and Adam, and my face feels like it's on fire. "Um. I've got it."

Logan frowns. "Dragonskin is light for something made out of metal, but it's still difficult to put on. Especially if you can't use your right arm. We'll help you."

The fire spreads down my neck and heads toward my toes. "Logan, I'm not wearing an undertunic. If you think I'm going to strip down to nothing in front of the two of you—"

"No," Logan says, just as Adam turns on his heel and says, "I'll go get a vest of my own."

"I sure know how to clear a room," I say, but my breath is shaky because Logan is so close to me. I can feel the heat of his skin through the thin cotton of his tunic. I look up to find his eyes watching me with an intensity that threatens to turn my bones to water.

"Yes, you do," he says softly, and reaches out to trail his finger over my cheek and down my neck until he reaches the hem of my tunic. "Turn around. I'll help you. I won't look at anything you aren't ready for me to see. I promise."

I turn to face the cot, and he rummages in a box against the wall until he finds a sleek undertunic in a shimmery white fabric that looks fancy enough to use for the first night after a Claiming ceremony.

Which is a really stupid thing to think about right now, because my skin refuses to keep secrets from Logan. It glows, my breath hitches in my throat, and a feeling just as real as the pain in my arm but infinitely more delicious spreads through my stomach in lazy spirals.

"This will work." Logan's voice is steady, but the fingers that reach around me to gently tug my tunic over my head tremble. His chest scrapes the sensitive skin along my back as he breathes in quick, little jerks as if he's been running.

I sound like I've been running too.

"Hold still," he whispers, and the shimmery undertunic flows over my skin like water. His hands cup my waist, and he pulls me against him. Pressing his mouth to the nape of my neck, he holds me in place for a long moment. Not that I'm tempted to move. Tiny shivers spark across the heat on my skin, and I wiggle even closer to him.

He lifts his head and says in a voice I barely recognize, "Walk away."

"I—what?"

"Walk away from me." His fingers dig into my hips. "Please."

I don't want to. I want to forget everything that haunts us, everything we still have to face, and just have this one perfect moment with him.

But something in Logan's voice compels me to move. I take three steps forward until my knees hit the cot.

"Thank you," he says after a long silence. Then he lifts the Dragonskin off the cot and carefully settles it over my head. It's lighter than my cloak, and flexible when I move, but it still feels strange to wear something constrictive so close to my body.

I turn to face Logan, tugging at the Dragonskin with my left hand.

"I'm sorry," he says.

"For what?"

"For . . . being tempted by you."

My smile feels just a little smug.

He smiles back. "Let's finish getting you ready."

He slides my outer tunic over the Dragonskin. Tugs on my boots and buckles them down. Straps my knife sheath where I can reach it with my left hand, but where it will be hidden from sight. And true to form, he spends the entire time giving me a litany of worst case scenarios, instructions, and plans. Finally, he drapes my cloak over my shoulders and pronounces me ready to go. The leather of my cloak smells like garlic and smoke, and I use the memories it evokes to focus on what matters in the next few moments.

Finding Ian. And making him regret that he was ever born.

CHAPTER FIFTY-FIVE

LOGAN

Rachel leans heavily on me as we climb down a set of stairs and hurry through the main hospital hallway. The walls are a brilliant white, and the floor beneath us is smooth, dark wood. Quinn refuses Willow's help as he walks, but his breathing is harsh, and his hands shake. Frankie and Adam walk in front of us.

Jodi, Drake, Smithson, and Nola meet us in the front hall, a circular room with a scattering of stiff-looking chairs covered in soft green cloth.

"Ian isn't in the building," Nola says. Her usually calm expression is set in angry lines. "No one's seen him in here all day."

"Well, if Clarissa was telling the truth, some of Ian's tracker friends are here from Rowansmark. Maybe he went to find them," Rachel says.

"Oh, good. More murderers to kill." Willow adjusts her quiver and doesn't look at Quinn.

"The triumvirate is expecting you in the council room now,"

Elim says as she crosses the stone floor with brisk steps. "I'll take you."

"We don't have time for this now," Adam says. "We need to find Ian."

I glance meaningfully at Elim and shake my head.

"We'll tell the triumvirate we know who the killer is and ask for their help in capturing him. They know this city, and the probable location of the Rowansmark trackers, better than we do," I say quietly. "But we aren't going to stand around and wait for them to reach a decision. We'll give them his identity, and then we're going to turn this city upside down until we find him."

We follow Elim out of the wide double doors, across the small, manicured courtyard, and through the stone archway that leads to the main road. With every step, I see Donny's eyes lit with eagerness as he remembers to keep his knife ready. Sylph smiling while she carefully bandages my head. Thom sacrificing himself so that I could live.

Ian's hands are covered with the blood of my people—my *friends*—and every breath I take is fueled by the cold, implacable fury that lives within me. Ian will die for what he's done. I only wish I knew how to reanimate him so I could kill him again and again and again until he's suffered the way he made us suffer.

Silencing the tiny voice that wonders if my motivations are so very different from his, I scan the streets as I walk and pray for a glimpse of him. My motivations might be similar, but I don't plan to kill innocent people to achieve my goal.

Lankenshire is a city of gray-white stone, tidy yards, and streets that curve in gentle circles around the cluster of government buildings that rest in the city's heart. Elim walks with her customary brisk strides, her dark hair swinging with every step. I'm thankful the hospital is only one street away from the council house. Rachel holds her head high, but I can tell every step she takes is harder than the last.

We follow the street as it spirals inward toward the city's center. Most of the buildings we pass look like businesses. One tall structure claims to be a library. I can't imagine what it's like to live in a city where every citizen has access to a huge collection of books.

I guess the triumvirate doesn't share the Commander's conviction that ideas can be threatening.

"You can rest in the council room," I tell Rachel as we round the corner and see the orderly square laid out before us. It's a testament to how weak she still feels that she doesn't argue.

The council building is an imposing structure made from polished gray brick. A tall statue of a man with a narrow face and an impressive sword stands in the middle of the square surrounded by pink and purple flowers.

Ahead of us, Elim halts in the middle of the paved path that leads to the council building's steps. Casting a quick, panicked look over her shoulder at us, she lifts trembling fingers to her throat.

I peer around her to see what's wrong and instantly reach for my sword. A line of Rowansmark trackers stretches across the steps leading into the council building. I scan the rest of the square and see more trackers stepping out of the shadows. In seconds, we're surrounded by no fewer than fifteen.

Ian isn't with them.

"Give us the controller, and your friends can walk away from this place unharmed." A tracker near the center of the square steps closer. His skin is nearly as dark as Oliver's, and his head is bare. His brown eyes are calculating as he assesses us.

Rachel lets go of me and draws her knife. Willow nocks an arrow on her bow.

"I don't have it with me," I say before anyone else can show aggression toward the trackers. If I can convince the trackers to separate me from the rest of my group, ostensibly to retrieve the device, I can keep my friends safe. As if she can read my mind, Rachel steps a little closer to me. Her hands shake as she holds her knife, but her face is a mask of furious determination.

I admire her courage, but on a day like this, when she's already struggling just to stay on her feet, her courage is going to get her killed.

"You wear the device on your chest," the tracker says.

Of course he knows that. Ian must have told his tracker friends every single detail he'd observed over the past few weeks.

I glance behind me. The trackers are closing in. If I'm going to derail what's about to happen, I need to do it soon.

Ripping at the laces on my tunic, I show the tracker my bare chest. "I told you the truth. I don't have it with me. And if you and your men so much as injure one of my people, I swear on my life I'll never tell you where I hid it."

The tracker doesn't seem surprised that I anticipated this moment. He got his information about me straight from Ian, who's had ample opportunity to observe the way I think.

Which means Ian will already have accounted for this possibility, and he'll be ready with a counterattack.

I stare the tracker down. "Where's Ian? Expecting you to do his dirty work for him while he hides his face from those he's betrayed?"

No sooner do the words leave my mouth than Ian separates himself from the thick hedges surrounding a meeting hall and walks toward us, clapping his hands in slow, deliberate movements.

"Well done, brother. Well. Done," he says. The sly sincerity in his voice is at odds with the anger in his eyes.

I'll see his anger and double it. I have the weight of Baalboden's destruction and the loss of thirty-eight of my people to fuel me. Ian has a twisted sense of patriotism and a mile-wide streak of insanity.

I step in front of my people and hold my sword steady.

Ian laughs, an ugly, vicious sound. "Isn't that heroic?" He turns to the other trackers and throws out his arms. "My brother, the hero! The boy who colluded with Jared Adams to steal from Rowansmark. Left his family to suffer the consequences. And then stole his followers away from their leader so that he could start his own city-state on the backs of Rowansmark technology and Baalboden labor."

"That's not what happened." Adam's voice is little more than a snarl.

"Well, look who's decided to become a devout Logan follower. It wasn't too long ago that I was vigorously defending his honor to you."

"Why bother defending him if you're going to turn around and do all this?" Adam gestures around us.

"I had to gain his trust, didn't I?" Ian looks at me and slowly tugs on the silver chain he wears until the tiny copper dragon charm is visible. "You know, until I called the *tanniyn* that day we stopped by the Ferris wheel in the Wasteland, I wasn't absolutely sure you still had the controller. I'd caught up with you a day before you met the Commander to give the tech to him. I'm afraid I lost sight of what happened to the controller after that. I was a little busy telling the *tanniyn* where to go."

My jaw hurts from clenching my teeth. "That charm calls the beast? Does it also override the controller? Is that what happened when the Cursed One went inside Baalboden?"

Ian's smile is fierce. "My father wouldn't build technology meant for the Commander without giving us a way to shut it down. And if you hadn't altered the strength of the controller with your little booster pack, I could've finished all of this that day on the field the way I finished your city."

My voice shakes. "You killed thousands of people. *Thousands.*"

"Justice requires sacrifice." He steps closer.

"Instead of listening to this lunatic, how about if I just put an arrow straight through his lying tongue?" Willow asks.

"If you shoot me, every single person inside Lankenshire will die."

Willow shrugs and pulls her bow string back. "I'll call that bluff."

Ian gestures toward the top of the council building. "Do you see that?"

I follow his arm and see a dark gray box attached beneath the eaves of the building's roof. The metal looks like the same that was used to make both the dart and the device.

"What is it?" Frankie asks, his tone belligerent.

"It emits a sonic pulse. A slightly stronger pulse than the one worn by every city-state's leader to keep the *tanniyn* at bay. If a city dishonors its protection agreement with Rowansmark, any tracker in the area can change the frequency to summon the beast instead." He smiles, a ghost of the charming Ian we'd come to know. "I did enjoy listening to you uneducated, superstitious people call the *tanniyn* the Cursed One. I bet you still believe there's only one *tanniyn* left, too. You really never once thought to challenge anything the Commander said or did. How pathetic."

"Neither did our father," I say. "If he had, we wouldn't be here now."

Ian's face flushes brilliant red and he stalks closer. Perfect. If I can make him angry enough to forget that he should stay out of sword range, I can end this.

End him.

My eyes graze the metal box attached to the building's eaves, and my stomach drops. I can't kill Ian while any Rowansmark trackers remain inside Lankenshire. Not if it means the Cursed One, or *tanniyn*—whatever we want to call it—will be summoned to turn Lankenshire into a pile of smoldering ruins. Not when I haven't examined the tech to know if the power boost I gave our device is enough to override this new signal.

Rachel trembles beside me, and I cast a quick look at Quinn, who stands on her other side. He doesn't look too good himself, but he wraps an arm around her and gently eases her back a few steps. The fact that she doesn't fight to stay by my side speaks volumes about her condition.

Ian takes another step forward, his fists clenched. "He was

not your father. He was mine. So was our mother. But you killed them." Ian's voice rises. "You killed them both. My mother couldn't stand to suffer over the loss of you, even though I was *right there*. She chose death instead. And my father—"

"Paid the price for his loyalty toward the Commander with his life while you watched. I know. You told me, remember? While you were busy lying to me about your background, because unlike a man of *honor*, you chose deception and murder as a means to get the vengeance you crave."

I step forward, as much to put distance between me and my friends as to get closer to Ian. Quinn has already moved Rachel back another few yards. Behind the trackers who line the council steps, the triumvirate exits the building and stops to stare. I look at Ian. "I guess you and the Commander aren't very different from each other, are you?"

Ian's entire body vibrates, and he spits his words at me. "I have more honor in my little finger than you could find in the entire group of pathetic refugees from Baalboden. I remained loyal to my leader. To my city. Even in the face of my family's disgrace."

"Honor and loyalty require you to murder children? To poison innocents?" My voice is rising too. "To burn an entire city to the ground because you thought your life wasn't fair?"

"Fair?" Ian is yelling now. "Let me tell you what isn't fair. You spent your life in the lap of luxury, coddled by the Commander as his precious investment, while I spent mine scrambling to stay one step ahead of the disgrace my mother's suicide and my father's theft brought down on my head."

"You idiot!" Frankie roars, whipping out his sword and

closing the gap between him and me. "Logan's Baalboden mother was flogged to death in front of him when he was just six years old. He was declared an outcast. He survived on the streets by begging or stealing or eating trash just to have enough to keep himself alive. Until you destroyed our city, most of us still wouldn't have anything to do with him. He had a mountain of loss, neglect, and downright cruelty to overcome, but he didn't turn around and start killing innocent people because of it."

"He betrayed his family!" Ian's voice rings across the square, full of terrible rage. "He left us to our disgrace."

"I didn't know." I speak quietly, hoping to calm Ian. Hoping to stop the violence I see in his eyes. "Until two hours ago when a Lankenshire man who'd spent significant time in Rowansmark nineteen years ago recognized me, I didn't know I was anything other than Logan McEntire from Baalboden."

Ian's laugh is harsh. "That's very believable, Logan. Very. You delivered that lie with all the false sincerity with which you live your life." He steps closer. "But I *know* you knew the truth. Jared Adams checked in with my father every six months, bringing progress reports on you and assuring us that you were healthy and happy. The same man who took you in as his apprentice and allowed you to court his daughter." His voice shakes. "You were close to Jared, connected to him in every way, so don't stand there and tell me you didn't know the truth."

"I didn't . . ." My voice dries up. My air runs out. My heart is a frantic, caged thing beating against my chest.

Jared *knew*? All this time, he knew who I was and why the Commander hated me so much, but he never told me? I thought he respected me. Maybe even loved me. Earning his regard was one of the touchstones by which I lived my life.

Ian is still speaking, but I don't hear a word he says. Who else knew? Oliver, who was closer to Jared than anyone but Rachel and who fed me, clothed me, and treated me like a son? Did he save me out of love, or was he tasked with making sure the Commander's investment didn't starve to death in an alley before I could be useful?

The pain of my mother's lies, Jared's secrecy, and Oliver's uncertain motives slices into me, but I don't have time to dwell on it.

Ian locks eyes with me and says, "Do you understand pain atonement, Logan? The pain must be commensurate with the crime. Most people survive the punishment. But if the crime is too big—if you've betrayed your family, your employers, your fellow citizens, and your leader by giving the power to rule the continent to the one man your leader hates beyond all others—the punishment is impossible to survive."

"Marcus died. I get that." My hand grips my sword with white knuckles. Two more steps and Ian will be in range. I can't kill him, but I can maim him. If I take him out of the equation, perhaps we have a chance at fighting off the rest of the trackers. Perhaps none of them will summon the beast while they're still well within its path of destruction. "But just because you lost your father—"

"I killed him!" Ian's voice sounds desperate. "It was my test to be accepted into the ranks of the military council without the taint of my family's disgrace clinging to me. I administered the pain atonement, and I watched him die."

I stare at him in horrified silence as the emotion on his face slowly subsides, replaced by a slick mask of charm that fails to contain the twisted creature he's become.

Had he always been like this? Always capable of murdering innocents and laying the blame on his inner demons? Or did he join our group hoping to find family with me, hoping to make me see things his way, only to be disappointed once again when I wasn't who he needed me to be?

It doesn't matter. All that matters is that the killings stop, and that he pays for his crimes.

Around me, my people fan out to flank me, weapons raised. My heart clenches as the trackers move closer. Only five yards separate us now.

"Tell your people to back off," Ian says as he reaches into his cloak pocket and withdraws two clay cylinders, each about the size of his palm.

"Or what?" Willow asks. "You'll call that unholy lizard—"

"The *tanniyn*," Ian sneers. "If you're going to talk about something, at least use the correct terminology."

"Would you like to hear the terminology I use for you?" Willow asks. "Or should I tell you that after I've cut out your tongue and fed it to the dogs?" She steps past me, and Ian retreats a step.

"Tell your people to back off, Logan, or once again, you'll be responsible for the consequences," he says.

"Funny how you seem to think everyone else should be responsible for what *you* do," Rachel says from ten yards behind me. Her voice sounds breathless. Pained.

I glance back to see her leaning on Quinn, her knife still in her hand, her skin as pale as the stone beneath our feet. Quinn meets my eyes. I beg him with my expression to get her away from here before all hell breaks loose. She's in no shape to defend herself, and if I'm worried about her, I'll be distracted while I'm fighting.

Quinn nods his understanding and begins moving Rachel away again, a task made difficult by the presence of trackers at his back. He'll have to make it look like he has no part in what's going on.

And I'll have to provide a distraction capable of buying him the time he needs.

"Give us the device, along with any modifications, designs, or replicas, and your people get to stay alive." The tracker who first addressed me speaks again, and Ian takes a sliding step to my right.

"What about Logan?" Adam asks. "You said his people get to live. What about Logan?"

"Oh, there's no scenario in which Logan survives this." Ian moves to the right again, and the other trackers step closer. The moves are coordinated. Rehearsed.

Planned.

"You see, the very second Logan hands everything over to me, he will die," Ian says, his thumbs rubbing the clay cylinders he holds.

"Then why would he ever give it to you?" Frankie says. "You've lost your mind."

What is Ian up to? I stare at the cylinders he holds while I edge toward him, my sword ready. Some sort of incendiary device? More tech involving the Cursed One?

"He never had his mind to begin with," Willow says. "He's nothing but a lunatic who lost his mommy and daddy and wants to burn the world down so he can sit back and watch."

Ian snarls at her, but then drifts farther to the right. Farther away from me.

"He'll hand it over—"

Farther toward the southern edge of the square.

"—because if he doesn't—"

The other trackers converge on us, weapons out.

"—if he holds back even one single piece of tech—"

Ian slides to the right again. Toward the edge of the square. Toward *Rachel*.

"—he'll lose everyone he loves." His blue eyes meet mine, and he smiles. "Just. Like. Me."

"No!" I shove Willow aside and start running.

CHAPTER FIFTY-SIX

RACHEL

Quinn's arm tightens around me as Ian raises his hands above his head and throws the clay cylinders onto the stones at his feet. They explode on impact and the southern half of the square is instantly filled with thick, gray smoke.

I raise my hand to cover my mouth, but it's too late. The smoke rushes down my throat and coats my lungs. I cough—harsh, desperate gasps that seem to tear at my throat—and feel Quinn coughing beside me as well. His hand fists into the back of my cloak and he pulls me toward him.

A bell starts clanging from the top of the council building. I don't know if it's calling for Lankenshire citizens to help us or if it's warning them to stay away.

My head feels too light, my knife too heavy, and I struggle to stay on my feet. Ian did this for a reason, and I'm not dropping my weapon or my guard until I see what that reason is.

Quinn coughs and hacks, one arm thrown over his face, and says, "Get down!"

He half pulls, half shoves, and it doesn't take much to convince my already-shaking knees that they can't hold me. I hit the pavement hard, and pain screams up my right arm.

"Keep your head down. The smoke is rising." Quinn sprawls on all fours beside me, his breathing erratic, his arms trembling.

We need to get out of this smoke. We can't help Logan fight off Ian and the trackers if we're too busy desperately gasping for clean air that never comes. If we can't walk, we're going to have to crawl.

Clutching my knife in my left hand, I lie on my belly, dig my elbows into the stone beneath me, and push myself forward. Agony blazes through me every time I put any weight on my right arm, but I don't have the luxury of stopping. Quinn drops to his stomach beside me and begins to move forward as well.

We're heading south. I think. There's too much thick smoke to tell, but it doesn't matter. What matters is getting clear of the smoke so that we can breathe again.

Muffled voices shout all around us. The harsh metallic clang of swords clashing fills the air, but we can't see the fighting. We can only see a handspan in front of us.

Digging my elbows in again, I shove forward and my hand slaps against a pair of dark brown boots. Before I can do more than gasp for a smoke-tainted breath, the owner of the boots crouches down and meets my gaze.

It's Ian, his mouth covered with a thick cloth. Brilliant rage glows in his eyes as he reaches out and grabs the front of my tunic. I slash with my knife, aiming for the artery in his wrist, but my movements are slow and sluggish as the smoke drifts through my lungs and settles over my brain like a fog.

He deflects the blow, sending my knife skittering across the square, and then pulls his mask to the side long enough to say, "This time, Rachel, I'm more than happy to let you sacrifice yourself for Logan."

He drags me to my feet, but Quinn is already there, crouched and shaking, his breath rattling in the back of his throat like a trapped animal. He lunges forward, but Ian snaps out a powerful sidekick, and his boot connects solidly with Quinn's head. Quinn falls to the ground and disappears beneath the cloud of smoke.

Ian pulls me roughly to the edge of the square and then into a side street, where the smoke thins enough to see where we're going. I can't get enough air, and my throat feels raw. I'm weak, my right arm is useless, my weapon is gone, and I can't even draw enough air to curse Ian's name.

It doesn't matter. I'm still going to kill him. For Sylph. For Donny. For Logan.

For me.

The street curves away from the square. The brick facades on the buildings that line the road are covered in a fine sheen of grit and dirt, as if no one really cares what this neighborhood looks like. My boots drag against the ground, and I let myself go limp. If Ian wants me to come with him so badly, he's going to have to expend the time and energy it takes to carry me. And if he lifts me over his shoulder where my boot has a clear shot at his manly parts, so much the better.

He grunts as I slump against him, and then he rips the mask off of his face. "I know what you're trying to do, and it won't work."

Since we've already slowed down, I beg to differ.

He bends down and scoops me up, cradling me against his chest. My feet can't reach anything but air, but my arms are another story. Dragging in as much of a breath as I can manage, I punch my left hand toward his face and jab my fingers into his eyes.

He drops me.

I land on my right side, and pain screams through me. I curl into a ball, holding my arm as if I can somehow make the hurt go away, and clench my teeth to keep from crying.

Ian crouches beside me and says, "You can't beat me, Rachel. All I have to do is squeeze your burned arm, and you'll come undone."

I roll slowly onto my back. "Undone is not the same as beaten."

Far behind us, shouts ring out as the trackers battle with the small group of Baalboden survivors inside the square. I stare up at Ian's eyes and remember that in the flickering light of the fires, when most of his face was covered by his cloak and I didn't know who he was, he reminded me of Logan. Now that I know they're brothers, I can see that Ian's eyes and the tilt of his chin resemble Logan's.

Ian's voice is calm, though the fury in his eyes hasn't abated. "Make this easy on yourself, Rachel."

I laugh—a choked, wet, desperate sound. "When have I ever made things easy on myself?"

His jaw clenches. Grabbing a fistful of my tunic, he lifts me partially off the ground and begins dragging me down the street.

I kick and thrash, doing my best to jerk myself out of his grasp.

He lets me fall onto the pavement, and my head bounces against the stone with a dull thud that instantly makes my skull ache. Letting go of my tunic, he punches my bandaged arm. I scream as the pain rips through me, but then I swallow it down.

I'm not going to give him the satisfaction of knowing how much he's hurting me.

Grabbing my tunic again, he continues to drag me as the street narrows and the buildings become rough-faced, broken-down things. I struggle against him, but the throbbing in my arm has spread to my neck, and my head feels fuzzy and unfocused.

"You should've kept your word," he says as he turns abruptly into a narrow alley overshadowed by tall brick buildings on either side. "You should've taken the controller from Logan and given it to me. You could've avoided all of this, but you broke your promise."

My feet bump against the uneven stones beneath me, sending jolts of pain through my arm. I'm still gasping for air with lungs that feel gritty and raw, but I say, "You'd already killed eight innocent boys before we had that conversation, even though you'd taken a position as a guard and given your word to protect our camp. You have *no right* to talk to me about broken promises."

"They were Logan's punishment." His voice is hard and cruel.

"What about the people you poisoned? What about *Sylph*?"

"Justice requires sacrifice." He crouches down, keeping one hand on me, and lifts a slim metal circle out of the center of the alley. "I thought you understood that."

"Justice sometimes requires sacrificing oneself. Not sacrificing others."

There's a hole in the ground. A metal ladder is attached to the edge of the opening.

"We're going down this ladder," he says. "In your current condition, I'd hang on tight. We wouldn't want you plummeting to your death before Logan has the chance to give his life for yours." His smile is twisted, full of pain and purpose. "Logan understands sacrifice, too."

"Yes, he does." I plant my left hand on the street and push myself upright, my right arm still cradled across my lap. "And so do I. But we also understand justice, something you don't seem to grasp."

"Climb down."

"No."

His eyes blaze. "Climb down or I'll make you regret ever breaking your promise to me."

I lift my chin and meet his gaze without flinching. "I'll make another promise to you, Ian. One I am wholeheartedly committed to keeping." I lean close, and a draft of moist, cool air rises out of the hole in the street.

"I, Rachel Adams, promise to kill you, Ian McEntire, for the crimes of destroying Baalboden and killing thousands of innocent people." I match the ferocity of his anger with a heaping dose of my own. "And I'll make it *hurt*. You like pain atonement. You should appreciate that."

His lip curls, and he says, "One last chance. Climb down."

"No." I hurl the word at him.

He balls up his fist and slams it into the side of my head. For one fleeting moment, I can still hear the distant sounds of fighting. Still feel the roughness of the stone beneath me. Still see Ian's eyes glaring into mine.

But then my ears ring, my eyes close, and darkness takes me.

CHAPTER FIFTY-SEVEN

LOGAN

My sword slams against a tracker's blade as I battle my way toward where I last saw Rachel. The smoke is lifting, shredding into long slices of gray, but I can't see her. The man I'm fighting spins, blade slashing, and I parry his blow.

Easily.

Another slash. Another parry. Fighting him is like sparring with one of our newer guards. It takes very little effort on my part to keep him at bay.

A quick glance behind me shows that Adam, Frankie, Drake, and Nola are holding off the trackers easily as well. Which means they aren't trying to kill us. They're just trying to slow us down enough to let Ian get away.

"Rachel!" I yell her name and cough as acrid smoke burns my throat. The tracker lifts his sword for another attack, but I'm done playing cat and mouse. Turning on my heel, I run toward the southern corner of the square—toward where I last saw Rachel and Quinn.

I lunge forward, holding my cloak to my nose, but I can't see more than a yard in front of me. The bell keeps clanging. Bodies brush past me in the smoky haze, but I can't tell if they're trackers or my own people. A hand grabs my cloak, and suddenly Willow is in my face, her dark eyes lit with fury.

"They're gone."

"Who's gone?" I ask, though the terrible fear coursing through me is answer enough.

"Quinn, Rachel, and Ian."

"The gate," I say, and she doesn't wait for more explanation.

The smoke is a thinning haze as we hurry out of the square. My people are all still standing, but most of the trackers are gone. Whether they left with Ian or just disappeared back into the depths of Lankenshire to keep an eye out for any perceived disloyalty toward Rowansmark, I have no idea.

We leap out of the square and onto the pale stone road that leads toward the gate and start running. It takes less than three minutes to race from the square to the gate. I spend the entire time alternately praying that Rachel is okay and thinking of terrible things to do to Ian.

We skid around the last curve of the spiraling road and find the gate locked. Coleman Pritchard, along with fifteen of his guards, stands in our way.

"Move," Willow snaps.

He acts like he didn't hear her.

"Did a tall boy about my age just come through the gate with a red-haired girl and a dark-haired boy?" I ask Coleman.

"No one's come through this gate in over an hour," he says, and there's something heavy in his tone.

"They used the tunnels," Willow says. "I know where those let out." She turns back to Coleman and snarls, "Get out of our way."

"I can't do that," he says.

"I'll make it easy on you." Willow nocks an arrow and whips it toward his face. "Move or die."

"You can kill me, but that gate isn't opening. We're on lock-down. No one can open the gate except the triumvirate, now."

"Lockdown? Why?" I grip my sword so hard it hurts. "We need out of that gate, Coleman. Ian is a killer, and he has the only people we can still call family."

He nods as if he's sympathetic, but there's something dark in his eyes. Something that worries me.

"I'll tell you why we're on lockdown, Logan McEntire of Rowansmark." He steps aside and gestures toward the gate. "Because you have yet another powerful enemy you neglected to tell us about, and now you've endangered all of Lankenshire."

I step past him as the other guards part to let me through, and despair washes over me as I see the Commander's army surrounding the city. It's a sea of red uniforms mixed with the blue of Baalboden guards as far as the eye can see, and near the front, the Commander sits astride his horse, his face turned toward the gate.

"That man is really starting to get on my last nerve," Willow says, and shifts her arrow to point through the bars of the gate at the distant Commander.

The Commander spurs his horse forward a few steps and shouts, "People of Lankenshire, this is Commander Jason Chase of Baalboden. I have no quarrel with you. Give me the

Baalboden citizens you have sheltered within your walls, along with their belongings, and you will remain unharmed. You have until dawn. If you choose not to comply, we will attack you with intent to destroy."

"You can give the Commander anything you want, but Logan McEntire and all of his belongings come with us." The tracker with the dark skin and shaved head who first spoke to me in the square approaches the gate, flanked by two other trackers. He holds a folded sheet of parchment in his hand.

Coleman draws himself up straight and speaks with enough authority to rival Clarissa. "Logan McEntire, you are under arrest. You will go before the triumvirate by nightfall. They will decide what to do with you." His voice leaves little doubt as to what he thinks they'll do to someone who managed to invite enmity with their Rowansmark keepers and embroil them in a war with Carrington all in the space of one day.

"You can't arrest him," the tracker says, his voice full of baffled indignation. "We're taking him. He's wanted for crimes against Rowansmark."

Coleman looks straight at the man. "Then you will be called as a witness when he goes before the triumvirate. You may be here to protect us from the *tanniyn*, but every person inside our wall is subject to our laws. Unless you wish to claim that your word is now law inside Lankenshire—which would, of course, potentially incite our thousands of people to protest and riot— you will stand aside and let me arrest this man. Your case against him will be heard by the triumvirate."

All things being equal, I'd rather be taken into custody by the tracker, because at least his goal to force me to bring the device back to Rowansmark lines up with my goal to arrive at Rowansmark with a means to destroy Ian and rescue Rachel.

Actually, all things being equal, I'd rather not be taken into custody at all, but that isn't an option.

The tracker sneers as if he smells something rotten, and steps toward me. Instantly, Coleman's guards surround me, their swords gleaming beneath the sunlight. The tracker's laugh seems to say that all the Lankenshire swords in the world couldn't keep him from me if he truly wanted to take me.

I figure his orders are to keep me alive and unharmed until I lead him to the device, the booster pack, and any designs I've drawn based on their tech. Coleman's orders are to keep me alive and unharmed until I can meet with the triumvirate and help them decide how to placate their Rowansmark keepers without inciting the army at their gate into declaring war against them.

The tracker shoves the folded parchment at me. "One last message from your brother. Better be sure to follow it to the letter. No one dies easily under pain atonement. Especially pretty little girls like your Rachel."

I match his sneer with one of my own. Rachel is stronger than he thinks. She isn't going to make the journey back to Rowansmark easy on Ian or the trackers helping him. She'll slow him down, sabotage his progress, and do her best to make his life hell.

Ian won't kill her, because she's his only leverage against me, but he'll wish with every fiber of his being that he could.

The tracker steps back as the guards begin dragging me toward the square. I look at Willow. "Go see Drake," I say.

"Make sure our people have enough food. If they don't, go hunt for small game."

The guards on either side of me look at me like I've suddenly lost my mind, but I can see that Willow understands I'm telling her to let Drake know what's going on and then go retrieve the device.

"Oh, I don't think so," Coleman says from behind me. "She's under arrest, too."

"Why? She had nothing to do with this. She isn't even from Baalboden." Desperation sharpens my voice. I need her freedom. The only person left inside Lankenshire who knows how to get out of the city and who can help me rescue Rachel and Quinn is Willow.

"None of you are going anywhere until the triumvirate decides your fates."

"No one decides my fate but me," Willow says as guards surround her and begin pushing her back toward the square.

I meet her eyes and shake my head slightly as I see her hand tighten on her bow. Even if we fought our way free of these guards, we still couldn't get the gate open without the triumvirate's help. And we'd be immediately surrounded by trackers. We'd have gained nothing but a certain verdict against us or Rowansmark watchdogs making it impossible to get to the device without an audience. We'll have to go peacefully and hope that what I can offer—a way to fight Rowansmark's tyranny and an end to the Commander—will be enough to secure our freedom.

If it isn't, then Willow can do what Willow does best, and we'll either fight our way out of the city or die trying.

The jail cell is in the basement of the council building. The stone floors are dark gray, and the bars are the same gleaming ebony as the gate. Our weapons are taken from us. Willow is placed in the cell next to mine, and she starts pacing its length the second the door clicks shut behind her.

I step into my cell, hear the door slam shut, and unfold the paper Ian left for me.

Bring the controller, along with all modifications, to Rowansmark or she will receive the punishment you deserve. I guarantee she won't survive it.

My hands shake as I sink onto the single stone bench within the cell. Rachel is badly wounded and at the mercy of a madman who has no qualms hurting innocents to get his way. The Commander and his borrowed army are camped outside the city's wall with a bounty on my head that I doubt Lankenshire can afford to refuse.

And I'm locked inside this cell, trusting the fates of everyone I love to the wisdom of three people I know nothing about.

Best Case Scenario: The triumvirate agrees to my bargain and sets me free to kill the Commander and rescue Rachel.

Worst Case Scenario: Everything else.

The wound of Jared's betrayal bleeds somewhere within me. The weight of it—the weight of all of this—sinks into my bones, an ache that rubs me raw from the inside out. Once, I was Logan McEntire—loved by the mother who gave her life to save me, rescued by the baker whose heart was bigger than his fear, trusted by the most respected courier in Baalboden, and loved by the girl whose honesty and courage were a beacon of hope in my darkest hour.

Now I'm Logan McEntire—raised on lies, kept alive until I proved useful, and locked away from my own story like a fool who cannot be trusted.

I can't demand explanations from my mother. I can't ask Oliver if he saved me for love, or if he was charged with keeping me fed until my father held up his end of the bargain. I can't confront Jared and ask him how he could look into my eyes and never tell me the truth.

The only person left who might know the answers is the girl I love, and she's gone.

For the first time since I lay on the filthy cobblestones beside my mother's lifeless body thirteen years ago, I am Logan McEntire—alone.

Taking a deep breath, I ignore the ache of betrayal within me and focus on what I can control. I don't have any solid exit strategies. I'm weaponless, tech-less, and I can't communicate with any of my people except Willow. A carefully reasoned plan full of logic and sound science isn't in my reach.

We have until nightfall before we see the triumvirate. That's more than enough time to put together a backup plan that hinges on sheer audacity and dumb luck. The odds might be stacked against us, but I have Willow. And I have the loyalty of the Baalboden survivors.

Plus, I once promised Rachel that I would always find her. Always protect her.

I refuse to fail.

Folding Ian's last message into a small square, I shove it into my cloak pocket and begin to plan.

CHAPTER FIFTY-EIGHT

RACHEL

Sunlight paints the backs of my eyelids red and sends a piercing shaft of pain straight into my brain. I try to lift my hands to push at the ache, but my arms refuse to move.

"Rachel," a voice says in a mocking, singsong rhythm. "I know you're in there. Come out and play." Something hard slaps my cheek, and the pain in my head doubles.

The familiar voice has lost its flirtatious charm, and the truth sinks into me like poison.

Ian.

Ian blew up the smoke bomb, dragged me through a side street, knocked me out, and . . . and what? I force my eyes to open, and immediately squint against the daylight that floods my head with agony.

"Oh, good. You're awake," he says, and I see him, crouched before me, his eyes glowing with hate like it's the only thing keeping him alive.

I turn away and scan my surroundings. I'm inside the

Wasteland, propped up against a thick oak in the middle of a vast sea of trees packed so close I can barely see the sky. Nowhere near the path. Probably nowhere near Lankenshire if Ian's smart. Logan will already be looking for me. And when he finds me . . . I meet Ian's eyes and bare my teeth in a smile.

"Logan will move heaven and earth to find me."

"Oh, I'm counting on it," he says, and a stray beam of sunlight gleams off the thick, double-edged knife in his hands. He flips the blade around to face me and cocks his head.

"We're going to be traveling a long way, Rachel. Logan has his hands full with Carrington at the moment, but I have no doubt he'll outsmart them somehow. And then he'll come to ransom you from Rowansmark with the device, just like my father tried to ransom him."

"You're crazy."

The knife plunges down, slicing through my bandage and digging into burned flesh. I scream as raw agony blisters my arm. Ian watches me with a terrible desperation in his eyes.

When he pulls the knife away, blood bubbles out of the jagged wound and pours over my hand.

He grabs my chin and tilts my face toward him. "You'll watch your mouth."

I spit on him.

The knife flashes, and the pain hits, and I scream until my throat fills with tears. Until the agony twists my stomach so that I gag.

"It's a long journey to Rowansmark," he says. "And I can inflict a lot of pain."

My voice is hoarse as I say, "I can take it."

He smiles, and something inside of me trembles. "There are all kinds of pain, Rachel."

"You can't break me," I say, and I mean it. I've already been through hell, and I know I can survive it. I can rise above it. I might break for a little while, but I won't stay broken forever.

"It will be a delight to prove you wrong," he says, and yanks me to my feet by the rope around my wrists. "Now start walking. We have a lot of ground to cover before my spineless brother figures out how to bypass the Carrington army that surrounds him."

"Let her go."

I turn and see Quinn a few yards from us, lethal fury spilling off of him in waves. Blood pours down the side of his face from a gash in his head, and he sways a little as he stands.

"That's quite a wound," Ian says, and smiles. "Almost like someone kicked you in the head. I was actually trying to kill you. Pity."

"You'll have to try harder," Quinn says.

Ian bows, his hands fluttering, and I see a second knife slide out of a wrist sheath and into his hand. The blades are dark gray metal and seem to absorb the sunlight that filters in past the canopy of leaves above us.

"Where did you get those weapons?" I ask, and pressure builds in my chest as the answer comes to me even before the pair of Rowansmark trackers step out of the trees behind us.

That's going to making catching Ian off guard and killing him a bit more difficult.

"The same place I got all that white phosphorous. And the

poison. And the smoke bombs. You didn't really think I'd come all this way to recover stolen Rowansmark property and neglect to bring a pair of law enforcers and a wagonload of supplies with me, did you?"

We're at a disadvantage. Ian's armed. The trackers are armed. And all three are expert killers. I'm injured and tied up with rope, my weapons gone. And Quinn, who doesn't want to be a weapon any longer, is barely able to stay on his feet.

"It's okay," I say to Quinn, because he can't save me, and I don't want him to try. I want him to live. Go back to Logan and Willow and *live*.

The trackers draw their swords. Ian flips both knives around in his palms. And Quinn takes a step toward them.

"*Quinn.*"

"She knows you can't save her," Ian says softly. "You can't even save yourself."

"I don't want to save myself."

My throat closes, and I whisper, "Quinn, please. Go back."

"Oh yes, Quinn. Go back. Obey the girl. That's all you do anyway, right? Obey others?" Ian's smile is dipped in venom as he moves forward, a tracker on either side.

Quinn looks at me. "I'm going to do the right thing."

"No." Tears streak down my face, and I jerk against the rope that holds me.

"Sometimes the right thing costs us the biggest piece of ourselves, but it still has to be done." He smiles at me, and there's peace on his face.

He turns to Ian, and the feral rage comes back. "Pretty

pathetic that you can't beat me without the help of not one, but two trackers." His voice mocks. "If I'm such a whipped dog, what does that make you?"

Ian snarls, and I start grasping at straws. If we separate the three, if Quinn only has to take on one at a time, he has a chance. The only way to separate them is to push Ian past logic and into rage.

"He's crazy," I say to Quinn. "Stark, raving mad."

Ian hisses and turns as if to teach me a lesson.

"Yes," Quinn says with soft menace. "He's stark, raving mad. No wonder he needs their help."

The trackers move toward Quinn, but Ian waves them off, his face purple with rage, his eyes pits of miserable hate. And then he lunges for Quinn, his knives slashing.

Quinn spins, strikes Ian in the face as he passes, and then drops into a crouch. Blood flows down his arm. Ian must have cut him as he passed.

Ian laughs, readies his knives, and comes at Quinn again. This time, Quinn is slower to move out of the way. He deflects Ian's right arm, sending one of the knives flying onto the mossy ground near me, and then elbows him in the face.

Ian fights like he's possessed. Slashing, hacking, and lunging with extraordinary grace. Grace Quinn could easily match if he weren't badly injured already. Quinn punches, parries, and kicks, but he's tiring. The head injury is slowing his reflexes. The weaker he gets, the harder Ian fights. My chest burns as I realize the truth.

Quinn isn't going to win.

I fall to my knees and struggle to breathe as Ian slams his fist into the wound on Quinn's head, and Quinn's arms go slack. It's just for a second, but a second is all Ian needs. Raising his knife into the air, he drives it into Quinn's chest.

"No!" I scream and scream until I have no breath. Tears blur the world into soft silhouettes, and I don't want blink them away. I don't want to see Quinn fall to the ground beside me. I don't want to see blood pouring over the bright green moss.

But Quinn deserves to have a witness to his courage. And I want the last face he sees to be someone who loves him. So I blink the tears away and crawl toward him as he lies on his back, his breath coming in halting, strangled gasps.

His hands grip the knife blade that's lodged in his chest, and blood seeps slowly through his fingers and onto the forest floor. Somewhere above us, Ian laughs, but I ignore him. Ignore the trackers who are driving a wagon into the clearing. Ignore everything but Quinn lying broken and beautiful beside me.

"Oh, Quinn," I whisper, and my tears drip from my face onto his.

He moves his lips, and I lean forward until my ear is next to his mouth.

"The knife," he whispers. "Get it."

For a moment I think he means he wants me to pull the knife out of his chest, but he isn't looking at himself. He's looking at the thick cluster of moss beside my feet. Suddenly, I know the truth, and I can't bear it.

When he said he was going to do the right thing, he didn't mean he was going to kill Ian and the trackers. He already knew he was too injured to beat them. He never intended to save us both. He simply wanted to find a way to give me the tools I needed to save myself.

"Rachel, please," he says, and I can barely hear him.

Grief tears at me with vicious fingers, and I let it take me. Sobbing wildly, I curl toward the forest floor until my hair covers my arms and hands, and my fingers touch the cold metal of a blade. I gather it to me and slide it into my boot, rocking back and forth to cover the motion.

Then I collapse onto Quinn's shoulder, pressing my palms to his chest, and beg him not to die. Not to leave me, like so many have left me. I beg and cry, and beneath my hands I feel . . . metal.

My fingers curve and scrape as I redouble the volume of my grief while triumph, brilliant and wild, surges through me.

The knife isn't in Quinn's chest. It's lodged in the Dragonskin he wears beneath his tunic. The blood leaking through his fingers isn't from his heart. He's gripping the blade tightly, letting his breath become shallow and faint, and hoping no one decides the amount of blood lost isn't enough to kill him.

I can help with that.

I slide forward until my hair curtains our faces and whisper, "Thank you."

He smiles.

And then I rip the blade out of his hands, clumsily slash the rope that binds my wrists, and charge Ian. Ian deflects my attack, but I don't mind. I wasn't trying to hurt him. That would give the trackers an excuse to take care of matters their own way. I was simply trying to divert everyone's attention away from Quinn.

Ian laughs as he wrenches the knife from my hands and ignores my pleading to let me stay until Quinn dies. Laughs as he tosses me over his shoulder while I scream and beat at him with my fists and Quinn's dark eyes close.

Laughs as he tells me he'd promised a lesson in pain, and he'd delivered.

He's wrong.

The lesson I just learned had nothing to do with pain and everything to do with courage. Sometimes the right thing to do is the thing that costs us the most. For Quinn, that meant putting his life on the line so that the daughter of the man who once saved him could live. For Sylph, it meant loving others without ever asking them to be someone they weren't. For Logan, it meant setting aside the heartbreak of his childhood to protect the people who once cast him out.

And for me, it means honoring those who've loved me and sacrificed for me by choosing to be the kind of warrior who delivers justice even when it threatens to hurt me.

Let Ian laugh. Let him believe pain will ruin me. I know better. I've already been ruined once, and I know how to rise from the ashes. I know how to find my broken pieces.

I know how to fight the battles that must be won.

As we move deeper into the Wasteland and the tiny clearing where Quinn lies disappears into shadow, I silently promise myself that I won't let the sacrifices of those who loved me be in vain. Not while I still have breath in my body.

Ian tosses me to the ground, and I climb to my feet, my chin held high while a single purpose burns fiercely within my heart.

I will do the right thing, no matter what it costs me. I will stop Ian. Tear apart Rowansmark brick by miserable brick until I dismantle the technology they would use to turn the Cursed One against innocent people. And then I will find Logan and help him destroy the Commander. I won't break. I won't falter.

I won't stop until the lives of everyone I've lost have been avenged.

ACKNOWLEDGMENTS

First and foremost, thank you to Jesus for loving me, broken pieces and all.

Another huge thank-you to my amazing husband, Clint, who tirelessly supports and understands me. Thank you for picking up all the slack around deadlines and for deciding that my inability to concentrate on anything other than the worlds inside my head is part of my charm.

Tyler, Jordan, Zach, and Johanna, thank you for putting up with my long work hours and for proudly telling your friends and teachers that your mom wrote a book. I am so blessed to be your mom.

Thank you, Mom and Dad, for understanding when I disappear off the face of the earth for weeks and for being huge fans of mine.

This book is the book that wanted to eat my soul. I can't count how many times I wanted to just kill the thing with fire and walk away. I didn't, though, and a lot of the credit is due to a handful of amazing people. Thank you to Kristin Daly Rens for being the kind of editor who pushes me hard and always believes in me. To Jodi Meadows for Gchats and scene reads and for saving me from the under-armor. (Worst. Name. Ever.) To MG Buehrlen for early reads, late reads, plot chats, and generally keeping me sane when nothing else could. (Ermahgerd!) Myra McEntire for reading early and fast, loving the story, and being one of my biggest fans. (Baby, you're a firework, too.) To Heather Lindahl for beta reading and for colluding with MG to call this book *Defiance II: Check Yourself Before You Wreck Yourself.* (The bag of orange Spree was awesome, too. Until you told me it was ten years old. AFTER it had been eaten.) To KB Wagers for being an awesome friend and for making sure my fight scenes are physically possible. (My own personal ninja!) To Julie Daly for being my buffer from the outside world, for managing the details so well, and for being a fan of my work. To Shannon Messenger, Sara McClung, and Beth Revis for supporting my crazy word count on the retreat (and for laughing at me over the Suitcase of Doom event). To Holly Root for remaining my champion through good and bad. To Caroline Sun for being a rock star of a publicist. And to Sara Sargent, the ninja of all things, and the rest of the team at Balzer + Bray for being in my corner and for being totally cupcake-worthy.

Thank you also to YOU, my readers. It's been amazing to hear your response to Rachel and Logan. I'm so very blessed that my book found a home on your shelf.

And finally, thank you, Donny Miller, for letting me kill you off in book two. I told you so. ☺

TURN THE PAGE FOR A SNEAK PEEK AT

DELIVERANCE

THE FINAL BOOK
IN THE DEFIANCE SERIES.

CHAPTER ONE

LOGAN

"Five minutes." The soldier guarding Lankenshire's dungeon raps sharply against the bars of the cell I've been in for the past three hours.

Three hours since the Commander showed up outside Lankenshire with an army and a demand that I be released to him by dawn or he'll attack the city. Three hours since the Rowansmark trackers inside Lankenshire demanded that I give them the device Willow hid in the Wasteland or they'll call the Cursed One—the *tanniyn*—to destroy Lankenshire. I'm assuming the gray metal boxes I saw mounted to buildings throughout the city while I was being marched from the gate to the dungeon—boxes that match the one Ian pointed out to me in the square—all contain a signal capable of summoning the beast. Maybe capable of summoning more than one beast, if Ian's claim about multiple *tanniyn* roaming the earth is correct.

Three hours since Ian took Rachel and disappeared.

"Five minutes until what?" Willow asks from the cell beside

mine. "Until you let us go? Why wait? Open our cells now, and we'll be gone before you can finish locking the doors behind us."

The soldier doesn't look amused. "Five minutes until I escort you to your trial, where the triumvirate will try to figure out a way to appease both the Rowansmark trackers you've managed to upset and the army waiting at our gates."

"It'll be fine." Willow sounds far more confident than I feel. "Logan has a plan. Right, Logan?" When I don't answer, Willow's voice sharpens. "*Right*, Logan?"

"Do you?" the soldier asks softly, his eyes locked on mine.

I open my mouth. Close it. Swallow against the lump of fear that wants to close the back of my throat and say, "I'm working on it."

"You're *working* on it?" The man steps closer to the iron bars that separate us. "You listen to me. This is my city. My *home*. I have family here, and I don't want to lose them because some refugee from Baalboden brought trouble down on our heads." He shoves his green cloak off his shoulders and points to the row of gold bars that line up neatly over his heart. "I'm a ranking officer in Lankenshire's army. I haven't pulled dungeon duty in years, but I'm here today because the triumvirate thinks you merit special treatment. They think you've got a way out of this impossible situation. So don't tell me you're working on it. Figure it out before all of us die. You have five minutes."

He turns on his heel and stalks toward the entrance of the dungeon, his boots slapping against the stone floor as he goes.

"That was dramatic," Willow says as she leans against the bars of her cell and looks at me.

"That was accurate." I close my eyes against the terrible image of Rachel, badly injured, traveling to Rowansmark at the mercy of my murderous brother Ian while I sit in a dungeon, faced with the impossible task of appeasing both the Commander and the trackers, unable to save her. "Every worst case scenario running through my head has come true."

"Oh, please," Willow says. "Knowing the way your brain works, I'm sure there are at least five scenarios worse than this one that you've spent useless hours worrying over. Besides, this isn't *that* bad."

"Not that bad? Willow, the Commander is sitting outside the gate with the Carrington army and what's left of Baalboden's guards and he's promise to attack the city at dawn if I don't give him the device by then. He's a man who keeps his word. And the trackers are going to call the *tanniyn* to destroy Lankenshire the same way Baalboden was destroyed if I don't give the device to *them* instead. But I can't give the tech to either of them, because if I do, I have nothing to use for ransom when I arrive in Rowansmark to barter for Rachel's life." I rub my eyes and try to think my way around the impossibility of it all.

There has to be a way out of this. Too many lives depend on it.

Willow's voice is steady. "If you give the tech to the trackers, it's the same as giving it to Rowansmark itself. That should satisfy the ransom for Rachel. Then we just have to deal with the old man and his stupid army."

I'm already shaking my head. "The second I give up the device, I've lost my leverage over both the Commander and Rowansmark. Plus, I doubt Ian's pain atonement vendetta against me will be satisfied by hearing that the device made its way back to

Rowansmark. He wants to hurt *me*, and what better way to hurt me than to hurt Rachel?"

My throat closes over her name, and I can't push away the fear that pounds through me, taunting me with images of Rachel hurt. Bleeding.

Dead.

"So the trackers, the Commander, and rescuing Rachel—those are all of your worst case scenarios?" Willow asks. "Because you forgot to mention that my brother, the bastion of self-sacrifice, went missing too. Presumably to track down Rachel, since no one would be crazy enough to kidnap Quinn. Of course, Ian is a lunatic who wouldn't recognize sanity if it slapped him in the face, so there's that."

"Thank you for summing that up. I feel so much better about the whole situation now."

"I thought we were just listing our problems. Nobody told me I was supposed to provide sympathy." Willow sounds irritated.

The fear pulsing through me makes it impossible to stand still, so I start pacing the small confines of my cell. "I don't need sympathy. I need a plan. My people are trapped. The clock is ticking. And I'm stuck inside a Lankenshire prison cell without a weapon or a shred of tech within reach."

I'm also stuck in an endless loop of thoughts that have nothing to do with my present circumstances and everything to do with the secrets I recently uncovered about my past. I was born in Rowansmark. Fine, I can adjust to that. I was kidnapped by the Commander as a newborn and kept in Baalboden to coerce my father into turning over his invention for calling and controlling the *tanniyn* once he completed it. I can adjust to that, too.

But knowing that the woman who called herself my mother was lying to me, knowing that Rachel's father, Jared, brought regular reports about me to my father in Rowansmark and never respected me enough to tell me the truth, and wondering if Oliver, the closest thing I ever had to a father in Baalboden, knew my secrets all along and only looked after me to protect the Commander's investment—I can't adjust to that. I can barely stand to look it in the eye.

The foundation on which I built my life is lying in pieces around me, but I can't stop to put it back together. I have a prison break to engineer, an innocent city to protect, a murderer to track down, and two power-hungry leaders who need to be stopped. Personal reflection will have to wait.

"I wouldn't say that we don't have any weapons," Willow says.

I jerk to a stop and whip my head toward Willow's cell. By leaning against my cell door, I can just see her. She's crouched against the front corner of her cell, her back pressing against the iron bars that lock her in. With deft movements, she unties the leather strap that binds her long, dark braid and slowly pulls it free. My eyes widen. A length of thin silver wire is attached to the end of the strap and is woven into her braid. She holds her braid secure and tugs until nearly half a yard of wire slides out of her hair and lies in her lap.

"Brilliant," I breathe.

"Agreed." Willow coils the wire around her left wrist and secures the loose end against the leather tie. It looks like she's wearing a simple silver bracelet, but I have no trouble imagining the kind of havoc Willow can wreak with that length of wire.

Picking locks.

Jabbing eyes.

Slitting throats.

"Have I told you recently that I'm grateful you and Quinn decided to stay with our group instead of trying to find another Tree Village to join? I don't know what I'd do without you."

Willow flashes me a smug little smile, and I make myself smile back, but inside, my desperation is growing. One weapon alone won't help us fix this. I need tech, supplies, people . . . a *plan*.

And I don't have a single workable idea.

The soldier picks up two lengths of chain and strides down the corridor toward our cells. Our five minutes are up.

"If you're going to make a plan, you'd better think fast," Willow says as the soldier stops before my cell, a heavy iron key in his hand.

"I'm *trying*."

I run through my options as the man opens my door, wraps chains around my wrists, and then puts a matching set on Willow while she gives him a look that would drop a lesser man to his knees.

Best Case Scenario: I think of a way out of this before we reach the courtroom, and no one dies.

Worst Case Scenario: Everything else.

My stomach cramps as Willow and I, flanked by another pair of Lankenshire soldiers, follow the man through the long stone hallways that lead from the dungeon to the courtroom.

Short of cutting myself and the device in half and giving a piece to both Rowansmark and the Commander, I can't think of a single way to keep this city and the Baalboden survivors who followed me across the Wasteland—survivors who are family to me now—safe.

"What's the plan?" Willow whispers as we turn a corner and begin climbing a set of steep steps carved into the stone. The torches that bracket the stairway are lit, their golden light gleaming against her dark hair as she looks at me.

"Um . . ."

"You don't have one, do you?"

I shake my head and force myself to think smarter. Faster. Rowansmark needs to believe that Lankenshire is turning me over to them, or they'll use the beacons. The Commander needs to believe that I'll be in his custody by dawn, or he'll attack the city.

And I need to be out in the Wasteland, free of them both, so that I can track down Rachel and Quinn.

"Do you have a plan yet?" Willow asks as we leave the stairs behind and enter a spacious corridor with white marble floors that sparkle beneath bronze gas lamps. A bank of wide windows to the right lets in the brilliant light of the setting sun.

Rachel has been missing for three hours now. Three hours is a decent head start in the Wasteland, but I know I can catch up.

I *will* catch up.

"Logan!" Willow shakes her bound hands in front of my face, the iron chain links slapping together harshly. When I meet her eyes, she leans close and says through gritted teeth, "We're about to walk into that courtroom. What. Is. The. Plan?"

Panic shoots through my stomach and somehow lands in my chest, where it feels like a vise is slowly crushing me.

I don't have a plan. I don't have a single viable scenario. All

I have is desperation and the terrible fear that I'm about to fail everyone I love.

The soldier leading us stops abruptly and motions to a narrow door situated between two bronze gas lamps. "You two wait in here until it's time for the trial to start." His eyes meet mine, and he lowers his voice. "And I certainly hope that in the time since you told me you were 'working on it,' you've come up with something, because in about two minutes, you're going to need to explain it to the one person who can make it happen."

Without another word, he motions us inside the cramped little box of a room, leaves the pair of Lankenshire soldiers to stand guard outside the door, and locks us in.

"The one person who can make it happen . . . we must be meeting with Clarissa Vaughn before the trial starts," I say.

Clarissa Vaughn—leader of Lankenshire's triumvirate and quite possibly the most formidable woman I've ever met. Enduring the soldier's frustration at my lack of a plan will be nothing compared to facing her.

Willow paces the room, scanning the plain white walls and the knotted pine ceiling like she thinks she can find a secret exit that will dump us straight into the Wasteland. I'm scanning the walls too, for all the good it will do me. We need a plan. A real one. And I've got no ideas and no more time to figure it out.

As if she can read my mind, Willow asks, "Still got nothing?"

I meet her eyes for a second, letting her see the sheer desperation churning through me, and then turn to the door. I have to tell Clarissa something. Maybe if I look at this from a different angle. If I examine ways we can neutralize the beacons to take the teeth out of the trackers' threats. If I talk to Coleman Pritchard, head of Lankenshire's security, about methods to defend the city against the Commander . . .

Who am I kidding? I know nothing about defending a city against an army, and I can't tell Clarissa how to neutralize the Rowansmark beacons without seeing one for myself, and even then . . . what if I can't figure it out? What if—

"Hey!" Willow smacks my shoulder lightly. "Stop disappearing into your head and listen. I know what to do."

I blink and stare at her. "You do?"

"Don't act so surprised. I just figure the fastest way to get out of here and into the Wasteland is to remove the obstacles in our way. We'll start with the trackers and then move on to the army—"

"You want to take out an entire contingent of Rowansmark trackers—"

"I don't see why not."

"—and then go after an *army*—"

"Don't be an idiot. Not the *whole* army. Just the leader. Cut off the head and the rest of the body just sort of flops around uselessly."

"You want the two of us, who are currently weaponless . . ." I pause as she wriggles her wrist at me. The silver wire she took from her braid shimmers. "Fine, you want the two of us who are *mostly* weaponless, and who are chained up like criminals, to take out a group of Rowansmark trackers. What are we supposed to use against them? We need a bigger weapon than chains and attitude."

"That's a very negative way to look at this."

A bigger weapon than chains and attitude.

I stare at Willow, but I don't see her. I finally see possibilities. Scenarios.

Plans.

The pain in my stomach eases.

"We can't kill all of the Rowansmark trackers," I say.

"Speak for yourself." She glares at me.

"We need to leave a few alive to testify that Lankenshire had nothing to do with our escape in case other trackers come to the city," I say slowly as a risk-filled plan for how we can break out of prison without endangering either Lankenshire or the Baalboden survivors takes shape inside my head.

"And how are we going to escape?"

"I have a plan." I can't believe what I'm about to suggest. "It's stupid and bold and could fail in a hundred ways before we even get fifteen yards."

She grins. "You cover stupid. I'll take care of bold. Now, what's the plan?"

"We're going to get the Commander to break us out of prison."

CHAPTER TWO

LOGAN

The air inside the little room grows stale while I pace the floor, talking through the details of the riskiest plan I've ever conceived and waiting for Clarissa Vaughn to tell me I'm crazy and that I've just cost her people their lives.

When I've finished, I meet Clarissa's gaze. Her expression tells me nothing. Beside her stands a girl who looks like a younger version of her—right down to the proud tilt of her chin and the air of power wrapping around her like she was born to it. Clarissa introduced her as Cassidy when they arrived. Cassidy's shoulders are ramrod straight beneath her white tunic and dark-green cloak. A black scarf is pinned to the right shoulder of her cloak by a gold medallion with a scale etched onto its surface. Books lie on one side of the scale. A dragon's head lies on the other. The books weigh more.

She's a courier for Lankenshire. An official emissary charged with handling state business with other city-states. For a moment, I imagine that if Rachel had been born in Lankenshire instead of Baalboden, she might've been an emissary for a city-state that valued her brains and her skill without worrying about her gender. Or she might be in the army. Or, eventually, in the triumvirate.

A small part of me wishes that had been her path. The rest of me holds fast to the girl with the fiery hair who defended me when schoolboys caught me scrounging for food in a trash heap, who challenged my ideas and my sparring skills, and who kissed me like I was the air she desperately needed to breathe.

Clarissa and Cassidy are still watching me in silence, and I clear my throat.

"That's it," I say. "That's the plan."

"Let me get this straight," Clarissa says. "You want me to send an emissary to the army outside my gates, tell the Commander that you will give him the device in exchange for freeing you from our dungeon, and then have that emissary lead him to the dungeon through the underground tunnels at midnight to break you out of prison."

"Yes." I try to sound like the prospect doesn't fill me with dread.

"In the meantime, you're going to plead guilty at your trial, and you expect me to hand you over to the Rowansmark trackers while somehow still keeping you in our custody until the Commander can come for you." Clarissa's eyes narrow as she studies me.

I resist the urge to break eye contact with her and say, "Yes, let the trackers have control of the dungeon, but keep them from leaving until dawn by telling them you have to sort out last-minute details like . . . I don't know . . . having me sign a confession to send to the Commander so that he knows to take up his cause against me with James Rowan? Think of something so that when the Commander comes for me—and he will—the Rowansmark trackers won't suspect that you were involved."

"It's not a bad plan," Willow says as she leans against the wall closest to the door.

"It's a terrible plan," Cassidy says, her dark eyes flashing. "We're deceiving the people who can press a button and call the *tanniyn* to destroy us while simultaneously allowing the army who is threatening our city to access our secret tunnel system. What part of that sounds like a good idea to you?"

"The part where you realize it's the only plan you've got," Willow shoots back, somehow managing to look menacing despite the chains that bind her wrists.

"This afternoon, before the trackers attacked you and the army surrounded my city, you told me you could build a replica of Rowansmark's tech in exchange for me offering asylum to your people." Clarissa's voice cuts through the room like a knife, silencing both Cassidy and Willow.

I hold her gaze. "I did. But I won't have time now."

"You'll have until midnight," she says.

"It's not just time. I need supplies. Sixteen-gauge braided copper wire, several high-voltage batteries, thin sheets of silver, and a transmitter capable of sending a signal for at least five hundred yards. And I'd need to be able to work without having trackers looking over my shoulder, which will be difficult given the fact that after the trial, I'll be in their custody." I meet Clarissa's gaze. "I'm sorry. I meant to keep my word. The best I can do now is to deflect Rowansmark's suspicion so that they have no reason to call the *tanniyn*."

"I'm not interested in apologies." She waves her hand through the air, a gesture at once regal and commanding. "I'm interested in results. Your plan might work, but it's hardly a guarantee of safety for my people or yours."

"I realize that. I don't know how to—"

"Cassidy, the beacon, please." Seeing my raised brows, Clarissa says, "I had one removed from one of the western outposts since the trackers are distracted with your presence in the dungeon and with the Commander outside the gate. It isn't likely to be missed, but I want to put it back in place as quickly as possible."

Cassidy pulls a dark-gray metallic box from the inside of her cloak and hands it to Clarissa. The beacon is about two handspans wide and as thick as the sole of my boot. When Clarissa pops the back off, revealing the powerful tech inside, I run my fingers over the intricate silver mechanisms and then examine a transmitter that's twice as powerful as the one inside the device Willow hid in the Wasteland. I'm surprised—and impressed— at the difference between the two. This piece of tech makes the device look like a harmless toy. I have to wonder why Rowansmark is expending so much effort to recover something so inferior to the tech they now possess.

Maybe it really is a matter of restoring honor, as Ian claimed.

Or maybe James Rowan knows the only way he can gain control over the rest of the city-states is by keeping them from copying and then improving on his tech. That would also explain why my father's pain atonement sentence alone wasn't enough to rectify the crime of letting tech like this out of Rowansmark hands. I'm guessing from James Rowan's perspective, Ian's mission has nothing to do with honor and everything to do with removing a threat to Rowansmark's plan to subjugate the rest of the city-states.

"Can you use any of these parts to make something we can use to protect ourselves?" Clarissa asks.

The transmitter may be more powerful, but unlike the device's ability to send the creature in any direction, there are only two frequencies. One to call the beast and one to keep it away. I smile grimly as I realize what this means. I can keep my promise. I can keep Lankenshire safe.

"I can do better than that." I tap the transmitter. "This has two active components. One component generates an ultrasonic sound wave, and the other produces an infrasonic wave. The infrasonic—the sound set low enough to cause the ground to rumble if there's enough power behind the transmitter—calls the *tanniyn*. If you disable the infrasonic in each of these beacons, the trackers won't be able to destroy your city unless one of them has the tech skills it takes to rebuild a transmitter and set it to an exact frequency."

"And if one of them does know how to fix it?" Clarissa asks.

I reach inside the beacon and gently disengage the transmitter from its position. "I assume you or one of the other members of the triumvirate has a necklace set to a sonic frequency that repels the beasts, right?"

Clarissa pulls a flat disk hanging on a thin silver chain from beneath her tunic.

"Good. Attach it to the transmitter like this." I show her how to splice the transmitter's wire onto one inside the tech she wears. "Now it will amplify your ultrasonic emission—the sonic frequency that repels the *tanniyn*—by at least three hundred percent."

She tucks the necklace and the transmitter away, and says, "Do we need to remove the transmitters from every beacon to disable them?"

I shake my head and show them how to disable the infrasonic component inside the tech.

Clarissa taps three times on the door and then studies me while Cassidy hides the now useless beacon inside her cloak again. "You upheld your end of our bargain. I'll do the same. I will send an emissary to the Commander with the terms of your deal. And your people will be offered asylum within our city as long as they agree to be governed by our laws."

"Drake is leader in my place." Something tight wraps itself around my chest as I realize I'm leaving the rest of the survivors behind, and I might not be coming back. I can't guarantee that I'll survive my encounter with the Commander, much less my attempts to rescue Rachel and bring down Rowansmark.

One of the soldiers guarding the room's entrance taps once before opening the door. "All clear, ma'am."

Clarissa nods but makes no move to leave the room. Instead, she continues to watch me. "What will you do?" she asks. "Once you give the device to the Commander—provided you survive that encounter—what will you do next?"

I meet her gaze. "I'm going to Rowansmark."